THE FRONTIER

University of Oklahoma Press   Norman

The Frontier

COMPARATIVE STUDIES

edited and with an introduction by

David Harry Miller and **Jerome O. Steffen**

Library of Congress Cataloging in Publication Data

The Frontier.
  Includes bibliographical references and index.
    1. Frontier and pioneer life—America—Addresses, essays, lectures. 2. Frontier and
pioneer life—Rome—Addresses, essays, lectures. 3. Frontier thesis—Addresses, essays,
lectures. I. Miller, David Harry, 1938-   II. Steffen, Jerome O., 1942-
E18.75.F76   970'.007'2   76-62507
ISBN 0-8061-1376-6

Preface

This book brings together certain studies on different facets of the frontier as an anthropological, geographical, or historical problem. It is the result, in part, of an ongoing program in comparative and interdisciplinary frontier studies at the University of Oklahoma. The goal is to extend communications between disciplines and to promote the comparative study of a variety of frontiers.

In April, 1975, the "First Oklahoma Symposium on Comparative Frontier Studies" gathered on the Norman campus. It was the result of the labors of Stephen I. Thompson of the Department of Anthropology, James Bohland of the Department of Geography, and William W. Savage, Jr., and Jerome O. Steffen of the Department of History. The "Second Oklahoma Symposium on Comparative Frontier Studies" gathered in March, 1976, for an expanded program, and in the interval between the two symposia publication of the *Comparative Frontier Studies Newsletter* was begun under the editorship of William W. Savage, Jr. The publication of this volume, therefore, is the fulfillment of an idea broached in the fall of 1974, and a complementary element in a rounded program in frontier research and discussion.

The editors have attempted to preserve some stylistic uniformity in citations to the articles while yet allowing for differences between the disciplines represented in the volume. Hence the reader will find two separate stylistic systems in the form of the notes and references, depending on the preferences of each author.

Publication of this book, as well as the holding of the symposia themselves, would have been impossible without the generous intellectual encouragement and substantial material support provided by Paul F. Sharp, himself a frontier and comparative historian, and president of the University of Oklahoma. This encouragement and support is gratefully acknowledged by the editors.

The editors would also like to acknowledge the aid and assistance of their colleagues on the executive committee of the *Comparative Frontier Studies Newsletter* and the symposium committee: James Bohland, William W. Savage, Jr., and Stephen I. Thompson. Special acknowledgment is due to Professor Savage, whose editorial expertise we exploited on numerous occasions.

The editors would also like to extend their appreciation to the following individuals who assisted with gathering manuscripts, typing and other secretarial work: Gloria Steffen, Alexis Rodgers, Josephine Gil, Jane Jones, and Vicki Williams. We also thank the Departments of Anthropology and History of the University of Oklahoma, which made this secretarial assistance available.

Norman, Oklahoma
July, 1976

David Harry Miller
Jerome O. Steffen

Contents

THE FRONTIER

Introduction

David Harry Miller and Jerome O. Steffen

THIS VOLUME brings together the work of anthropologists, geographers, historians and sociologists for the comparative study of frontiers as meaningful aspects of the human experience. Since comparative studies are not particularly new to most of the fields of social science, the methodological implications and possibilities of comparative study will not, perhaps, seem very novel to some readers. Historians, however, have never been particularly concerned with viable comparative study and, though the term *comparative history* has been used commonly enough, it is doubtful that its implications are much appreciated. It seems desirable, then, given the indulgence of colleagues in anthropology, geography, and sociology, to discuss some aspects of comparative methodology from the historian's point of view.

The interest in comparative historiography among historians in the United States is relatively recent. Traditional historiography was emphatically non-comparative in its outlook and theoretical aspect. There was, of course, some discussion of comparative history among American historians of the late nineteenth and early twentieth centuries, but the results were without much merit. There was little methodological sophistication underlying this approach, and most of these studies involved a search for direct or exact analogies of institutional development; an attempt to find exemplary patterns of wide-scale and long-range developments in one social tradition more or less exactly reproduced in other social traditions. Inevitably, these efforts involved the distortion of most of the evidence in order to make the preconceived patterns fit other situations.[1] Essentially, the theoretical assumptions on which early professional historiography in the United States was based belied the possibility of meaningful historical comparison.

From its origins, professional historiography in the United States was based on two major assumptions. The first was that historical phenomena are incorrigibly unique; that is, unique in

3

a sense, or to a degree, that other types of phenomena are not. Because of this assumption, historians found themselves driven to the necessity of arguing that historiography must have resort to some methodological procedure distinct from that commonly called the scientific method. In company with this argument historians were also constrained to argue that, whereas the purpose of other disciplines may be to focus on the general similarities of types of phenomena, historiography ought to treasure, even savor, the uniqueness of particular phenomena.[2] The second major assumption was that historiography ought not to indulge in generalization. Some historians came to this conclusion by way of a conviction that historical generalization was ultimately possible, but premature for the present, and others simply believed generalization to be out of place in any case.[3] Either way, the results were the same. Given these assumptions, there could obviously be no meaningful interest in historical comparison.

This general intellectual stance of professional historiography led, almost inevitably, to a sense of crisis in the profession in the United States. The fundamental problem was that the traditional theories of historiography led to a self-perpetuating system which led eventually to a lack of confidence in the possibility of historical knowledge. Meaningful general truths were not sought because it was assumed that they could not be attained; the fact that meaningful general truths were not developed was taken as proof that they could not be developed.[4] This impasse led to a dissatisfaction with historiography on the part of both younger historians and other social scientists. Within the profession the result was the proclamation of a "New" historiography early in the twentieth century.

Fundamentally, the new historiography was based on the acceptance of the proposition that historical truth, as such, was unobtainable, and that historical interpretation was inescapably influenced by the biases, personal and social, of the historian. The attempt to salvage a relevant historiography, under the influence of these assumptions, involved an attempt to put historiography at the service of the society itself—to produce the socially useful myth.[5] Again, these assumptions constituted a self-perpetuating system: if historiographical statements are relative, historiography might as well put itself to some utilitarian service of present need; and if historiography consciously served present utility, it showed the total relativity of historiographical statements. The New History represented no more than the logical degeneration of traditional historiography.

The dead-end to which the theoretical assumptions of the traditional historiography have led has been the occasion of a variety of responses by historians concerned with the intellectual and scholarly integrity of their profession. Among these responses has been an increased interest in comparative historiography. As must be obvious, comparative historiography implies a departure from the methodological stance traditional with historians. To assert the theoretical possibility of the comparative approach is to affirm that historical phenomena may be dealt with as representatives of types or categories of phenomena. There is no need, in making this affirmation, to deny the uniqueness of historical phenomena. The uniqueness of historical phenomena is an overworked cliché based on a failure to realize that *all* phenomena are unique and that the treatment of phenomena as *generalia* is an arbitrary procedure fundamental to human understanding.[6]

The obvious purpose of comparative historiography is comparison and categorization of phenomena and the articulation of general explanatory hypotheses, which may be tested by further comparative study. Ultimately, the rationale of a comparative approach to the historical enterprise is the understanding that it is impossible to avoid the use of general conceptions in any intellectual endeavor. The rigid antipathy to generalization notwithstanding, traditional historiography was thoroughly saturated with general theories. Because, however, of that antipathy, most such generalizations were vague, unarticulated, and impressionistic—hence they often turned out to be ridiculous clichés or oversimplified varieties of (untested, or untestable) conventional wisdom. Hence also the tendency of historiography to manifest only too obviously the partisan, religious, or social biases of historians. The function of comparative historiography is to bring historical generalizations into the open forum of scholarly discussion as explicit, formally articulated hypotheses, which may be subjected to analysis and testing. By these means superficial explanations, biased selection, and false analogy should be made more obvious and thereby discouraged.

Comparative historiography should by no means be supposed to imply a greatly lessened role for the narrative form in historical literature. On the contrary, it should permit the development of more sophisticated and accurate narration of events.

More importantly, the application of comparative hypotheses to the elucidation of processual patterns of development in specific historical sequences should become one of the major ways of testing the validity of these hypotheses.

Discussion of the possibilities of comparative frontier studies among historians generally involves the implicit assumption that the frontier theories commonly identified with Frederick Jackson Turner offer a sufficient theoretical base. The application of Turnerian frontier notions to other frontiers often proves, however, to be unproductive.[7] There are several reasons for this. It is difficult to say what the Turner thesis is, or was. Turner's essay, "The Significance of the Frontier in American History," usually assumed to be the manifesto of frontier historiography, did not really state a hypothesis as such, except for Achille Loria's theory of the function of free land.[8] The real thrust of Turner's essay was a vague statement of the need to find a theme for a nationalistic historiography in American terms. Turner was a representative of the New History and his impact was based on his ability to articulate a serviceable American historical interpretation.[9] Subsequent historiographical discussions of Turner's ideas led to a number of alternative statements of a thesis, but still in more or less vague terms.

There is a very definite necessity for continued discussion of the theoretical orientations of comparative frontier studies. What is a frontier? What different types of frontiers might be discussed? The chapters in this volume do not represent a singular view on the meaning of the term, frontier, just as they are not confined to one geographical area or one historical period. In one chapter, an anthropologist, Emilio Willems, uses the term to indicate "an area of highly variable size into which migrants have moved to exploit some of its known resources." Based on this definition, Willems explores contemporary Latin American social change in three contexts: mining, agriculture (family farm and plantation), and urban development. Latin American social change is also the focus of the chapter by an urban planner, Martin Katzman, who compares plantation and farm family agricultural frontiers with three questions in mind. Who is in control of the work? What are the rules of distribution of resources? Finally, how is capital and land distributed among the workers?

Contemporary Latin America is also the setting for a cultural ecology study by anthropologist, Stephen I. Thompson. Thompson reviews the current literature on the subject as it relates to the Amazon Basin and concludes that the outlook for successful agricultural colonization of the region is not as bleak as some scholars have predicted. The study concludes that successful colonization will depend on how well colonists pay heed to the environmental demands of the region.

The Canadian Shield provides the setting for two additional chapters on agricultural colonization by geographers Brian Osborne and Geoffrey Wall. Osborne's is a historical study of the differing perceptions of land usage during the early colonization period of the region. He explores entrepreneurial efforts to sell the Shield's lands to potential agriculturalists even though the environment of the region was unsuitable for farming. Geoffrey Wall's chapter focuses on Muskoka, a region on the southern margin of the Shield. Wall reviews government colonization plans which resulted from a concern over the lack of settlement in the region, and also discusses the interaction between lumbering interests and agrarian settlers lured to the region.

Colonization and environmental adaptation is also the focus of a chapter by an archaeologist, Kenneth Lewis, on colonial Jamestown, Virginia. Lewis defines the frontier as a "zone of contact between an expanding society and the environment (including aboriginal cultures) of the new territory. Employing this perspective, Kewis analyzes social change by relating economic subsystems to existing archaeological hypotheses on environmental adaptation.

The essays on Latin American and Canadian agricultural colonization share an emphasis on environmental adaptation. In the same tradition, geographer David J. Wishart presents a geographic synthesis of the American Fur Trade. He views the fur trade as an ecosystem represented by a fusion of biological, physical, and cultural environments. Wishart discusses the relationship between defined ecological subsystems and the total ecological system controlling the fur trading frontier.

Comparative frontier studies need not necessarily be confined to contemporary or early modern topics. For example, a historian, William Cooter, focuses on Roman expansion using the frontier concept as "groups and institutions juxtaposed to preindustrial states which are neither eliminated nor integrated as full-fledged provincial areas." Specifically, he employs the "interaction-sphere" concept, first formulated by Joseph Caldwell in 1964, to analyze the relationship between Romans and less complex societies in Northern Europe. Historian John Eadie also discusses Roman relations with cultures peripheral to the Empire. Eadie, focusing on Roman expansion into North Africa, pays tribute to the inter-action sphere studies represented by William Cooter's work in this volume. He suggests, however, that this approach may be too interested in the military aspects of Roman expansion to allow for a full appreciation of the acculturation process at work.

Roman expansion is also the concern of a co-authored chapter on ethnic stereotypes by two historians, David Harry Miller and William W. Savage, Jr. The authors suggest that stereotypes are a necessary subelement of an expansionist ideology and from this perspective proceed to compare Roman and American attitudes towards encountered indigenous population. The defined stereo-type views indigenous population as sub-human, and consequently served to normalize behavior otherwise thought to be illegal and immoral.

Whereas Miller and Savage concentrate on comparative racial attitudes, two sociologists, David T. Bailey and Bruce E. Haul-man, examine ethnic differentiation. The authors employ vari-ables such as occupation, migration, family status, and illiteracy to compare Anglo and Mexican Americans in Santa Fe, New Mexico, and San Antonio, Texas, in the mid-nineteenth century.

John Hudson, a geographer, and Leedom Lefferts, an anthro-pologist, discuss demographic models and typologies that can be successfully employed in comparative frontier studies. Hudson outlines several existent demographic approaches ranging from an emphasis on the duration of residency, population turn over, land-use competition, and diffusion from outside the frontier con-text. He combines the latter two models to offer three additional demographic techniques. Hudson's suggested methodology cen-ters on environmental continuity and conflict as well as group conflict within the frontier. Lefferts' chapter on demography sug-gests that population increase is not a true indicator of growth in frontier regions. Other factors such as individual versus house-hold migration, sex ratios, and age structure are more accurate indicators of true regional growth.

It is clear from the studies in this volume that no one definition of the frontier has emerged, just as it is apparent that no singular methodology will suffice for every frontier study. However, be-cause of the nature of the field, it is incumbent upon comparative frontier scholars to expose themselves to the broad spectrum of available methodologies.

Notes

1. A prime example of this sort of pseudo-comparative historiography may be found in the germ-theory of American institutional development so popular in the late nineteenth century.

2. John W. Burgess, "Political Science and History," *American Historical Review,* 2 (1897), 402; and Fred Morrow Fling, "Historical Synthesis," *ibid.,* 9 (1903), 1–22.

3. W. Stull Holt, *Historical Scholarship in the United States* (Seattle, 1967), p. 43; and "The Idea of Scientific History in America," *Journal of the History of Ideas,* 1 (1940), 352–362; John Hermann Randall, Jr., and George Haines, IV, "Controlling Assumptions in the Practice of American Historians," *Theory and Practice in Historical Study* (SSRC Bulletin 54, ed. by M. Curti [New York, 1945]), p. 32; and John Higham, Leonard Krieger and Felix Gilbert, *History: the Development of Historical Studies in the United States* (Englewood Cliffs, 1965), pp. 98–99.

4. Patrick Gardiner, *The Nature of Historical Explanation* (Oxford, 1952), p. 30.

5. W. M. Sloan, "The Substance and Vision of History," *American Historical Review,* 17 (1912), 235–252; James Harvey Robinson, *The New History* (New York, 1965, [originally published in 1912]); Carl Becker, "Some Aspects of the Influence of Social Problems and Ideas on the Study and Writing of History," *Publications of the American Sociological Society,* 7 (1913), 73–107; and "Everyman His Own Historian," *American Historical Review,* 37 (1932), 221–236; Charles A. Beard, "Written History as an Act of Faith," *ibid.,* 39 (1934), 219–229; and Beard and Alfred Vagts, "Currents in Historiography," *ibid.,* 42 (1937), 460–483.

6. Nicholas Rescher and Carey B. Joynt, "The Problem of Uniqueness in History," *History and Theory,* 1 (1961), 150–162; and William Dray, *Law and Explanation in History* (Oxford, 1957), p. 45.

7. A pertinent example may be found in James Westfall Thompson, "East German Colonization in the Middle Ages," *Annual Report of the American Historical Association, 1915* (Washington, 1917), pp. 123–150.

8. Frederick Jackson Turner, "The Significance of the Frontier in American History," *The Early Writings of Frederick Jackson Turner,* ed. by F. Mood (Madison: 1938), pp. 186, 198. Cf. U. Rabbeno, "Loria's Social System," *Political Science Quarterly,* 7 (1892), 261, and 276; and Lee Benson, *Toward the Scientific Study of History* (New York, 1972), pp. 175–180.

9. Frederick Jackson Turner, "The Significance of History," *The Early Writings,* pp. 52, 55, and 58; and "Problems in American History," *ibid.,* p. 72. Cf. Joseph Schafer, "Turner's Frontier Philosophy," *Wisconsin Witness to Frederick Jackson Turner,* comp. by O. Burnette, Jr. (Madison, 1961), p. 28; H. Hale Bellot, *American History and American Historians* (Norman, 1952), p. 19; Randall, et al, pp. 43–50; Becker, "Frederick Jackson Turner," *American Masters of Social Science,* ed. by H. Odum (New York, 1927), p. 300; and *Publications of the American Sociological Society,* p. 99; Carlton J. H. Hayes, "The American Frontier—Frontier of What?" *American Historical Review,* 51 (1946), 199–216; and Richard Hofstadter, "Turner and the Frontier Myth," *American Scholar,* 18 (1949), 435. Ironically, though the work Turner is most famous

for is of dubious value as a comparative hypothesis, some of his earlier work, most notably his Ph.D. dissertation, has distinct value in this regard. Consult *The Character and Influence of the Indian Trade in Wisconsin: A Study of the Trading Post as an Institution,* ed. by David Harry Miller and William W. Savage, Jr. (Norman, 1977), especially the editors' introduction.

Theory and Methodology
in Comparative Frontier Studies*

John C. Hudson

COMPARATIVE FRONTIER STUDIES were first suggested in 1904 by the inventor of the frontier, Frederick Jackson Turner.[1] The idea was taken up by Herbert Heaton in 1946, extended by Paul Sharp in 1955, and was the subject of considerable discussion by historians during the nineteen-fifties.[2] Marvin Mikesell introduced comparative frontier studies to geographers in a 1960 review paper which assessed some of the problems and prospects for this line of research.[3] Although the literature is not abundant and is scattered through books and journals whose publication spans more than seventy years, it seems that there is an inherent appeal in comparative frontier research that has transcended criticism of the frontier thesis itself. This is important since the original purpose and perhaps the most commonly stated justification for doing comparative studies has been to "test" Turner's thesis.

Tests of the frontier thesis have been no less but scarcely more successful than tests of the Holy Scriptures, yet this has not discouraged those who would attempt to perform such tests. The words of Frederick Jackson Turner are as stimulating, aggravating, and worthy of discussion today as they were seventy-five years ago. In turn, comparative frontier studies have proven little but they have contributed much to our general knowledge of pioneer settlements around the world.

It is a fundamental proposition of statistical research that a hypothesis must not be tested on the same data that suggested the hypothesis in the first place. Taken at face value, this proposition suggests that Turner's thesis ought to be tested only outside the United States. That the most successful test of the thesis to date was done by Merle Curti in Turner's home state of Wisconsin seems to cast doubt on the validity of Curti's general confirmation of the thesis and to strengthen the position of those who argue it must be tested elsewhere.[4]

The difficulty with such tests is that Turner did not write a theory capable of testing. There is no unique, unambiguous way to translate Turner's words into a theory out of which testable hypotheses might be deduced. Under such circumstances, those who defend the thesis can always claim that a hypothesis is invalid and hence the outcome of the test cannot affect the validity of the thesis. This is a common problem in the social sciences and is by no means peculiar to the frontier thesis or even to historical studies in general. It does, however, offer one clue as to why social scientists are so fickle in their attachment to objectivity and hypothesis testing.[5] At present, statistical hypothesis tests are all but ignored in geography but they are very much in vogue in quantitative historical research; ten years ago, the situation was reversed. Today, geographers believe their theories—more or less—and are not much interested in hypothesis tests since they are seldom instructive. Historians may sense a lack of theory and believe they can produce some by adopting methods used by those disciplines which have theory.

These introductory remarks are by way of saying that I see little to be gained from making "Turner-testing" the principal thrust of comparative frontier research. This may not seem a very propitious beginning for a work on theory in comparative frontier studies since the Turner thesis is virtually the only theoretical basis for the whole endeavor. What is possible is to outline the methodologies that overlap frontier research and to organize the relevant concepts into a few heuristic models of the frontier process. Various aspects of Turner's theory appear in these models and research strategies, but the focus is not on that grand theory of 1893.

Vocabulary

All theorizing must begin with some definitions—some mutual agreements about how words are to be used. The term "frontier" has had various definitions that reflect beliefs of those who used the concept. It is most easily defined in spatial terms—a fringe or an outer boundary. The 1890 Census maps that so influenced Turner used two persons per square mile as the boundary between settled and unsettled; others have argued that this definition is misleading.[6] In any case, such spatial/cartographic definitions are easily implemented. The position of the frontier can be traced without having much idea of the nature of the thing being studied.

A second usage of "frontier" is less capable of operational definition; this is the notion that the frontier is a peculiar type of society and, moreover, that the movement of the frontier zone is a kind of social process, not merely a series of isolines on a map. In 1893 Turner called it the "meeting point between savagery and civilization." Later, as he formulated his ideas about sectionalism, the frontier became a "migrating region" and a "moving section."

The spatial definition of the frontier was easy; definition in terms of a stage of society with an objective list of traits was more difficult; definition in terms of a process—the crucible in which democratic institutions were forged—was far-fetched. Fascination with the frontier idea came in a direct ratio with fuzziness of definition. An isoline on a map is not very controversial but a hypothesis about the source of American institutions is bound to be debated.

The vocabulary of frontier theory contains a number of geological terms; "waves," "stages," and even "strata" are common terms in social-spatial theories born in the late nineteenth century. The vocabulary of culture-area studies in anthropology and geography is much the same. Turner was a bit more specific in his analogues and was probably influenced by his Wisconsin colleague, the Pleistocene geologist T. C. Chamberlin, when he referred to the "traces" left behind the frontier as being like successive terminal moraines.[7]

It would be pleasing to report that, seventy-five years after the geological metaphor was given vogue, thinking has been substantially advanced and that these early attempts have been improved with our increased knowledge of urbanization, migration, and group behavior. Such is not the case. There is a new vocabulary, containing such terms as network, hierarchy, competition, and adaptation, but this has been superimposed on the same old ideas about behavior in space. When historians discovered in the 1950's that urbanization had slipped out ahead of Turner's agricultural frontier in the Middle West, this did not bring about any new locational models; it was treated merely as evidence against Turner's waves and stages.

There are other problems in terminology. For example, how long is an area to be considered a frontier? If we believe in stages of civilization it is possible to designate a time point after initial settlement when a region is no longer to be considered a frontier. Could developments in Indiana politics in the 1920's be considered as fair game for a study of frontier institutions? Probably not, but Alberta politics of the twenties could be so considered. If we disavow the notion of stages and replace it with nothing better, then such questions are harder to answer, not easier.

If the vocabulary of frontier studies has grown in length more than it has changed in composition it is not surprising that frontier theory has changed but little; and if this is so, then comparative frontier studies cannot have had the benefit of much new theory, either.

Principles of Comparison

The nature of the comparison usually suggested from frontier studies can be succinctly summarized: given a set of n variables $(X_1, X_2, \ldots X_n)$ thought to be important in understanding frontiers, hold $X_1, X_2, \ldots X_m$ constant, or at least exogenous, and let $X_{m+1}, X_{m+2}, \ldots X_n$ vary. The exogenous variables include climate, soils, landforms, time of settlement, and ethnic background of the settlers; the endogenous variables are those suggested by Turner and are operational definitions of economic success, land ownership, population turnover, political institutions, forms of livelihood, and so on. This strategy is a common one employed in a variety of scientific endeavors where control groups are used.

What will we learn about frontiers if we employ such an approach? If the problem was really as simple and as "succinct" as just described we could probably learn much. Unfortunately it is impossible to "hold $X_1, X_2, \ldots X_m$ constant" due to the well-known, but not terribly useful, dictum of the areal differentiationists that regions are unique. Furthermore, it would probably be impossible for researchers ever to agree on a single list of relevant variables, much less formulate them into a model. Even given these technical drawbacks, which are not absolutes, but instead represent a kind of friction against systematic understanding, there remains a question of purpose.

Is it useful to compare frontier A with frontier B if A's frontier does not significantly differ from the "core" of A? (The core refers to the longer settled, perhaps industrial portion of a nation and must logically exist if not all the nation is called frontier.) For example, high labor mobility and population turnover on the settled fringe have often been explained in terms of frontier conditions. Recent studies of nineteenth-century cities in the American core indicate that similar high rates of mobility occurred there as well.[8] This forces us to rethink the entire causal sequence that produced high mobility rates and at least temporarily to disassociate the idea from its position in frontier theory—in other words, to remove it from the endogenous category.

The problem of what and how to compare becomes more critical as the influence of the frontier is reinterpreted. As this reinterpretation takes place it will probably become more useful to focus on a spatial rather than a social definition of the frontier and to employ more general models to study all regions—frontiers, cores, and everything in between. If in the process of doing this, frontier zones turn out to be meaningfully different, then cross-frontier comparisons will be useful and will no longer be motivated only by assertions about their significance.

Methodology

Three dimensions or variables are required to identify frontier studies among social studies in general. These dimensions form a basis which contains many other kinds of research traditions that overlap the problems of frontier study. A brief examination of these complementary themes suggests some new approaches that might be of interest to the comparative frontier historian.

The dimensions are *time* (measured continuously or in discrete units), *location* (the set of all places being studied), and *population* (the collection of individuals studied). Various slices and layers through this "cube" are easily recognized as familiar research orientations (Fig. 1).

There are three types of background studies contained in this basis. Biographies and genealogies trace individuals and their families through time, but seldom discuss location. Synoptic population studies usually ignore time or process, and instead focus on the distribution of population at a single point in time; it would not stretch common usage to call such studies population geographies. Both of these kinds of studies may be useful to the frontier scholar, but each lacks information on one of the necessary dimensions. Community studies are an example of a third viewpoint; in presenting a detailed study of a place and its population over time they provide much information but can only speculate

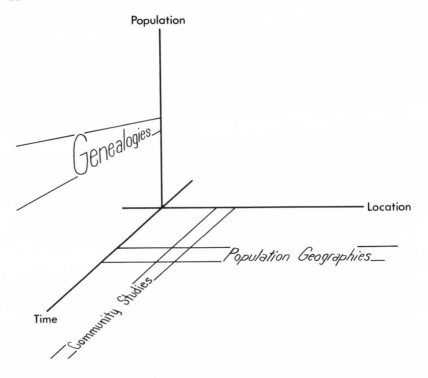

Fig. 1. Background studies

about the situation of the community vis-a-vis others like it, although nearly all such case studies are chosen in advance in hopes
that they are representative of some larger whole, such as "all
small towns," "all medium-sized industrial cities," "all countries
on the Middle Border," or some other such criterion referring to
a large subset of locations.

Historical geographers speak of "changing geographies and
geographies of change" indicating that they are beset with the
problem of how to slice this cube, as it were. Historical geography
and most historical research traditions which lack a theoretical
foundation are, for purposes of this classification, treated as background studies since they do not admit to any focus "smaller"
than one of the three planes defining the basis. Theory, if it is
sufficiently rich, suggests what to study; if theory is lacking, it
is difficult to know what (not) to study.

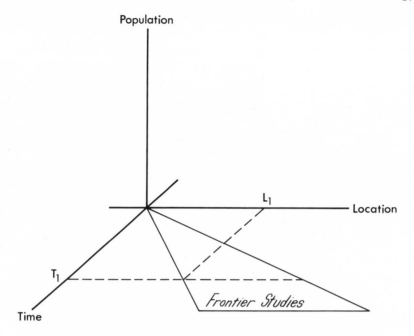

Fig. 2. Conceptual background for frontier studies

Frontier investigations do have a theoretical foundation that defines the limits of study (Fig. 2). A given location, L_1, is on the frontier for a limited amount of time; also, at a given time, T_1, only a small proportion of all locations are on the frontier. Such a limitation on what to study is meaningful regardless of the merits of frontier theory in all its detail. Viewed in this way, frontier studies naturally stand to gain much from those other research traditions (background studies) which overlap. This rather simple diagram was not necessary to show us this, which we already know; it does suggest, perhaps, why theory plays such an important role in defining research traditions.

In the years since frontier studies were first begun several new formal structures have "appeared" inside the same basis. Two of these relatively newer models worth mentioning come under the general heading of migration studies; specific attention is drawn to *duration-of-residence models* and to *migration field models* (Fig. 3).

The duration of residence theme had two independent origins.

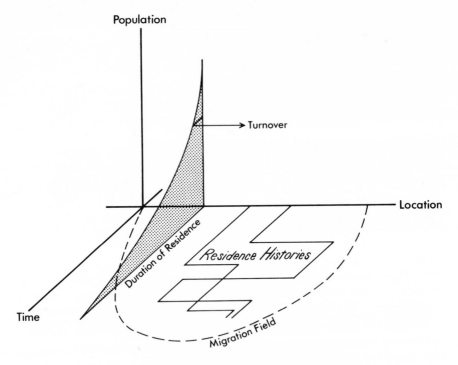

Fig. 3. Migration analysis

James Malin was one pioneer in the field, although he called it the study of population turnover.[9] Replacement or turnover in a population, frontier or otherwise, is the logical complement of duration of residence—the greater the turnover the shorter the duration of residence. Malin's studies of Kansas frontier populations first suggested the importance of turnover as a significant element in frontier life. The frontier was not a stable zone in which pioneer agriculturalists settled once and for all, but instead was a zone of considerable inflow *and* outflow. Malin's conclusions were reaffirmed in subsequent studies of other frontiers.

A decade ago, demographers discovered the other side of the coin, apparently unaware of Malin's work. They were trying to fit theoretical models to migration-flow data. They found that the longer a person lived in one place, the less likely it was for him to move.[10] The simple Markov chain models of migration they had been trying to use could not handle this phenomenon, which was given the high-sounding title, "axiom of cumulative inertia."[11]

When the "new" urban historians began studying turnover in the city and compared their findings with the data gathered by Malin, Curti, and others they apparently failed to see the connection with cumulative inertia, although the generalization has now been confirmed in the United States, the Netherlands, Great Britain, and Mexico. Further research has shown that places with large per-capita migration volumes (high turnover) are likely to be growth areas. This was recently demonstrated in a regional planning study in England where a conventional migration model was "upgraded" by including a turnover component.[12] The authors of this study conclude that growing regions have high turnover and that declining regions have a small turnover, per-capita. These findings from an entirely different time and place are quite supportive of what started out as a generalization about Kansas frontier populations. If areas experiencing rapid per-capita population growth due to net migration commonly have a large turnover then it is not surprising that the generalization also applies to frontiers. What Malin discovered forty years ago is now subsumed into a larger body of generalizations about migration among regions in general.

The theme might be extended just a bit more. If we classify frontier zones in the category known to contemporary regional planners as "growth regions," which is indeed how they are designated in countries currently trying to develop their pioneer fringes, then the high outmigration rates observed in frontier regions are in line with expectations and need not be rationalized.

Taking the Great Plains as an example, in the latter part of the nineteenth century, we see that the region grew rapidly owing to a positive net migration that was accompanied by much turnover (large per-capita volume of gross $1/M$ and positive net migration). Later, when economic opportunities shifted elsewhere, the region declined in population although per capita turnover decreased (smaller per-capita volume of gross $1/M$ and negative net migration).[13]

People who move to an area do so in response to real or perceived opportunities in that area with respect to other areas. Also, people who have recently moved are the most likely ones to move again in a short time. The great debate over whether there was an urban safety valve or a frontier safety valve becomes much less interesting in light of these findings, as do the various "push-pull" theories of migration.

The knowledge gained from these studies has been made possible in part by manuscript censuses and other records specific to a single place. Data on where people come from and where they move once they leave a place are lacking in such sources. Turnover studies thus "crosscut" the frontier at specific locations but no amount of such analysis will allow conclusions about the distance and direction of migration.

Twenty years ago, Swedish geographers of the Lund school made good use of the widely acclaimed migration register data available in that country to study the distance effects in migration, repeated migrations, step-wise migration, and many other topics.[14] These studies revolutionized population geography but seem to have had little impact elsewhere. Torsten Hagerstrand's concept of the *migration field* (the area from which migrants are drawn or sent) has been applied mainly to urban regions. The classic form of the model describing distance effects on migration is one of an inverse relationship between migration frequency and distance. The residence histories from which migration fields are constructed show a clustering around the origin of the field, or the ultimate destination, depending on whether immigration or emigration is being mapped. The inverse-distance formulation, as proposed by Hagerstrand and by others who wrote before and after his contribution, has become a universal component in models predicting migration flows.

The inverse-distance generalization, however, is not a universal. At the very least it is inappropriate for studying frontier migrations such as those which occurred in this country. By and large, frontiers did not draw large numbers of immigrants from nearby areas. New residents came from "behind" the frontier, but not from newly settled areas. In the northern plains, for example, there was about a twenty-five- to fifty-year lag (two to five hundred miles) in pioneer migration fields.[15] Counties which were colonized in the eighties drew heavily from areas colonized in the fifties, and so on. Such a time lag was necessary to put population pressure on land resources and to thus stimulate an out-migration to the current homestead frontier.

Preliminary study of a sample of approximately one thousand residence histories of pioneer settlers in North Dakota reveals that frontier migration fields were exceedingly haphazard.[16] There was much moving about both on and behind the frontier which accompanied many shifts in occupation. An example of one residence history will illustrate the point.

Mr. Carroll was born to Irish parents in Oshkosh, Wisconsin in 1863. From 1879 to 1883 he worked in upper Michigan lumber camps; 1883—returned to Oshkosh to do carpentry work; 1884—went to Dakota to look for land; 1885—returned to Oshkosh; 1886—moved to Carrington, North Dakota and did farm work, took a tree claim near Sykeston and did summer work on the Dalrymple "bonanza" at Casselton; 1887—had an elevator job at Hunter, North Dakota; 1888—returned to Carrington and went into carpentry business, but worked in Wisconsin lumber camps each winter; 1891—returned to Oshkosh and married a Miss Vogel, originally from Milwaukee; 1895—returned to Carrington and established a permanent home.

What kind of theory, frontier or otherwise, could explain such behavior? Mr. Carroll made a shambles of Turner's stages, completely disregarded the fact that there is supposed to be a friction of distance on migration, evidently shifted occupations at the slightest urge, going both up and down the ladder of occupational status with ease, and apparently had no trouble finally settling down in a single place with a single job after sixteen years spent criss-crossing the upper Middle West. Mr. Carroll was more migratory than most, but was certainly not unusual in the records I have examined.

This example shows the value of residence histories; in comparison, census data would only show three of the moves and two occupations even if all the relevant census schedules could be located. The price of the added detail comes in the baffling array of moves and job changes that are revealed. Is this a frontier phenomenon or is it just one instance of the high turnover and long-distance mobility widespread in America? Did such individuals, although perhaps they were a minority, keep the gross migration rates high across the nation by their constant moving about? Answers to such questions demand careful research. The kinds of questions illustrate the importance of studying non-frontier areas simultaneously in order to capture the relevant geographical scale of human behavior.

Models of Frontier Dynamics

The three dimensions (location, time, population) used here to classify various methodologies are not proposed to be all-inclusive. The classification can do little more than suggest alternative approaches within a limited framework. Factors left out include environment, economy, culture, and many other topics not usually studied by counting. In fact, what is left out is the very stuff which makes frontiers most interesting, namely, the interactions between people, institutions, and environment on the edge of settled territory.

If we move away from glacial analogues and the like in our frontier theories, these broader concepts ought to be included. New theory clearly has to come from outside the frontier thesis as handed down from Turner. Two bodies of what can loosely be called theory were suggested above, in the subject area of migration studies. Two more bodies of theory are proposed in this section. One is the fairly well-developed theory of land-use competition from spatial economics and the other is an amorphous body of generalizations concerning innovation diffusion.

Frontier history is often written as a history of conflict and succession. Apart from the general lawlessness that is portrayed as endemic on the frontier there was much competition for land between groups who had different ideas about how the land should be used. Since the cost of land per acre on the frontier was relatively cheaper than its cost in the core, frontiers were and still are logical places for competition among alternative land users who have large land requirements. Thus cattle ranchers and wheat farmers were often put into conflict with one another. Cattle ranchers and gold miners were not in conflict since the land requirements for one were very large and were negligible for the other. Cowboys and prospectors certainly fought, but it was over their relative shares of the water supply, the whisky supply, women, and other dear commodities they both treasured. They were compatible in the sense that both could simultaneously exist in the same area without competing for land.

A link with Turner's stages is easily established, since each of his successive waves represents a more competitive form of land use; each wave, in turn, bid up the price of land and had a higher ratio of capital and labor inputs per acre. Frank Owsley's description of the retreat of livestock ranching in front of the agricultural frontier in the South is another example.[17] Assuming a favorable physical environment, one would thus expect that all battles between homesteaders and cattlemen would be won by the homesteading farmer.

The principle probably should not be extended to the fall of hunting and gathering cultures in front of the white man's fron-

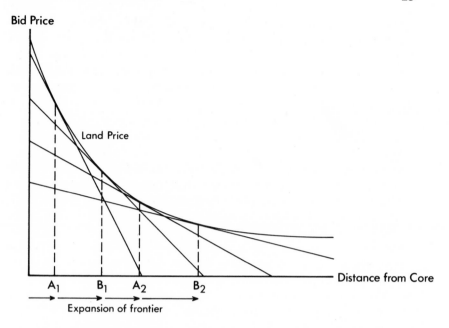

Fig. 4. Land-use competition and the frontier

tier since one frontier was subsistence, the other commercial. The aboriginal population already owned the land and hence had no need to pay a higher price for it when the competition arrived. Furthermore, the competition had little inclination to pay for the land it coveted. It was not a free market.

The land-use competition model was first developed to study agricultural land-use zones around a city.[18] Later it was commandeered for service in urban economics where it was used to explain the distribution of land users having various income elasticities of demand for land within a concentric city.[19] There ought to be no objection to sneaking it back out into the countryside and pressing the model into service once again, this time to describe frontiers (Fig. 4).

Two land users, A and B, compete for land. One is more willing to trade off a central location for cheaper land than is the other; in this case, A uses land more intensively than B does. As population grows, the frontier expands and the more remote the land parcel is from the core, the cheaper its price. This ignores the geographically constant prices of land offered from the public domain and instead concentrates on the prices which soon evolve once land passes into private ownership. Assuming that no innovation or catastrophe occurs which would substantially alter the ratio of labor and capital to land inputs, A and B will remain in the same relative positions as progressively more distant areas are linked to the core with suitable transport routes. Bid-price curves fall as a larger area is settled and the market expands in proportion.

There is nothing new or startling in this model; it is neo-Turnerian at best. It is implicit in many accounts of frontier expansion and the diagram simply makes more explicit what is already a popular notion about frontier economic activity.

Not all land-use conflicts are between groups of people; the frontier is also a study in adaptation and adjustment to environmental restraints. Innovations permit formerly strict limits set by climate and terrain to be overridden. An example is offered by Sharp in his comparison of Australian and North American frontiers.[20] Parallel adjustments in arid region agriculture occurred as settlement pushed westward. Environmental restraints call forth innovation and improvisation to overcome the old limits.

Studies of innovation and innovation-diffusion are not usually approached in such terms. It is more common to treat innovation as a process of cultural change which originates in the core and then diffuses outwards until a large area is covered. The frontier, wherever it might be, is the last to know. In contrast, Turner, Webb, and other frontier historians emphasized the role of both material and non-material culture-change due to the frontier. Cultural geographers and anthropologists with their diffusion models tend to see the situation reversed, with the frontier as the outer fringe of the trait-complex held by the core. Clearly, both approaches have something to offer and should not be treated as rivals.

Land-use competition and innovation-diffusion are implicit if not explicit in frontier studies. They are interesting especially because of their importance in the process of settlement expansion. A simple, four-fold classification of frontier models is suggested by combining the two sets of ideas (Fig. 5).

1. *Adapted Spread* (Fig. 6). The simplest of the four models is suggested in a recent paper by Milton B. Newton, who explains the rapid spread of Upland South culture in terms of pre-adapta-

Stimulus or source of innovation

	Core	Frontier
Single group (no territorial conflict)	Adapted Spread (Fig. 6)	Environmental Conflicts (Fig. 7)
Several groups (territorial conflict)	Stages of Occupance (Fig. 9)	Group Conflicts (Fig. 8)

Fig. 5. Models of frontier dynamics

tion.[21] According to Newton, culture-traits were "selected" in the core (or, rather, *hearth,* in the terminology of cultural geographers) in the northern Appalachians, and the entire trait-complex spread southward with little competition from other groups or from the environment. Another example of adapted spread is Webb's explanation of a northward, Texas-based diffusion of the range cattle industry. The trait-complex originated in south Texas and followed the cattle drives northward through the plains, spreading rapidly in the immediate post-Civil War era.[22]

2. *Environmental Conflicts* (Fig. 7). In this case, a population encounters environmental conflicts on the frontier which stimulates innovation to overcome the conflict. As settlement spreads down the environmental gradient (i.e., toward harsher zones) adjustments need to be made. Webb took the gradient idea to the limit and turned it on end on top of the 98th meridian, calling it a "cultural fault."[23] Many innovations, such as windmills, dry farming, and the development of frost-hardy plant varieties were

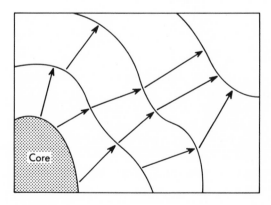

Fig. 6. Adapted spread

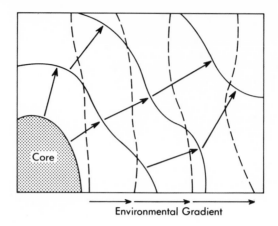

Environmental Gradient

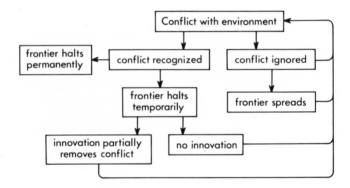

Fig. 7. Environmental conflicts

stimulated on frontiers around the world in such a fashion, although the manufactured copies of the inventions were often produced back in the industrial core.

The accompanying diagram illustrated that innovation does not necessarily occur in such situations and that frontiersmen do not always heed environmental cues, at least in the short run. Eventually, innovation to overcome environmental limits will occur if there is a sufficient demand for new land on the margins, creating a market for innovations.

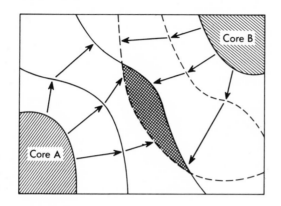

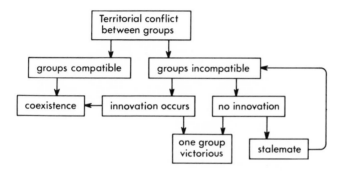

Fig. 8. Group conflicts

3. *Group Conflicts* (Fig. 8). Here innovation is a product of conflict on the frontier, but between groups of people of separate
origins rather than between people and environment. If one group
is not inherently stronger than the other an innovation may enable
one eventually to dominate the other. The adoption of various
strategies of warfare is an example of this process. Colonial
strategies for pacifying aboriginal populations are another. If
there is no territorial conflict, as would be the case if the two
groups exploited different resources in the same environment,
they may coexist or even be symbiotic. If the same resources are
desired by both and neither group possesses an advantage, protracted conflict over boundaries is likely.

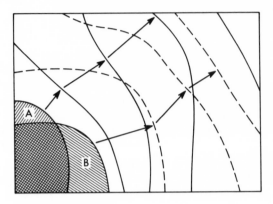

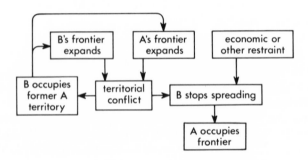

Fig. 9. Stages of frontier occupance

4. *Stages of Frontier Occupance* (Fig. 9). If innovations occur largely in the core or if they are first adopted there, after invention outside the region of study, then land use competition spreads along with the frontier. This is the neo-Turnerian model (Fig. 4). The outer limit of frontier spread depends on economic, cultural, and environmental factors, exogenous to the model. For example, in the semi-arid grasslands, grain farming encroaches on non-agricultural fringe land when grain prices are high and capital to intensify agriculture elsewhere is lacking. The grain farming frontier pulls back when prices fall.

Conclusion

Comparative frontier studies do not suffer from a lack of theoretical and methodological guides for further study. The field, broadly defined, seems to be relatively well stocked with models which are of immediate or potential usefulness. Although it was claimed at the outset that this study would not focus on Turner's frontier thesis, it is obvious at the end that Turnerian ideas are lurking behind many of the concepts discussed. Some of the models have their origin in the same era that gave us the frontier thesis; some of them were proposed in direct reaction to the thesis; all of them deal in part with things Turner treated in a single, general theory. The attempt here has been to break out of some of the relatively manageable aspects of frontier theory and put them in a more contemporary framework.

It is fashionable nowadays to conclude with a section on policy implications, whether or not there are any in the study and whether or not there should be any. In this case, policy implications at least ought to be mentioned.

Dozens of countries scattered over all the world's continents are currently engaged in efforts to promote growth on their unsettled margins. Pioneer fringes today are mainly tropical or subpolar and are by no means like the fertile, middle-latitude temperate zones which suggested the frontier thesis and which have provided most of the examples for comparisons. A large literature has accumulated over the past several decades concerning settlement policies, the selection of settlers for new land colonization efforts, land-use decisions, marketing strategies for products grown in remote areas, and many other topics. Most of these studies were and are directly concerned with policy making. If they are derivative of any tradition it is probably Isaiah Bowman's *Pioneer Fringe,* rather than Turner's frontier thesis.[24]

Another research tradition which parallels these settlement policy studies comes from regional economics; growth poles, cost-benefit analysis, and other planning devices are now an accepted part of frontier research, if one wishes to call it that.[25] Most of this literature will probably remain outside the realm of expertise of the comparative frontier historian on grounds of division of labor, if nothing else. Yet it does suggest some research possibilities.

What would be the result if we applied modern techniques to answer the questions that bothered policy makers one hundred, or even two hundred, years ago? For example, what would have been the result if John Wesley Powell had known about cost-benefit analysis? Powell was a planner and policy maker who attempted to change the course of latter-day American frontier history by radically changing the land policy. He failed in his major objectives, which in retrospect was probably just as well since he believed in water and in little else—but he might have done better if he had had better tools.

Much debate has taken place concerning public land policies, whether they were good or bad and whether they proved to be wise in the long run. Today, planners are using a wide array of tools to make decisions about how to develop pioneer fringes for the future. Some argue that their tools are dull, which is certainly not beyond the realm of possibility, making it even more interesting to apply them to past problems. If they proved to be useless in light of developments up to the present then that fact might be of interest to today's planners concerned with the future.

Notes

*This chapter is based on a paper prepared for Oklahoma Symposium on Comparative Frontiers, University of Oklahoma, Norman, April 11-12, 1975.

1. Frederick Jackson Turner, *The Significance of Sections in American History* (New York, 1932), pp. 18–19.

2. Herbert Heaton, "Other Wests Than Ours," *Tasks of Economic History,* supplement to *Journal of Economic History,* 6 (1946), 50–62; Paul F. Sharp, "Three Frontiers: Some Comparative Studies of Canadian, American, and Australian Settlement," *The Pacific Historical Review,* 24 (1955), 369–377; Walker D. Wyman and Clifton B. Kroeber, eds., *The Frontier in Perspective* (Madison, Wis., 1957).

3. Marvin Mikesell, "Comparative Studies in Frontier History," *Annals, Association of American Geographers,* 51 (1961), 62–74.

4. Merle Curti, *The Making of an American Community: A Case Study of Democracy in a Frontier County* (Stanford, 1959).

5. Some alternative viewpoints are given in Denton Morrison and Ramon Henkel, *The Significance Test Controversy: A Reader* (Chicago, 1970).

6. Frederick Jackson Turner, "The Significance of the Frontier in American History, *Annual Report of the American Historical Association,* 1893, 199; John Fraser Hart, "The Middle West," *Annals, Association of American Geographers,* 62 (1972), 258–282.

7. Turner, "The Significance of the Frontier," p. 201.

8. Stefan Thernstrom and Peter R. Knights, "Men in Motion: Some Data and Speculations about Urban Population Mobility in Nineteenth-Century America," *Journal of Interdisciplinary History,* 1 (1970), 7–35.

9. James Malin, "The Turnover of Farm Population in Kansas," *Kansas Historical Quarterly*, 4 (1935), 339–372.

10. Peter A. Morrison, "Chronic Movers and the Future Redistribution of Population," *Demography*, 8 (1971), 171–184.

11. George C. Myers, "The Duration of Residence Approach to a Dynamic Stochastic Model of Internal Migration: A Test of the Axiom of Cumulative Inertia," *Eugenics Quarterly*, 14 (1967), 121–126.

12. M. Cordey-Hayes and D. Gleave, "Migration Movements and the Differential Growth of City Regions in England and Wales," *Papers, Regional Science Association*, 33 (1974), 99–123.

13. Richard G. Bremer, "Patterns of Spatial Mobility: A Case Study of Nebraska Farmers, 1890–1970," *Agricultural History*, 49 (1974), 529–542.

14. Torsten Hagerstrand and Bruno Odeving, eds., *Migration in Sweden*, Lund Studies in Geography, Series B, No. 13, 1957.

15. John Hudson, "Two Dakota Homestead Frontiers," *Annals, Association of American Geographers*, 63 (1973), 442–462.

16. Research in progress by the author.

17. Frank L. Owsley, "The Pattern of Migration and Settlement on the Southern Frontier," *Journal of Southern History*, 11 (1945), 147–176.

18. Reference is to von Thünen's classic formulation of 1826; see Michael Chisholm, *Rural Settlement and Land Use* (London, 1961).

19. William Alonso, *Location and Land Use* (Cambridge, Mass., 1964).

20. Sharp, "Three Frontiers," p. 377.

21. Milton B. Newton, "Cultural Preadaptation and the Upland South," *Geoscience and Man*, 5 (1974), 143–153.

22. Walter Prescott Webb, *The Great Plains* (Boston, 1931), Ch. 6.

23. *Ibid.,* p. 8.

24. Isaiah Bowman, *The Pioneer Fringe* (New York, 1931).

25. For example see Michael Nelson, *The Development of Tropical Lands* (Baltimore, 1973).

Frontier Demography: An Introduction

H. L. Lefferts, Jr.

> The population of Terra Nova was initially established with great deliberation, based on the experience with American frontier towns. The overwhelming number of people were in the 21-45 age group (74%). Sixteen percent were younger, and 10% were older.[1]
>
> Sexually they were split at 43% male, 41% female, and the rest children under 21 whose sexual make-up was not controlled . . .
>
> That is a more productive society than the average small American town in the 70's (where 58% were not in the work force), and a far more adult one. (Shurkin 1975)

Although written as if these events had taken place in past time, cognoscenti of 1975 will recognize that Terra Nova does not yet exist. To give away the secret, it is the proposed space colony designed to provide a source of continuing energy to the industrialized nations of Terra Firma.

But, more to the point, on what basis were "great deliberations" made regarding the demographic structure of this colony? Do we have collections of data describing the initial demographies of frontier areas, with periodic updatings to show how this structure evolved? Or, must we rely primarily on our own impressions of how these events progressed?

Simply put, extensive evidence on what may or may not be the unique dynamics of the population structure of an area undergoing human colonization has not yet been collected. Moreover, it appears that little research in this area has been attempted which has been designed to define major questions. In a modest way, this chapter attempts to initiate such work. This is done in the belief that intensive analysis of the evolving population structure of frontiers requires better knowledge than that which intuitive comprehension gives us. Furthermore, such knowledge may pay dividends in terms of understanding the more involved social and cultural characteristics which are thought to be indicative of frontier situations. Finally, such work may provide a comparative perspective against which to look at other questions of a demographic or developmental nature.

In exploring these topics, this study has been divided as follows: First, there will be a brief discussion of how a demographic approach may lend some quantitative precision to frontier studies. Second, we will consider some data available from several sources which may enable us to generate initial hypothese concerning the evolutions of such populations. And, third, we shall attempt to place these formulations in a context of theoretical and practical importance that may, in turn, generate further questions.

The Value of Demographic Analysis in Frontier Contexts

Stephen Thompson, in his summary of anthropological research in pioneer colonization, notes that frontier studies permit the establishment of a "base line (which) is relatively recent and relatively reliable, and (by which) the delineation of culture change in the frontier area is therefore greatly facilitated" (1973:3). It is this striving toward precision and reliability and the opportunity for the analysis of change under conditions of "surprising rapidity" which, to him, make frontier studies of greater noteworthiness than they traditionally have been accorded for anthropology.

Demography has a great calling for quantitative data. The uses of these data, while at times inexact and subject to differing meanings, are organized by a mathematical statement, a fiction called a stable population. The value of demography is that it provides material for cross-cultural and cross-national comparison which, in turn, can be placed against this over-arching mathematical statement (cf. Keyfitz 1975). However, there are three contexts in which the seeming universality of demography can be questioned and, significantly, each one of them arises most prominently in the study of frontier demography. How is this so?

Demography, formally conceived, "is concerned with the size, distribution, structure and change of populations" (Shryock, Siegal and Associates 1973:2). It takes as its touchstone the universality of certain definitions, the most important being the birth and death of the individual, and the aging which takes place between these two events. Without getting into philosophical esoterics, anthropologists are quite familiar with definitional problems and, more importantly, with the problem of eliciting the occurrence of supposedly universal events from individuals in systems which have defined the world in different ways. Because a frontier encompasses a rapidly changing system, definitions which have been imported from the culture of origin of the frontier people might very well have changed. Elicitation regarding these universal events, not to mention problems of gathering data of a more ephemeral nature such as migration, occupation, and household and family histories, becomes even more difficult in this context.

The second major problem of applying demography to a frontier setting is that of data collection: not only collecting basic data on births, deaths, and numbers, but also of collecting data which might be more appropriate to the problem, such as migration and living arrangements. Frontiers are by definition beyond the range of organized settlements within which official demographic data collection usually takes place. While the world has now been divided between various nation-states, this does not mean that all of the included area will be routinely covered. This is, of course, in addition to the often incomplete coverage that obtains within areas of older settlement of many nations, especially in the "developing" world. By its nature, frontier settlement is peripheral and it is only through time that one observes the permanence of what has been begun.

On the basis of a survey of the literature, I am compelled to state that most work in frontier demography must take place retroactively, once someone has observed that a frontier situation has progressed to a relative stage of permanency. This is not normally the type of work that would be undertaken by official government agencies but rather by researchers who become involved in retrospective questioning in an area which has been involved in frontier movements.

To put the point bluntly, except possibly for making very broad statements about general population growth, the pioneer demography of settlements far in the past does not appear possible. Here and there, as for instance with colonial New England and the spread of the population west from the Atlantic, sufficient written information may be available to make detailed efforts worthwhile. But, again, it is interesting (cf. Lockridge 1970; Thornthwaite 1934; Thomas, Kuznets, et al 1957, 1960, 1964) that the data are not primarily organized in terms of frontiers, but rather, in the first instance, of household structures and, in the latter two, of inter-state migration patterns.

For the following section, attempting to construct hypotheses regarding population dynamics in frontier contexts, I have generally relied on three sources: (1) a study of settlement in a Philippine valley, (2) my own field work, which, perhaps fortuitously, took place in what had been a frontier community, and (3) what I would expect to be the case in these situations. If I had more data, I would feel more comfortable. Under these circumstances, we must be most open to references to other sources and to further work on the subject.

The third problem for population statistics in frontier contexts concerns interpretation. By this is meant the relative weight to be given intrinsic demographic processes versus those played by characteristics peculiar to the frontier. Stable population theory states that, given constant age-specific birth and mortality rates, a certain age structure will result that will hold as long as these vital rates remain the same. In turn, these define the rate of growth that will inhere to this population. The essential question that frontier demography must answer here is: To what extent does the population under consideration differ from the condition of stability, and how can this condition be attributed to frontier rather than other dynamics?

At the conclusion of the next section I propose a set of statements that appear to reflect the characteristics of population in frontiers. Basic to these statements is that what happens is different from the condition of stability. As part of this approach, I propose a concept of time that, while not specifiable in terms of specific years, is meant to take place at rates faster than would be the norm if the condition of stability were present. A consideration of frontier populations not only includes time as a basic element but, on the basis of what little evidence is available, it appears that the passage of this time is much more rapid than with normal processes. Thus Thompson's "surprising rapidity" becomes not only a tool for the researcher, but a fact of the definition of demographic change itself.

The presentation of these three problem areas is not meant to turn individuals away from the study of frontier demography, but rather to induce people to enter into it. Frontier demography is itself a frontier. In the following section, I present some ideas which will make this area of endeavor more accessible. But let no one think that work in frontier demography is so difficult. In my search of frontier material, I have been amazed at the number of qualitative statements which appear subject to quantitative verification. And, to put it simply, the social sciences are far beyond the period during which qualitative statements are going to be permitted to stand without argument.

In a very real sense we know that a frontier is or has been such because we have sensed or been told that a rapid or drastic change in population size or characteristics has taken place there. Usually, this has meant an increase, accompanied by a great amount of migration into the area, a greatly biased sex ratio in favor of males, and/or an age structure slanted toward individuals or young adulthood. But few of these facets have been explicitly noted, whereas much attention has been paid to ascertaining settlement patterns, studying frontier character, and developing typologies of frontiers, among other topics. Perhaps (to play devil's advocate for a minute) the differing qualitative statements are the result of different kinds of population movements brought about by different cultures meeting relatively unoccupied territory. It remains frontier demography's task to note these conditions of population structure so that differing qualitative statements can be based on comparative substrata.

In addition to these questions, I would propose frontier demography as another topic for further study. As Mikesell wrote, "the aim of comparative study is to build a foundation for generalization that extends beyond the particular conditions found in a given area at a given time" (1960: 65). I propose that demography provides one of the most salient techniques for comparing the similarities and differences between frontiers. While I highlight similarities here, it is the differences which may have more impact in defining specific processes, and I trust this study will contribute to that.

On the basis of these thoughts, then, let us investigate the population dynamics of frontiers as we are able to ascertain them today.

A Trial Formulation of Frontier Population Dynamics

Discussions of the demography of the frontier, just as with discussions of other facets of the frontier, are concerned with the juxtaposition of two foci—the frontier in comparison or in interaction with its place or places of origin, and the frontier in its own dynamics. Nowhere does this Janus-like approach become more apparent than in discussing the population of the frontier.

First of all, the population of the frontier originates outside of it, and thus we must be concerned with the migratory stream that initiates and perpetuates an interaction between one area and another. But, at the same time, we are concerned with how the frontier area itself evolves and the changing characteristics of its evolving population.

This distinction between interaction with an external population and internal development is a major point of departure for Simkins and Wernstedt's (1971) consideration of settlement in the Digos-Padada Valley of Davao Province, the Philippines. Here they place the major stress on migration, seeing the truly pioneer phase of settlement completed by 1939 and denoted by a decrease in the percentage of migrants *into* the valley. However, this does not mean that the pioneer phase was ended for all parts of the valley. Substantial movement within the valley continued through the 1950's. Thus, the authors speak of a relative balance between migration into the valley as the major source of population increase, versus the later period when in-migration becomes relatively less important, when natural increase rises as the major factor in population growth, and when movement within the valley to localized pioneer areas is of major importance in defining frontier life. This was the case even though in-migration into the valley increased *in numbers* up through 1950; as the major factor in total growth, however, it had been supplanted by natural increase, more people being born than dying.

Simkins and Wernstedt's study, since it concentrates on the migration of people from the rest of the Philippines to the valley, is particularly interested in indentifying the nature of migrants and the factors which were correlated with their leaving their place of origin. At first, males in the migrant stream outnumbered the females quite heavily, with the sex ratio tending to increase with the distance between the origin and destination and to decrease over time. For the whole valley, 1918 statistics show the sex ratio (number of males per one hundred females times 100) is 209, while in 1939 the ratio is 135. Even later, they describe the "major towns of the valley (as) either female-dominant or only slightly male-dominant (while) away from these centers, sex ratios increase" (ibid:85). Thus the sex ratio of the whole valley is tending toward more equality. This contrasts with certain areas within the valley where the sex ratio is as unbalanced as the 1918 statistics for the whole area.

Similarly, they describe the age structure of the early population as young adult. However, with increasing settlement, even though fertility increased with the importation of women, the median age of all inhabitants rose. While this is a valley-wide phenomenon, they say that "the median ages of the population . . . show significant decreases away from the more accessible and more mature areas toward the frontier of settlement where services, facilities and amenities become progressively less available" (ibid:84).

As the sex ratio of the migratory stream became more balanced and as its age composition broadened, more in-migrants married, and more of them came as members of family or household units. Simkins and Wernstedt note that more often than not, even at the beginning when in-migrants were overwhelmingly male, they were married at the time of their arrival. This trait became increasingly dominant as settlement progressed. Of those who came as members of families, the average size of household was concentrated among medium-sized families, that is, fewer were members of small families (6 or fewer persons) or large (10 and more persons) than comparable figures for the Philippines as a whole (ibid:88). However, this would seem to be at least partly counterbalanced by the statement that the "migrant population was characterized by extremely high fertility" (ibid:87). Thus middle-range families probably would experience an increase after in-migration so that by the end of the child-bearing span of the wife they would have become large-size.

Because the major thrust of the Padada Valley study is on migrant characteristics, a large part of it covers economic and social descriptions vis-a-vis place of origin. The stream of migrants from the nation to this valley was not random. As a matter of fact, the authors state, "The origins of the first 10% of the migrants . . . can be used to predict . . . the origins of all subsequent migration." Thus, while the initial movement may be unpredictable, owing to chance factors, "once a migration stream begins pumping in a given direction it continues to flow in that direction despite considerable change in the circumstances that prompted the initial movement. [This] is largely determined by informational and aid links between actual and potential migrants from a given area" (ibid:61). This results in the formation of destination communities dominated by persons from a particular locality, with "each barrio (having) a predominant share of its total population from the same province" (ibid:75).

Migrants also appear to be neither the richest nor the poorest in their locations of origin, having "been selected from among those who had at least some degree of economic success in their home communities" (ibid:94). The "correlation is strongly *inverse* between the rates of out-migration (from origin communities) and economic pressure" (ibid:59, emphasis added). This is so in spite of "economic pressures," or hopes for economic gain, reported as primary stimuli for the move (ibid:60).

Most of the migrants appear to have been urban dwellers, with the movement to the valley meaning a concomitant shift in occupation to farming. Along with this was not only an increase in size of land owned, but labor productivity also increased, making surplus production possible. Of course, this was more characteristically true at the beginning of settlement and there has been a slow tapering off since then. However, productivity and size of land holdings for the valley are reported still high.

However, to summarize the demographic findings of Simkins and Wernstedt's study, it appears we can say that a population that was overwhelmingly male gradually moved toward parity with the opposite sex, that was limited to the ages of young adulthood gradually broadened out, and that, as females began to move into the stream and take up residence with their husbands, natural increase supplanted migration as the major force for expansion. Furthermore, not only do these dynamics exist for migrants from the population of origin to that of destination, but also they hold for areas within the valley.

In microcosm, my field work replicates and expands some of these findings. However, I must state that it was not undertaken in the expectation that this had been a pioneer settlement, nor did the possible impact of this occur until after I had returned to the United States. Perhaps this experience may be illuminating for other field workers and might make profitable a reexamination of the work of others.

From 1970 to 1972 field work was conducted in Baan Dong Phong (read Pong) in Khon Kaen Province, Northeast Thailand. This is a wet-rice community of some 700 souls in 104 households in 1972. My original intention was to explore the cultural ecology of this settlement—the relation of people to landscape as mediated by technology, including conceptual framework, land tenure, material culture, household structure. (Results of this analysis and some data substantiating the conclusions presented here are contained in Lefferts 1974, 1975a, b.) However, in collecting materials through the usual introductory framework of

a census, and while establishing necessary genealogical connections, I elicited an increasingly rich source of historic materials.
This has been organized in a fashion similar to that used by Henry
(1956), Wrigley (1966), and their associates, in the technique
known as family reconstitution. Because my data were collected
orally they therefore can be made to relate to actual households.
I have dubbed the technique "household reconstitution," which
also has the advantage of divorcing it from the somewhat arcane
term "genealogical census." However, no one should think that
this work was not done in the tradition of Rivers (1900, 1910),
who first established its potential on the Torres Strait Expedition.

In contrast to the experience of the Digos-Padada Valley, the
pioneer demography of Baan Dong Phong involves a consideration of pioneer demography in small scale. Thus the establishment of this community some fifty years ago was part of the ex-
plosion of the Thai-Lao population from hearths along the major
rivers of the Korat Plateau to sites that were generally less favored
and further away. In addition, the settlement of Baan Dong Phong
was not part of the moving edge of a frontier, but rather was
part of an interstitial filling-in of locations that had been bypassed
by other settlements whose origin appears lost to the technique
of oral reconstruction. Thus, in 1923, when some 30 households
migrated from a village 25 kilometers to the south to this point,
there were villages already situated in favorable up-land locations
some 3–5 kilometers distant which, even in 1972, maintained their
advantage in numbers. Sometime before 1923 three households
had moved to this location and, by this date, increased to 8 with
62 members. In 1923, 167 individuals organized in 29 households,
all but four of which were related consanguineally or affinally
to each other, moved to this location. The sex ratio of this population was 111.6 males to 100 females, and although exact ages
are difficult to determine, it appears probable that there was a
heavy concentration of adults with younger children, or in other
words, incomplete families.

Following this initial spurt, migration for the next fifteen years
supplied the major increment of growth for the village. While
the rate for the period 1922 to 1927 approaches infinity (because
the denominator of the equation is close to zero), for the period
1927–37 the annual growth rate is 3.65 per cent, of which migration forms the larger factor. This is graphically displayed in Figure
1, which gives one curve (A) showing "real village growth" by
five or ten year periods, and another (B) showing what the growth

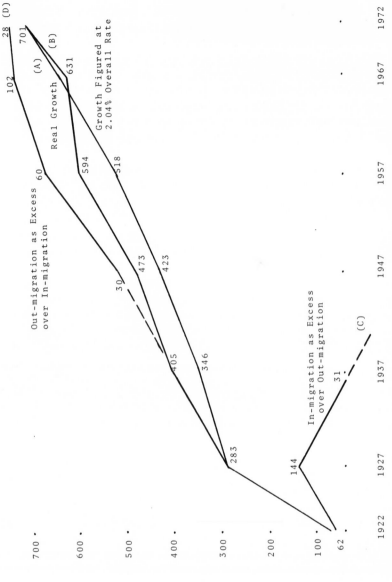

Fig. 1. Population growth and migration, Baan Dong Phong, 1922–1972 (Source: Lefferts 1974)

would be if it were figured at the annual 2.04 per cent rate which held from five years after the initial migration to the closing date of field work.

In Figure 1, two other curves are depicted which form one line extending for the fifty-year existence of the village. This curve demonstrates the influence of migration as a factor in village growth by, in the bottom line (C), showing in-migration as an excess over out-migration which, sometime between 1937 and 1947 (D) transfers to out-migration as an excess over in-migration. If I had no other information, it is for this latter period that I would say, in a statement similar to that of Simkins and Wernstedt, that the village evolved from pioneer status to that of an established settlement.[2]

Coincident with this change from that of a community receiving migrants to that exporting them came a change in the social structural position. Figure 2 shows the percentage of migrants that

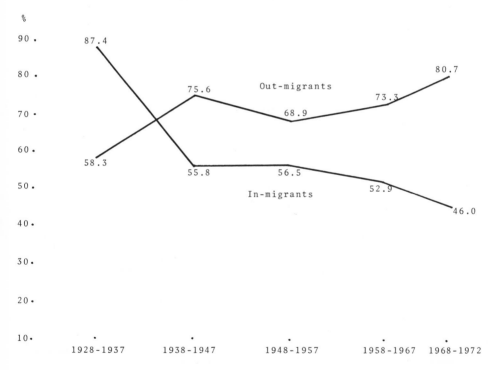

Fig. 2. Percentage of migrants who were members of households Baan Dong Phong, 1928–1972 (Source: Lefferts 1974)

arrived or departed as members of households. It should be re-
membered that the initial analysis of this village occurs after
the time of discovery that would correspond with Simkins and
Wernstedt's period of exploration when single adult men would
be ascertaining the possibilities of this and other locations. Thus
almost all persons before 1928 and 87.4 per cent of in-migrants
for the following ten years were members of households. In opposition to this is the curve of out-migrants. At first Baan Dong
Phong sent out males to establish connections and ascertain new
locations. Later, as these new locations in turn became increasingly settled, the village sent out households to fill the available
niches.

In this way, an observer can see a kind of leap-frog pattern to
settlement. Villages of origin first send out scouts and then families to settle. These are succeeded by second-generation villages
doing the same while the more settled villages reach an irreduc-
ible minimum in in-migrants. In Northeast Thailand these in-
migrants are predominantly males who marry into their wives'
families' households under the prevailing arrangement of uxori-
locality.

Finally, another index of the condition of frontier life is the
skewing of the age distribution towards the age group 20–40.
This has the effect of increasing the number of individuals in
the more productive age categories, a point made in the opening
statement regarding the settlement of Terra Nova.

While Simkins the Wernstedt presented no quantitative data
on this point, the Baan Dong Phong experience may give some
perspective. Figure 3 presents the population distributed by 20-
year age groups, the top of each column being represented by
the group 40 years and over. The last column to the right presents
the current age distribution for Northeast Thailand presented by
the 1970 census (Kingdom of Thailand 1973). If we remember
that we are seeing the initial settlement of young families for
the 1937 and 1947 periods, the figure can be seen as illustrating
the point being made. In addition for the 1937 column, the older
people of the 20–39 age group and those 40+ are under-repre-
sented. Almost 25 per cent of the people reported living as of
that date are of unknown ages.

Taking those factors into account, it appears that the column
for 1947 may be appropriately viewed as the end of a trend that,
if extended back into time, would make the 20–39 age group for
1937 approximately 40 per cent, and be even larger before then.

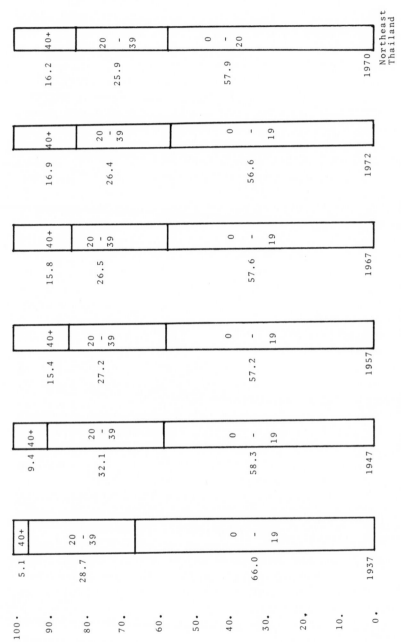

Fig. 3. Age structure of Baan Dong Phong, 1937–1972 of Northeast Thailand, 1970 (Source: Lefferts 1974, Kingdom of Thailand 1973)

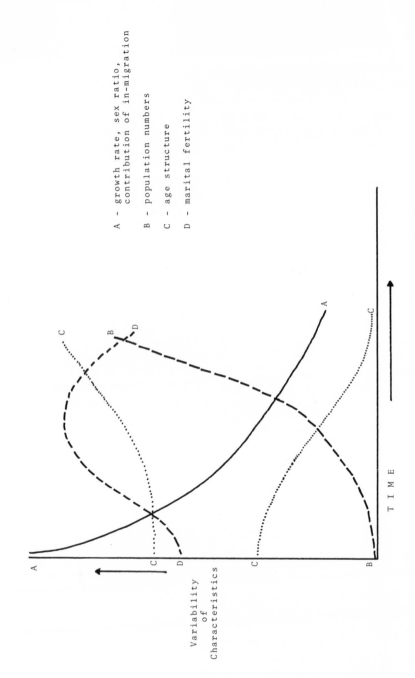

Fig. 4. Regularities in frontier demography

A – growth rate, sex ratio, contribution of in-migration

B – population numbers

C – age structure

D – marital fertility

TIME

Variability of Characteristics

We certainly see that a definite break occurs between 1947 and the columns of later dates, with the latter in substantial agreement with that holding for the surrounding region today.

Figure 4 is a summary statement of these two studies. Each of these curves depicts one or a number of the characteristics of population which have been observed to vary regularly under frontier conditions. These are: numbers, growth rate, sex ratio, in-migrants as individuals rather than as members of households, and age structure. They are plotted with time represented on the horizontal axis and variability of the characteristic noted on the vertical axis. No absolute time or standard measure of change in the characteristic is proposed; the figure is meant to display the changes in the characteristics that have been considered and give indications of their possible interrelationships.

Curve A represents the direction in which the growth rate, sex ratio, and the contribution of in-migration are expected to move. These are, for growth rate, in a relatively smooth flow from high, reaching almost to infinity, to low or almost no growth; for the sex ratio, from one biased strongly towards males to relative equality between the sexes; and for migration as a factor in growth, from a very high to almost negligible role.

Curve B is the logistics curve by which population growth in absolute numbers is usually depicted. At this point it should be noted that none of these curves define their concluding endpoints. Rather, the emphasis in their depiction is on beginnings and the carry-over effects of these beginnings on the mid-range of population characteristics for areas that had been frontiers. Most demographic and social scientific discussion has concerned the end-states of these curves, a position which distinguishes those studies from this one, and to which we shall return towards the conclusion of the next section.

Finally, in order to represent the changes in the age structure, two curves (C) which bear an asymetric relationship to each other are given. The area between them is meant to represent the broadening of the age structure that we have observed taking place in pioneer contexts. The lower line, representing the impact of the changing sex ratio and the rapid rise in fertility is meant to move downwards more rapidly, while the upper line, representing indigenous expansion in the older ages and probable heightened mortality during the pioneer phase moves more slowly. (Curve D will be explained in the following section.)

In conclusion, the purpose of this section has been to present data and draw preliminary conclusions concerning regularities in the demography of differing pioneer situations. It has been summarized by a figure which, while incorporating many in-puts, seems to indicate, at least on a trial basis, that some regularities may exist. These regularities, in turn, have much in common with demographic phenomena pertaining to other contexts. It is my contention that in pioneer situations they are seen to occur in a differing configuration, and to happen over a much more compressed time span. The next section is concerned with discussing theoretical positions which may explain and at the same time direct further research to the dynamics of frontier population growth.

Theoretical Underpinnings of Frontier Demography

The preceding section attempted to develop, on the basis of too few studies, a statement concerning the dynamics of population in frontier areas. It was essentially descriptive, and gives a basis from which to depart for further work. However, this description leaves much to be desired. We must pit it against theoretical statements that would give it meaning or that would at least pose as basis for further questions.

In this section two hypotheses will be sketched which might make further work in frontier demography more worthwhile. In other words, there come to mind two theories which depend on demographic statements of frontier life for their foundation and which therefore would provide the impetus for developing continuing research in this field. The first of these theories has to do with the course of fertility under frontier conditions, a discussion which leads to the Malthus/Boserup controversy. The second, more of a perspective than a theory, is concerned with bringing the study of human frontier populations into the purview of the discussions in biological ecology regarding colonization.

One of the many advantages in studying frontier demography is the possibility of observing in microcosm and rather rapidly how human populations adjust to changing environmental conditions. The contrasting theories of Malthus and Boserup use population pressure, induced by rapid growth, as a major focus to propose, in the case of the former (Malthus 1960), that human populations must necessarily outrun their resources or, in the case of the latter (Boserup 1965), that population growth is an inducement toward social and economic change.

These are large questions which have, at times, been approached in sweeping terms. But the study of frontiers may make it possible to break them down into specific, approachable components. For instance, it appears in both of the cited cases, the Digos-Padada Valley in the Philippines and Baan Dong Phong in Northeast Thailand, that the people developed some methods by which they controlled the amount of people per land area, even though the population of each location continued to grow. The specific control mechanism in these cases would have to be one or a combination of out-migration, a reduction in fertility, or an increase in mortality.

Richard Easterlin of the University of Pennsylvania and Marvin McInnis of Queen's University, Canada, have been concentrating on changing fertility patterns in frontier contexts as a prime question to explain North American rural adaptation as a part of the demographic transition. Using 1860 and 1861 census materials which are available for each household, they have classified the areas in which these households exist by their closeness to the frontier. They find that:

> Fertility rises consistently as one moves from older to newer settlement areas with one exception. Average fertility in the "frontier townships," if we may use this term, while higher than in the oldest area, is perhaps 5 to 10 percent lower than in the newly settled areas slightly behind the frontier, those with, say 20 to 40 percent of their land improved. (Easterlin 1975:5).

Following this, Easterlin and McInnis (1974) analyze their data regarding possible statistical biases and the relative importance of various factors, such as origin of in-migrants, dependency ratios, education, employment opportunities for women, children, and adult males, economic conditions, and selective migration. None of these appears to explain adequately the rise and decline of fertility that they observe. Consequently, Easterlin proposes an inter-generational effect as follows:

> A distinction may be drawn between (1) first generation settlers, recent migrants who have often had at least some of their children somewhere else than their current place of residence, (2) second

generation settlers, who may be born in an area or have migrated there with their parents, and (3) third or later generation settlers. The implication of our data is that as a given area moves through these successive generations of settlers, marital fertility rises between the first and second generation, and then starts to decline as the third generation takes over. The highest level of marital fertility occurs with the second generation, that comprising the first group of what might be called "home grown" residents. (Easterlin 1975:19) (Curve D on Figure 4 is designed to represent this finding.)

From this Easterlin deduces that the situation is not so much that of a condition of pro-fertility conditions in a frontier situation, but rather of "anti-fertility pressures that emerge as an area becomes more settled — pressures to which the first wave of 'home grown' settlers (the second generation) are largely oblivious, but which become increasingly apparent to their successors." This, then, resolves itself into a theory of land scarcity, the problem eventually posed is that it might be a component of delayed child-cost, "namely, the cost of establishing children on nearby farms when they reach adulthood" (ibid:19).

McInnis, in his discussion, also points out that some kind of long-term adjustment must be built into whatever model is proposed. In discussing Easterlin's hypothesis he says:

> The second generation, brought up in the austerity of frontier conditions has modest expectations about levels of consumption of material goods yet inherits productive assets capable of generating a significantly higher level of income than their parents were able to enjoy. It is their children — the third generation — that feel the pinch of higher standards of material goods consumption with relatively less farm land to go around and more pressure to choose carefully and rationally between children and material goods.

His concluding sentences are that "Even if the evidence points in this direction, though, it is slim evidence. It might, however, suggest a direction for further investigations (ibid:48)."

One can only agree, therefore, that further research must be done in comparative, preferably non-Western, contexts to establish these events as having taken place, and then to derive possible causal sequences. On the basis of this kind of discussion, though, it is possible to give free rein to one's thoughts and propose that perhaps a good portion of the developing world, in terms of its fertility experience, may be going through the equivalent of a second-generation effect in which economic and social horizons are relatively open. As the third generation has its children the effect of preceding fertility joined with a relative decrease in economic opportunities may bring about a reduction to more temperate levels. In any case, it is only through more careful research at the micro, household level that we will be able to observe the occurrence of this permutation of transition theory, if, indeed, that does happen.

As social scientists, we can appreciate the intricacies of discussing the various rates of change and growth of human frontier populations. But, at the same time, we must recognize that human populations are part of the total spectrum of populations in general and that they therefore deserve to be compared across species boundaries. Demography is perhaps the key study in this regard, since it permits quantitative statements about change by which to compare populations of many kinds with the ability to disregard for the moment qualitative statements of meanings and values.

Since I do not pretend to be conversant with all of the materials of biological ecology, it would perhaps be best to give an indication of the kind of effect a dialogue between human and biological frontier demography might have on the social sciences. I am led to this consideration by *Geographical Ecology* by Robert MacArthur (1971) and a review of it by Scott Boorman which appeared in *Science* (1972).

The thrust of MacArthur's book is to concentrate on patterns of extinction and colonization, an emphasis different from other volumes on ecology which stress equilibrium and stasis. In doing so, the author eschews the use of complex model building, believing that such limits a comprehension of the trends taking place in these conditions. "The theme running through this book is that the structure of the environment, the morphology of the species, the economics of species behavior, and the dynamics of population changes are the four essential ingredients of biographic patterns (MacArthur 1972:1)." However, in describing the distribution of species he notes that "environmental heterogeneity is necessary to co-existence" (ibid:25). In instances of homogeneity, populations run either to extinction or to superabundance. Envrionmental heterogeneity permits prey to survive hidden from omnipresent predators.

Also regarding predator-prey relations, MacArthur cites studies which show that these ". . . interactions have a built-in time lag. When the prey are commonest, the predators are increasing the fastest, but there is some delay before they reach their commonest, and by that time they have overeaten their prey, which have decreased" (ibid:30). However, under more complex environmental conditions, the longer the predators take to increase (in reality, the more easily prey can hide and the less easily predators can find them), the less risk the predators have of overreaching their source of supply. It is interesting to speculate on a homology between this and the cycle of human fertility that Easterlin and McInnis observed for North American frontiers.

MacArthur also discusses the relative merits of migration. "Can we ever," he asks in conclusion, "find a situation where a unidirectional and continuous migration is beneficial? The answer is unknown" (ibid:152). What about the human colonization pattern? Does such a statement apply?

Finally, Boorman's review epitomizes what may be the value of frontier demography in comparative perspective and to symposia on comparative frontiers: "Sociological model-building seldom progresses beyond dealing with processes involving fixed sets of categories such as attitudes or social classes. The ontogeny of dissolution of such a categorical system, even in a highly local environment, is almost never tackled from a formal standpoint" (Boorman 1972:393).

Traditionally, populations that are growing or approaching extinction have been "embarrassing" to the social sciences. They have conceived the world as made-up of a number of relatively self-sufficient units that neither expand nor die. Populations of hunters and gatherers and of industrialized states do not behave in this manner and this model is even beginning to be discarded as appropriate to peasantry to which it has been traditionally applied. The use of ecological examples as touchstones for organizing data on and comprehending human pioneer populations may be one way to continue to import this dynamism into the social sciences.

Conclusion

This chapter has presented ideas, data, and theory ranging from Terra Nova to the Philippines, Thailand, the frontier United States, and general ecological considerations. Primarily, it is meant to generate new ideas by concentrating on an area of discourse which seems neglected. What new ideas can we say have come to the fore?

These new ideas can be summarized as pertaining in two contrasting directions—theoretical implications and methodological considerations. Theoretically, we must bear in mind that the study of pioneer demography may have important implications—if Terra Nova seems too distant—for the following areas:

1. It has implicit within it a comparison with ecological studies of colonization.

2. By definition it is possible to utilize frontier studies to test the Malthus/Boserup hypotheses concerning the effect of population pressure on the landscape and on its own characteristics.

3. Within demography, pioneer studies have the potential of examining the interrelationships between several demographic characteristics. The condition of rapid change implicit in most frontier situations provides a ready-made test for analyzing these relationships over relatively short time periods.

4. For frontier studies generally, it is proposed that the study of demography provides access to a precision which may be helpful.

5. Finally, there may arise a time when it might be useful to turn the idea of a frontier demography around and analyze situations in which a similar constellation of demographic characteristics occur as reflecting features of the frontier. Thus, pioneer demography may become a predictive device, and pinpoint "hidden" frontiers, such as may occur with technological expansion, social structural invention, and so forth.

Methodologically, what do studies of frontier demography hold for us? Two results may be important:

1. When discussing populations in frontiers, it is not enough to chart growth as the sole characteristic. This study shows that other changes are perhaps more indicative than expansion or rate of growth alone. Studies of frontiers can rely on demographic data and techniques which at first may seem hidden. The work of historical demographers and historic enthographers and archaeologists are cases in point. For comparative work, demography provides a valuable tool.

2. As an anthropologist, I would make the appeal that demog-

raphy is a usable resource in ethnographic studies, and that work in the area can be profitable. The questions are there to be addressed; the techniques are available. It remains to do the work. The foundations of Terra Nova exist on Terra Firma today.

Notes

1. This paper was written while the author was employed under USAID Contract CM/pha-C-73-25, Culture and Population Programs. Thanks are due the contractor and Dr. Vera Rubin, Director, Research Institute for the Study of Man, for their indulgence during the paper's composition and typing. Presented at the Second Oklahoma Symposium on Comparative Frontier Studies, University of Oklahoma, March, 1976.

2. This last statement is not to be construed as implying, however, that in- and out-migration did not continue to be a major factor in community life. It appears that at no time in the fifty years of Baan Dong Phong's existence has the percentage of migrants within a ten-year period dropped below 40 per cent of the total population. Thus, while the switch from net migration to natural increase as the major factor for population growth signifies the conclusion of the pioneer phase of settlement for the village, the "turnover" rate continues high and appears to be endemic to life on the Korat Plateau.

References Cited

Boorman, Scott A.
  1972   Analogies in the Social Sciences, Review of MacArthur 1972. Science 178:391–393.
Boserup, Ester
  1965   The Conditions of Agricultural Growth. Chicago: Aldine.
Easterlin, Richard A.
  1975   Factors in the Decline of Farm Family Fertility in the United States: Some Preliminary Results, Revised Draft. Paper presented at American Historical Association, Chicago, 1974. Forthcoming in *Journal of Economic History.*
Henry, Louis
  1956   Anciennes Familles Genevoises: Etude demographique: XVIe-XXe siecle. Cahier No. 26, Institut National d'etudes demographiques. Paris: Presses Universitaires de France.
Keyfitz, Nathan
  1975   How Do We Know the Facts of Demography? Population and Development Review 1(2):267–288.
Kingdom of Thailand
  1973   1970 Population and Housing Census, Northeastern Region. Bangkok: National Statistical Office, Office of the Prime Minister.

Lefferts, H. L., Jr.
1974   Baan Dong Phong: Land Tenure and Social Organization in a North-
        eastern Thai Community. Unpublished Ph.D. Dissertation, Depart-
        ment of Anthropology, University of Colorado.
1975a   Change and Population in a Northeastern Thai Village, *In,* Population
        and Development in Southeast Asia, ed. by J. F. Kantner and L.
        McCaffrey. Lexington, Mass.: D. C. Heath, pp. 173–178.
1975b   The Historical Demography of Developing Areas: A Research and
        Theoretical Frontier, *In,* Sociological Research Symposium V, ed. by
        W. S. Williams, A. M. Schwartzbaum, and R. F. Ganey. Richmond:
        Virginia Commonwealth University, pp. 64–69.
Lockridge, Kenneth
1970   A New England Town: The First Hundred Years. New York: Norton.
MacArthur, Robert H.
1972   Geographical Ecology: Patterns in the Distribution of Species. New
        York: Harper and Row.
Malthus, Thomas
1960   On Population. New York: Modern Library.
McInnis, R. M.
1974   Childbearing and Land Availability: Some Evidence from Individual
        Household Data. Paper presented at conference "Behavioral Models
        in Historical Demography." Philadelphia.
Mikesell, Marvin
1960   Comparative Studies in Frontier History. Annals of the Association
        of American Geographers 50:62–74.
Rivers, W. H. R.
1900   A Geographical Method of Collecting Social and Vital Statistics. Jour-
        nal of the Royal Anthropological Institute 30:74–82.
1910   The Genealogical Method of Anthropological Inquiry. Sociological
        Review 3:1–12.
Shryock, H. S., J. S. Siegel and Associates
1973   The Methods and Materials of Demography. Washington: U.S.G.P.O.
Simkins, Paul D., and Frederick L. Wernstedt
1971   Philippines Migration: Settlement of the Digos-Padada Valley, Davao
        Province. New Haven: Yale University Southeast Asia Studies #16.
Shurkin, Joel N.
1975   Colonies in Space: A Princeton Professor is Dreaming the Possible
        Dream. Today (Sunday Magazine of the Philadelphia Inquirer) 23
        November:12–20.
Thomas, D. S., S. Kuznets, et al.
1957, 1960, 1964 Population Redistribution and Economic Growth in the
        United States, 3 vols. Philadelphia: American Philosophical Society.
Thompson, Stephen I.
1973   Pioneer Colonization: A Cross-Cultural View, Addison-Wesley Module
        in Anthropology #33.
Thornwaite, C. Warren
1934   Internal Migration in the United States. Philadelphia: University of
        Pennsylvania Press.
Wrigley, E. A., ed.
1966   An Introduction to English Historical Demography. New York: Basic
        Books.

Civitates and Clients: Roman Frontier Policies in Pannonia and Mauretania Tingitana

John W. Eadie

ALTHOUGH the accumulation of archaeological data has gradually reduced the ancient historian's dependence on literary sources, the classical image of the barbarian as cultural assassin and the perception of the Roman frontier as a military barrier continue to dominate discussions of Roman relations with tribal groups on the borders. Only within the past twenty-five years have some historians renounced the centrist bias of the literary sources and begun to approach the frontier experience from the periphery. The most instructive of these alternatives to the conventional conceptual framework have been the attempts to reconstruct the internal organization of the "barbarian" tribes in Europe. By establishing new ways of measuring the impact of Roman expansion on regional interaction spheres, these studies have provided a radically different perspective for frontier studies.*

Whether this new approach is flexible enough, or comprehensive enough, to account for the diversity of Roman responses to tribal practices and initiatives is uncertain. The principal defect, in my judgment, is that it assesses the Roman intrusion into the tribal areas primarily in military terms—so much so that the image of the barbarian as cultural assassin is simply replaced by the Tacitean portrayal (expressed in Calgacus' speech, *Agricola* 30, 4) of the Romans as insatiable plunderers *(raptores orbis)*. Thus, neither the revisionists nor their predecessors have adequately appreciated the Roman attempt, fundamental to the development of their frontier policies, to establish the regions on both sides of a border as zones of acculturation.

Early on in their conquest of the "civilized" Mediterranean states the Romans learned that the control of politically and culturally diverse populations could not be effected by military means alone. By the end of the third century B.C. they had already developed the policy (modeled on the existing patron-client system that regulated Roman social relations) of governing overseas territories through alliances with native rulers and aristocrats.

Recognizing that interference with local institutions and practices could only inspire further resistance, the Romans entrusted much of the administration to these surrogates, buttressed by the presence or promise of Roman military support.

The transfer of supreme authority in provincial affairs from the senate to the emperors did not alter this policy. Throughout the Mediterranean the Roman emperors continued to rely on the managerial expertise of the native elites and from time to time rewarded their services with grants of citizenship and special privileges. This policy was so effective that Augustus and his immediate successors were able to disarm most of the provinces bordering the Mediterranean, the civilized zone, and to concentrate their armies on the periphery under the direction of the commanders and governors whom they appointed.

Because they were ethnically and culturally different from the interior provinces, the frontier zones offered peculiar challenges to imperial ingenuity. Even in these remote and uncivilized areas, however, the emperors were not inclined to abandon traditional responses without a trial. Just as the Republican commanders and the senate had selected urban aristocrats to govern territories they did not wish to administer directly, the Roman emperors and their representatives attempted to use tribal leaders to maintain order on both sides of the provincial border. Within the frontier provinces the Romans agreed to respect the customs and institutions of the incorporated tribal groups so long as they remained within the authorized political units *(civitates)* and consented to supervision by a Roman military official *(praefectus)*. With the tribes inhabiting the regions adjacent to the provincial borders the Romans entered into alliances which converted their leaders into clients and their warbands into supernumerary members of the Roman defense network. In exchange for the tribe's friendship *(amicitia)* and tangible support, the Romans were prepared to grant certain privileges: unrestricted movement within existing regional interaction spheres; opportunities for trade with Roman merchants; and on occasion, when their loyalty had been adequately demonstrated, citizenship for royal and noble families.

Not surprisingly the clients (the "outer barbarians") were less content with this interlocking and highly stratified system than the tribes living inside the Roman borders (the "inner barbarians"), who participated more directly in provincial affairs and gradually acquired Roman status and privileges. Rarely was a client's disaffection, however, the direct result of Roman military intervention. By the end of the first century A.D. the Romans had abandoned thoughts of world conquest, if indeed they had ever entertained them, and for the most part (Dacia, Armenia, and Syria excepted) were prepared to live within the established borders. Only when a tribal chief decided to annul an existing arrangement by leading his warband into Roman territory were the military units stationed on the periphery committed to battle. If those garrisons were not able to repel the attack, the local commanders or the emperor himself would attempt to appease the insurgents by renegotiating the earlier arrangement, hoping thereby to achieve through diplomacy the stability his troops could not ensure.

During the first two centuries of the Empire military failures could be put right by diplomatic concessions of this sort, occasionally involving promises of annual payments of tribute to the restive tribe or tribal confederation. It was only in the third century, when external pressures impaired relations with the clients, that military action, rather than diplomacy, became for a time the foundation of Roman frontier policy.

This brief, and admittedly simplified, survey describes Roman responses in Europe, but it does not take into account the variations found elsewhere in the Empire. To illustrate the diversity of Roman policies I propose to examine Roman relations with tribal groups in two geographically, and ethnographically, dissimilar frontier provinces, Pannonia and Mauretania Tingitana. The specific purpose of this exercise is to demonstrate that relations with tribal groups determined the shape and character of Roman frontiers and that the security of the border zones was usually maintained through diplomatic rather than military initiatives.

Pannonia

The Romans established a foothold in the Balkans during the third century B.C. and gradually expanded this to include most of modern Yugoslavia and Albania, but it was not until the campaigns of Augustus in 35 B.C. that they acquired a portion of the Pannonian territory. Augustus apparently did not undertake the conquest of the Pannonian tribes in the Sava Valley in order to increase opportunities for colonization or simply to establish a natural frontier in northern Illyricum. Rather, it seems that he

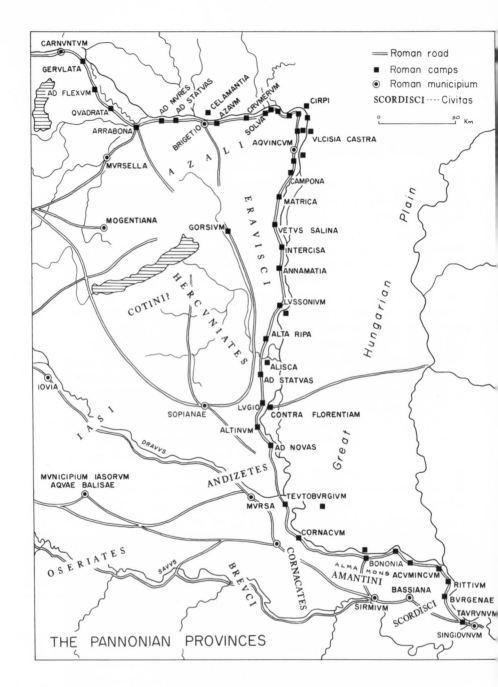

Fig. 1. The Pannonian Province

envisaged the campaign as a first step in a major confrontation with the Dacians. The Pannonian tribal center of Siscia, which he captured after a thirty-day siege, was to be the staging area for the larger effort; in it Augustus stationed twenty-five Roman cohorts, roughly 12,000 men, who would constitute the core of his Dacian army.[1] Augustus never implemented his grand strategy, but his initial foray into the Sava Valley opened the way for the conquest of the middle Danube. How the establishment of a Roman garrison in Siscia affected existing tribal associations cannot be determined from the literary evidence we possess, but it is not unreasonable to suppose that the displacement of the Celtic Scordisci was in some way connected with the Roman intrusion.

Although we do not know when the Scordisci first occupied the region of Srem, between the Danube and the Sava, it is clear that they had established themselves as a major power in the area several decades before the Roman attack on Siscia (35 B.C.). The Romans did not immediately march into Srem, but their advance into the Sava Valley was evidently enough to drive the Scordisci into an alliance with the Dentheletai in southern Illyricum (16 B.C.). Whether this movement into the south should be considered a migration, perhaps to reclaim lands they had once held in this area, or an attempt to force the Romans to campaign on two fronts cannot be determined. In any event, the resistance ended the following year when a large army under the command of Tiberius, Augustus' stepson, defeated the Scordisci and forced the tribe to resettle in Srem as Roman clients.[2]

Five years later (12–11 B.C.) the Scordisci joined their patron in a successful campaign against neighboring tribes, the Breuci and Amantini, which culminated in the annexation of the territory between the Sava and the Danube to the province of Illyricum. Their loyalty to Rome was tested again in A.D. 6–9, when the Breuci rebelled, besieged the town of Sirmium—in which some Romans resided—and occupied the nearby Alma Mons, the Fruška Gora region which belonged to the Scordisci. Whether members of the tribe participated militarily in the campaign to expel the Pannonians is not certain, but the decision not to defect to the insurgents demonstrates clearly their continuing commitment to *amicitia* with the Romans.[3]

We are not told how the Romans rewarded the Scordisci for their loyalty during this last rebellion of the Pannonian tribes, nor do we know the status of these tribes in the years following the Roman victory. By the reign of Claudius, however, all the tribal groups in the Sava Valley had been reconstituted in *civitates*. In a sense, a *civitas* was nothing more than a successful variant of the patron-client system the Romans had perfected during their conquest of the "civilized" Mediterranean states. Unlike the client-state, however, a *civitas* did not necessarily include all the original territory of the tribe and in many cases was defined for administrative convenience. Moreover, although some of the *civitates* in Pannonia may have been *liberae* or *foederatae*—that is, at the time of their surrender the chiefs had negotiated treaties which did not place their tribes under the supervision of Roman military officials—most were assigned a military *praefectus,* usually a centurion from a Roman unit stationed in the vicinity, who managed tribal affairs and represented the tribe before his superiors. As a condition of their preservation some of the *civitates* may have been required to pay tribute and all were encouraged to contribute recruits to the Roman army. If a *civitas* met its obligations, remained loyal, and gradually adopted Roman practices, it would be permitted in time a measure of self-government. By the end of the first century, in fact, the military prefects had generally been replaced by leading members of the tribe, the *principes.*[4] This gradual elevation to self-government indicates that the primary goal of internal Roman policy in Pannonia, as in the other European provinces, was the Romanization of native groups. The final step in the process, of course, was the grant of citizenship, and by the beginning of the second century the *principes* of many *civitates* in Pannonia had received this stamp of approval.[5]

With the extension of their control north of the Drava the Romans gradually were able to organize all the Pannonian tribes into *civitates,* and these remained the basis of Roman-tribal relations for the next two centuries. Even when the Romans established permanent forts in the Danubian zone and sponsored the growth of towns *(municipia* and *coloniae)* in both of the Pannonian provinces, Inferior and Superior, these *civitates* survived. Most of the original *civitates,* in fact, were still in existence at the beginning of the third century.[6]

The Romans could not impose the *civitas* organization on the tribes beyond the Danube which had not surrendered, however, and were required to revert to the older patron-client relationship. The fact that the Germanic and Sarmatian tribes across the river were ethnically distinct from the Pannonian tribes undoubtedly facilitated the development of a different policy. The aim of both internal and external policies, however, was the same—that is, pacification through diplomacy rather than war. A brief review of Roman relations with the Sarmatian Iazyges will indicate the effectiveness of Roman policy toward their clients in Pannonian frontier zones.

At the time of Augustus' campaign in 35 B.C. the Iazyges were still in the Carpathians, but by the middle of the first century they had migrated into the Great Hungarian Plain and later settled in the Tisza Valley. In his *Res Gestae* (31, 2), Augustus boasted that the Sarmatians had dispatched an embassy to establish friendly relations with the Romans, but there is no way of knowing whether the Iazyges participated and there is no reason to believe that they became clients at this time. It was their alliance with the Suebi under Domitian that evidently disrupted the pattern of peaceful coexistence and brought them into direct conflict with Rome. Unfortunately, only Dio Cassius—or rather the fragments of Dio Cassius Byzantine excerptors in the eleventh century chose to preserve—provides an account of the Suebian-Sarmatian War. From this it is clear that the war lasted until the early years of Trajan's reign, but it is not certain that the treaty the Iazyges signed reduced them to client status. More secure information is supplied by another fragment, usually dated to A.D. 117, which mentions an embassy from the Iazyges seeking renewal of the client treaty. It is safe to conclude, therefore, that at some point during Trajan's reign the Iazyges did become clients.[7]

The best evidence of Roman-Iazyges relations is associated with the Marcomannic Wars, which completely disrupted existing client relationships in the Pannonian zone during the 170's. To suppress the rebellious clients Roman armies crossed the Danube and attacked the Quadi and Marcomanni, the two major tribal groups situated on the northern Pannonian border. Operations against the Iazyges, who were initially allied with the Quadi, began somewhat later (173) and continued until their defeat in 175. The terms the Romans imposed were harsh. The Iazyges king, Zanticus, and the chief men of the tribe who accompanied him agreed not to inhabit a ten-mile "no-man's-land" on their side of the Danube, to return 100,000 [*sic*!] captives, and to provide the Romans each year with a contingent of 8,000 cavalrymen.[8]

This apparently did not resolve all the issues, however, since the Iazyges a few years later (179) joined with the Buri, a tribe from the Carpathians, in an unsuccessful attempt to revoke the agreement. They were again defeated, but their effort did persuade the Romans to renegotiate the earlier treaty. The terms were now more acceptable—only their access to Roman markets and their right to keep boats on the Danube were restricted. Moreover, the Romans agreed that the Iazyges could pass through Dacia to associate with their kinsmen, the Roxolani, so long as the governor of Dacia consented.[9]

These terms compare favorably with those imposed on the Marcomanni and Quadi at the end of the war. To prevent attacks in the future Marcus Aurelius ordered the construction of forts in their territory which could accommodate 20,000 Roman troops.[10] One ancient source reports, in fact, that the emperor intended to annex all the tribal territory, incorporating it into two new provinces, Marcomannia and Sarmatia.[11] The death of Marcus Aurelius precluded implementation of this scheme, if it had been envisaged, and the outposts he had established were dismantled by his son and successor, Commodus. Roman surveillance continued for some time under the direction of a centurion, however, who supervised the monthly assembly of the tribes at a site selected by the Romans. Although this is the same military officer who initially served as *praefectus* of the Pannonian *civitates,* one should not assume that the Romans intended to organize the Marcomanni and Quadi into *civitates.* On the other hand, the appointment of a centurion is clearly consistent with existing Roman policy toward tribal groups.[12]

Whether Marcus Aurelius intended to annex the Iazyges kingdom, incorporating it in a new province called Sarmatia, cannot be determined. His relatively lenient treatment of the tribe following their rebellion certainly does not point in this direction. It is possible, of course, that the creation of Sarmatia was discussed at some point during the period, perhaps in the course of the first campaign (173–175), and then rejected. In any event, garrisons and forts apparently were not constructed in their territory, and the tribe was reinstated as a client in good standing.

The Marcomannic Wars did not cause the Romans to abandon their bi-level frontier policy—pacification through the organization of tribal *civitates* and the neutralization of potentially dangerous groups across the Pannonian border through clientage. The *civitates* survived the conflagration and for several decades remained the principal medium for Roman relations with the "inner barbarians." Indeed, epigraphic evidence of grants of citizenship to members of the Pannonian *civitates* and the incorporation of entire *civitates* into the towns during the third century suggest that these groups did not require the *Constitutio Antoniniana* (A.D. 212) to establish their Roman status. Romanization of the Pannonian *civitates* proceeded so smoothly, in fact, that there is not the slightest hint of internal friction in our sources.

The same cannot be said, of course, for Roman relations with the clients. Yet, only once during the first two centuries of Roman rule in Pannonia was the disruption serious enough to require a prolonged military campaign. For most of the period the border was relatively secure and lesions in Roman relations with "barbaricum" were quickly repaired by negotiation. Even the Marcomannic Wars did not persuade the Romans to jettison the client system. It was only in the third century, when the familiar groups— Marcomanni, Quadi, Iazyges—were forced to share their kingdoms with less Romanized immigrants that the client system began to disintegrate. Neither the clients nor the Romans were able to absorb the new groups quickly enough to prevent their migration across the provincial borders.

The elaborate system the Romans developed and their determination to preserve it at all costs clearly indicates that the Pannonian frontier extended beyond the provincial borders. That the Romans included barbaricum in the zone of acculturation is attested by the treaties that alternately permitted or denied access to Roman markets and Roman civilization, by their attempts to regulate royal succession within the client system, and by their decision to settle large numbers of clients on Roman soil following the Marcomannic Wars.[13] Romanization of clients may have progressed more slowly, but the Romans clearly considered it no less important than Romanization of the *civitates*.

Mauretania Tingitana

The frontier in Tingitana developed in a very different political and geographical context. Since the second century B.C. the Romans had monitored North African affairs and had periodically supported the incumbent Numidian/Mauretanian monarchs or their rivals in domestic quarrels. Their interference in one succession crisis in Numidia, in fact, had triggered the long and frustrating war with Jugurtha (last decade of second century). It was the Numidian involvement in the civil war between Pompey

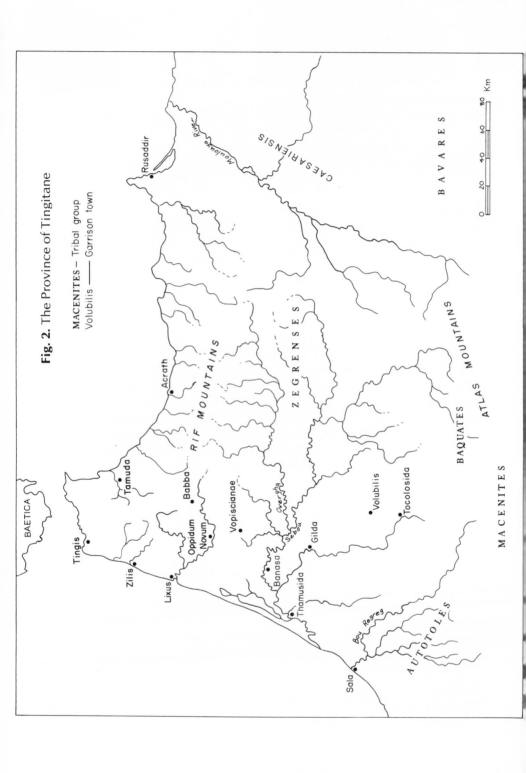

Fig. 2. The Province of Tingitane

MACENITES – Tribal group
Volubilis —— Garrison town

and Caesar (they supported the loser), however, that persuaded the Romans to annex their kingdom. With Numidia under direct Roman rule, Augustus' decision to convert the neighboring, and politically connected, kingdom of Mauretania (Caesariensis and Tingitana) into a client state was almost inevitable.

The Romans had good reason to believe that a Mauretanian client would protect their interests; the obvious candidate, Juba II, the son of the former king of Numidia, had impeccable credentials. Educated in Italy, where he had lived as a hostage from the age of four, Juba had earned Roman citizenship and had frequently accompanied Augustus on campaigns. Perhaps the only blemish on his record was his marriage to Cleopatra Selene, the daughter of Antony and Cleopatra. But this did not dissuade Augustus from recognizing him as client-king of Mauretania (25 B.C.). Because Juba was thoroughly Romanized and was anxious to please his patron, Mauretania was now effectively in Roman hands. So much so that Augustus did not hesitate to establish Roman colonies in Tingitana at Babba and Banasa, presumably under the supervision of the governor of Spain.

With Roman assistance Juba survived several attempted assassinations and rebellions and remained on the throne until his death in A.D. 23 (at which time the Romans were preparing for their final campaign against his most serious rival, Tacfarinas). His son and successor, Ptolemy, was less fortunate. Although he had served the Romans well, and had earned the title "rex, socius atque amicus" (Tacitus, *Annales* 4, 26), Ptolemy was executed in A.D. 40 on orders from Caligula, who evidently had decided that the Mauretanian protectorate should be abolished.[14] Thus, Tingitana, unlike Pannonia, became a Roman province by imperial fiat rather than military conquest.

The southern boundary of Juba's territory in Tingitana cannot be determined from the later Roman sources, but it is clear that Volubilis, his western capital, was even then a frontier town. The well-watered Plaine du Sais immediately to the south was certainly included within the kingdom and it is not impossible that the narrow green belt which extends into the Middle Atlas range was also under Juba's control. Unfortunately, we do not know the extent and character of Juba's relations with the indigenous tribes, the sedentary groups around Volubilis or the pastoral nomads of the Middle Atlas, and consequently cannot assess the progress of pacification in this area before the Roman annexation.

Nor is it certain that Juba commanded the loyalty of all the tribes in the region north of Volubilis (that is, north of Fez-Meknes-Rabat) or in the Moulouya valley to the east. Only in the western regions did Ptolemy's murder incite his subjects to rebel, under the leadership of Aedemon, one of his courtiers, and this was quickly suppressed by Roman units from Spain and "auxiliaries" resident in Volubilis. In recognition of the latter's loyal service in the campaign Claudius, Caligula's successor, made Volubilis *municipium* and granted to the inhabitants *(incolae)* the right to marry natives *(peregrini)* and exemption *(immunitas)* from certain civic duties. Since the prefect of the "auxiliaries," M. Valerius Severus, was a Roman citizen and the right to marry natives is intelligible only if the recipients were Roman citizens, it is probable that a fairly sizable group of Romans had been living in Volubilis for some time.[15]

The existence of Roman settlements in Volubilis, Babba, and Banasa, however, does not imply that Tingitana was thoroughly Romanized before annexation. Although the tribes in the environs of Volubilis may have been incorporated by Claudius' grant into the new *municipium,* there is no reason to believe that this became official Roman policy throughout Tingitana. In his *Geography* (compiled in the second century A.D.) Ptolemy supplies the names of nine tribes (presumably sedentary) situated within the official boundaries of the province, but he does not indicate their status vis-a-vis the Romans. We can say with some confidence, however, that they had not been organized as *civitates.* The epigraphic evidence from the garrison towns of Tingitana is unusually good and one would expect to find in the inscriptions some mention of *civitates* if such existed.[16] Their absence cannot be attributed simply to the North African setting, since in the eastern provinces of North Africa, Africa Proconsularis and Numidia, the Romans did organize some of the tribes in the traditional European manner. Why, then, did they not do so in Tingitana?

The distribution of the tribes was undoubtedly a major factor in the Roman decision. Of the nine "interior" tribes Ptolemy places six on the Atlantic coast, between Tingis/Ceuta and Sala, and three in the oued Ouergha/Rif Mountains region. The latter (Oueroueis, Zegrenses, Maurosii) were settled within the official boundaries of the province—Sala-Volubilis in the south, the oued Moulouya in the east—but in fact should not be considered interior tribes.[17] The Romans were never able to pacify the region from the confluence of the Ouergha and the Sebou near Banasa to the Moulouya Valley, a distance of 250 kilometers. They did not build forts in this area and, as far as we know, did not attempt by military means to subdue the tribes. Whatever their maps or rhetoric might claim, their actions reveal that the Ouergha and Rif were independent frontier zones.[18]

The six tribes along the coast, on the other hand, were clearly situated within "Maroc utile," the only sector of Tingitana the Romans actually occupied (Tingis/Ceuta–Banasa–Volubilis–Sala). No legions were stationed within this zone—there was only one, III Augusta, for all of North Africa—but auxiliary units were posted to the garrison towns (especially Banasa, Volubilis, and their satellites) during the first century and their numbers were dramatically increased in the second. The Roman army of occupation can be reconstructed with some precision from the twenty-nine military diplomas found in the garrison towns, principally in Banasa and Volubilis. The diplomas (issued between A.D. 88 and 165) record the discharge of soldiers from twenty-three auxiliary units that had served in the province. In the first half of the second century there were five *alae* and nine cohorts distributed among the garrison towns, but by the end of the century at least five additional cohorts had been transferred to the province (raising the total strength to roughly 12,000 men).[19] At least one-third of those troops were garrisoned in the forts around Volubilis; the remainder were accommodated in other existing camps, especially in the Banasa zone, or in new camps built during the second century.

Unfortunately, literary accounts of events in Tingitana are so inadequate that we cannot say whether the new troops were brought in to suppress an internal tribal revolt or to repel an external invader. Ancient writers uniformly attribute disturbances in the area under Antoninus Pius and Marcus Aurelius to the "Mauri," but it is not certain that these "Mauri" were operating in Tingitana.[20] Mauri is often and indiscriminately used to describe the inhabitants of both Mauretanian provinces. Inscriptions from Spain, however, independently corroborate the literary account of a Mauri attack on Baetica in the 170's.[21] Since their expeditions were launched from the northern coast of Tingitana, these Mauri have been identified with the Maurosii (or Maurensii), a tribal group usually located in the Rif Mountains.[22] In any event, the invasion of Baetica did not directly threaten the Roman garrison towns in Tingitana.

Inscriptions on a statue from Sala, on the other hand, suggest that the Mauri attack under Antoninus Pius may have been directed against that Roman settlement. Dedicated to M. Sulpicius Felix, the prefect of ala II Syrorum C. R. (otherwise unknown), the inscriptions (A.D. 144) record the services of this "liberator and patron" to the Roman community—he repelled attacks, prevented a famine, and built a defensive wall round the town.[23] The crisis in Sala may have been caused by the Mauri, but which Mauri? If they were Maurosii from the Rif, then *en route* they must have passed through the garrison towns north of Sala. Rachet, on the other hand, believes they were *("sans doute")* Autololes, a tribe usually located in the oued Bou Regreg area. Neither the Maurosii nor the Autololes, it should be noted, were settled within the zone of Roman occupation.

Nothing in the available evidence, in short, suggests that the six interior tribes rebelled against the Romans. It is not inconceivable, of course, that Ptolemy's list included tribes which had once been independent but by the second century were incorporated into the Roman towns. Alternatively, the tribes may have been too weak militarily to challenge the Roman garrisons. Either hypothesis would explain their apparent passivity. This much is certain: the Romans did not attempt to Romanize the interior tribes through the creation of *civitates* or through widespread recruitment of natives into the army. Only one native is known to have served in an "auxiliary" unit stationed in Tingitana (ala Gallorum Tauriana), and his name, M. Publilius Publicus, suggests that he was Romanized before enlistment.[24] L. A. Thompson, on the other hand, has argued that a sizable number of natives with Roman citizenship appear in inscriptions from Banasa and Oppidum Novum.[25] Whether these native citizens (if indeed they are all natives of Tingitana) received citizenship on discharge from auxiliary service or through a special grant to the inhabitants of Banasa and Oppidum Novum is not certain.

In any event, the Romans did not pursue within Tingitana the active policy of Romanization we have observed in Pannonia. Whatever the reason—because they considered the tribes too insignificant, or too "foreign," or too hostile—the Romans for the most part were content to remain within the enclaves they had established and were prepared to defend.

We are on much firmer, and more familiar, ground when we turn to Roman relations with the "outer barbarians." Inscriptions from the principal military centers, Banasa and Volubilis, permit us to trace in some detail Roman diplomatic efforts to neutralize, perhaps even to Romanize, the tribes outside the zone of occupation. Especially important in this context is the *Tabula Banasitana,* found at Banasa in 1960, which documents Roman attempts to win the support of tribes in the oued Ouergha area.[26]

The *Tabula* records two separate grants of citizenship, each recommended by the governor (procurator) of Tingitana, to members of a leading Zegrenses family. In the first (A.D. 168) the co-Emperors Marcus Aurelius and Lucius Verus confer citizenship on Julianus—who is said to be one of the *primores,* the equivalent of *principes* in Pannonia—and his wife and children (the latter have Roman names). The second, issued by Marcus Aurelius and Commodus (A.D. 177), elevates another Julianus, probably the son of the preceding Julianus, and his wife and children (again the names are Roman). This Julianus, unlike the first, was *princeps gentium Zegrensium*—not just a noble, but the chief of the tribe.[26a]

The word *civitas* does not appear in either document, and nothing suggests that the tribe was under the supervision of a Roman military official. On the other hand, since the grant of citizenship did not include immunity from taxation—*sine diminutione tributorum et vect(i) galium populi et fisci*—the Zegrenses *in strictu sensu* may have been provincial subjects.[27] The denial of *immunitas,* however, raises a number of difficult questions. Had the Romans previously collected taxes from the Zegrenses (a *populus stipendarius?*) or were they simply announcing their intention to do so? Was the entire tribe now required to pay taxes or tribute? Would the Juliani have agreed to this condition simply to gain citizenship, or was their agreement secured by force or the threat of military intervention? Since the Romans did not restrict the family's participation in tribal affairs (implied by the formula *salvo iure gentis,* which precedes the denial of *immunitas*), did not station troops in the area, and did not create a *civitas Zegrensium,* it is safe to conclude that the Romans did not intend to occupy the oued Ouergha area. On the other hand, these grants, and particularly the denial of *immunitas,* would establish their authority in the zone and would give weight to their claim that the Moulouya was the eastern boundary of Tingitana.

The timing of the grants—the first in the same year that the fortifications of Volubilis were strengthened, presumably in response to a military crisis; the second in the midst of the "Mauri" attacks on Baetica—suggests that the Romans were attempting to co-opt the Zegrenses in order to create a buffer zone between themselves and the restive tribes. Whatever their earlier relationship with the tribe may have been, the friendship of the Zegrenses in 168 was needed to protect the Roman garrisons on the perimeter—Banasa, Souk el Arba, Rirha, Ain Chkour, Sidi Said—from a surprise attack and to prevent the formation of a tribal confederation in the Rif area.

The oued Ouergha basin was not the only invasion route into Roman territory. The peculiar geography of Tingitana (that is, the zone of occupation) made the province even more open to attack from the Atlas region, inhabited by the Baquates, Bavares, and Macenites. Roman relations with these tribes from the early second century down to the reign of Diocletian, a period of more than 150 years, can be traced in a unique series of inscriptions from Volubilis that record treaties with the Baquates and their confederates.[28]

Unfortunately, we know almost nothing of Roman contacts with these "outer barbarians" before the reign of Hadrian and consequently cannot assess the earlier development of Roman policy. Our literary sources record only two major forays into the south—the expeditions of Suetonius Paulinus and Hosidius Geta in the Moulouya valley, the northwest passage from the Middle Atlas to the Mediterranean—and both occurred soon after annexation (A.D. 42–44).[29] That the Romans recognized the strategic importance of the Moulouya is not surprising, but the immediate objectives of these campaigns are unclear. Although their armies traced the oued to its source and even engaged the desert tribes beyond the High Atlas range, the expeditions did not produce major victories in the field or establish permanent diplomatic ties with the tribes.

It is unlikely that this brief encounter disrupted the seasonal migratory regimes of the pastoral nomads in the region, and on occasion these groups must have passed through, or at least near, Roman territory. The Romans, however, did not attempt to interdict this traffic by constructing forts along the oued. Nor is there any certain evidence of Roman settlement south of Volubilis and its satellite forts.[30] In the south, as in the Banasa district, the Romans evidently were more interested in developing the existing urban centers than in establishing new settlements in "barbaricum." This does not mean, of course, that Roman troops never penetrated this zone or that skirmishes with tribesmen were un-known, only that skirmishes did not trigger major invasions or Roman campaigns before the reign of Hadrian.

The first documented conflict with the tribes occurred around A.D. 120 when the Baquates attacked, probably through the Mou-louya Valley, the port city of Cartennae in Mauretania Caesar-iensis.[31] Since the Baquates' motives cannot be determined, and the Roman response—apart from the defense of the city—is not recorded, it is impossible to say whether this marks a new phase in Roman–Baquates relations. By A.D. 140 the Baquates were on good terms with the Romans. In that year Aelius Tuccuda, *princeps gentis Baquatium,* dedicated an inscription in Volubilis to Antoninus Pius, Hadrian's successor.[32] As the name Aelius indicates, Tuccuda had received Roman citizenship from Hadrian (Publius Aelius Hadrianus). If Tuccuda's expression of friend-ship accurately reflects the tribe's attitude toward the Romans, we may assume that the Baquates did not participate in the "Mauri" raids on Sala in the early 140's. Moreover, Tuccuda's elevation to Roman citizenship under Hadrian indicates that Romans had begun to develop a new policy toward the tribes. Or rather, they had begun to implement their traditional policy.

Between 140 and 173/175 the leadership of the tribe changed and the Baquates formed a confederation with the Macenites. The Romans would not have welcomed such changes in leader-ship, which invariably required them to renegotiate the existing agreements, and may well have been alarmed by the emergence of a tribal confederation on their southern border. The con-struction of a wall around Volubilis in 168/169 indicates that the Romans expected, or had already suffered, an attack from some quarter.[33] Perhaps from the Mauri, who were at that time tooling up for their attack on Baetica, or possibly from the new confederation: activities of either group may have convinced the Romans that the fortifications should be strengthened. Or they may have been responding to earlier incidents, which had inspired the transfer of additional army units to Tingitana.

An inscription set up in Volubilis by Ucmetius, *princeps gen-tium Macennitum et Baquatium* in 173 or 175, is often cited as evidence of military conflict.[34] But this simply commemorates a meeting *(conlocutus)* between the leader of the new confed-eracy and the procurator Epidius Quadratus; there is no mention of warfare or of the restoration of peace. On the other hand, the fact that Ucmetius had not acquired Roman citizenship—the imperial name (e.g., Aelius) is missing—suggests that the Romans mistrusted the confederacy.

By 180 the confederacy had been dissolved and a new dynasty ruled the Baquates. In this year another conference involving the *procurator* and the new *princeps,* Canartha, was held in Volubilis.[35] An unusual element in this inscription, which otherwise adheres to the earlier formulation, is the designation *princeps constitutus gentis Baquatium.* Whether *constitutus* denotes selection by the tribe or appointment by the Romans is uncertain. It is not inconceivable that the Romans—who appointed kings elsewhere, as the coins with the legend REX QUADIS DATUS prove—attempted to break up the confederacy by manipulating the succession.

The decision to send Canartha's son to Rome for an "education"—attested in a later inscription from Rome—does not imply a loss of confidence; sons of client kings (e.g., Juba II) often went to Rome as hostages. Indeed, while he was in the capital the royal family was awarded Roman citizenship.[36]

Between 180 and 200 there was another dynastic change—perhaps the result of the premature death of Canartha's son—but this did not occasion any alteration of the contract.[37] The first sign of difficulty is the reference to a *pax firmanda* in an inscription from the reign of Alexander Severus (A.D. 226–229).[38] This political/military significance of *pax firmanda* is uncertain (does this refer to the restoration of peace following a war or simply to the confirmation of an earlier agreement?) but some change in the relationship is implied.

A few years later (A.D. 232–234) the Baquates joined with the Bavares, a tribe normally resident in Caesariensis, to form a new confederacy. This cannot have pleased the Romans and they may well have taken steps to correct the situation. The reference in the *SHA (vita Alex. Severi* 58, 1) to a victory won by Furius Celsus in Tingitana and the dissolution of the Baquates–Bavares confederacy by 239 or 241 certainly point in that direction.[39]

Over the next four decades the Romans maintained the established procedures, rewarding trustworthy *principes* with citizenship and renegotiating agreements with the Baquates on the accession of each new *princeps.* The assumption of the title *rex* (king) by Julius Matif, however, implies that the status of the tribe vis-a-vis the Romans changed during the 270's.[40] If so, the new status, whatever it may have been, was short-lived; Matif's successors did not inherit the title, even though they were members of the same dynasty (all were "Julii").

Doubtless the Romans initially considered the Baquates a threat to Volubilis and to the province generally, but by the end of the second century their skillful diplomacy had transformed this liability into a significant asset. Their diplomatic efforts not only neutralized a potentially dangerous opponent, but also facilitated the extension of the frontier without a commitment of additional manpower. With the Baquates as clients the threat of invasion from the south was considerably reduced; the "peace," periodically renewed, established a buffer zone between Volubilis and the desert.

But what did the Baquates gain, or hope to gain, from their association with the Romans? Apparently not an annual subsidy. The only "gift" was the grant of citizenship to the family of the *princeps*. This undoubtedly pleased the royal family, but it did not materially improve the lot of the tribesmen.[41] The principal benefit may have been .the Roman agreement, implied if not explicitly included in a separate treaty, not to interfere with the tribal migratory regime.

In modern times the Beni Mguild have established a rather complex migratory regime in the Middle Atlas–Upper Moulouya area.[42] In spring/summer they sow cereals in the lowland areas and transfer their herds to the high mountain pastures; in autumn/winter they harvest their crops and leave their herds to graze on the harvested fields and lowland pastures. This regime is clearly dependent upon the maintenance of reasonably good relations with one's neighbors. If another tribe seized the lowland pastures and arable fields the Beni Mguild would be forced to fight or to relocate.

The Baquates may have established a similar regime in the area, engaging in seasonal agriculture either in the upper Moulouya Valley or in the green belt south of Volubilis. They did not require Roman consent to pass through the Moulouya corridor—with the exception of Paulinus and Geta, no Roman commander had seriously challenged their access to this route—but they would want to protect the pastoral and agricultural operations which ensured their survival. Their seasonal oscillation between highlands and lowlands may well have alarmed the Romans in Volubilis and may have led to conflict. Periodically, therefore, conferences between the procurator and the Baquates chief would be needed to restore peace. It is precisely this pattern of diplomatic initiatives that is reflected in the inscriptions ("altars of peace") from the Volubilis document.

Hadrian's decision to withdraw from the "provinces" Trajan had created in the East undermined belief in the invincibility of the legions. The army was now instructed to defend the existing frontier zones, a less glamorous task than conquest and one that called for an ever greater expenditure of manpower. Lacking the required manpower reserves, the Romans quickly discovered that the *Pax Romana,* precarious in the best of times, could not be maintained on every front by military means alone. The legions and auxiliary units stationed on the periphery were a visible deterrent, but the total strength of the army in a given zone was not sufficient to dissuade or repel a determined opponent. In these circumstances diplomacy necessarily became the cornerstone of frontier policy.

It was a necessity consistent with Roman experience and preferences. They had exported Romanitas for decades and had developed practices which would permit them to impose their concepts of civilized behavior on the indigenous populations. As we have seen, practices were adapted to meet particular conditions, but the aim was always the same—the neutralization and, if possible, eventual Romanization of the inner and outer barbarians. In both Pannonia and Tingitana the frontier was defined by these groups; their settlement patterns, and not the geography of the area, determined the limits of the frontier zone. The diversity of Roman policies and the vigor with which the Romans pursued Romanization were also conditioned by these settlement patterns and by the responses of the indigenous groups to Roman diplomatic and cultural initiatives. In Pannonia and Tingitana the policies toward the outer barbarians developed on similar lines; the Romanization of the inner barbarians (the six inner tribes) in Tingitana, on the other hand, proceeded much more slowly, if one can speak of progress at all, than in Pannonia.

As a defensive strategy Roman frontier policies in both provinces were successful: Pannonia remained an imperial province until the end of the fourth century, Tingitana until the end of the third (at which time Diocletian ordered the evacuation of the garrison towns, with the exception of Sala, south of Lixus). In political and social terms the acculturation of indigenous groups in the frontier zones was essential to the survival of the Empire. Had the Romans decided on a more exclusive policy, the Maginot

Line mentality some have attributed to them, the so-called barbarization of the Empire during the third and fourth centuries would have been an even more traumatic experience.

Notes

1. Campaign of 35 B.C.: Appian *Illyr.* 22–24; A. Mócsy, *Pannonia and Upper Moesia,* tr. by S. Frere (London, 1974), pp. 22 ff.

2. Confederation with the Dentheletai: Dio 54, 20, 3; for an account of their settlement in Srem and their earlier activities in the south see Mócsy, pp. 12 ff.

3. Campaign of 11 B.C.: Dio 54, 31; Pannonian Revolt of A.D. 6–9: Dio 55, 29–34; cf. Augustus, *Res Gestae* 30, 1; Velleius Paterculus 2, 110 ff.

4. Late in the first centruy T. Flavius Proculus, a *princeps,* was serving as *praefectus Scordiscorum:* A. and J. Šašel, "Inscriptiones Latinae . . . in Iugoslavia," *Situla* 5 (1963), 100, #280. In the second century, *principes* also administered the *civitates Eraviscorum* (CIL III 3546) and *Azalorum* (AE [1937], 138).

5. For an assessment of the evidence see A. Mócsy, pp. 137 ff. Members of four Pannonian *civitates*—Scordisci, Boii, Azali, Eravasci—are known to have served in Roman *alae* and *cohortes* before the Marcomannic Wars: K. Kraft, *Zur Rekrutierung der Alen und Kohorten an Rhein und Donau* (Bern, 1951), 64 ff.

6. For the epigraphical evidence see P. Oliva, *Pannonia and the Onset of Crisis in the Roman Empire* (Prague, 1962), pp. 145 ff.; A. Mócsy, pp. 141 ff.; cf. A. Alföldi, *Cambridge Ancient History,* XI (1936), 545 ff. A notable exception was the *civitas Amantinorum,* which had been incorporated into the colonia of Sirmium under the Flavians. Whether the *civitas Scordiscorum* was suppressed by Septimius Severus when he founded the colonia of Bassiana on their territory (G. Alföldy, "Des territoires occupés par les Scordisques," *Acta Antiqua* 12[1964], 127) or was absorbed when Bassiana became a municipium under Hadrian (S. Dušanić, "Some New and Revised Roman Inscriptions from Eastern Srem," *Živa Antika* 17 [1967], 214 [English summary]) is uncertain. The fragmentary inscription on which Dušanić bases his hypothesis, however, is scarcely conclusive, and I am inclined to favor the later date.

7. J. Klose (*Roms Klientel-randstaaten am Rhein und an der Donau* [Breslau, 1934], pp. 115 ff.) and J. Fitz ("Pannonien und die Klientel-staaten an der Donau," *Alba Regia* 4/5 [1963/64], 80 ff.) provide succinct accounts of Roman–Iazyges relations. Individuals who served in a Suebian–Sarmatian campaign, probably in the reign of Domitian, are commemorated in three inscriptions: CIL III 6818 (cf. Mócsy, p. 102 and n. 85, p. 376); CIL V 7425; CIL X 135. The client-treaty: Dio 69, 15, 2; Eutropius 8, 3, 1.

8. Peace terms: Dio 71, 16. J. Klose, p. 121, rightly considers the number of captives "improbably high."

9. Dio 71, 18–19.

10. Dio 71, 20.

11. Because the literary accounts are so fragmentary and ambiguous, it is impossible to ascertain Marcus Aurelius' intentions. A. Mócsy (pp. 184 ff.) believes that Marcus Aurelius proposed annexation in the course of his ne-

gotiations with the Marcomanni and Quadi, but abandoned the plan when attacks by the Lombards and Obii unexpectedly propelled the Marcomanni/ Quadi across the Pannonian border. The sources, however, do not support this intriguing domino theory. The *Vita Marci* in the *Scriptores Historia Augustae* mentions the proposed annexation in two different chronological contexts (in A.D. 175 [24, 5] and at the end of the war [27, 10]), and Dio omits it altogether. Dio's silence is not conclusive, but it cannot be discounted—*pace* A. R. Birley, "Roman Frontier Policy under Marcus Aurelius," in *VIIth International Congress of Roman Frontier Studies 1967,* ed. by S. Applebaum (Tel Aviv, 1967), pp. 10 ff. Neither source, it should be noted, connects the proposed annexation with attacks on the Marcomanni/Quadi.

12. Commodus evidently supplemented this surveillance (Dio 72, 2) with new fortifications on the right bank of the Danube (CIL III 3385).

13. Coins of Antoninus Pius (A.D. 140–144) with the legend REX QUADIS DATUS point to Roman interference in tribal affairs: H. Mattingly, et al., *Roman Imperial Coinage* III (1930), 620; cf. R. Göbi, "Rex . . . datus," *Rheinisches Museum* N. F. 104 (1961), 70 ff. In the third century, Caracalla is credited with the assassination of Gaïobomarus, King of the Quadi: Dio 77, 20, 3–4. According to Dio (71, 11 ff.) and the *SHA (Vita Marci* 22, 2), Marcus Aurelius settled some members of the tribes on Roman soil, in the frontier provinces and even in Italy.

14. Murder of Ptolemy: Suetonius, *Caligula* 26 and 35; Dio 59, 25, 1; M. Rachet, *Rome et les Berbères,* "Collection Latomus" 110 (Brussels, 1970), p. 126; D. Fishwick, "The Annexation of Mauretania," *Historia* 20 (1971), 467 ff.

15. I agree with Fishwick (pp. 473 ff.; *contra* Rachet, pp. 127 ff.) that the revolt of Aedemon was "a partisan attempt by a narrow clique to keep Mauretania in the hands of the royal court" and was not supported by Ptolemy's subjects outside Tingitana. The grant of Municipal status to Volubilis is recorded in an inscription from Volubilis: L. Chatelain, *Incriptions latines du Maroc* (Paris, 1942), no. 116; cf. U. Laffi, *Adtributio e Contributio* (Pisa, 1966), pp. 74 ff.

16. The literary evidence has been assembled and assessed by J. Desanges, *Catalogue des tribus Africaines de l'antiquité classique* (Dakar, 1962), pp. 27 ff.

17. *Ibid.,* pp. 32 ff.

18. Some still believe that the Romans built a camp at Bou Hellou, in the Taza pass east of Volubilis, but close inspection of the area has not revealed any trace of the camp or the East-West road that supposedly joined Tingitana and Caesariensis: J. Baradez, "Deux Missions de recherches sur le *limes* de Tingitana," *Comptes-rendus de l'Academie des Inscriptions et Belles-lettres* (1955), pp. 295 ff.; J. Marion, "Liaison terrestre entre la Tingitana et la Caesarienne," *Bulletin d'archeologique* 4 (1960), 442 ff.; M. Euzennat, "Le limes de Volubilis," *Studien zu den Militärgrenzen Roms: Vorträge des 6. Internationalen Limeskongressus in Suddeutschland* (Cologne, 1967), pp. 194 ff.

19. For a list of the military diplomas see M. Euzennat, "Fragments inédits de bronzes épigraphiques morocains," *Antiquités Africaines* 3 (1969), 126–127; previous assessments of the diplomas, and other military inscriptions, are cited in his notes.

20. Unrest under Antoninus Pius: *SHA, vita Antonini* 5, 4; Pausanias 8, 43, 3; attack on Baetica under Marcus Aurelius: *SHA, vita Marci* 21, 1; *vita Severi* 2, 4.

21. See Rachet, pp. 205 ff.

22. Desanges, pp. 35 ff.; Rachet (pp. 177 ff., *passim*), on the other hand, consistently—and, in my opinion, wrongly—links the "Mauri" with the Atlas and pre-Saharan tribes (Baquates, Bavares, Macenites).

23. Rachet, pp. 194–195.

24. CIL XVI 173 (A.D. 129/132).

25. "Settler and Native in the Urban Centres of Roman Africa," in *Africa in Classical Antiquity,* ed. by L. A. Thompson and J. Ferguson (Ibadan, 1969), pp. 132 ff.

26. The *Tabula* has been published, with extensive commentary, by W. Seston and M. Euzennat, "Un dossier de la chancellerie romaine: *La Tabula Banasitana,* Etude de diplomatique," *Comptes-rendus de l'Academie des Inscriptions* (1971), pp. 478 ff.; cf. A. N. Sherwin-White, "The Tabula of Banasa and the Constitutio Antoniniana," *Journal of Roman Studies,* 63 (1973), 86 ff.

26a. M. Euzennat—"Les Zegrenses," *Mélanges d'histoire ancienne offerts à William Seston* (1974), 185—suggests that the Iuliani were not elevated by the tribe itself but by the Romans (i.e., they were *principes constituti*).

27. Sherwin-White, p. 89.

28. The texts (to which one should add *Année Epigraphique* [1966], v. 602) are reproduced and discussed by E. Frézouls, "Les Baquates et la province romaine de Tingitane," *Bulletin d'archeologique Marocaine* 2 (1957), 65 ff.; see also R. Thouvenot, "Rome et les barbares Africains," *Publications du Service des Antiquités du Maroc* 7 (1945), 166 ff.; P. Romanelli, "Le iscrizioni volubitane dei Baquati e i rapporti di Roma con le tribù indigene dell'Africa," in *Hommages à Albert Grenier,* ed. by M. Renard, 3 vols. (Berchem, 1962), 3, 1347 ff.

29. On the campaigns, see Fishwick, pp. 475 ff.

30. Aerial photographs of the Moulouya Valley do not reveal any trace of Roman settlement (see *supra* n. 17); similarly, attempts to place the Romans at Anoceur in the Middle Atlas are not convincing—see M. Euzennat, "Anoceur (Kasba des Aït Khalifa): Faux poste romain dans le Moyen Atlas," *Bulletin d'archeologique du Maroc* 4 (1960), 381 ff.

31. Frèzouls, 1, p. 66.

32. Frèzouls, 2, p. 67.

33. Wall: E. Frèzouls, "Inscriptions nouvelles de Volubilis, II," *Mélanges d'histoire et d'archeologie de l'école francaise de Rome* 68–69 (1956–57), 95 ff.

34. Frézouls, 3, p. 67.

35. Frézouls, 4, p. 68.

36. The addition of "Aurelius" to the family name is attested in the son's epitaph (he was sixteen years old when he died in Rome): Frézouls, 5, p. 68.

37. Frézouls, 6, p. 69; the new chiefs apparently did not receive Roman citizenship.

38. *Année Epigraphique* (1966), 602.

39. The Bavares are not mentioned on an "altar of peace" from the reign of Gordian III (between 239 and 241): Frézouls, 8, pp. 69–70.

40. Two "altars" from this period have been found in Volubilis: Frézouls, 10 (A.D. 277) and 11 (A.D. 280), pp. 71–72.

41. Since all members of the tribe did not receive citizenship, Sherwin-White (p. 97) concludes that the Baquates were classified as *dediticii,* the only group specifically excluded from the universal grant of citizenship in A.D. 212 *(Constitutio Antoninana).*

42. See D. Johnson, *The Nature of Nomadism. A Comparative Study of Pastoral Migrations in Southwestern Asia and Northern Africa* (Department of Geography Research Paper no. 118 [Chicago, 1969]), pp. 105 ff.

*My research on Mauretania Tingitana, which included an inspection of the principal sites in 1974, was made possible by grants from the National Endowment for the Humanities, the American Council of Learned Societies, and the Rackham School of Graduate Studies (University of Michigan).

Preindustrial Frontiers and Interaction Spheres: Prolegomenon to a Study of Roman Frontier Regions

William S. Cooter

SEVERAL crucial factors would seem to figure into the types of frontiers usually studied by American historians working within the framework of the Turner thesis,[1] in the work of anthropologists concerned with contemporary pioneer communities, or in the work of many economists studying the development of so-called "regions of recent settlement."[2] All such frontiers have pervasive ties with highly developed, industrialized societies, and the settlers within such frontiers, settlers often recruited from neighboring developed societies, are heavily dependent at all stages of their frontiers' evolution on connections, economic, political, social, and military, with these larger societal nexes. Especially in economic matters, such industrial frontiers are significantly indebted for their survival on a variety of market, credit, and trade ties with external areas. Highly developed nation states may view frontier development as a desirable way to bolster regional economies, expand sources of food supplies or raw materials for industrialized or industrializing regions, or to facilitate other types of changes. In turn, the people of the frontier zones will probably view as highly desirable their steady integration with national level institutions, this seen as the most efficacious way to ameliorate "harsh" frontier environments[3] often lacking in all manner of locally based facilities or the means to provide for transportation, communication, financial, and other services.

Through the mediation of external agencies, credit can be obtained, goods and services can be acquired whose production would be awkward or impossible given the technological and organizational potentials of local artisans or manufactures, and various social overhead costs may be minimized; for example, the costs of roads, canals, railroads, or schools can be shifted onto or shared with outside public or private agencies. Local production within industrial frontiers is thus able to specialize and adapt to such external linkages. Pioneer productive units may have to make do with a degree of homespun self-sufficiency unnecessary in more highly developed or urbanized regions, but many cash crops and products—"staples"—will be complementary to the needs of nonlocal market outlets, and, under propitious conditions, economic diversification and balanced growth may build on the initially narrow export base.[4] Such, in brief, are the features of industrial frontiers, a class containing examples ranging from the nineteenth century American West to modern South American colonization schemes in Peru, Ecuador, or Bolivia.[5]

Economic variables then, and economic variables clearly associable with modern market institutions, are important in industrial frontiers. Modern market institutions arose during the course of the complicated interplay of agricultural, commercial, and industrial revolutions beginning in early modern Western Europe.[6] Although Europe and other areas, for example, Islam, India, or China, have witnessed prior cycles of economic expansion, the earlier norms were still those of pre-capitalist, preindustrial societies. Within this general category of preindustrial societies, two major, if somewhat overlapping, categories can be distinguished. On the one hand are societies featuring appreciably high population densities, fairly intensive agricultural systems, complex divisions of labor with many non-agrarian roles, and considerable specialization and centralization in political and military spheres. As opposed to such preindustrial states are those societies with lower population densities, more extensive agricultural systems, less complex divisions of labor, and considerably less political or military centralization, such "primitive" groupings being commonly referred to as tribes. A rough definition of an important type of frontier situation in preindustrial contexts may be taken to involve the juxtaposition of preindustrial states with their less complex neighboring societies and the various institutional linkages between the two types of societies. The following discussion will advance a model framework for the study of such preindustrial frontiers, Roman frontier regions being singled out for the bulk of the illustrative material, although a host of other contexts fall within this same category, the hallmark of which is the conspicuous unimportance of the market ties, credit relations, or capital exchanges which are the cardinal features of industrial frontier relationships.

As a preliminary exercise, it is illuminating to consider a range of responses and developments conceivably, though awkwardly, assignable to the tentative definition of preindustrial frontiers given above. Such an exercise will be of use in refining the types of relationships and the types of developmental contrasts likely to ensure the more pronounced or longstanding imposition of frontier conditions. To begin with, a preindustrial state may find it possible to incorporate neighboring groups with relative ease as integral parts or dependencies. For Rome, the creation of provinces within the eastern Mediterranean—for example, in Greece, Anatolia, Syria, and Egypt, areas already boasting state machinery comparable to Rome's—was readily accomplished. Other areas—for example, portions of Africa, Spain, or southern Gaul previously exposed to strong Carthaginian or Greek influences—were also provincialized in short order. In areas such as these, the notion of a preindustrial frontier is either not applicable or is of restricted or minimal utility.[7]

Comparable types of rapid provincialization might also be possible even where the indigenous foundations were insubstantial. If some readily accessible region offered potentials in terms of soils, grazing lands, or mineral resources, it could be rapidly developed for cash-crop farming, ranching, or mining concessions. Crucial would be cheap transportation, usually by sea or river, providing access to large urban centers which would generally offer the only sources of commodity demand. Another consideration would be a ready supply of cheap labor, e.g., slaves, recruited either from the erstwhile natives or from sources farther afield. In the ancient world, much of peninsular Italy, and, subsequently, vast areas in Sicily, Spain, Africa, and Gaul, were developed in this manner. Once again the notion of a preindustrial frontier would seem of limited use, such areas being the ancient world's closest approximations to the processes associated with modern industrial frontiers.[8]

Proceeding to another possibility, even if certain of these latter variables, perhaps most important of all being transportation, were lacking, sparsely populated or minimally developed regions might still witness rapid provincialization if they offered convenient dumping grounds for excess population from within preindustrial states. In the Graeco-Roman world, the Greeks of the archaic period had paved the way, their colonies in Sicily, southern Italy, and southern Gaul boasting long histories before Roman influence had spread far beyond the confines of the plain of Latium.[9] By the end of the Second Punic War, massive disruptions in the local economies of central and southern Italy and the problem of how to pension off thousands of displaced veterans sparked a growing interest on the part of Rome in colonies in areas such as the Po Valley and later in areas outside the peninsula entirely, e.g., in Gaul, in Spain, or in Africa. Often the lands for such foundations were seized forcibly from pre-existing groups, who were either displaced or forced to adapt to or amalgamate with the new colonists. The Po Valley region, i.e., Cisalpine Gaul, provides the classic Roman instance, a former Celtic stronghold being converted into a bastion of the Latin and Roman small farmer.[10] A certain amount of wool and processed meats found their way to markets in central and southern Italy, but the relative isolation of Cisalpine Gaul put severe limitations on the development of commercially oriented agriculture or ranching. Once again, the rapid transformation, even elimination, of the indigenous institutional systems in instances of this sort renders the preindustrial frontier concept of limited use.

These developmental alternatives are a warning of the limitations of the tentative definition given earlier. For the notion of a preindustrial frontier to have utility, what is clearly entailed are situations where groups and institutions juxtaposed to preindustrial states are neither eliminated nor integrated as fullfledged provincial components even though pre-contact patterns may be considerably altered by a host of acculturation pressures. Within such nexes, various types of processes, structures, and roles may emerge, the whole of such a socio-cultural complex being a frontier. From this preliminary discussion, a more precise definition of preindustrial frontiers begins to emerge, the features of which are most conveniently appreciated by appeal to some of the salient characteristics of Roman frontiers in Europe.

Especially for Roman frontiers, a glance at the Rhenish or Danubian *limes,* or the grandiose scheme of Hadrian's Wall in northern Britain, gives the impression that such concentrations of military works marked a decisive dividing point, the Roman world on one side, the world of the barbarians on the other. However, this neat picture of barbarians on one side, Romans on the other, and some occidental version of the Great Wall of China between the two, will not work. Roman frontiers, even when festooned with all manner of walls, palisades, forts and signal stations, were seldom hermetical seals. Ample, if sometimes carefully selected and administered arenas for exchange and communication were provided, even along such obstacle courses as Hadrian's Wall.[11] Many regions, e.g., marcher regions like Wales or southwest England, as well as the lower Rhenish frontier and certain stretches of the Danubian *limes,* defy ready demarcation as lines on maps since here military strongholds, signal stations, and roads were scattered over considerable swashes of territory. Even in northern Britain, the predecessor to the neat line of Hadrian's Wall was a much more amorphous collection of military structures, and even after Hadrian's time, the northern frontier of Britain was hardly a static affair. Even considered as a line on a map, this frontier fluctuated, now jumping north to the line of the wall of Antoninus Pius, now retreating to older positions, and so on for a half century and more. For this north British frontier, evidence, documentary and otherwise, indicates that these successive military zones were designed as much to control affairs to the south as to the less pacified north. Indeed, in this context the concept is suggested that the military structures of such frontiers, while bending at times to take advantage of tactical or strategic considerations of location and terrain, were consciously situated squarely in the midst of pre-existing tribal interfaces or lines of articulation.[12] Such nodal points would provide ideal bases from which to control local and regional affairs. If this concept is accepted as a trial hypothesis, then a number of implications are suggested, implications that pave the way for a fairly rigorous definition of preindustrial frontiers and an elucidation of the processes and variables involved in their functioning.

Preindustrial frontiers were seldom built from whole cloth, nor did they always involve the complete dismantling of pre-existing indigenous patterns. Rather, such frontiers often preserved many of the core features of pre-existing institutional structures, altered and controlled, to form subsystems within the overarching frameworks of preindustrial states and empires. Various factors, perhaps chief among these being difficulties in realizing more than a limited agricultural potential from such regions in the face of pressures stemming from frontier incorporation, hindered trends toward full integration as provincial areas, thus perpetuating the zones' status as frontiers.

From these initial considerations, several types of questions follow, which demand fuller discussion. Some more detailed delineation of the pre-frontier baselines would be desirable, pinpointing the types of variables and organizational features associated with the native institutional structures. From such a baseline, the types of alterations imposed by the creation of a frontier zone and the impact of these alterations on the functioning of the indigenous systems could be better gauged. Some conclusions might then follow on the types of crucial tolerances and threshold associated with the continued functioning of preindustrial frontiers as well as insights into the types of factors that could exceed these thresholds and throw a frontier into some dysfunctional state. A set of trial hypotheses dealing with these problems will be formulated, hypotheses which further research may then show to be of general import. The first task is to outline the pre-frontier, "tribal" baselines.

The concept of "tribe" is one of the more vexing problems in anthropology, archaeology, and other disciplines obliged to employ the notion.[13] Several types of competing and sometimes mutually incompatible ways of defining tribes and tribalism are commonly used, which for convenience can be reduced to a group of "subjective" and a group of "objective" criteria. One approach commonly used by legal historians, ethnologists, or colonial administrators relies heavily on the informants' own notions of what and who they are, such subjective classifications perhaps bolstered by attention to language affiliations, kinship norms, and the like. Built nearly entirely on considerations of this latter sort are the somewhat less subjective methods of historical linguists, folklorists, archaeologists, or museum curators whereby tribes are pinpointed from distributions of various traits, e.g., language, manner of dress, technology, or subsistence practices. The more idiosyncratic the traits the better, and the implicit hope is that the degree of trait overlap will be considerable and that neat, closed "culture areas" corresponding to tribes can be discerned. Where troubles arise, the somewhat unscrupulous double check can be resorted to by asking the natives who they are, mixing subjective and objective criteria, this provided, of course, that natives exist to ask. Neither of these approaches is genuinely theoretical. Present concern must center on the second approach since for the matter of ancient tribalism contemporary ethnographers such as Caesar or Tacitus were often confused as to who the natives were, forcing one to rely heavily on linguistic treatments working from old personal or place names and on archaeology, the latter being especially invaluable.

Well into the twentieth century, the study of the proto-historic "barbarians" of the immediate pre-Roman, Roman, and early medieval periods in temperate Europe has been a muddled exercise in associating archaeological cultures with tribal names or other references gleaned from ancient authorities or, where specific names failed, on supposed groups and sub-groups concocted by historical linguistic studies.[14] The proto-history of temperate Europe was seen as a record of the growth, spread, or decline of supposed tightly drawn, closed, tribal entities, a tale usually punctuated with all manner of conquests, invasions, and migrations, footnoted perhaps with a smattering of "trade," and embellished with an admixture of that usually undefined ingredient, diffusion, the whole cast in a decidedly nontheoretical "historical" framework.[15]

In recent decades, this perspective has been challenged, especially on the basis of its fetish for explaining the bulk of culture change by the unexamined *deus ex machina* of invasions or migrations. Continuity and development from local roots would save the appearances as well, it is argued.[16] While proponents of this newer persuasion have sometimes been too intrigued by the metaphysics and polemics of the continuity-discontinuity controversy, they have made a case for rethinking the types of models that can be reared on the basis of the traits of archaeological evidence.

The desirability for new and more flexible conceptual frameworks has been underscored in recent years as new analytical techniques have broadened the types of evidence that can be derived from archaeological materials. For instance, pottery has long provided a crucial source for the traits used to pinpoint culture areas, with the distribution of the wares of tribal potters— the implicit assumption being that pot-making among the barbarians was a very nonspecialized household industry—taken to be roughly equal to the territory of a tribe. A growing number of analyses of the fabrics of such pottery has resulted in the discovery of centers of extraction and manufacture, and in many cases, the distributional hinterlands of such pottery have scarcely respected supposed tribal boundaries.[17] In instances where there is a paucity of linguistic or literary evidence, there is the possibility that such fancied boundaries can be redrawn. In many other instances, where linguistic boundaries can be reasonably distinguished or where literary accounts—usually by their Roman conquerors—clearly indicate the locations of tribal spheres of influence, the pottery evidence has proved disquieting. Clearly, proto-historic tribal groupings in Europe were not necessarily closed monads, but traditional conceptualizations of tribes give scant indication of how to handle the manifest presence of intertribal linkages and articulations.[18]

Such problems are not unique to European archaeology. Similar anomalies have bedeviled attempts to carve aboriginal America into tribal culture areas, the scope of such anomalies having prompted—from an even earlier date perhaps than in Europe—efforts to develop alternative descriptive and explanatory frameworks. A seminal region is that of the Hopewellian complex of eastern United States. Here, the archaeologists were confronted with a number of locally differentiated sub-groups of diverse subsistence bases (with most, however, practicing intensive hunting and gathering strategies centered on riverine areas), all these local groups sharing in some sort of over-arching Hopewellian culture reflected in a range of ceremonial centers and ritual artifacts. During the period around the beginning of the Christian era, this inclusive Hopewellian complex ranged over the whole of the eastern United States, a staggeringly large area. This far-flung complex could hardly have reflected any cohesive political unit, but, at the other extreme, efforts to explain this distribution by a series of migrations and invasions have proved unsatisfactory.

A more workable conceptualization would picture the Hopewellian culture as the result of a series of trade and exchange linkages focusing on the larger ceremonial centers, these larger centers in turn articulating with lower-level regional population groups.[19] These lower-level groupings, which would traditionally be labeled as tribes, were obviously not closed systems, and on-going research is beginning to flesh out the roles and functions of their supra-local articulations. While a good many of the exchanges can be expected to have simply centered around efforts to maintain the far-flung ties of the "interaction sphere" and to regulate the role structures and status differentials associated with the higher level activities, the higher-level systems very probably served to regulate and redress various sorts of variations and imbalances at the local levels.[20] Subsistence system failures or deficiencies, local difficiencies of other natural resources, and regional demographic imbalances are among the factors that could have impinged—sometimes disastrously—on local groups. Manipulation of kinship ties or limited types of aggressive activities would be one class of strategies to redress such imbalances, but use of the intermediatory services and redistributive capacities of the institutions of the higher-level interaction sphere would also accomplish the same ends in many situations.

The exact range of the variables involved, their relative importance, their degree and incidence of variability as well as the types of associated regulatory mechanisms, and the capacities and effectiveness of these mechanisms would, of course, vary

from context to context. The general features of the interaction
sphere concept, though, offer a valuable model framework from
which to view the problem of tribalism, with tribes viewed not as
closed entities, but as open systems capable of various linkages
and articulations with more inclusive institutional supra-systems.
As level after level of hierarchical structuring is added to such
systems, one is eventually faced with situations where, in terms
of complexity and centralization in political or economic spheres,
the appellation state becomes appropriate, and recently, scholars
such as Kent Flannery have emphasized the utility of the interaction sphere concept in the study of the evolution of state
systems.[21] For present purposes, however, attention will be focused on less complex, more tribal, types of interaction spheres.
With concentration given to temperate European contexts, several
possible interaction spheres will be proposed and a range of variables, processes, and mechanisms explored for such systems in
order to provide baselines from which to gauge the probable
impact of the subsequent linkage of several of these regions into
the framework of the Roman Empire.

Joseph Caldwell, the formulator of the interaction sphere concept, has suggested that late Neolithic–Early Bronze Age cultures
such as the Battle Axe groups of northern Europe may have
ranked as interaction spheres.[22] Highly crafted objects such as
polished stone axes imitative of metal artifacts would indicate
the operation of Hopewell-type institutions while lower-level systems would be represented by regionally differentiated objects,
e.g., hammer stones or lithic cutting implements associated with
more mundane subsistence activities. An interesting research as-
signment would be to test Caldwell's notions against a broad
range of prehistoric European cultures, a task obviously beyond
the scope of the present study. By Iron Age times, however, the
task is rendered somewhat easier. Conspicuous structures, e.g.,
hill forts, brochs, duns, raths, rounds, hillslope forts, and other
types appear throughout temperate Europe, and many of these
structures very probably served as analogues to the ceremonial
centers of the Hopewellian complex. For lower-level systems,
excavated settlement sites and their associated artifacts become
more abundant by Iron Age times than for earlier periods. From
this mass of material, three probable interaction spheres will be
described, two of which subsequently figured in Roman frontier
systems.

In north Scotland, and in the adjacent island groups of the

Orkneys and the Shetlands, the pre-Roman Iron Age saw the emergence of cultural systems associated with massive dry-stone towers called brochs, which probably served as the political, military, and ritual focal points for resident and surrounding population groups.[23] The subsistence base of these groups was mixed farming[24] with an appropriately accentuated stock farming component since the cool, damp climate and short growing season militated against an over-reliance on cereal crops. These resources were augmented by a certain amount of hunting, chiefly of fowl, but more importantly by exploitation of the abundant marine life, e.g., shellfish, fish, and marine mammals. Contacts between island groups could have been readily accomplished by sea, such contacts and the presence of trade and exchange linkages being indicated archaeologically by the distribution of steatite (soapstone) used as a tempering agent in ceramic vessels or ground down to form stoneware containers, this mineral having a notably restricted natural distribution.[25]

Around the time of Roman contact, the broch groups were very probably engaged in a gradual southerly encroachment on the territory of somewhat similar cultural groups centered in Scotland itself who, instead of brochs, used hill forts with timber-laced ramparts which, when burned, often vitrified to produce an archaeologically more durable variant, the vitrified fort. This encroachment by the broch groups was perhaps sparked by demographic pressures building up on the outward island groups. Such contact was sometimes violent.[26] But there are also indications of more peaceful exchanges, these in the form of trade in hides, hemp, bone implements, marine foodstuffs, and other items of the broch builders for the metals, pottery, and grain of groups to the south. The north Scottish area, then, may very possibly have supported two regional interaction spheres, one associated with the hill fort groups, another with the broch groups, and a higher-level inter-regional interaction sphere associated with trade and exchange mechanisms articulating the two lower-level spheres.

Another intriguing region consists of the North Sea coast from Flanders into Jutland and its associated hinterland. From the late Iron Age and into the early Middle Ages, this region included the range of groups such as the Frisians, middlemen for much of Northwest Europe, responsible, so it is argued, for shuttling goods of various sorts between Gaul and Scandinavia, and between

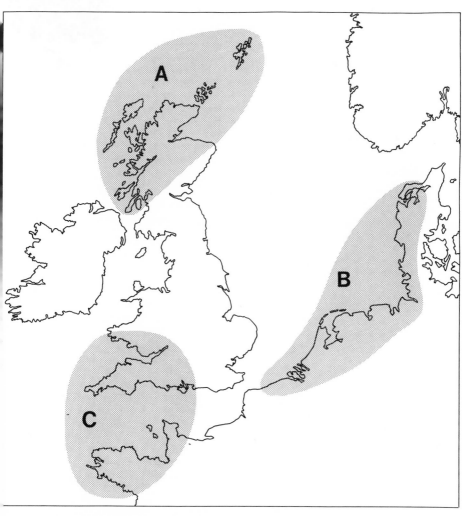

Ranges of some probable interaction spheres: A, North Scotland;
B, North Sea Coast; C, South Wales, Southwest England, and Armorica

the continent and Britain.[27] The roots of such trading acumen go back into the Iron Age when a lowering in the level of mean sea level opened up sizeable new areas along the braided river mouths of the North Sea coast for human occupation, this hydrological optimum lasting into the Roman period. Concurrent with this trend, the sandy uplands of the interior, prior to this time the primary demographic focus, became less hospitable as over-clearance and over-grazing culminated in widespread soil degradation, erosion, and the spread of poor quality heath vegetation.[28] Farmsteads and hamlet sites, often built on artificial mounds or *terpen,* rapidly began to fill in the coastal regions.[29] Cereals and other crops could be harvested from well-manured infields on or near the *terpen* and from fields laid out along silted-up water courses off the *terpen* while the marshy grassland provided pasturage for large numbers of livestock, especially for cattle. Provision of adequate cereal supplies was probably a perennial problem, though, with periodic flooding to be reckoned with even under the best of conditions and a gradual rise in mean sea level beginning in the late Roman period further aggravating the difficulties. Exchange of animal and cereal products among groups along the coast was an obvious adaptation, such strategies supplemented by exchanges of craft items as well as income from trade in foreign goods passing through the region. Provision for the small-scale movement of people within kinship and other networks along the coast may also be assumed. Mechanisms for larger-scale movements may have also existed, shuttling excess population into the interior along the numerous river channels or even across the North Sea into Britain or along the English Channel into Gaul, such movement following established trade routes. From such adjacent areas, various items, e.g., manufactured goods, metals, salt, or grain, could be acquired. None of these networks were associated with large-scale centers, but, nevertheless, the North Sea coast ranks as a probable regional interaction sphere with numerous pervasive ties with adjacent areas. Much of this region was also to become linked to the Roman Empire and its frontier on the lower Rhine.

The last region to be considered comprises southern Wales, southwest England, and Armorica (modern Brittany). This region, a portion of Europe's Atlantic fringe,[30] has, from the Neolithic period on, been a major arena for movements and exchanges of various sorts. Agriculture itself first spread to the British Isles from France within this sphere, and subsequent exchanges and movements in raw materials, skills, and personnel were responsible for the development of copper and bronze metallurgy within this region and immediately adjacent areas.[31] On the eve of Caesar's conquest of northern Gaul, Armorica was the center of groups like the *Veneti,* who had extensive trade connections along the coasts of Gaul and even farther afield in Britain.[32] The processes underpinning such regional and inter-regional contacts can be seen from an analysis of a few selected regions in southwest England. These regions are the Land's End district at the tip of Cornwall and the adjacent Lizard Peninsula jutting southward into the English Channel.

The Land's End district reveals with some clarity the dynamics of subsistence activities within the Atlantic fringe. Here, as in the other regions discussed above, one is faced with a mixed farming system with an emphasis on stock-farming, but here with considerable spatial adaptation to the recurrent pattern in Atlantic Europe of coastal lowlands rising into higher moorland and mountain reaches. The rugged nature of the landscape offers scant meadow-land but abundant rough pasture in the higher-lying areas. The full potential of the rough grazing can only be realized, however, by resort to various types of seasonal transhumance involving movements of persons and stock over distances of several miles. The result is generally a bifurcation of settlement foci into a lowland focus, where stock can be over-wintered and where the limited agricultural activities are concentrated, and a highland focus used primarily for summer grazing.[33] Distinctive settlement structures commonly emerge in these two zones, the settlements adapted to variant subsistence functions. Upland sites, or shielings, may boast a number of simple shelters and storage facilities used seasonally to tend stock, care for young animals, and process dairy products or wool. Wintering zones may boast more substantial dwellings and more ample storage facilities and work areas.[34] Prehistoric settlement distributions in the Land's End reflect such a bifurcation in settlement foci, with substantial, palisaded farmsteads, called rounds, concentrated in lower-lying regions and with the higher reaches dotted with less substantial hutcircles and enclosures occurring whether singly or in loose compounds. However, certain settlement types, the courtyard house type found along the juncture between highland and lowland zones and the cliff castle type found on coastal promontories, may represent variations in the more general bifurcated pattern.[35]

The all but frostless winters of the Land's End encourage over-wintering of limited numbers of animals along the highland focus. This is further facilitated by the lack of bogs or other hazards such as occur on high moorland tracts in most other regions of the Atlantic fringe. Permanent or near permanent occupancy along the highland-lowland juncture in the Land's End may have been possible in a certain number of sitings which also offered sufficient land for cropping. Even in sitings relatively unsuited for agriculture, surplus stock, textiles, and dairy products could have been exchanged for agricultural products with other groups. Courtyard house settlements, then, may have sacrificed a considerable measure of agricultural productivity to concentrate almost solely on stock farming. This strategy would be quite understandable along the north coastal strip of the Land's End, the narrow lowland apron below the highland zone nowhere exceeding a mile or so in extent and offering extremely limited potentials for agriculture.

Cliff castles and other sites lying immediately on the coastal cliffs may represent another variation in the multiple focus pattern outlined above. Some of these coastal settlements, when located on extensive promontories, may in fact be perfectly understandable as lowland components within a bifurcated framework. Such extensive headlands offer appreciable areas of grassland and, except for the extreme tips of the promontories near the sheer cliff faces, can often be cropped. Studies of similarly situated sites in Ireland have suggested that locating along cliffs gave relief from strong gale winds coming off the sea, the cliff faces deflecting the force of the winds upward for a considerable distance inland.[36] Coastal sitings of this sort, then, may present no anomaly at all. Other sites, however, may have represented adaptations to take advantage of marine resources, e.g., sea plants, shell fish, fish, cliff-dwelling birds, and even marine mammals of the sea.[37] Other types of resources may then have been obtained by exchanges with neighboring groups. Many cliff castles, then, may have sacrificed their highland components for more ready access to the sea.

Various factors impinged on these mobile subsistence frameworks, creating a wider range of exchange ties within the Land's End district and adjacent regions. For instance, as outlined above, the limited amount of arable land on the north coast of the Land's End probably prompted exchanges of livestock and craft products in return for cereals. Furthermore, the whole of the Land's End, and many other regions in Cornwall, are deficient in a number of important resources, among these being good-quality potting-clay[38] and salt springs or tidal estuaries which provided the major foci for saltworking in prehistoric Europe.[39] One region in the Lizard Peninsula, the area around modern Trebarveth in St. Keverne parish, at least boasted ample supplies of potting-clay. Petrological analyses of Cornish ceramics dating from the Neolithic onward indicate that a surprisingly large percentage of the clay and usually the actual pottery originated from this one region in the Lizard Peninsula, to be transported by pack animal or by sea throughout the whole of Cornwall.[40] Ample supplies of potting-clay also encouraged the construction of saltpans and drying troughs, as recent excavations at Trebarveth have demonstrated.[41] In return for ceramics and salt, the inhabitants of the Lizard Peninsula could have received agricultural goods, the serpentine bedrock of much of the peninsula producing poor quality soils relatively useless for cropping and nutrient-poor forages undesirable even for rough grazing.

From the Bronze Age onward, a further factor impinged on these symbiotic ties. Cornwall is one of the few areas in Northwest Europe with surface deposits of tin, a vital ingredient in the alloying of copper to form bronze. One area within Cornwall boasting such easily worked tin deposits is found in an arc flanking the north coast of the Land's End.[42] Bronze was a significant item in metal artifacts long after the advent of iron, its ornamental use in fact probably increasing even though it was no longer employed in a growing range of tools and weapons. The production of tin, either as ore or in smelted form, would be a welcome adjunct to the precariously balanced mixed farming bases of tin-rich regions such as the north coast of the Land's End. And while the demand for tin and bronze within Cornwall was limited, the demand throughout northwest Europe was enormous, even when the factor of the recasting of old bronze is allowed for. In this manner, an already complex series of symbiotic networks within Cornwall was tied to other networks in other portions of the Atlantic fringe with their own variants of the Cornish theme of inter-regional imbalances in resource endowments or other factors made good by complementary exchange relations.[43] These networks of the Atlantic fringe were in turn articulated with trade routes and institutional linkages in adjacent portions of northwest Europe.

From this brief consideration of several regional and inter-regional interaction spheres in pre-Roman northwest Europe, a number of common themes emerge. In all these instances, a variety of supra-local institutions, networks, and processes, some centered on fairly conspicuous central structures or centers, some only perceptible by close attention to regional resource endowments and the provenances of artifacts and materials figuring in exchange networks, fulfilled probably regulatory functions vis-a-vis variations and imbalances in subsistence and demographic factors affecting affiliated local groups. Flows of goods, services, and persons within the interaction spheres on an ongoing or periodic basis served to redress these imbalances. A certain amount of friction—at times outright warfare—undoubtedly occurred, but a more general trend was probably for imbalances and grievances to be redressed by peaceful means. Within certain limits and tolerances, then, these interaction sphere mechanisms were remarkably effective.[44] In many of the regions involved, it is arguable that without the interaction sphere mechanisms and the specializations and symbiotic ties these allowed, the existing subsistence bases and technologies could only have supported much reduced population densities, and these at much impoverished levels of material culture.

It is also obvious that the mechanisms of these interaction spheres in some instances involved a degree of central control, at the very least its potential. The ability to manipulate such institutional nodes by select groups, strata, or classes is, of course, at the crux of the process by which state systems can evolve from less centralized interactions sphere frameworks.[45] Where such trends are the result of slowly accumulating pressures with sufficient time for the efficient selection of the more effective means to exercise such control, lower-level groups may in the end still find themselves slotted into low-prestige roles, but the higher-order institutions and elite groups may still effectively regulate lower-level variables. There is always the possibility, however, that such trends toward centralization may result in all sorts of dysfunctional structural adaptations, with massive coercion but with grossly inadequate control.

With these comments in mind, developments along Rome's frontiers become more intelligible. The location of Roman frontiers in Europe was seldom a matter of chance, but it was also not merely a matter of judicious strategic and tactical appraisal of terrain. These factors might dictate the siting of individual forts or roads or even ostentatious displays of wall-building such as Hadrian's Wall. Military complexes such as these, however, are best seen as attempts at controlling the institutional corridors of power presented by the pre-Roman foundations, i.e., interaction spheres.

It is interesting to pursue the notion that even extended frontiers such as those along the Rhine or the Danube represented in effect chains of interaction spheres loosely, then ever more tightly, strung together under unified military commands. The impact of such strong-arm tactics on the efficiency of pre-existing mechanisms was often, as one might expect, disastrous. Mechanisms of regulation turned overnight into instruments of coercion must have simply collapsed in many instances. In many other instances, their effectiveness was probably severely impaired. The whole period of the *Pax Romana* was dotted by recurrent rebellions at one point or another of the frontier system, some regions being the scenes of almost incessant troubles, e.g., Wales, North Britain, and the awkward region fronting Raetia and Noricum that the Romans would have liked to have provincialized after the manner of Dacia, Moesia's trans-Danubian nemesis.[46] In some areas, Rome may have slowly learned to soften her propensity for coercion without regulation, but in other areas, e.g., along the middle Rhine, her response was Draconian in the extreme, taking the form of the creation of a forcibly depopulated no-man's land on the east bank of the Rhine.[47]

Even the best intentioned of Roman efforts at frontier control could have all sorts of dysfunctional side effects. The situation of a huge military establishment and its logistics train in the midst of, or close to, erstwhile native centers usually caused a rapid proliferation of commercial activities. The productive and distributive capacities of the pre-Roman frontier groups were seldom able to keep up with Roman criteria of quality and quantity. As a result, whole ranges of cheap and readily available goods and services and whole classes of petty entrepreneurs and vendors came to pervade the frontiers and the areas beyond. Where this led to competition with native craft production, the latter was likely to succumb in the face of the Roman novelties. Where displaced native craftsmen could not retool and compete with the new products, a whole range of livelihoods and supplementary incomes were jeopardized. Where such craft activities had previously allowed specializations, which in turn allowed the support of population densities in excess of the capabilities of a more undifferentiated subsistence base, the resultant dislocations could be severe. The proliferation and spread of commercial activities might also spread social competition into spheres where such competition had been minimal or nonexistent before the Roman advent. One key arena where this commercial onslaught might unleash deleterious side effects stemmed from Rome's appetite for cheap labor fed by a trade in barbarian slaves.

Numerous studies have examined the deadening effect on the internal Roman economy and technology of the use of slave labor.[48] Hardly any studies have considered the impact of slaving on the areas which provided these human chattels, but if early modern African analogies are *a propos,* the result must have been extremely unsettling.[49] Not only the Romans but native groups themselves would have become involved in the acquisition of this new commodity, and once again drawing on African analogies, the slave trade may have been a powerful triggering mechanism whereby aggressive behavior and Roman military techniques were diffused through barbarian Europe, steeling nascent exploitative tendencies in native institutional frameworks with brutally efficient new coercive techniques.[50]

This new way of shuttling persons out of the native systems entirely may have replaced older, more subtle ways of relieving demographic or other imbalances, but its liabilities probably more than overshadowed its advantages. One liability may have been to retard the development of more efficient subsistence and technological practices among frontier groups and barbarians even farther afield.[51] Such avenues effectively hamstrung, the only viable remaining strategies in the face of demographic or other pressures would either be to shunt off excess population into the Roman world or, where this was not possible, to depress drastically the standard of living of an increasing segment of the native populations, paving the way for the post-Roman norm of seigneurial military elites on the one hand and low-status peasants on the other.

And these devices, violent, exploitative, and inefficient even when they worked, may not have always sufficed to regulate fluctuations in the variables affecting frontier societies. Kent Flannery has outlined a number of "pathologies" to which highly complex societies are subject, prominent among these being what he calls "coherence."[52] Coherence becomes dysfunctional where too many aspects of socio-cultural life become too tightly linked with each other. A violent oscillation in one sector may spark other undesirable reactions throughout the system. Efforts by higher-order mechanisms to initiate regulatory responses may then be stymied. In fact, such additional inputs may only make matters worse, and further efforts at control may unleash utter chaos. Too many things may happen too fast for regulatory agencies to digest the information properly, and their responses based on this inadequate information may then become ineffectual shots in the dark.[53] If the system is "lucky," the disturbances may damp themselves out. If the system is "unlucky," its prior structural arrangements may prove impossible to retain.

The history of Rome's frontiers, especially in their latter phases leading into the early Middle Ages, is highlighted by those recurrent migratory maelstroms known collectively as the barbarian invasions, and Flannery's notion of coherence may go far to explain this phenomenon. Pre-Roman regional and inter-regional interaction spheres were seldom as extensive as the unified *limes* systems which supplanted them. Such unified zones, spanning hundreds of miles along the Rhine or Danube, opened the door to the destabilizing tendencies of coherence. What influenced one interaction sphere might now influence very drastically and directly events in another. Rome's ability to monitor the scope of such interplays was impressive, but not even the Romans were aware of all the potential consequences of their frontier policies. And while Rome's coercive ability—its chief control mechanism—was enormous, this had its limitations too. There were only so many legions; troops could march only so far in a day; and the empire's ability to funnel funds and manpower into massive regulatory endeavors was strictly limited. A variety of conditions could develop that could throw the whole system into disarray. Gross demographic imbalances, crop failures, or epidemics along the frontiers, often coupled with suitable external inputs, e.g., demographic surfeits beyond the frontiers or internal embarrassments such as civil wars within the empire, might trigger a sudden collapse of the whole system of control along some stretch of frontier.

Trouble in one frontier zone could necessitate frenzied redeployments and vexillations of troops along other stretches to underwrite the costs of patching up the initial collapse. This could easily induce a flare-up in the areas from which manpower or ordnance had been stripped. Likewise, some incident, even a minor incident, at some point on a frontier might persuade vindictive or frightened generals or emperors to initiate campaigns of reprisal along the whole length of a frontier, perhaps sparking in the process the disaster they had sought to avoid, only in an unsuspected quarter. Once some chain reaction had started, the Roman capacity to respond appropriately, or even to respond at all, might be exceeded. Responses would then amount to in-effectual shots in the dark. This lack of regulation would leave the situation to work itself out. One such chain reaction, which began on the Danubian frontier in the late second century under the reign of Marcus Aurelius, took nearly a century to work itself out. Only under Diocletian was a semblance of control restored, but in short order, a new round of massive disruptions began, and this time the price of restoration for Rome was the abandonment of the whole of the West, both frontiers and prov-inces.

Generalizations from the Roman experience may be over-hasty, but on this basis, the conclusion must be that preindustrial fron-tiers are prone to all the dysfunctional aspects of preindustrial states in an extremely glaring form. The maintenance of such frontiers would seem to provide minimal long-term rewards, eco-nomic or otherwise, for any of the parties involved, and the long-term norm would not seem to be the preservation of the frontier but its periodic or permanent dissolution, entailing in the process all manner of rapid and drastic structural alterations, both on the part of the preindustrial states and their highly ac-culturated frontier societies.

Many of the dysfunctional aspects of preindustrial frontiers stem from their coherence and the resultant crudeness manifested by those in positions of control frequently forced to act on the basis of inadequate information using regulatory machinery it-self too inefficient or indiscriminate to effect desired changes. These observations point the way, however, to how models of frontiers intermediate between the industrial and preindustrial types outlined in this study might be delineated. In the types of preindustrial frontiers described above, control was usually ob-tained only through the extreme tactic of seeding the institutional landscape thickly with military hardware. Over and beyond brute force, control via such military complexes hinged on flows of information, which was often inefficiently communicated, e.g., in the Roman world by couriers laboriously treking from post-station to post-station along Roman roads or trusting to the quicker but still grossly inefficient mercies of the Roman navy or merchant marine. Furthermore, the types of articulations be-tween frontiers and provincialized interiors were seldom a stimulus to sustained economic growth in either type of region, and the liabilities of the frontiers inexoriably had a way of reacting disadvantageously on the "barbarians" and on the whole social fabric of the preindustrial states, tying the states' hands and necessitating a perpetual readiness to pour the resources of a vast and expensive military establishment into the job of frontier restoration. Even if all went well for a preindustrial state, its frontiers were liabilities, especially as regards the diversion of a large share of their productive, distributive, and consumptive capacities to non-productive ends.

The dysfunctional aspects of such frontiers could be partially minimized if the task of gathering, processing, and transmitting information were made more efficient. Better transportation facilities, especially by sea, and better communications systems, perhaps mere appendages of the transportation facilities, in more modern times via means even more efficient, e.g., telegraph, wireless, or telephone—all these would offer obvious advantages. Better organizational techniques, e.g., efficient bureaucratic systems, would make possible similar advances. Such developments might lessen the need to rely so much on brute force to exercise control in frontier regions. At least, the military forces could be pared down, made more mobile, and made more efficient. At the very least, such trends might enable the controlling society to screen out the undesirable effects, especially bad economic feedbacks, from frontier activities. Frontiers would then offer more lucrative arenas for commercial and entrepreneurial ventures based within the controlling societies. Low-risk "enclave economies"[54] might then be established in the frontier zones, and if frontier conditions became unsettled, the enclaves could be abandoned, if need be, with no fear of such actions spreading losses beyond readily calculable bounds. For lack of a better name, these might be called commercial frontiers. Historians such as Charles Verlinden and Joshua Prawer would trace the origins of such frontiers to the activities of medieval Italian merchants and city republics in the Levant,[55] the techniques which in slightly altered form were brought to relative perfection by the Dutch in the East Indies or even by the English in colonial schemes beginning with Jamestown.[56] The techniques and skills worked out in the evolution of these commercial frontiers were much more compatible with advanced capitalistic, industrial practices, hence serving as the nexes—in some cases the actual territorial nexes—from which the patterns of industrial frontiers developed.

Notes

1. Much of the research for this paper was made possible by a year of study at Oxford University's Institute of Archaeology as a result of an N.D.E.A. Title IV Fellowship. I warmly acknowledge the help and support of all the persons, agencies, and institutions involved.

2. See J. D. Gould, *Economic Growth in History* (London, 1972), pp. 164–82, 235–40, 257–65; and R. E. Baldwin, "Patterns of Development in Newly Settled Regions," *Manchester School of Economic and Social Studies,* 24 (1956), 161–79.

3. This harshness is both a matter of the local environment, natural *and* social, as well as—and perhaps more importantly—a matter of the difficulties in affecting external institutional linkages.

4. E.g., D. C. North, "Location Theory and Regional Economic Growth," *Journal of Political Economy,* 63 (1955), 243–58; M. H. Watkins, "A Staple Theory of Economic Growth," *Canadian Journal of Economic and Political Science,* 29 (1963), 141–58; J. W. McCarty, "The Staple Approach in Australian Economic History," *Business Archives and History,* 4 (1964), 1–22; and A. G. Hopkins, *An Economic History of West Africa* (New York, 1973), pp. 124–31, 168–71.

5. For an anthropological perspective on modern pioneer colonization schemes, see S. I. Thompson, *Pioneer Colonization: A Cross-Cultural View* (Reading, Mass., 1973).

6. On these matters, see the following convenient anthologies: E. L. Jones, ed., *Agriculture and Economic Growth in England, 1650–1815* (London, 1967); R. M. Hartwell, ed., *The Causes of the Industrial Revolution in England* (London, 1967); and W. E. Minchinton, ed., *The Growth of English Overseas Trade in the Seventeenth and Eighteenth Centuries* (London, 1969).

7. Analogies for this Roman experience from Spanish South America are given in Elman R. Service, *Cultural Evolutionism: Theory and Practice* (New York, 1971), pp. 75–90.

8. On the growth of commercial farming in peninsular Italy, see the concise treatment in P. A. Brunt, *Social Conflicts in the Roman Republic* (New York, 1971), pp. 19–41.

9. See Erik Sjoeqvist, *Sicily and the Greeks* (Ann Arbor, 1973); and Jaques Heurgon, *The Rise of Rome to 264* B.C., trans. by James Willis (Berkeley, 1973), pp. 75–105, 212–18.

10. Arnold J. Toynbee, *Hannibal's Legacy: The Hannibalic War's Effects on Roman Life,* 2 Vols. (London, 1965), II, 197–205.

11. See B. Dobson and D. J. Breeze, *The Building of Hadrian's Wall,* 2nd ed. (Durham, 1970); Peter Salway, *The Frontier People of Roman Britain* (Cambridge, 1965); and George Jobey, "Homesteads and Settlements of the Frontier Area," in *Rural Settlement in Roman Britain,* ed. by Charles Thomas (Council for British Archaeology Research Report No. 7 [London, 1966]), pp. 1–14.

12. My thanks to Professor Barry W. Cunliffe for valuable suggestions on these matters. See further Olwen Brogan, "Trade between the Roman Empire and the Free Germans," *Journal of Roman Studies,* 26 (1936), 195–222, and esp. at p. 197, where Brogan notes how Roman forts along the Rhine frontier were almost invariably sited at points where older pre-Roman trade routes crossed the frontier.

13. Morton Fried, "On the Concepts of 'Tribe' and 'Tribal Society'," in *Essays*

on the Problem of the Tribe, ed. by June Helm (Proceedings of 1967 Annual Spring Meeting of the American Ethnological Society [Seattle, 1968]), pp. 3–20.

14. For a critical review of this approach, so very much indebted to the German archaeologist Gustav Kossinna, see Reinhard Wenskus, *Stammesbildung und Verfassung: Das Werden der Fruehmittelalterlichen Gentes* (Colgne, 1961), pp. 113–42. For a critique of the types of linguistic arguments often used to bolster the delineation of archaeological tribes, see Friederich Mauer, *Nordgermanen und Alemannen: Studien zur germanischen und fruehdeutschen Sprachgeschichte, Stammes und Volkskunde,* 3rd ed. (Munich, 1952).

15. See the criticisms raised in Colin Renfrew, "Wessex without Mycenae," *Annual of the British School at Athens,* 63 (1968), 277–85; and "Trade and Culture Process in European Prehistory," *Current Anthropology,* 10 (1969), 51–78.

16. The seminal article is J. G. D. Clark, "The Invasion Hypothesis in British Archaeology," *Antiquity,* 40 (1966), 172–89.

17. See esp. D. P. S. Peacock, "A Contribution to the Study of Glastonbury Ware from South-Western Britain," *Antiquaries Journal,* 49 (1969), 41–61.

18. For an appraisal of the consequences of research such as that of Peacock for received views on tribal boundaries, see Richard Bradley, "Trade Competition and Artefact Distribution," *World Archaeology,* 2 (1971), 347–52.

19. See the studies in Joseph R. Caldwell and Robert L. Hall, eds., *Hopewellian Studies* (Illinois State Museum Scientific Papers, 12, No. 3 [Springfield, Ill., 1964]). See further Stuart Struever, "Woodland Subsistence-Settlement Systems in the Lower Illinois Valley," in *New Perspectives in Archeology,* ed. by Sally R. Binford and Lewis R. Binford (Chicago, 1968), pp. 285–312.

20. Stuart Struever and Gail L. Houart, "An Analysis of the Hopewell Interaction Sphere," in *Social Exchange and Interaction,* ed. by Edwin N. Wilmsen (Anthropological Papers, Museum of Anthropology, University of Michigan, No. 46 [Ann Arbor, 1972]), pp. 47–79, where an attempt is made to break the large Hopewellian sphere into a number of nested local, regional, and interregional networks. While their study does not tackle in any depth the processes associated with such component sub-systems, other studies by Struever connect the growth of interaction sphere ties with rising population densities, increasingly sedentary village settlement patterns, and increasingly intensive hunter-gatherer procurement systems. See further Stuart Struever and Kent D. Vickerby, "The Beginnings of Cultivation in the Midwest-Riverine Area of the United States," *American Anthropologist,* 75, No. 5 (1973), 1197–1220.

21. Kent Flannery, "Summary Comment: Evolutionary Trends in Social Exchange and Interaction," in *Social Exchange and Interaction,* pp. 129–35.

22. Joseph Caldwell, "Interaction Spheres in Prehistory," in *Hopewellian Studies,* pp. 138–39.

23. The following sketch is based on J. R. C. Hamilton's work at two broch sites, Jarlshof and Clickhimin, in the Shetlands. The excavation reports appeared as J. R. C. Hamilton, *Excavations at Jarlshof, Shetland* (Edinburgh, 1968) and *Excavations at Clickhimin, Shetland* (Edinburgh, 1968). Hamilton's conclusions involving the Iron Age phases of these sites are set out in his "Brochs and Broch Builders," in *The Northern Isles,* ed. by F. T. Wainwright (Edinburgh, 1962), pp. 53–90 and "Forts, Brochs and Wheelhouses in Northern Scotland," in *The Iron Age in Northern Britain,* ed. by A. L. F. Rivet (Edinburgh, 1966), pp. 111–30. Hamilton's conclusions should be compared with the slightly variant

opinions of Euan W. MacKie, e.g., his "The Scottish Iron Age," *Scottish Historical Review,* 49 (1970), 1–32.

24. "Mixed farming" refers to subsistence systems combining both stock farming and arable cropping. The relative importance of these two major components would reflect the level of technology, the level of population, the types of external pressures, and the ecological features and tolerances of the region within which the mixed farming activities were set.

25. Within the region under consideration, steatite outcrops are only found on the Shetlands. The use of steatite backing in the fabric of clay pottery may have been a local eccentricity, but finished stoneware vessels definitely show a wide distribution throughout the whole of this proposed regional interaction sphere. See Hamilton, "Brochs and Broch Builders," pp. 71–72.

26. Hamilton, *ibid.,* pp. 64–65, emphasizes the hostile nature of such contracts, noting that the interface between the broch and hill fort zones is marked by a noticeable concentration of vitrified forts, produced by the firing—perhaps during the sack—of the hill forts and the vitrification of portions of their ramparts. The phase that produced this concentration of vitrified forts, however, falls squarely within the period of maximum Roman meddling in north Scottish affairs. The pre-Roman norm was perhaps not so bellicose. See MacKie, "The Scottish Iron Age," pp. 26–28.

27. Good introductions to the early medieval period include Herbert Jankuhn, "Der fraenkisch-friesische Handel zur Ostee im fruehen Mittelalter," *Vierteljahrschrift fuer Sozial-und Wirtschaftsgeschichte,* 40 (1953), 193–243; and D. Jellema, "Frisian Trade in the Dark Ages," *Speculum,* 30 (1955), 15–36. A valuable corrective to modernist notions of the nature and importance of such trade is Philip Grierson, "Commerce in the Dark Ages: A Critique of the Evidence," *Transactions of the Royal Historical Society,* 5th ser., 9 (1959), 123–40. My thanks also to Mr. Dafydd Kidd for much stimulating discussion on the problems of North Sea coast groups.

28. H. T. Waterbolk, "The Lower Rhine Basin," in *Courses Toward Urban Life,* ed. by Robert J. Braidwood and Gordon R. Willey (Chicago, 1962), pp. 227–53.

29. See the excellent syntheses in B. H. Slicher van Bath, "The Economic and Social Conditions in the Frisian Districts from 900 to 1500," *A.A.G. Bijdragen,* 13 (1965), 97–133; and Werner Haarnagel, "Die Grabung Feddersen Wierde und ihre Bedeutung fuer die Erkenntnisse der baeuerlichen Besiedling im Kuestengebiet in dem Zeitraum vom 1. Jahrhundert vor bis 5. Jahrhundert nach Chr.," *Zeitschrift fuer Agrargeschichte und Agrarsoziologie,* 10 (1962), 145–57.

30. E.g., E. Estyn Evans, "Ireland and Atlantic Europe," *Geographische Zeitschrift,* 52 (1963), 224–41 and "The Atlantic Ends of Europe," *Advancement of Science,* 15 (1958), 54–64.

31. For the Neolithic period, see Humphrey J. Case, "Neolithic Explanations," *Antiquity,* 43 (1969), 176–86. For the introduction of metallurgy, see H. H. Coughland and Humphrey J. Case, "Early Metallurgy of Copper in Ireland and Britain," *Proceedings of the Prehistoric Society,* 23 (1957), 91–123. My thanks to Mr. Case and to Professor Cunliffe for helpful advice and criticism on many of the points that follow.

32. A good introduction to such contacts can be found in Nora K. Chadwick, *Early Brittany* (Cardiff, 1969), pp. 1–123.

33. See esp. Glanville Jones, "The Multiple Estate as a Model Framework for Tracing Early Stages in the Evolution of Rural Settlement," in *L'Habitat et les paysages ruraux d'Europe*, ed. by F. Dussart (Les Congès et Colloques de l'Université de Liège, 58 [Liège, 1971]), pp. 251-67.

34. Many useful insights and analogies can be found in D. MacSween, "Transhumance in North Skye," *Scottish Geographical Magazine*, 75 (1959), 75-88; W. Kissling, "The Character and Purpose of the Hebridean Black House," *Journal of the Royal Anthropological Institute*, 73 (1943), 75-100; and E. Estyn Evans, "Dairying in Ireland through the Ages," *Journal of the Society of Dairy Technology*, 7 (1954), 179-88.

35. A good introduction to Cornish settlement patterns of the Iron Age and Romano-British periods is Charles Thomas, "The Character and Origins of Roman Dumnonia," in *Rural Settlement in Roman Britain*, pp. 74-98. Much of the following discussion stems from the author's own research based on locational analysis techniques applied to the data contained in Vivien Russell, *West Penwith Survey* (Truro, 1971).

36. V. B. Proudfoot and B. C. S. Wilson, "Further Excavations at Larrybane Promontory Fort, Co. Antrim," *Ulster Journal of Archaeology*, 24-25 (1961-1962), 106.

37. Useful comparisons can be made between coastal sites from the Land's End and settlements in the Isles of Scilly some twenty-five miles off the tip of Cornwall. See Paul Ashbee, "Excavations at Halangy Down, St. Mary's, Isles of Scilly, 1965 and 1966," *Cornish Archaeology*, 5 (1966), esp. at p. 26 and "Excavations at Halangy Down, St. Mary's, Isles of Scilly, 1967-1968," *Cornish Archaeology*, 7 (1968), 26-31. My thanks to Mr. Ashbee for private discussion on problems associated with his excavations at the Halangy Down site.

38. On potting-clay, see Henry Hodges, *Artifacts: An Introduction to Early Materials and Technology* (London, 1964), pp. 21-24. Cornwall was not glaciated, depriving it of boulder clays. Likewise, Cornwall lacks lakes, depriving it of lacustrine clays. Cornwall is well endowed with primary clays, e.g., china clays formed from the breakdown of felspathic rocks like granite, but such clays are hard to form into a useable paste and are even harder to fire without sophisticated kilns. This leaves secondary clays deposited by stream or river action. In Cornwall, deposits of good secondary clays are restricted to a handful of watercourses along the southern coast. This conclusion is borne out in H. L. Douch, "Cornish Potters and Pewterers," *Journal of the Royal Institution of Cornwall*, new ser., 6 (1969), p. 34. My thanks to Mr. Douch for private comments concerning the observations of Cornish potting-clays contained in this note.

39. For prehistoric salt-working, see Jacques Nenquin, *Salt: A Study in Economic Prehistory* (Bruges, 1961). Much useful information can also be found in Ethel H. Rudkin and Dorothy M. Owen, "The Medieval Salt Industry in the Lindsey Marshland," *Lincolnshire Architectural and Archaeological Society Reports and Transactions*, new ser., 8 (1959-1960), 76-84. Lindsay Scott, "Gallo-British Colonies: the Aisled Round House Culture in the North," *Proceedings of the Prehistoric Society*, 14 (1948), 124-25, notes that a poor quality salt may be obtained by simply boiling sea water or salt-impregnated seaweed, and that in place of salt, ashes may be used as a preservative. However, Nenquin, pp. 108-12, notes that these poorer quality preservatives may discolor butter or cheeses and impurities may impart a disagreeable taste.

40. On the pottery, see D. P. S. Peacock, "A Contribution to the Study of Glastonbury Ware for South-Western Britain," *Antiquaries Journal,* 49 (1969), 44, and "Neolithic Pottery Production in Cornwall," *Antiquity,* 43 (1969), 145–49. For a discussion of the evidence for an actual trade in finished ceramics, see A. M. ApSimon and E. Greenfield, "The Excavation of Bronze Age and Iron Age Settlements at Trevisker, St. Eval, Cornwall," *Proceedings of the Prehistoric Society,* 38 (1972), esp. at pp. 341–44, 368. My thanks to Dr. Peacock and Mr. ApSimon for private communications concerning Cornish ceramics.

41. D. P. S. Peacock, "A Romano-British Salt-working Site at Trebarveth, St. Keverne," *Cornish Archaeology,* 8 (1969), 47–65. Saltworking and pottery manufacture in the Lizard Peninsula probably predate considerably the Roman period date suggested for the Trebarveth site.

42. The geological facts are indisputable, on which see Henry Dewey, "The Mineral Zones of Cornwall," *Proceedings of the Geologists' Association,* 36 (1925), 131–32. Unfortunately, the very simple technology required for tin-smelting has left very few archaeological traces. Much useful information on tin mining and extraction can be found in Denys Bradford Barton, *Essays in Cornish Mining History,* 2 Vols. (Truro, 1968), I, 130–48.

43. Poor preservation of organic and metallic artifacts in Cornwall's acid soils limits attempts to define the points of origin or fabrication for anything besides lithic and ceramic objects. Iron Age sites such as the Glastonbury and Meare Lake Villages offer a much more impressive array of artifacts preserved by the peaty deposits of the former lake margins. For an attempt to show how such sites were articulated into regional and inter-regional societal hierarchies, see David L. Clarke, "A Provisional Model of an Iron Age Society and its Settlement Systems," in *Models in Archaeology,* ed. by David L. Clarke (London, 1973), pp. 801–69.

44. For the systemic framework employed in the present study to amount to anything more than metaphor or jargon, system tolerances, thresholds, and parameters need to be specified as carefully as possible, a task attempted in the author's "Preindustrial Frontiers and Interaction Spheres: Aspects of the Human Ecology of Roman Frontier Regions in Northwest Europe," (unpublished Ph.D. Dissertation, University of Oklahoma, 1976). For a discussion of the logical and methodological points underlying such types of systemic or functional analysis, see Paul W. Collins, "Functional Analyses in the Symposium 'Man, Culture, and Animals,'" in *Man, Culture, and Animals,* ed. by Anthony Leeds and Andrew P. Vayda (Washington, D.C., 1965), pp. 270–82.

45. Kent V. Flannery, "Summary Comments: Evolutionary Trends in Social Exchange and Interaction," in *Social Exchange and Interaction,* pp. 133–35. See also Maurice Godelier, *Rationality and Irrationality in Economics,* trans. by Brian Pearce (New York, 1972), pp. 289, 312–13.

46. See Fergus Millar, *The Roman Empire and its Neighbors* (New York, 1967), pp. 221–38, 297–99.

47. Ulrich Kahrstedt, "The Roman Frontier on the Lower Rhine in the Early Imperial Period," in *The Congress of Roman Frontier Studies, Newcastle upon Tyne, 1949,* ed. by Eric Birley (Durham, 1952), pp. 46–47. This depopulated zone was maintained throughout the Julio-Claudian dynasty.

48. E.g., Moses I. Finley, "Technological Innovation and Economic Progress in the Ancient World," *Economic History Review,* 2nd ser., 18 (1965), 29–45.

49. See briefly Paul Bohannan, *Africa and Africans* (Garden City, N.Y., 1964),

pp. 105–109. See further Richard Gray and David Birmingham, eds., *Pre-Colonial African Trade before 1900* (London, 1970); Claude Meillassoux, "Introduction," in *The Development of Indigenous Trade and Markets in West Africa,* ed. by Claude Meillassoux (London, 1971), pp. 3–86; and Karl Polanyi, *Dahomey and the Slave Trade: An Analysis of an Archaic Economy* (Seattle, 1966).

50. Rolf Hachmann, Georg Kossak, and Hans Kuhn, *Voelker zwischen Germanen und Kelten* (Neumuenster, 1962), pp. 130–32; and C. M. Wells, *The Germanic Policy of Augustus: An Examination of the Archaeological Evidence* (Oxford, 1972), pp. 30–31, 244.

51. Slavery and the slave trade probably favored the perpetuation of structural inefficiencies both among frontier and barbarian populations as well as in the core provinces of the empire. See Moses I. Finley, *The Ancient Economy* (Berkeley, 1973), pp. 62–94, 150–76.

52. Kent Flannery, "The Cultural Evolution of Civilizations," *Annual Review of Ecology and Systematics,* 3 (1972), 412–21. Flannery calls this pathology "hypercoherence," but the prefix will be deleted here. It should be borne in mind, however, that some coherence, i.e., some interaction among component parts of a system, is both inevitable and necessary.

53. Such situations would be favored by what Flannery, *ibid.,* pp. 413–14, calls "linearization." As the effectiveness of lower-level native institutions waned, the Romans would be tempted to intervene from time to time through various political-military channels. Many of these overriding mechanisms would be more appropriate to general policy matters affecting the whole of a province or frontier. When called upon to deal with the specifics of local-level problems, these higher-level control mechanisms would frequently prove ineffective and inefficient (as shown by Rome's predilection for crude, military remedies) or would risk dereliction in their proper spheres of authority and competence.

54. On enclave economies, see Gould, *Economic Growth in History,* pp. 247–51. Such enclaves, e.g., mining or oil concessions, are export oriented and heavily dependent on foreign capital inputs. They seldom promote self-reinforcing sectorial linkages and economic growth within their host regions.

55. Charles Verlinden, *The Beginning of Modern Colonization,* trans. by Yvonne Freccero (New York, 1970); and Joshua Prawer, *The Crusaders' Kingdom: European Colonialism in the Middle Ages* (New York, 1972).

56. For Jamestown, see Kenneth E. Lewis, "An Archaeological Consideration of the Frontier," *Papers in Anthropology,* 14, No. 1 (1973), 84–103. My thanks to Dr. Lewis for much stimulating discussion on frontiers, preindustrial or otherwise.

Ethnic Stereotypes and the Frontier: A Comparative Study of Roman and American Experience

David Harry Miller and William W. Savage, Jr.

THE SOURCES of North American frontier history are rife with stereotypes of various aboriginal groups. White men, whether from Spain, France, England, or Holland, were compelled, perhaps by the novelty of their encounter with the aborigines, to comment upon the appearance, manners, customs, and behavior of the people who became known collectively as Indians. Stereotypes emerged from these observations—stereotypes that became increasingly important in the political relationship between Indians and whites, particularly after 1763 and 1776. Anglo-American stereotypes of Indians have certainly not escaped scholarly scrutiny, but the political implications of those stereotypes have not been examined to any real extent. Nor have scholars generally been concerned with the role of the frontier in developing politically useful stereotypes. The purpose of this chapter is to explore that role in a preliminary manner and to offer a comparative model based on the Roman and Anglo-American experiences that may be useful in analyzing the development of stereotypes in other frontier situations. It is hoped, additionally, that the model will suggest to historians of the North American frontier a dimension of the frontier experience often overlooked in favor of the exceptional or spectacular event.[1]

The function of the stereotypic barbarian in Roman imperial life is a historical problem of some importance since it is one which may be traced in the sources over a relatively prolonged chronological span and the study of which may, therefore, be very useful for comparative discussion. The entire subject of Roman views of barbarians, however, is clearly beyond the scope of this paper. In order to delimit the problem and restrict the discussion to a manageable proportion, we shall restrict our attention to considerations of the stereotyped German. We shall also restrict our discussion to the period before the *Völkerwanderungen.*

The stereotypic Roman image of the German had little to do with any actual Germans. Even in the last years of imperial sur-

109

vival in the west, when the Germans, organized as war-confedera-
tions, approached the stereotyped model more closely than at
any other time, the relation between the real and the myth was
not even approximate. The stereotype was founded to a degree
on observation. But that observation was selective, and subject
to interpretations determined by the goals of Roman policy and
Roman perceptions of themselves and the empire. Once the fully
developed stereotype had become generally accepted as part of
the intellectual and emotional world-view of the majority of those
Romans who would either have contact with Germans or determine policy towards them, it became self-perpetuating. The stereotype led Romans to expect specific phenomena which they,
therefore, easily found; it led the Romans to interpret any phenomenon associated with the Germans in terms of a logical structure inherent in the stereotype itself. The stereotype was created
to rationalize or justify specific behavior towards specific groups
of "germanic" peoples, and afterwards it predetermined behavior
towards Germans in general in conformity with patterns already
set during the period of its formation.

The original Roman stereotype of the German was largely the
creation of Julius Caesar. It has been argued by some authorities
that the Roman attitude towards the Germans at the time of
Julius Caesar's first military contacts with them in the trans-
alpine regions, was one of fear inspired by memory of the invasion
of Italy by the *Cimbri* and *Teutones* in the time of Marius. This,
it has been argued, was why the Romans felt the need to extend
their control across the Alps; dread of the *furor teutonicus*.[2]
The Romans were in fact apprehensive on the subject of the
Cimbri and *Teutones,* and they may for that reason have been
anxious about alpine security. The argument, as it refers to the
Germans, is in error, however, and reflects too credulous a reading of Caesar's propaganda, which deliberately made an attempt
to link the peoples he called Germans with the *Cimbri* and *Teutones* to exploit popular fears and by that means to justify, after
the fact, a policy he had already put into force.[3] Earlier Greek
and Roman ethnographers had not, in fact, been certain how
to classify the peoples of the Rhineland and the area to the east,
and Caesar was the first ancient authority to identify the *Cimbri*
and *Teutones* as Germans. Indeed, the very idea of a radical
dichotomy between a celtic people in Gaul and a germanic people
in the Rhineland, and the lands east of the Rhine, is probably
untenable. The La Tène culture-style characteristic of celtic Gaul

extended, in Caesar's time, east as far as the Carpathian Mountains and, in the regions east of the Rhine, as far north as the Lippe. While there may have been some linguistic distinctions within this culture area, peoples as primitive as Caesar described the Germans to be were located only in the region of the lower Elbe and in regions northeast and east of the Elbe.[4]

Caesar, then, deliberately attempted to convince Roman opinion that a group of "barbarians," distinct from the Celts, and more dangerous than they, and related to the *Cimbri* and *Teutones,* were threatening to conquer Gaul and potentially posed an ultimate threat to Italy itself. These Germans he described as ferocious, war-loving brigands, of incredible courage and military skill, and of powerful and commanding presence.[5] Caesar's propaganda would appear to have been successful in Rome,[6] and the idea of the Germans as a people wild, savage, and war-like, to be crushed and confronted by either extermination or thorough subjugation, was born. It was successful enough, in fact, to survive long after its creator, and became a permanent feature in Roman imperial thought.

Caesar, of course, intended his version of his German wars to attain several specific goals. As a potential military dictator waiting for his main chance in Rome, he required to enlarge his command so far as possible, and reap a harvest of victories to enhance his reputation. Victories require wars, however, and wars require enemies. Hence Caesar's policy in Gaul was to provoke hostilities wherever he could, and in his reporting of these wars to inflate the magnitude of his victories by touting highly the valor and strength of his opponents.[7]

The stereotype of a people as a savage and ferocious mass intent upon rapine and slaughter, in short as sub-human, has other results, however. It justifies those who use it in making war, but it also sets a certain style for that kind of warfare. Given an opponent so blood-thirsty and dangerous, any tactic may be adopted in making war. A stereotype such as that cultivated by Caesar and perpetuated among the Romans, puts those who are thus labeled, whether implicitly or explicitly, beyond the protection of any humane convention. And so it turned out even in the first military encounters conducted by Caesar himself. Caesar's Germans clearly had no rights except to grovel before Caesar, or if obstinate enough to refuse to grovel, to have unlimited war waged upon them. Hence, acting consistently with his portrayal of the Germans, Caesar attacked the people of Ariovistus without warning, and put both women and children to death along with the warriors. During negotiations with other groups, the *Tencteri* and *Usipetes,* the villages of these groups were attacked by Caesar's troops while the negotiations were still in progress and while the leaders of these peoples were in his camp.[8]

Caesar's propaganda against the Germans, intended to establish an image of them as dangerous, powerful and hostile, and used to justify aggressive warfare in the Rhineland and on the right bank of the Rhine, areas normally outside his province, was a success. Henceforth the myth of Caesar's Germans was accepted at face value in Rome and Italy, and war against the Germans could always be justified and would always be regarded as proper in public opinion. It ensured as well that Romans would continue, in their dealings with Germans, to assume that uncivilized savages such as these had no human rights and could be subjugated or destroyed as chance, necessity, or whim might dictate.

It has often been alleged that Caesar's nephew and heir, Augustus, in his administration of the empire, had definitely decided on an end to imperial expansion and the inauguration of a period of peace. Indeed, this interpretation of Augustus' policy was current even among Romans themselves after his death in A.D. 14.[9] It is an interpretation which cannot, however, be taken seriously, so far as the frontier was concerned. While his uncle was merely a potential military dictator, in competition with a serious rival for supreme power, Augustus was a successful one, whose power rested on an enormous military establishment. But while the army might keep Augustus in power, it was also a major source of danger to his state. Large bodies of troops could not be kept in Italy, nor could they be kept idle. And while ambitious generals could not be allowed too much chance of winning glory in battle, neither could they be altogether denied the opportunity of enhancing their renown. More importantly, a dictator who would pass his power securely and successfully to the next generation would be forced to give his prospective heirs the chance to make their names as generals. Untried men, unknown or unrespected by the armies, would not rule for long once Augustus himself was dead. Hence, every practical consideration dictated that Augustus pursue a policy of controlled military operations, and the frontiers were the only place such a policy could be pursued. Caesar's Germans were as good an enemy as any other.[10] Given the acceptance of Caesar's propaganda, war against the Germans required no extensive psychological preparations. That no campaigns were prosecuted until 16 B.C., was due to the fact that Augustus had other immediate problems. After the battle of Actium in 31 B.C., Augustus had the task of consolidating his position in Rome and encouraging people to believe that the civil wars were over for good. This period immediately after 31 B.C., then, was no time for military adventures, especially when the Germans themselves were no real threat, Caesar to the contrary. Until Augustus was ready to open operations on the Rhine, garrison duty could be entrusted to auxiliary troops.[11]

The lull was broken, then, after 16 B.C. In that year a Roman column on a raid was annihilated by the *Sugambri*. This had not been the first Roman raid across the Rhine, casual expeditions to keep the troops in trim being occasionally adopted. The annihilation of an entire troop command, however, forced Augustus' hand. It would be seen publicly as a dangerous situation and a loss of face and hence the *imperator* had to take action. The decision was for the conquest of Germany itself, and several years were spent in preparation for a prolonged offensive campaign conducted by members of Augustus' family.[12] As a result of these campaigns, the frontier was pushed from the Rhine to the vicinity of the Elbe, and Germany was regarded as pacified. During this period the court ports celebrated the policy of imperialist expansion in no muted terms.[13]

The policy of conquest in Germany was, however, brought to a halt suddenly and unexpectedly. In A.D. 9, the military governor on the Lower Rhine, Quintilius Varus, was slaughtered along with three full legions by supposedly cowed and submissive Germans. The Roman forces on the Rhine were thrown into disorder and confusion.[14] The magnitude of the defeat cannot be overlooked; the legions that had been lost could not immediately be replaced and Augustus took the extraordinary measure of reinforcing the Rhine garrison with slaves, freed specifically for the purpose. As is probably typical in such instances, the response in Rome was an over-reaction, and it is reported that Augustus feared an invasion of Italy. In alarm over the situation he dismissed his bodyguard of German mercenaries, and took measures to prevent public disturbance, fearing that the defeat might encourage empire-wide revolt.[15] The Germans, however, being a collection of relatively small groups, rarely at peace with each other, and poorly armed,[16] and having never, therefore, been the sort of danger the Romans believed them to be, did nothing further.

After the initial shock had passed, the Romans adopted a policy of retrenchment on the Rhine accompanied with a series of extermination campaigns against various German groups across the River. These extermination campaigns indicate the degree to which the Romans' stereotype of the Germans now determined their policies. None of the German groups attacked were heavily involved in the uprising against Varus, and none of them had taken advantage of the episode to revolt. The general conducting the raids, Germanicus, exhorted his troops to take no prisoners, but to exterminate all. No distinction being made between hostile and peaceful communities, it is obvious that in this situation the Romans acted on the assumption that one German was the same as the other. Hence the raids, which were made in ridiculously overwhelming strength, were directed against villages asleep, or engaging in religious festivities, and expecting no violence, and the killing was indiscriminate as to age or sex.[17] "The troops escaped without harm—they had been killing men half-asleep, unarmed, and unorganized."[18]

This policy proved a failure, however. The extermination raids only caused a further inflamation of the situation, and once the Germans were well stirred up, Germanicus' engagements with hostile forces tended to result in defeats or drawn engagements. Finally, in A.D. 16, Tiberius called a halt to this policy, and in doing so put an end to the project of creating a trans-Rhenish province.[19]

The massacre of Varus in the *Teutobergerwald,* and the subsequent decision of Tiberius to withdraw to the Rhine, ended the first prolonged period of Roman contact with the Germans, but it did not involve any really substantial change in the pattern of frontier Roman-German contact. The basic nature of the Roman policy between 16 B.C. and A.D. 16 was the use of the German frontier as a theater of limited war in which a major segment of the military establishment could be kept busy and removed from any uncomfortable proximity to the seat of power, and in which the male members of the imperial dynasty could develop their military reputations. Germany was the main theater for these operations because it offered—or was assumed to offer—a frontier region inhabited by undesirables where war could be casually waged at no great cost, and where the attitudes or interests of the population thus attacked were of no great importance. Germany was the natural place for this military charade since the Germans themselves were popularly supposed to be a

threat of significant proportion to Italy itself. And, being assumed
to be total savages, of no redeeming nature, Germans could be
blatantly mauled from time to time without undue concern.

The loss of three legions, then, meant only that the creation
of a trans-Rhenish province was abandoned, and that the stereotype of Caesar's Germans became more convincing. From this
point on the German's were both more highly feared and more
highly detested. Though imperial policy dictated a more conservative defensive position on the Rhine, the basic pattern which
the stereotype imposed on military practice remained. This outcome was practically guaranteed in fact, since the rising against
Varus had been a fluke, and there was not, in the period after
Tiberius called a halt to ambitious trans-Rhenish operations, any
genuine military threat posed by the Germans.

Hence between Tiberius' death and A.D. 68, the policy toward
the Rhine frontier could be allowed to lie in the hands of local
military commanders under a succession of markedly non-military
emperors. During this whole period, the only real problem on the
Rhine was the loyalty of the garrisons themselves. This problem
in itself prompted Tiberius' successor, Gaius, to participate in
a military promenade across the Rhine to revive his dwindling
reputation with the troops.[20] His successor, Claudius, while following a different course, proved motivated by similar considerations in holding a limit on the independent activities of Rhine-
garrison commanders lest they acquire too high a popularity.[21]
In general during this period the main goal of Rhine policy was
to secure a defensible frontier in the region. This involved the
settlement of Suebic allies on the Upper Rhine and Neckar, and
the clearing of the Lower and Middle Rhine banks of population.[22]
Beyond these actions the government pursued no specific purpose, though the dismissal of Corbulo by Claudius probably may
be taken as an indication that local commanders continued the
habit of periodically using the Germans as the target of training
missions for their troops. The obvious implication of all of this is,
of course, that while the Germans were not a serious problem
for Roman security, the stereotype of Caesar's Germans continued to determine the behavior of the troops.

Imperial policy towards the Rhine frontier after the accession
of the Flavians was not substantially different, although the Flavians and the Antonines after them were for the most part genuine
military emperors. Some attempts were made to dress up the frontier line and improve the fortifications, but, aside from this, cam-

paigning on the Rhine was probably a matter of the discretion of local commanders, except for a brief excursion carried out by Domitian. The military attention of the Flavian regime, especially under Domitian, was concentrated on the Danube frontier against the Dacians. Flavian military policy on the Rhine was supplemented by a diplomatic policy, followed also by the Antonines, of forming alliances with various German leaders and the promoting of wars among the Germanic groups. This situation continued until A.D. 89, when the revolt of the Upper German garrison resulted in the conversion of the Upper Rhine region from an army command to a provincial status with a weakened garrison.[23]

The Antonines also placed their main attentions on the Danubian frontier, where the rising confederacy of the *Marcomanni,* identified by them as a Germanic group, and the *Dacii,* who were conquered and annexed, were their main concerns. This policy involved the reduction of the Rhine garrisons and the general de-emphasis of the Rhine region. Except for a period of general inactivity in the reigns of Hadrian and Antoninus Pius, this remained the basic pattern of Roman policy through to the period of Marcus Aurelius. By this time, however, conditions among the Germans themselves were radically changing as a result of Roman pressure, and new confederations were appearing which had not been previously known to the Romans, and which, along with the *Marcomanni,* began to put greater pressure on the frontier defenses. The mixed military and diplomatic policies of containment failed totally and the government, given its views of the Germans, resorted to a policy of military subjugation and extermination. The empire was, from this point on, entirely on the defensive.[24]

Through the period up to the time of Marcus Aurelius, then, additional experience of the Romans with Germans did nothing to deter the stereotyped view of the Germans as barbarians fit only for slaughter or slavery. Indeed, the stereotypes became, if anything, more entrenched, and broadened out to take on most of the cliches of a "civilized" man's sense of superiority over the primitive. The fact that most of this received wisdom was inconsistent did not apparently damage its credibility with the public. The Germans, then, were both a great potential threat to civilized life, and a petty nuisance: they were both incredibly stupid and fiendishly clever. They combined great valor, delighting in war, and base cowardice. Fundamentally, the Germans were seen as a useless people; lazy, dirty, without ambition, and politically incapable of organization. They were both a simple, unsophisticated and primitive people, poor beyond measure and uncorruptible by desire for wealth, and greedy, plundering, bandits, to whom no crime was foreign.[25]

In general, then, the Germans were seen as incorrigible and worthless brutes, hardly human at all. Roman attitudes towards the methods of conducting war with the Germans did not change. From the Roman point of view, the more Germans killed, the better. Certainly they had no rights, and it must be assumed that low-level atrocities against them were simply too common to be recorded. In this context it is an important measure of attitude that even the official extermination campaigns after the defeat of Varus, as well as those under Marcus Aurelius, could be reported in the literature with no sense of either guilt or protest, so well did they conform to public feeling.[26]

After the death of Marcus Aurelius the situation on the frontiers deteriorated rapidly, partly due to the ineffectiveness of his successors, and partly to the crisis over the succession after the assassination of Commodus. Eventually Septimus Severus made some effort to control the frontiers, but his efforts were not continued, and, after A.D. 235, the nearly permanent state of civil war meant total neglect of frontier defense. The result was a serious problem of German raiding into the Roman interior, produced by the combination of a long period of Roman provocation, German economic dependence, and the sudden relaxation of the Roman position. Under the Illyrian emperors an attempt was made to refortify the Rhine and Danube lines, and this policy was held with general success until the period of the mid-fourth century, although this was only done at the expense of abandoning the *Agri Decumates* in Upper Germany and withdrawing the frontier back to the Upper Rhine.[27]

By the middle of the fourth century the frontier policies and civil wars of the Constantinian dynasty had further allowed the defenses to deteriorate. In response to the latter situation Julian was sent to the Rhine frontier to restore order. Various groups of Germans had crossed in some numbers and occupied the right bank for some distance inland.[28] This restoration of order, however, was ephemeral and by the end of the century the permanent settlement of Germans in the western provinces had begun.

The period between the death of Marcus Aurelius and the beginning of German settlement in the west was a period of expanding intensity in the development of Roman stereotypes of Germans. For Romans, the contrast between Romanism and barbarianism had become much more pointed. The extension of the citizenship under Caracalla had led, ideologically, to the view that all the world was either Roman or barbarian, and the Romans were, in this view, the *genus humanus,* from which barbarians were excluded.[29] But the Romans were forced increasingly to recognize that the Germans could not, now, be too casually dismissed or ignored.

From the late third century on, German artifacts and mortuary customs began to inspire imitation in the frontier provinces, and Germans, like barbarians of all sorts, were filtering into the empire through imperial service, and ascending even as high as the imperial office. Though Romans might feel contempt for such men, they had to live with the situation. Though under Julian there was some effort to cut down their influence, the empire could not do without the barbarian officers, whose presence was only the logical result of a thorough barbarization of the armies.[30] In addition, though they might try to pretend otherwise, most Romans could perceive that the military balance was shifting in favor of their enemies, even though the military technology of the Germans had not really improved in any significant degree. The emperors might adopt fancy titles, as Constantine did that of "Conqueror of barbarian peoples, Victor over all nations," but that did not change the fact that the barbarians were now sometimes the victors, and were in general increasingly difficult to beat.

The empire had been forced into an increasingly defensive posture and the focal points for the conduct of affairs had clearly shifted to the frontiers themselves. With a lack of proper leadership the empire might easily be deluged by barbarians, and, true to the stereotypical image, the barbarians were assumed to be waiting for just that occasion. Hence, as Romans perceived, however dimly, the prospect of eventually being overwhelmed by their enemies, the psychological role of the barbarian stereotypes, and especially those related to the Germans, became increasingly important. The more endangered the empire was, the more clearly the Romans perceived the barbarians as their exact opposites on all counts.[31]

The stereotypes applied by the Romans to the Germans through the third and fourth centuries, A.D., showed, therefore, perfect continuity with earlier stereotypes in a developing sequence. The changes were very gradual. There was greater fear and greater contempt as well. The Germans of the third and fourth centuries were described as being not only fierce, but as commonly gnashing their teeth in fury at the prospect of battle. They were said to fight without regard for their own lives, and they were not only uncontrollable in their battle-rage, but stronger and taller than Romans, and capable of carrying on the combat even when forced to their knees by fatigue. They were held to delight in slaughter even more than ever, and were becoming supremely energetic. They were, in short, without fear.

There was no longer any feeling that any noble quality of simplicity clung to these Germans, but they were seen as uniformly base and treacherous. Most of the old character flaws of Caesar's Germans remained features of these later stereotypes. Germans were said to be unstable, unpredictable, rash, boastful, and overly proud, although easily humbled. Despite being such formidable foes, however, the Germans, while dying without qualm one moment, might become cowards the next. Indeed, these terribly dangerous and extraordinary warriors were so childish that they might be awestruck by the baubles and insignia of a caesar, or even the majesty of his mere person, before which they would tremble, and in this state of bedazzlement be struck dumb or petrified. The Germans, then, were regarded even in this later period as inferior to the Romans, and though fearsome, as ungraced by the more important human qualities. A barbarian life was regarded as indistinct from a life of crime.[32]

Hence, even though the odd German or two might unexpectedly prove redeemable,[33] the rest were thought fit only for the slaughter. A virtuous emperor's chief responsibility was to kill them, and he might do so without distinction of age or sex. The highest praise accorded the emperor Probus was that had he lived longer, the world would contain no more barbarians. Certainly no odium would attach to a commander who attacked them while supposedly at peace with them or negotiating with them. Germans who did not have to be slain were held to be fit only to be slaves.[34]

The attitude of the Romans toward the Germans can best be summed up in the episode which preceded the battle of Adrianople. The Visigoths, having crossed the Danube in flight, were left starving in Thrace where they had been promised supplies of food by the emperor. The local authorities took advantage of this situation and allowed merchants to approach them offering them dog-meat for sale at the price of one slave from among them for each dog carcass. This caused considerable resentment, especially as the Goths had no other choice than to fight, which they had promised not to do, or starve, and many bought the dogs. As the grumbling and unrest reached a peak, the local military commander invited the Gothic leaders to a banquet that was really an ambush, from which some of them escaped. At this point the Goths went to war.[35] With the defeat of the emperor by the Goths at Adrianople, the long process was initiated by which the Germans began progressively to take over the western empire.

The creation of the stereotypic German by Caesar, and the acceptance of the stereotype by the authors of the imperial period can be partly explained by the argument that the urge to stereotype the stranger is a universal human trait. That, of course, is true. But the specific aspects of the Roman stereotype of Germans are associated directly with the creation of an empire and the frontier context which that implied. The empire itself was a product of what one writer has called an atavistic, irrational, impulse to forceful expansion, and not a creation of policy. Hence, the Romans did not develop a theory to justify the existence of the empire until after it had been, more or less, achieved.

Ideologically, it was necessary to couch a justification of empire in morally positive terms. It had to be argued that being conquered was good for those who were vanquished, that the empire was a product of natural Roman superiority,[36] or, alternatively, that the gods had selected the Romans for a specific role as masters.[37] One of the functions of an effective ideology, as of an effective stereotype, is that those who create it come themselves to believe it and act on it. Hence the assumption common among Romans even as late as the second century, A.D., that a proper emperor's responsibility was to pursue the course of continued imperial growth.[38]

Eventually, of course, the conquered had to be admitted to membership, else the idea of the imperial mission should lose its appeal. Hence, the extension of citizenship to all subjects by Caracalla was only the logical entailment of imperial ideology. This, in its turn, implied that the dichotomy between Romans and non-Romans became a more simplified dichotomy between civilized men and barbarians. Given the ideological assumption that the function of empire was to improve the people taken under its paternal care, the continuing existence of unregenerate free savages necessitated that those peoples become, ideologically, great foes, intent upon destruction of the empire, their only reason for destroying such a manifestly beneficent institution being sheer viciousness. Such peoples could not, unless the ideology were at fault, possibly be fully human. For as we have already seen, the Romans were the *genus humanum*.[39]

The same conclusion follows when we pursue the development of the stereotypic German himself. To begin with, it would be absurd, of course, to assume that the Roman writers and leaders who created the stereotypes and propagated them over the years had no opportunity to avail themselves of less inflamatory data. Indeed, the authors deliberately ignored the archival accumulations of ethnographic data which, even in the first century, B.C., were in the possession of the government. The stereotypic German, then, filled a demand and added to, or was an essential element in, imperial justification. The psychological and moral examples of a free people outside the empire was intolerable,[40] no matter how insignificant they were in military terms. Hence the concept of barbarism of which the stereotypic German was an example.

The empire's policy toward the Germans was also, in the early period, dictated by the fact that the empire was governed by military despotism. Despotism needed armies and generals, who had to be kept occupied and in readiness, although the generals had to be managed in such a way to prevent their aspiring to power. Prospective or actual emperors needed a reputation as military leaders. These considerations necessitated a steady, but not major, war, which could be used to train troops and officers and gild reputations, without blazing into major problems. The logic of the imperial system dictated that this military zone be a frontier. The German frontier was ideal, partly because no diplomatic problems would be created there and partly because the Germans were, in this period, militarily negligible. It was necessary, however, on a psychological plane, to define the Germans in such a way that they could be regarded as having none of the ordinary human rights. Hence, the implied proposition that they were not really human at all, but sophisticated animals, a proposition that, while not articulated until relatively late, was indispensable to the functional role of the stereotype, both logically and psychologically. Only when so identified would they be routinely deceived, murdered individually, massacred collectively, or enslaved.[41] The final necessary element in the concept of the Germanic barbarian was to argue that the Germans were a viable and powerful threat to civilized society as such. Great victories demand greater foes.

Hence, both the ideological and mundane practical implications of Roman imperialism demanded a classic barbarian—a barbarian more barbarous than all the rest: the German. The Romans acted predictably, conforming to a nearly universal pattern.[42]

The Roman stereotype of the Germanic barbarian was not, however, a racial stereotype. It was not based on inirradicable differences of pigmentation or physiognomy, but on the simple fact of cultural primitivism.[43] It was only necessary that the German seem uncouth and wild. Out of this, the myth of the sub-human/superhuman warrior hordes could be conveniently created.

The pattern of Roman relations with the Germans is in itself of considerable interest. In the time of Caesar and Augustus the stereotype of the Germans and the practical implications of that stereotype in frontier policies functioned as they might be expected to function. The defeat of Varus temporarily suspended this function, but the Romans resumed their normal role, vis-a-vis the stereotype, on the Rhine frontier. The stereotype became, if anything, more securely embedded in the Roman consciousness. It was only when the more severe indications of imperial instability began to become obvious that the Germans became a problem in any practical sense. Ironically, the stereotype of the German barbarian and the role it assigned the Germans as victims of Roman frontier defense proved to be a self-fulfilling proposition—the frontier barbarized a primitive people and alienated them while rendering them in some terms dependent on Rome.[44] As the empire weakened the problem became more severe. The Roman sense of imperial identification strengthened and the stereotype became more shrill. Beginning as a peripheral element in the Roman consciousness, the stereotypes of the Germanic barbarian progressed to the point at which the German became a slayer of empires. Even more ironically, though predictably, the stereotype lasted long after the Roman world had become a memory. It is to the stereotype that we owe the myth of a world destroyed by a savage horde.

The histories of Roman and Anglo-American frontier experiences demonstrate a number of striking parallels and important differences with regard to the formulation of stereotypes of aboriginal peoples. The differences result from contrasting reasons for expansion of the dominant culture, contrasting institutional forms transmitted to the frontier, and incongruent levels of technology among aboriginal peoples, precisely the sorts of distinctions that might reasonably be expected after twenty centuries of social and political evolution and technological development. In this context, the similarities between Roman stereotypes of Germans and Anglo-American stereotypes of Indians become even more striking: the points made about the one may be made with considerable certainty about the other. Stereotypes of Indians (1) had little to do with real Indians, (2) were founded upon a degree of selective observation, (3) became self-perpetuating, and (4) led Anglo-Americans to find, in subsequent contacts with Indian groups, exactly what they expected to find. If the sequence of Anglo-American stereotype development differed from the Roman, the effect was nevertheless much the same.

From almost the very beginning—from the very beginning, if one excludes Viking evaluations of aborigines as inconsequential, owing to the brevity of Viking tenure in North America—Indians were considered from two perspectives by the Europeans who encountered them, and accordingly, they were dealt with on two levels. First, Indians were prospective subjects for the monarch whose agent discovered them, and second, they were potential Christians. Columbus emphasized both points to Ferdinand and Isabella, reporting that he had bestowed gifts upon the Arawaks "in order that they might be fond of us, and furthermore might be made Christians and be inclined to the love and service of their Highnesses."[45] Those who persisted in idolatry, he went on, would be available as slaves. The notion of religion as a determinant of political status appealed to European monarchs and clergy alike and provided a fundamental procedure for dealing with aboriginal peoples; and the history of European involvement in the Western Hemisphere reveals a pattern of state support of Church acquisition of souls in return for Church support of state acquisition of labor. Columbus's news that Indians were without religion, timid, and naked initiated the Spanish conquest of Middle America and inaugurated a protracted discussion of the Indians' place in matters spiritual and temporal, which, although it resulted in no rigid political or religious dogma, established the standard for subsequent European dealings with North American aborigines.[46] It is worth noting also that, while Spaniards assessed and evaluated the role of Indians within the empire,

Indians became a factor in Spanish international relations, as far as Spain's treatment of them could be exploited as propaganda by Spanish rivals abroad.[47] This, too, was a pattern to be repeated in the various colonial histories of the Western Hemisphere.

The century after Columbus saw the production of a quantity of fabulous literature dealing with the New World and its aborigines—people with one normal foot and one huge foot (to be held above the head as an umbrella on hot or rainy days), people with enormous ears (in which they wrapped themselves at night for warmth), and the like. These travel narratives, or "voyages," produced as they often were for equal measures of vanity and money, contained and perpetuated a considerable amount of misinformation. As a consequence of this literature, many English colonists arrived in North America already prejudiced against the Indians. Theirs was a prejudice born of fear. Thus, William Bradford could record the Pilgrims' preoccupation, while still in the Netherlands, with tales of "savage and brutish men which range up and down" in North America "little otherwise than the wild beasts."[48] The Indians were assumed to be:

> . . . cruel, barbarous and most treacherous, being most furious in their rage and mercilous where they overcome; not being content only to kill and take away life, but delight to torment men in the most bloody manner that may be; flaying some alive with the shells of fishes, cutting off the members and joints of others by piecemeal and broiling on the coals, eat the collops of their flesh in their sight whilst they live, with other cruelties horrible to be related.[49]

The reality of life in proximity to Indians hardly staunched the flow of fabulous narratives.[50] It produced instead a new literary genre, the captivity narrative, which was the first popular American literature. Here again was a religious prejudice, Anglo-American this time, which dictated that capture by Indians was a horror to be endured only by those possessed of a deep faith in God. Captivity narratives remained a basic item in the cultural baggage of Anglo-Americans until well into the nineteenth century.[51]

The exaggerations of both the voyage and the captivity literature provided the justification for frontier violence by fixing Indians in the Anglo-American mind as subhuman beings. Indians remained objects of curiosity to English spectators, who found in their observations of Indian life precisely the evidence they sought in order to confirm that subhuman status. Indians wore few clothes, ate strange or ill-prepared food, spoke unintelligible languages, and engaged in devil worship.[52] At the same time, however, there was a benign, but equally distorted, view of Indians as people essentially innocent, possessed of many of the finer sensitivities—in short, Noble Savages.[53] The two attitudes often existed side by side on the North American frontier, but the harsher view prevailed because it had a political application. The benign view was preserved by a few clerics, philanthropists, and reformers on through the nineteenth century, but it had no political application and was never a consideration of government. Moreover, it could be argued that the benign view obtained largely in areas where Indians were tractable and where warfare was uncommon. Such was the case in the Caribbean, where Englishmen encountered the remnants of the Arawaks, enslaved them, and then idealized them.[54]

That Englishmen were at first unsuited to survive in the New World is axiomatic to the early colonial history of North America. Preconceived prejudices were less than useful in the face of the myriad problems of adapting to a new environment, and the colonists, however reluctantly, laid them aside to learn what Indians could teach them about their surroundings. The instruction was of importance to the success of English colonial ventures, for the Indians in large measure explained and interpreted nature for Europeans, dispensing in the process practical knowledge of food, shelter, transportation, clothing, and medicine. Once the lessons were learned, colonists could abandon Indians in favor of the old prejudices. In the struggle for empire among England, France, and Spain on the North American frontier, Europeans would find use for Indians as military auxiliaries, but their services were required for little else. The importation of African slaves resolved the problem of supplementing and then replacing the labor of indentured servants, so there was no other purpose to which persons classified as subhuman could be put, in the colonial context.[55]

The colonial wars ended with the establishment of English supremacy in North America in 1763. Thereafter, England sought to simplify the problem of colonial administration by controlling colonial expansion and confining Anglo-American settlement to specified areas, thereby reducing instances of frontier violence between Indians and colonists. These efforts resulted in a series of proclamation lines, boundaries imposed by the Crown to segregate Indian and colonial populations. Boundaries were determined by treaties negotiated with various tribes by British agents.

The patterns and procedures of the treaty-making process were to be, for the United States, a direct inheritance from the colonial period. The application of that process, however, was to be guided by radically different motives. England's frontier policy was paternalistic, toward colonists and Indians alike, and it was predicated on the belief that colonists, not Indians, were primarily to blame for frontier violence. Both colonists and the Crown were interested in trade with Indians, but abuses by the one led to attempts at regulation by the other. Boundaries and treaties were violated by colonists almost as soon as they were made, and England found itself unable to police the frontier adequately.[56]

Frontier problems were subordinate to the larger question of the colonies' status within the British Empire, a question that was resolved by the American Revolution. It is significant—and ironic—that the catalogue of colonial grievances against George III, the Declaration of Independence, contained the assertion that the king had "endeavored to bring on the inhabitants of our frontiers, the merciless Indian Savages, whose known rule of warfare, is an undistinguished destruction of all ages, sexes and conditions." The stereotype of the malevolent Indian thus appeared in the first pronouncement of the new nation, in rhetoric little different from that of voyage and captivity narratives and memoirs and histories prepared by colonists.[57]

The policies of the United States government under the Articles of Confederation and later the Constitution owed much to the forms established by England. The new nation and its component states measured their wealth in land—a practice that would find particular application in federal and state subsidies to canal and railroad builders in the nineteenth century—but much of that land, though nominally acquired from England, was occupied by aboriginal tribes. The government did not extend its claim on the land to the people resident thereon, but rather treated with the tribes as it would with foreign powers. Federal procedures for dispensing land to settlers first required the extinction of Indian title by treaty, at bottom a legal fiction which remained a part of the bureaucratic textbook on frontier administration as long as there was a frontier. The treaty process was meaningless in any legal sense because the government consistently ignored violations by its own citizens and punished any violations by Indians.

Indeed, the government ignored treaties in any situation in which honoring treaty commitments would impede the expansion of the frontier or thwart the ambition of settlers who, despite whatever else they were, belonged to the electorate. The government, through its various institutions, made clear to all observers its intention to ignore Indian treaties and thus lent its sanction and approval to even the most outrageous acts directed against Indians. The removal of aboriginal tribes from the cis-Mississippi East during the 1820's and 1830's was not the culmination of federal response to Indians, but merely a phase of it. Indian removals of one sort or another were to continue in the trans-Mississippi West wherever the line of Anglo-American settlement touched Indian domain.[58]

Given the federal support for individual and corporate expansion into Indian territory, it was left to those involved to develop justification for such expansion. The motivation of the government within the land-as-wealth context (or those later afforded by the doctrine of Manifest Destiny and the idea of expansion to the Pacific Coast to facilitate overseas commerce) was insufficient reason for the individual settler to remove to the frontier and provided no justification for violent means of wresting land for homes, a promise extended by the government or by land speculators sported by federal land policies, and homes could be protected—justification enough for violence on the frontier.

Settlers were preoccupied with Indians and the threat, real or imagined, that they posed to frontier security. They considered Indians from the perspective of two centuries of cultural prejudice, and, like the colonists before them, they found what they expected to find. Selective observation reinforced all the old myths and added new ones. There were few systematic attempts to study aboriginal peoples anywhere in the world before 1800, and although Thomas Jefferson made some studies in that direction, the American Indian hardly benefited from the effort.[59] John Heckewelder, a minister and advocate of the Indians of Pennsylvania, and whose observations lent much to James Fenimore Cooper's fictional Indians, partial though he was to the Indians, nevertheless characterized them as "revengeful and cruel" people who tortured and killed defenseless prisoners and were given over to superstition, drunkenness, and lying.[60] Henry Rowe Schoolcraft, whose transcriptions of Indian tales were the basis for Longfellow's *The Song of Hiawatha,* described them as "food

for whisky," people who would eat anything, including dead
horses, "Red Devils" given to idleness and possessed of "little
fixity of purpose" and "a defect of business capacity."[61]

Prejudices were reinforced at other levels. A survey of nineteenth-century schoolbooks reveals the prevalent image of inherently cruel and merciless Indians. Children perused accounts
of Indian warfare—there was one in every reader—and examined
illustrations showing Indians preparing to murder white women
and infants, learning in the process that Indians ultimately lost
the wars because they were inferior people.[62] To journalists like
Horace Greeley, Indians were "children" who did "little credit
to human nature" and were slaves "of appetite and sloth, never
emancipated from the tyranny of one animal passion save by the
more ravenous demands of another."[63] Greeley's description of
a group of warriors is a prime example of journalistic stereotyping: "Squalid and conceited, proud and worthless, lazy and
lousy, they will strut out or drink out their miserable existence,
and at length afford the world a sensible relief by dying out of
it."[64]

A decade later, Mark Twain described the Gosiute Indians
as "treacherous, filthy and repulsive" and observed that "wherever
one finds an Indian he has only found the Goshoots more or less
modified by circumstances and surroundings—but Goshoots,
after all."[65]

Such comments were ever before the public, underscored by
the federal government's response to Indians. After the Civil
War, the government abandoned the idea of maintaining a separate domain west of the Mississippi River for the Indian tribes
and adopted instead a policy of confining Indians to smaller
reservations, thereby releasing most western lands for occupation
by Anglo-American settlers attracted by the Homestead Act and
subsequent pieces of land legislation. Indian removal was no
longer a possibility, and in its place arose the dual (and contra-
dictory) policies, pursued in tandem, of cultural assimilation and
annihilation. The notion of private ownership of land as an instrument for civilizing Indians, espoused by Henry Knox at the end
of the eighteenth century, found application in the Dawes Sever-
alty Act at the end of the nineteenth, and in the century between,
it became a part of the stereotype that Indians could be assimi-
lated only by becoming small farmers. If they resisted, the argument ran, they deserved to die. "These people must die out—
there is no help for them," Greeley remarked of the Indians in

1859. "God has given this earth to those who will subdue and cultivate it, and it is vain to struggle against His righteous decree."[66] Indians, therefore, were socially useless and could be discarded. That task became the Army's primary responsibility.[67]

The military conquest of Indian populations west of the Mississippi River produced yet another literature of Indian stereotypes, one based on the selective observations of Indians by those responsible for their extermination. Richard Irving Dodge produced volumes of such observations that may be taken as typical examples. Dodge believed that the Indians were descendants of the lost tribes of Israel—hardly a new idea, since it dated from the time of the Spanish conquest—and saw scalping (a Syrian custom adopted by the Hebrews) and massacres (a Hebrew custom) as evidence of the fact. He wrote of the "horrors of captivity" in clinical detail and noted that, for the Indian,

> Cruelty is both an amusement and a study. So much pleasure is derived from it, that an Indian is constantly thinking out new devices of torture, and how to prolong to the utmost those already known. His anatomical knowledge of the most sensitive portions of the human frame is most accurate, and the amount of whipping, cutting, flaying, and burning that he will make a human body undergo, without seriously affecting the vital power, is astonishing.[68]

This sort of literature served notice to readers that they would be well advised to avoid falling into Indian hands. The promise of such cruel and unusual treatment was sufficient reason to kill Indians, and works like Dodge's were recommended to the reading public as antidotes to those of "sentimentalists" like Helen Hunt Jackson.[69] Savages, the federal government announced through its minions, were not so noble after all. For them, acculturation would be an ordeal, but they would suffer it, the government concluded, or die.

At about the same time that the federal government made clear to the Indians the unacceptability of their secular way of life, missionaries came among them in large numbers to criticize their spiritual values. Distinctions between Protestants and Catholics disappeared under the impact of their message, which, combined with that of federal Indian officials, announced that Indians must abandon their communal ways, become small farmers, and embrace both Jesus and the plow. The effect was predictably debilitating and hardly differed from that of the old Spanish policies of decimation, subjugation, and salvation. Indians were still both souls and subjects, and both potentialities were there to be exploited by the dominant culture. Thus, in his history of Catholic missions to the aborigines of North America, John Gilmary Shea could write in 1865:

> The discovery of America, like every other event in the history of world, had, in the designs of God, the great object of the salvation of mankind. In that event, more clearly perhaps than it is often given to us here below, we can see and adore that Providence which thus gave to millions long sundered from the rest of man by pathless oceans, the light of the gospel and the proffered boon of redemption.[70]

The massacre of some two-hundred Dakota Sioux at Wounded Knee in 1890 marked the end of the government's war against the Indian tribes, and that year, according to Turner, saw the passing of the frontier phase of American history. The political ends of Indian stereotypes had been served, but the stereotypes did not disappear. Rather, they became ingrained in American popular culture and yet serve as entertainment in novels, motion pictures, and television.[71] This phenomenon owes much to the persistence of a "frontier mentality" in contemporary American affairs that determines the way in which Anglo-Americans view their past. Stereotypes remain because the memory of them per-haps justifies their impact on American history—a circular argu-ment, to be sure, but one that allows the Anglo-American to take comfort from the necessity of Indian destruction and, in effect, to say in the 1970's what Antonio de Ulloa said in the 1770's: *"Visto un Indio de qualquier region se puede decir que se ha visto todos en quanto al color y contextura."*[72]

Roman and Anglo-American encounters with aboriginal peo-ples on the frontier suggest a model that may be applicable to other instances of culture contact in frontier zones. The model may follow this general outline:

1. Stereotypes provide a simplified system for processing in-formation that would otherwise be difficult to handle, for exam-ple, culturally conflicting ideas, such as conceptions of property and the function of social and political institutions.

2. Stereotypes function in the same manner as ideologies, by defining the world and allowing for the classification of phenom-

ena. They also posit the predictability of phenomena and con-dition individual and group behavior.

3. Frontier stereotypes are not necessarily racial stereotypes. Indeed, they may be exclusively cultural.

4. Frontier stereotypes are a necessary aspect of expansionist ideology. They encourage occupation of the frontier zone by defining it as uninhabited, that is, only subhuman beings reside there.

5. Frontier stereotypes justify behavior that would normally be defined as illegal or immoral but which, on the frontier, di-rected toward the aboriginal people, becomes a predictable norm. Such behavior assumes that the aboriginal people are something less than human and reflects a radical human-versus-subhuman dichotomy.

6. Frontier stereotypes make atrocities possible and, indeed, even encourage them.

7. Levels of technology possessed by respective cultures on the frontier do not affect the development of stereotypes.

There are frontier regions—South Africa, Australia, and Brazil come immediately to mind—where this model might apply his-torically and, indeed, where it might be tested in a contemporary frontier setting. It is to be hoped that investigations of the political utility of stereotypes will broaden general knowledge of the fron-tier and the functions of human institutions in frontier contexts.

Notes

1. Research into white stereotyping has centered largely on the problem of Negro slavery, and many of the assumptions of scholars working on Negro slavery have been applied without modification to explain the nature of Indian-white relationships. Wilbur R. Jacobs, *Dispossessing the American Indian: Indians and Whites on the Colonial Frontier* (New York, 1972), for example, presents a superficial discussion of stereotypes of Indians based on propositions gleaned from Winthrop D. Jordan, *White Over Black: American Attitudes Toward the Negro, 1550–1812* (Chapel Hill, 1968). Beyond that, Jacobs (pp. 4–5) is inclined to accept whatever Freudian psychology has to offer in the way of an explanation of why people develop stereotypes, which customarily has something to do with feces. See, for example, Joel Kovel, *White Racism: A Psychohistory* (New York, 1970), *passim.* The assumption, then, is that stereo-types are racially inspired and the political responses to aboriginal peoples are racist in conception, design, and execution. Scholars who have not accepted this position have instead approached stereotypes in a manner similar to that of a literary critic contemplating *Moby Dick.* Accordingly, the Indian, like the white whale, is a symbol of something, the something to be determined by anal-

ysis of the stereotypes. To Roy Harvey Pearce, *The Savages of America: A Study of the Indian and the Idea of Civilization* (Baltimore, 1953), p. 5, the Indian was, to the English mind, a symbol of what civilized men were not and what they must not become. More recently, Richard Slotkin, *Regeneration Through Violence: The Mythology of the American Frontier, 1600–1860* (Middletown, Conn., 1973), views the Indian as central to American mythology for reasons mostly literary, but Slotkin also resorts to psychology (Jungian, this time) to argue (p. 560) that the Indian is "the image or symbol of the American libido." The literature, then, suggests the analysis of particular stereotypes and their generalization to the entire Anglo-American population. The implication is that cultural attitudes, whatever they happen to be, find expression in political responses and, conversely, that political necessities, whatever they are perceived to be, do not influence cultural attitudes.

2. D. B. Saddington, "Race Relations in the Early Roman Empire," *Aufstieg und Niedergang der römischen Welt,* 2.3, ed. by H. Temporini (Berlin, 1975), p. 120; and Paul MacKendrick, *Romans on the Rhine* (New York, 1970), p. 4.

3. Caesar, *De Bello Gallico,* 1.33.

4. Gerold Walser, *Caesar und die Germanen: Studien zur politischen Tendenz römischer Feldzugsberichte* (Historische Einzelschriften, 1 [Wiesbaden, 1956]), pp. 37, 42–44, 55–57; C. M. Wells, *The German Policy of Augustus: An Examination of the Archaeological Evidence* (Oxford, 1972), pp. 14–30; and Gustav Stümpel, *Name und Nationalität der Germanen* (Kilo Beiheft, 25 [Wiesbaden, 1932]), *in toto.*

5. Caesar, *De Bello Gallico,* 1.31, 33 and 39, 4.1–4 and 16, 5.29, 6.2, 21–24, and 35.

6. Cicero, *De Provinciis Consularibus,* 8.19, 12.29 and 31, 13.32–33.

7. Caesar, *De Bello Gallico,* 1.39, 6.21–24 and 35; Suetonius, 1.24.3; and Cassius Dio, 38.31.1 and 38.34.3–4. Walser, *Caesar und die Germanen,* pp. 22–31, 86–88; and Dieter Timpe, "Caesars gallische Krieg und das Problem des römischen Imperialismus," *Historia,* 14 (1965), 189–214.

8. Caesar, *De Bello Gallico,* 1.53; and Cassius Dio, 38.36.1, 38.46.4, 38.50.1–5, and 39.48.1–2.

9. Cassius Dio, 56.33.5–6.

10. This thesis has been suggested in William S. Cooter's "Roman Frontiers and Interaction Spheres: Aspects of the Human Ecology of Roman Frontier Regions in Northwest Europe," a dissertation at the University of Oklahoma, 1976.

11. Ronald Syme, "The Northern Frontiers under Augustus," *Cambridge Ancient History,* 10.12 (Cambridge, 1934), p. 359. For a dissenting view see H. Schönberger, "The Roman Frontier in Germany: An Archaeological Survey," *Journal of Roman Studies,* 59 (1969), 144.

12. Cassius Dio, 54.32.1–54.33.5, 54.36.3, 55.1.2–5, 55.6.1–3, 55.8.3, 55.10a.2–3; and Florus, 2.30.12.21–22. Karl Christ, "Zur römischen Okkupation der Zentralalpen und des nördlichen Alpenvorlandes," *Historia,* 6 (1957), 416–428; Syme, p. 360; Schönberger, p. 144; and Wells, pp. 3–13, 93–99, and 154–161.

13. Horace, *Odes,* 4.2, 4.5, 4.14 and 4.15; and Vergil, *Aeneid,* 6.847–853. Hans D. Meyer, *Die Aussenpolitik des Augustus und die augusteische Dichtung* (Kölner historische Abhandlungen, 5 [Cologne, 1961]), *in toto.*

14. Cassius Dio, 56.18.1–56.22.2–4; *ibid.* (Zonaras), 56.22.2a–2b; and Velleius Paterculus, 2.118.2. Dieter Timpe, *Arminius Studien* (Bibliothek der klassischen

Altertumswissenschaften, 2.34 [Heidelberg, 1970]), *in toto*; Walter Kolbe, "Forschungen zur Verusschlacht," *Klio,* 25 (1932), 141–168; Walther Judeich, "Zur Verusschlacht," *Klio,* 26 (1933), 56–66; H. E. Stier, "Zur Varusschlacht," *Historische Zeitschrift,* 147 (1933), 489–506; Carl Schuchhardt, "Der Varuszug," *Historische Zeitschrift,* 149 (1934), 1–9; and Ludwig Schmidt, "Zur Schlacht im Teutobergerwalde," *Klio,* 35 (1942), 220–226.

15. Cassius Dio, 56.23.1; and Suetonius, 2.23, 2.25 and 2.49.1; Syme, p. 376.

16. E. A. Thompson, *The Early Germans* (Oxford, 1965), *in toto*; and "Early Germanic Warfare," *Past and Present,* 14 (1958), 2–29.

17. Tacitus, *Annals,* 1.49–51, 1.55–56, 2.21; and *Germania,* 33.1. Erich Koestermann, "Die Feldzüge des Germanicus, 14–16 n.Chr.," *Historia,* 6 (1957), 438; Schönberger, p. 147; E. Kornemann, "Die neueste Limesforschung im Lichte der römisch-kaiser-lichen Grenzpolitik," *Klio,* 7 (1907), 78–79; John Cecil Mann, "The Frontiers of the Principate," *Aufstieg und Niedergang der römischen Welt,* 2.1, ed. by H. Temporini (Berlin, 1974), p. 511; and Wells, p. 241. The groups attacked were the *Marsi, Bructeri,* and *Chauci,* whereas Varus had been attacked by the *Cherusci.*

18. Tacitus, *Annals,* 1.51: Sine vulnere militis, qui semisomnos, inermos, aut palantis ceciderant.

19. Wells, pp. 243–44; Syme, p. 379; and Schönberger, p. 147.

20. Suetonius, 4.45.1 and 4.47. Peter Bicknell, "The Emperor Gaius' Military Acitivities in A.D. 40," *Historia,* 17 (1968), 496–505.

21. Cassius Dio (Xiphilinus), 61.30.4; and Tacitus, *Annals,* 11.19.

22. Tacitus, *Annals,* 13.55. Ulrich Kahrstedt, "The Roman Frontier on the Lower Rhine in the Early Imperial Period," *First Congress of Roman Frontier Studies 1949,* ed. by Eric Birley (Durham, 1952), pp. 46–52; and Schönberger, pp. 153–154.

23. Cassius Dio (Zon.) 67.3.5; and *ibid.* (Xiph.) 67.4.1. Contrast Cassius Dio with Frontinus, *Stratagems,* 1.3.10. Cassius Dio's account is much to be preferred. Kornemann, *Klio,* 7.80; Mann, "Frontiers of the Principate," p. 518; B. W. Jones, "The Dating of Domitian's War Against the Chatti," *Historia,* 22 (1973), 79–90; Schönberger, pp. 155–156, 170; Thompson, *The Early Germans,* p. 90; and J. Fitz, "A Military History of Pannonia from the Marcomann Wars the the Death of Alexander Serverus, A.D. 180–235," *Acta Archaeologia* (Magyar Tudomanyos Akademia, 14 [1962]), 25 and 28.

24. Cassius Dio (Petrus Patricius), 72.3.1ª; *ibid.* (Xiph.), 72.3.2; *ibid.* (Excubitor), 72.13.1. Cf. *Das Rheinische Germanien in den antiken Inschriften,* ed. by Alexander Riese (Berlin, 1914), p. 25, no. 186: . . . III id. Aug. in capitolio ante cella[m] Iunonis Reg. fratres Arvales convenerunt, quod dominus n. imp. sanctissim[us] pius M. Aurelius Antoninus Aug. pont. max. per limitem Raetiae ad hostes extirpandos barbarorum [terram] introitus est, ut ea res ei prospera feliciterque cedat. Schönberger, pp. 160, 171–175; Robert Sherk, "Specialization in the Province of Germany," *Historia,* 20 (1971), 118; Mann, "Frontiers of the Principate," pp. 512–513; and Fitz, p. 34.

25. Tacitus, *Annals,* 11.16–17, 13.54; *Germania,* 6–7, 11, 14–17, 19–24, 30, 37; *Histories,* 4.13, 4.16; Florus, 1.38.3.5, 1.38.3.12–18, 1.45.10.9–15, and 2.30.31–32; Frontinus, *Stratagems,* 2.1.16, 1.3.10, 1.1.8, 2.4.6; Velleius Paterculus, 2.118.1–2, 2.106.2; Herodian, 1.6.9; and Cassius Dio (Exc.), 78.20.2 Timpe, *Arminius Studien,* pp. 126–127, 131–133. On Florus see William A. Oldfather and Howard V. Carter, *The Defeat of Varus and the German frontier policy of Augustus* (Uni-

versity of Illinois Studies in the Social Sciences, 4.2 [Urbana, 1915]), p. 29. The whole issue of whether Tacitus idealized Germanic life in the *Germania* seems pointless, and will not be discussed herein. Those who wish to follow the discussion, however, may begin with the following works: Herbert W. Bernario, "Tacitus and the Fall of the Roman Empire," *Historia,* 17 (1968), 37–50; and Karl Christ, "Germanendarstellung und Zeitverständnis bei Tacitus," *Historia,* 14 (1965), 62–73.

26. Tacitus, *Annals,* 13.56; *Germania,* 33. Saddington's remark, p. 120, on the attitudes of the officer corps in general, seems indicative. Cf. Koestermann, p. 439 (in reference to *Germania* 33).

27. Geza Alföldy, "Der Friedensschluss des Kaisers Commodus mit den Germanen," *Historia,* 20 (1971), 84–109; Harald von Petrikovits, "Fortifications in the Northwestern Roman Empire from the Third to the Fifth Centuries," *Journal of Roman Studies,* 61 (1971), 178–193; Schönberger, pp. 177–186; and Franz Oelmann, "The Rhine Limes in Late Roman Times," *First Congress of Roman Frontier Studies 1949,* pp. 80–81.

28. Julian, *Letter to the Athenians,* 279A–B.

29. F. M. Walbank, "Nationality as a factor in Roman History," *Harvard Studies in Classical Philology,* 76 (1972), 167; and Joseph Vogt, *Kulturwelt und Barbaren: Zum Menschheitsbild der spätantiken Gesellschaft* (Akademie der Wissenschaften in Mainz: Abhandlungen des geistes und sozialwissenschaftlichen Klasse, 1967.1 [Wiesbaden, 1967]), pp. 8–12.

30. *Scriptores Historiae Augusti, Miximini Duo,* 8.9–10. Ramsay MacMullen "Barbarian Influence on Rome Before the Great Invasions" (XIV International Congress of Historical Sciences, San Francisco, August 22–29, 1975); W. Ensslin, "Zum Heermeisteramt des spätromischen Reiches," *Klio,* 23 (1930), 306–325; 24 (1931), 102–147, 467–502; Friedrich Vittinghoff, "Zur angebliche Barbarisierung des römischen Heeres durch die Verbände der *Numeri,*" *Historia,* 1 (1950), 389–407; Karl Friedrich Stroheker, "Zur Rolle der Heermeister fränkischer Abstammung im späten vierten Jhts.," *Historia,* 4 (1955), 314–330; Ronald Syme, "Danubian and Balkan Emperors," *Historia,* 22 (1973), 310–316; Hermann Peter, *Geschichtliche Literatur über die römische Kaiserzeit bis Theodosius I,* 2 vols., reprint ed. (Hildesheim, 1967), II, 117 (original edition by Teubner, Leipzig, 1897); Alexander Schenk von Stauffenberg, "Die Germanen im römischen Reich," *Die Welt als Geschichte,* 1 (1935), 81–100; M. P. Speidel, "The Rise of Ethnic Units in the Roman Imperial Army," *Aufstieg und Nidergang der römischen Welt,* 2.3, *in toto;* Erich Sander, "Die Germisierung des römischen Heeres," *Historische Zeitschrift,* 160 (1939), 1–34.

31. Libanius, *Orations,* 18.290, 24.16; and Ammianus Marcellinus, 15.8.6. Thompson, *The Early Germans,* pp. 116–121; Vogt, p. 13; and Donald Earl, *The Moral and Poltical Tradition of Rome* (London, 1967), pp. 101–111.

32. Ammianus Marcellinus, 15.4.9, 15.8.7, 16.2.6, 16.3.2, 16.5.17, 16.12.47–61, 17.12.9–10, 17.16.3–4 and 9, 17.1.13, 27.2.6, 27.10.13, and 28.5.3; Julian, *Orationes,* 2.56B; *ibid., Against the Galilleans,* 116A; Claudian, *In Eutropiam,* 1.250–251, 2.153–155, 2.226–228; Herodian, 1.6.9, 1.3.5; *SHA, Firmus, etc.,* 13.4–5; *ibid., Divus Aurelianus,* 21.1–3; *ibid., Maximini Duo,* 12.3; Libanius, *Orationes,* 18.91, 24.12.

33. Ammianus Marcellinus, 15.5.33.

34. *Ibid.,* 16.1.1, 16.11.9, 30.5.14, 17.1.3–4, 17.8.3–4, 18.2.1–19, 28.5.4–7, 22.7.8; *SHA, Tacitus,* 16.6.7. Vogt, p. 12. Concerning Julian's deliberate use

of terror tactics against the Alemanni cf. Ilse Müller-Seidel, "Die Usurpation Julians des Abtrünningen im Lichte seiner Germanenpolitik," *Historische Zeitschrift*, 180 (1955), 231.

35. Ammianus Marcellinus, 31.4.11 and 31.5.5–6.

36. Mason Hammond, "Ancient Imperialism: Contemporary Justifications," *Harvard Studies in Classical Philology*, 58–59 (1948), 106–107, 116–119.

37. Gerold Walser, *Rom das Reich und die fremden Völker in der Geschichtsschreibung der frühen Kaiserzeit* (Baden-Baden, 1951), p. 20.

38. Hammond, p. 120.

39. Vogt, pp. 8–12.

40. Gerold Walser, "Die römische Uberlieferung vom staatlichen und kulturellen Zustande der Barbaria," *Carnuntina: Vorträge des internationalen Kongresses der Altertumsforscher* 1955, ed. by Erich Swoboda (Römische Forschungen in Niederösterreich, 3 [Graz, 1956]), pp. 195–199.

41. Cf. Andreas Alföldy, "The Moral Barrier on Rhine and Danube," *First Congress on Roman Frontier Studies 1949*, pp. 5–8.

42. Cf. Denis Sinor, "The Barbarians," *Dogenes*, 18 (1957), 49–50.

43. Cf. Lellia Cracco-Ruggini, "Pregiudizi razzili, ostilita politiche e culturali, intoleranza religiosa nell'Impero Romano," *Athenaeum*, 46 (1968), 139–144; and Saddington, pp. 112–135. These may be compared with A. N. Sherwin-White, *Racial Prejudice in Imperial Rome* (Cambridge, 1967), *in toto*.

44. Thompson, *The Early Germans, in toto*.

45. Samuel Eliot Morison (trans. and ed.), *A New and Fresh English Translation of the Letter of Columbus Announcing the Discovery of America* (Madrid, 1959), p. 10.

46. *Ibid.*, pp. 9, 14. See also Walter O'Meara, *Daughters of the Country: The Women of the Fur Traders and Mountain Men* (New York, 1968), especially Part One, "Sex on the American Indian Frontiers,"; Fred Olsen, *On the Trail of the Arawaks* (Norman, 1974), Chapter I; Charles Gibson, *Spain in America* (New York, 1967), Chapter 7; and Lewis Hanke, *Aristotle and the American Indians: A Study in Race Prejudice in the Modern World* (London, 1959), pp. 13–16, 74.

47. See William S. Maltby, *The Black Legend in England: The Development of Anti-Spanish Sentiment, 1558–1660* (Durham, N.C., 1971), especially Chapter II.

48. William Bradford, *Of Plymouth Plantation, 1620–1647*, ed by Samuel Eliot Morison (New York, 1970), p. 25.

49. *Ibid.*, p. 26.

50. See Percy G. Adams, *Travelers and Travel Liars, 1660–1800* (Berkeley, 1962), and, for the ways in which book production techniques preserved stereotypes, Howard Mumford Jones, *The Frontier in American Fiction: Four Lectures on the Relation of Landscape to Literature* (Jerusalem, 1956).

51. Samuel G. Drake, *Tragedies of the Wilderness; or, True and Authentic Narratives of Captives, Who Have Been Carried Away by the Indians from the Various Frontier Settlements of the United States, from the Earliest to the Present Time, Illustrating the Manners and Customs, Barbarous Rites and Ceremonies, of the North American Indians, and Their Various Methods of Torture Practiced upon Such as Have, from Time to Time, Fallen into Their Hands* (Boston, 1841), a basic compilation of such narratives, contains eight seventeenth-century items and twenty dating from the eighteenth century. In 1975,

Garland Publishing, Inc., announced the publication of *Narratives of North American Indian Captivities,* a series of 111 volumes containing 311 titles, the original publication dates of which range from 1682 to 1962.

52. See J. Ralph Randolph, *British Travelers Among the Southern Indians, 1660–1763* (Norman, 1973) for examples of such observations. A typical account, dating from the early 1770's, may be found in Louis De Vorsey, Jr. (ed.), *De-Brahm's Report of the General Survey in the Southern District of North America* (Columbia, S.C., 1971), pp. 108–114.

53. See Hoxie Neale Fairchild, *The Noble Savage: A Study of Romantic Naturalism* (New York, 1928), and, for a specific application, Gary B. Nash, "The Image of the Indian in the Southern Colonial Mind," *The William and Mary Quarterly,* 3rd ser., 29.2 (April, 1972), 197–230.

54. Carl Bridenbaugh and Roberta Bridenbaugh, *No Peace Beyond the Line: The English in the Caribbean, 1624–1690* (New York, 1972), pp. 30, 153–54.

55. *Ibid.,* pp. 98–99; A. Irving Hallowell, "The Backwash of the Frontier: The Impact of the Indian on American Culture," in *The Frontier in Perspective,* ed. by Walker D. Wyman and Clifton B. Kroeber (Madison, 1957), pp. 229–58; and Virgil J. Vogel, *American Indian Medicine* (Norman, 1970). The use of Indians in colonial wars is discussed in Russell F. Weigley, *History of the United States Army* (New York, 1967).

56. See Georgianna C. Nammack, *Fraud, Politics, and the Dispossession of the Indians: The Iroquois Land Frontier in the Colonial Period* (Norman, 1969) for a case study.

57. For comparison, see Robert Beverley, *The History and Present State of Virginia* [1705], ed. by Louis B. Wright (Charlottesville, Va., 1968), pp. 192–93. See also Howard Mumford Jones and Sue Bonner Walcutt, *The Literature of Virginia in the Seventeenth Century,* 2nd ed., (Charlottesville, Va., 1968), Chapters 2 and 3.

58. See Grant Foreman, *Indian Removal: The Emigration of the Five Civilized Tribes of Indians,* new ed. (Norman, 1953) and, for an overview, William T. Hagan, *American Indians* (Chicago, 1961).

59. Joseph-Marie Degerando, *The Observation of Savage Peoples,* trans. by F. C. T. Moore (Berkeley, 1969), pp. 65–69; Thomas Jefferson, *Notes on the State of Virginia,* ed. by William Peden (Chapel Hill, N.C., 1955); and Paul Russell Cutright, *Lewis and Clark: Pioneering Naturalists* (Urbana, 1969), pp. 23, 60.

60. Rev. John Heckewelder, *History, Manners, and Customs of the Indian Nations Who Once Inhabited Pennsylvania and the Neighboring States* [1819], rev. ed. (Philadelphia, 1876), pp. 106, 217, 239, 263, 321.

61. Henry R. Schoolcraft, *Personal Memoirs of a Residence of Thirty Years with the Indian Tribes on the American Frontiers* (Philadelphia, 1851), pp. 98, 103, 295, 311, 674.

62. Ruth Miller Elson, *Guardians of Tradition: American Schoolbooks of the Nineteenth Century* (Lincoln, 1964), pp. 73–74.

63. Horace Greeley, *An Overland Journey from New York to San Francisco in the Summer of 1859,* ed. by Charles T. Duncan (New York, 1964), p. 119.

64. *Ibid.,* p. 121.

65. Mark Twain, *Roughing It:* Vol. 2 of *The Works of Mark Twain,* ed. by Frederick Anderson (Berkeley, 1972), p. 146.

66. Greeley, *An Overland Journey,* p. 120.

67. Military policy toward Indians is discussed in Russell F. Weigley, *The American Way of War: A History of United States Military Strategy and Policy* (New York, 1973), pp. 153–63, and two volumes by Robert M. Utley, *Frontiersmen in Blue: The United States Army and the Indian, 1848–1865* (New York, 1967) and *Frontier Regulars: The United States Army and the Indian, 1866–1891* (New York, 1973). On the interrelationship between federal Indian and land policies, see Preston Holder, *The Hoe and the Horse on the Plains: A Study of Cultural Development among North American Indians* (Lincoln, 1970); Wilcomb E. Washburn, *Red Man's Land— White Man's Law: A Study of the Past and Present Status of the American Indian* (New York, 1971); William W. Savage, Jr., *The Cherokee Strip Live Stock Association: Federal Regulation and the Cattleman's Last Frontier* (Columbia, Mo., 1973); and D. S. Otis, *The Dawes Act and the Allotment of Indian Lands,* ed. by Francis Paul Prucha, new ed. (Norman, 1973).

68. Richard Irving Dodge, *Our Wild Indians: Thirty-three Years' Personal Experience Among the Red Men of the Great West* (Hartford, 1882), p. 536. See also pp. 512, 524, 531. The confusion of Indians with Hebrews is discussed in Samuel Eliot Morison, *The European Discovery of America: The Northern Voyages,* A.D. *500–1600* (New York, 1971), pp. 106–107, and in greater detail in Robert Wauchope, *Lost Tribes and Sunken Continents: Myth and Method in the Study of American Indians* (Chicago, 1962).

69. Theodore Roosevelt, *The Winning of the West: An Account of the Exploration and Settlement of Our Country from the Alleghanies to the Pacific,* I, vol. VII of *The Works of Theodore Roosevelt,* National Edition (New York, 1926), pp. 81–82.

70. John Gilmary Shea, *History of the Catholic Missions among the Indian Tribes of the United States, 1529–1854* (New York, 1855), p. 19. See also Robert F. Berkhofer, Jr., *Salvation and the Savage: An Analysis of Protestant Missions and American Indian Response, 1787–1862* (Lexington, Ky., 1965) and Howard L. Harrod, *Mission Among the Blackfeet* (Norman, 1971).

71. See Ralph E. Friar and Natasha A. Friar, *The Only Good Indian . . . The Hollywood Gospel* (New York, 1972).

72. For an example of the persistence of stereotypes, compare Joseph G. McCoy, *Historic Sketches of the Cattle Trade of the West and Southwest* (Kansas City, Mo., 1874), pp. 68–70, with white testimony concerning Indian diet in William W. Savage, Jr., "Monologues in Red and White: Contemporary Racial Attitudes in Two Southern Plains Communities," *The Journal of Ethnic Studies,* 2.3 (Fall, 1974), 24–31.

An Archaeological Perspective on Social Change —
The Virginia Frontier

Kenneth E. Lewis, Jr.

ARCHAEOLOGY has long been recognized as a means by which the investigator can increase his knowledge of past events because it utilizes a form of data apart from documentary sources which bears directly upon these events. The potential value of the archaeological record differs, however, depending on the framework in which one seeks to interpret the past. First, it is possible to look upon the past as a collection of particular developments, each unrelated to the others and unique unto itself. This approach almost inevitably limits the use of archaeological evidence to an auxiliary role of clarifying or elaborating a particular historical event or sequence of events which has been defined through documents or other sources. For example, one may know that an eighteenth-century trading post was built at or near a certain location. Archaeological excavations may then be conducted at this site in order to determine if, indeed, it once stood there, as well as other related information such as its appearance, its size, its length of operation, and types of goods traded. The results stemming from this kind of archaeological research are necessarily restricted by the narrow scope of the problems. As long as the latter are tied to the interpretations of particular events as ends in themselves, archaeology must, in turn, be limited to the elaboration of such events.

A somewhat wider and more profitable role for archaeology may be seen in the study of past events in terms of processual models. Cultural processes are merely regularities of change in the organization and/or content of cultural systems, and in the manner in which new formal components are integrated into them.[1] Such processes are best observed through the comparative study of the distribution of cultural forms through time and space.[2] In recent years anthropologists and other social scientists have increasingly sought to define cultural processes in hopes of explaining change and variation among present-day societies. Because most such studies are necessarily of short duration, however, it has, in general, been impossible to deal adequately with many suspected processes. For this reason it has often been necessary to utilize archaeological data in the study of long-term culture processes if other forms of evidence are lacking.

Unlike the ethnologist who can directly observe human behavior, the archaeologist confines his research to the material remains left behind as the by-product of past behavior. In order to make meaningful inferences from this type of data the investigation must operate under the assumption that man's behavior now, and in the past, is patterned or structured, and that the distribution of its archaeological remains reflects this organization.

Cultures are viewed basically as adaptive mechanisms by which a human society adapts to its larger environment, including the physical world, other societies, and even the consequences of its own past adaptions. This operation of this mechanism may be likened to that of a system[3] composed of a complex of components interrelated in a causal network to form an integrated whole which may be delimited by spatial boundaries.[4] As many of these components are environmental variable, it is possible to see a sociocultural system as part of a larger ecosystem. Changes within the system may be seen as the result of its constant readaptation to variation of particular components. Such adjustments often lead directly to emulative changes in the entire system or at least in large portions of it.[5] Human behavior must then be understood in terms of the operation of such a system as a whole rather than as the result of a series of point-to-point deterministic relationships between paired variables of the cultural and natural variety.[6]

Just as all members of society do not participate equally in a culture, not all of the components of a sociocultural system interact directly with all others. For this reason it is often desirable to define subsystems which involve only the interaction of selected variables.[7] A sociocultural system is composed of sets of interdependent subsystems each of which may be artificially conceptualized by the investigator to suit the nature of his inquiry.[8] As it is possible to define subsystems within the total configuration of the sociocultural system it should also be possible to observe them in the distribution of the archaeological record.[9] The change and variation within the systemic structure of a culture thus recorded should, in turn, allow the observation of the operation of culture processes in the archaeological record.

This chapter will attempt to summarize the manner in which the archaeological record has been used to investigate a particular process of culture change in frontier America. The model of culture change employed here is one developed by anthropologists studying contemporary pioneer colonies to explore the regularities in the development of intrusive cultures in frontier situations.[10] The term "frontier" is here understood to mean the zone of contact between an expanding society and the environment (including aboriginal cultures) of the new territory. The term "area of colonization" refers to the total territory occupied by the intrusive culture.[11] The characteristics of this model may be converted readily into a series of hypotheses for changes based upon the systemic organization of the intrusive culture prior to colonization. These hypotheses will also reflect changes which may be discerned by an examination of either the archaeological record or documentary evidence. By examining a particular frontier situation it should be possible to demonstrate the relevance of the frontier model on the basis of archaeological evidence alone. Such a situation also provides another source of information by which to check the accuracy of this evidence as a means of elucidating processes of culture change.

Perhaps one of the most extensively investigated frontiers in North America in terms of archaeology is that along the Virginia peninsula formed by the York and James rivers. This area contains the site of Jamestown, where the earliest settlement was established, as well as those of a large number of other settlements was established, as well as those of a large number of other settlements occupied during the seventeenth and eighteenth centuries.[12] The area of colonization in Virginia has been defined archaeologically on the basis of settlement site locations occupied during the seventeenth century (Fig. 1). Archaeological work has been conducted here on a broad scale since the 1930's by a number of public agencies, including the National Park Service, the Smithsonian Institution, the Colonial Williamsburg Foundation, the Virginia Historic Landmarks Commission, and the College of William and Mary, as well as by several private individuals. Because of the significance of this area in colonial American history both primary and secondary historical sources on the development of the Virginia frontier are also plentiful.

This chapter will be concerned primarily with one aspect of culture change in early Virginia, that associated with what is termed the "economic subsystem" of the intrusive English culture. This subsystem may be defined to include those productive, distributive, and consumptive processes centering on goods and

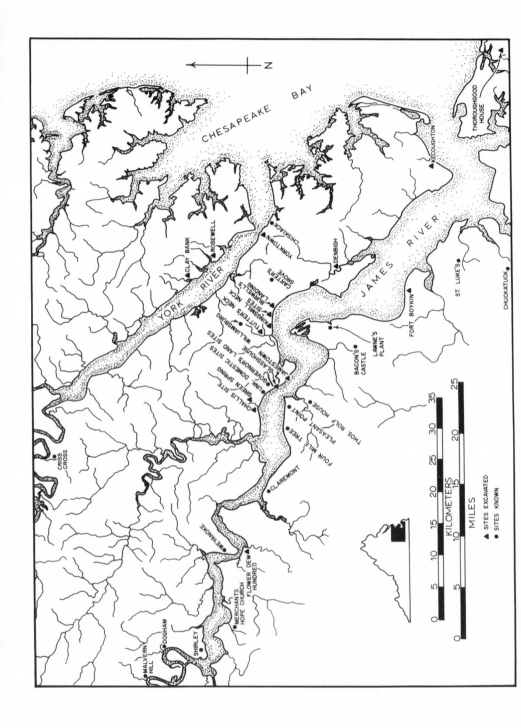

CHESAPEAKE BAY

THOROUGHGOOD HOUSE

LECOUGHTON

CHUCKATUCK

ST. LUKE'S

FORT BOYKIN

LAWNE'S PLANT.

BACON'S CASTLE

DENBIGH

JAMES RIVER

YORKTOWN

CHISKIACK

CARTER'S GROVE

MARTIN'S HUNDRED SITES

BIRKETT'S LANDING

TUTTER'S NECK

WILLIAMSBURG

KINGSMILL SITES

ASHSHOUSE

JAMESTOWN

GOVERNOR'S LAND SITES

UNIV. DOMESTIC SITES

GREEN SPRING

CHALLIS SITE

PLEASANT POINT

THOS. ROLF HOUSE

FOUR MILE TREE

CLAREMONT

CLAY BANK

ROSEWELL

YORK RIVER

CRISS CROSS

WEYANOKE

MALVERN HILL

DOGHAM

SHIRLEY

MERCHANTS HOPE CHURCH

FLOWER DEW HUNDRED

N

MILES

KILOMETERS

▲ SITES EXCAVATED
● SITES KNOWN

0   5   10   15   20   25

0   5   10   15   20   25   30   35

economically relevant services.[13] The significance of this sub-system with regard to the Jamestown frontier may be seen in light of the importance of economic activities in a "commercial" frontier such as Jamestown. The use of the term here follows the distinction made by Cooter in another chapter in this volume.

The Economic Subsystem of Sixteenth Century Britain

Early post-medieval England was predominantly a rural agricultural nation in which industrial production was still conducted largely on a regional basis for local use. Local areas frequently duplicated one another in providing limited and inelastic markets for local craftsmen and tradesmen.[14] Industry was organized in terms of small-scale units which usually consisted of the worker and his apprentices. Those enterprises requiring large amounts of labor, such as the manufacture of cloth, were often divided into a series of separate smaller stages, representing a horizontal rather than a vertical organization.[15] For this reason most areas were characterized by a lack of economic diversity. In part, this organization was determined by the technology of the time. Not only was post-medieval technology limited to the use of human and animal energy as well as that provided by early wind and water machines but, with minor exceptions, it did not require elaborate processes of manufacture.

The natural resources upon which these industries depended were not, however, equally distributed. Certain localities or regions served as sources of raw materials for industries throughout a wide area. Often the actual manufacture of certain products was confined to particular areas near the source of materials, and this situation led to the establishment of local and regional industries. Such areas, most notably the Highlands, were usually characterized by a somewhat more diversified economic structure in which industrially oriented activities often rivalled the importance of agriculture.[16]

In the remainder of this section, the scope of the economic subsystem of post medieval England will be examined in light of the ecological factors affecting its development. These factors were significant in the readaption of the subsystem to the area of colonization.

Any discussion of the distribution of early industrial activities in England must take into consideration the division of Britain

into two basically contrasting regions, the Highlands and the Lowlands. The former lies to the north and west and includes much of
Scotland, Wales, Ireland, and the Southwest peninsula of England,
while the latter is confined to the southern and eastern parts of
Britain. Highland Britain is characterized by wet upland terrain
with mountains and moorland predominating. Plains and valleys
occur but are generally limited in size and extent. Cultivation and
settlement are confined to these areas. Lowland Britain is a region
characterized by low undulating terrain, more moderate rainfall,
and richer soils. The Lowlands are extensively cultivated and
settlement is virtually continuous.[17]

Typical of Lowland Britain are the Midland counties. They
form an almost landlocked region which, in the sixteenth century,
was still devoted almost entirely to agriculture and pastoral subsistence activities. The efficiency and reliability of large-scale
farming and herding in this abundant environment precluded the
need for a diversified economy capable of responding rapidly to
the vagaries of a climatically less moderate zone such as the
Highlands.

Those economic activities which did arise here were basically
extractive in nature and were generally restricted to areas bordering the Midlands where natural deposits of raw materials
occurred. Few activities of a full-time specialized nature existed
in the Midlands by the end of the sixteenth century. Chief among
these were coal mining and iron smelting which were conducted
at the locations of the deposits of raw materials. These produced
semi-finished commodities primarily for use by local small-scale
industries such as smithing, dyeing, brewing, lime burning, and
smelting.[18] It is of some significance to note that in the sixteenth
century the use of charcoal in smelting had not yet been replaced
by that of coal, as attested by wholesale destruction of the English
forests at this time,[19] indicating the necessity of forest resources
in the development of post-medieval industry. The generally retarded development of industry in the Midlands seems to be linked
to the suitability of this region for agriculture and the lack of
natural resources that could be exploited with the contemporary
technology. At the end of the century ecological factors appear
to have still favored a non-diversified economy in most of Lowland
Britain.

In contrast to the Lowlands, the Highland Southwest was characterized by a multi-faceted adaptation to its varied environment,
an adaptation which involved numerous strategies apart from

agriculture. Indeed, agriculture was only a segment of what Hatcher[20] has called a "diversified economic structure," which also included mining, fishing, textile-making, quarrying, and ship-building as major industries. Rather than competing with agriculture, these activities provided an alternate, productive use of land and resources which were only of marginal agricultural value. The rugged terrain of the Southwest contained many easily exploitable natural resources as well as access to the resources of the sea along an extensive shoreline. Access to running water greatly aided the development of mechanization, an important factor in the evolution of early industries here. Specialized technological activities have a long history in southwestern England and they seem to have been integrated early into the total socio-cultural system of this area.

Hypotheses for Change in the New World

An examination of the potential area of colonization indicates that there were no conditions which were likely to impede seriously the establishment of an English colony in coastal Virginia. The physical environment of this area is similar to that of most of Lowland Britain in terms of its moderate climate and the rich alluvial soils of the coastal plain. An abundance of navigable rivers and streams allowed easy access to much of the territory below the fall line,[21] making settlement and subsequent expansion here a likely outcome of an initial colonization attempt. The indigenous inhabitants of the area, although maintaining a complex level of sociocultural integration, were not capable of competing successfully with the technology of a seventeenth-century European state,[22] and while they may have presented an initial threat to colonization they would not have comprised a significant barrier to an established expanding colony.

Given an area with the potential of supporting a new colony, and the nature of a portion of the sociocultural system existing in seventeenth century England, it is now possible to predict those types of changes one would expect to occur in an English colony here in terms of the frontier model. The anticipated changes will take the form of a series of hypotheses. For illustrative purposes this paper will discuss only those concerning the economic sub-system. These five hypotheses are as follows:

1. The contact of English and aboriginal cultures should have resulted in the mutual diffusion of technology and manufactured items between both groups, especially during the early period of contact when access to European products would have been more restricted. Because of the overall superiority of sixteenth-century English technology, the acceptance of native items should have been limited to those situations in which their European counterparts were either unavailable or nonexistent. Conversely, the adoption of English items by native cultures would have been more rapid and extensive. It is important to note that subsistence items do not form a component in the economic subsystem and for this reason the New World cultigens which were to form such an important part of the colonists' diet are not to be considered here.

2. An increase of small-scale technological activities should occur within the area of colonization. These are necessitated by the need for products normally obtained through trade from local or regional manufacturers in England.

3. Because the "horizontal" organization of sixteenth-century English industry often broke down industrial processes into geographically dispersed units, certain industries may be represented only in part in the area of colonization. That portion most likely to appear would include the earlier stages of manufacturing processes entailing the production and preliminary treatment of raw materials.

4. In contrast to subsistence activities which are usually dispersed, technological activities, especially those of a specialized nature, should be concentrated at the focus of the colony, the frontier town.

5. Finally, the geographical shift of such activities through time should indicate the development of new frontier towns as the area of colonization expands and the settlements within it assume different roles in relation to one another.

The Examination of the Archaeological Record

This section constitutes the main test of the utility of archaeological methodology in investigating the relevance of the frontier model. For each of the hypotheses outlined above certain test implications based upon historical and ethnographic analogy will be set down and the data compared to them.[23]

1. The first hypothesis concerns the effects of contact between the intrusive and indigenous cultures. As the physical environment of coastal Virginia did not differ appreciably from that of much of Europe, it did not necessitate the outright adoption of new technological methods to ensure the survival of the English, though it did require their use of indigenous subsistence items. This is obvious from an examination of general aspects of colonial technology. Structures followed English prototypes, as did most tools used in agricultural and industrial tasks in the area of colonization.[24]

Because of the potentially wide adaptability of semi-industrialized European technology to the Virginia environment, the value of adopting elements of aboriginal technology would be necessarily reduced. The great technological disparity between the two cultures, one of which still remained at a basically neolithic level, further diminished the probability of European tools being replaced by indigenous items. For these reasons it is highly improbable that archaeological evidence of the employment of aboriginal artifacts or techniques of manufacture will occur except on a small scale.

Only two types of artifacts bearing evidence of aboriginal techniques of manufacture were present in the area of colonization. These are brown clay pipes of colonial manufacture but of aboriginal design[25] and a ceramic ware exhibiting European forms but constructed in the same manner as aboriginal pottery. The latter has been called "Colono-Indian" ware,[26] and, together with the pipes, is found in sites throughout the Virginia peninsula.[27] Colono-Indian pottery occurs on a broad scale as a utility ware in seventeenth- and eighteenth-century sites throughout the Southeast,[28] and seems to have formed an important component in the acculturation of remnant Indian groups after contact, representing a means of survival by adapting to a marginal position in the colonial economic subsystem.[29]

In contrast to the lack of extensive borrowing by the Europeans, the acceptance of their items by the Indians should be much more widespread, owing to the inherent superiority of European technology. To confirm this statement, the data should indicate the replacement of aboriginal items by their European functional equivalents as well as the appearance of totally new artifacts. The presence of items manufactured especially for the Indian trade in both aboriginal and colonial sites is also expected.

Perhaps the most direct evidence of acceptance by the Indians of English material culture is the presence of such artifacts in burial contexts. These historic aboriginal burials occur at Jamestown and each is associated with European items.[30] European material is also common in Indian burials throughout the Tidewater region of Virginia.[31] An incomplete survey of protohistoric Indian sites in the James River area has yielded a wide variety of European items,[32] including ceramics, metal containers, clothing items, pipes, and glass fragments which were often reworked into implements. A number of items manufactured as trade goods were also found in aboriginal and colonial sites. These include Venetian glass beads, bells, hatchets, knives, and small brass pans.[33] Among the more unusual trade items encountered are brass casting counters, commonly used in Europe for making mathematical calculations.[34]

It may be concluded that while cultural borrowing occurred on the Virginia frontier, the archaeological evidence indicates that it involved the English primarily as donors rather than receivers. The technological disparity between the two cultures is affirmed by the heavy borrowing of European items and techniques by the indigenous inhabitants of Virginia.

2. The second hypothesis involved the nature of industrial activities in the colony. As colonial technology is necessarily an altered form of that found in the homeland, it is most likely that the industrial activities of the early Virginia colony differed from those of England. It is proposed that within the area of colonization such activities will consist primarily of small-scale operations designed to provide products not obtainable from England, or at least to supplement supplies from the homeland. The small size and limited production of these industries would preclude their supplying goods for widespread distribution. They would function similarly to village industries in the Old World in that they would provide finished and semi-finished goods for the immediate area only, but would differ because a much greater variety of activities would be represented at a single location.

The first test implication for this hypothesis is that settlements in the area of colonization should be characterized by specialized industrial structures distinguished by the presence of archaeological subassemblages associated with technological activities. Six types of specialized activities are distinguishable in the James River area. The most common activity is that of pottery making.

Four pottery kilns were uncovered at Jamestown[35] and one at Green Spring, a plantation site about three miles northwest of Jamestown.[36] The Challis Site, just west of Green Spring, consisted entirely of the waste dumps from a kiln,[37] and the possible site of a pottery kiln at Kecoughton, near the tip of the peninsula, was explored but not described.[38] Brick kilns were present at Jamestown,[39] all of which were similar to their English counterparts of the second half of the seventeenth century.[40] Three lime kilns were constructed at Jamestown[41] and are similar to English lime kilns of the seventeenth century.[42] One partly intact lime kiln was unearthed at Kecoughton.[43]

A fourth industrial activity in seventeenth century Virginia was glass making. The most extensive site with evidence of this activity is Glasshouse Point, located at the terminus of the peninsula connecting the island upon which Jamestown was erected with the mainland.[44] This site contained three glass furnaces and a pot kiln, indicating an operation similar to that carried out at sixteenth- and seventeenth-century English glass houses,[45] but one which was apparently of short duration.[46] A second glassmaking activity near Green Spring is suggested by scanty evidence.[47]

Iron working and the manufacturing of metal artifacts is attested to by the presence of a large forge at Jamestown. Associated with this structure were tools, forge debris, and partly completed iron artifacts, including weapons.[48]

Other activities indicated by the presence of specialized tools or artifacts alone are brewing, baking, distilling, wine making, timbering, coopering, furniture-working, and metal-working.[49]

A second test implication for this hypothesis calls for the presence of products of these industrial activities throughout the area of colonization. Evidence of products manufactured in the colony includes the widespread occurrence of locally made pottery traceable to the Jamestown and Green Spring kilns.[50] Clay pipes of local manufacture are also quite common, although it is not possible to trace them to particular kilns.[51]

Evidence of the products of Jamestown's brick kilns is obvious to the observer of colonial structural remains. Nearly all of the foundations exposed at Jamestown and other sites were constructed from what appear to be locally made bricks which were becoming slightly shorter and thinner than contemporary English statute bricks.[52] Bricks recovered from colonial kilns encompass the entire range of bricks used in the structures at Jamestown.[53] The lime used in the mortar holding the brick walls together was undoubtedly manufactured in local kilns.[54]

Iron objects from Jamestown are especially difficult to identify because they do not visibly differ from those made in Europe during this time;[55] however, the wide range of artifacts recovered from the forge site suggests that many of the metal items found at Jamestown and other sites may have originated there.

In summary, at least six specialized industrial activities have been defined archaeologically in the area of colonization. These were primarily concentrated in two areas, Jamestown and Green Spring. All represent small-scale undertakings with a greater diversity than that common to most European settlements of the time.

3. The third hypothesis states that many industrial activities in the colony will represent the earlier stages of more extensive manufacturing processes, usually the procurement of raw materials. As early as the mid-sixteenth century, England was importing large quantities of such items as wax, tallow, flax, hemp, and naval stores from Russia and Baltic Sea countries;[56] and the desirability of obtaining such products was emphasized in the first charter of the Virginia Company.[57]

An examination of archaeological data from peninsular Virginia yields evidence of the preparation of several types of raw products. The first of these is a smelting pit located at Jamestown. It is similar in size and shape to earth ovens used to produce bar iron in England during the first half of the seventeenth century,[58] and was presumably used to smelt bog ore from deposits in nearby swamps and shallow ponds.[59] In addition to the smelter, a pit containing deposits of pitch and tar was uncovered.[60] These products, obtained from the destructive distillation of pine wood, were used by shipbuilders to caulk the seams of wooden vessels.[61] An area bearing evidence of the continuous burning of wood, presumably for the manufacture of charcoal or potash, was also investigated at Jamestown, and seems to indicate the manufacture of these products here.[62]

Although somewhat less abundant than the small-scale finished industries in the area of colonization, the production of raw or semi-finished commodities is evident at Jamestown. The short duration of most of these industries suggests that they did not become permanent. They may represent experiments which failed because they proved to be an overspecialized response to a frontier environment in which survival was more closely linked to subsistence production.

4. The fourth hypothesis involves the siting of the industrial activities discussed above. The frontier model depicts the frontier town as playing a crucial role as the colony's social, political, industrial, religious, and commercial center as well as being its principal link to the homeland which, in this case, lay across the Atlantic. In a frontier which is chiefly oriented toward subsistence, the frontier town assumes the role of providing technological services for the other settlements in the area of colonization. For this reason it is postulated that archaeological evidence of industrial activities should be concentrated primarily around the frontier town in coastal Virginia.

In the case of Virginia only one seventeenth century settlement contains evidence of extensive industrial activity. This is Jamestown, which was shown above to have had twelve industrial activity areas representing six separate industries operating within the nucleated settlement sometime between 1650 and 1690. A survey of other sites shows such activities appearing in only three, Green Spring, Kecoughton, and the Challis Site (see Fig. 1). These sites contain three pottery kilns and one possible lime kiln. It will be noted that none of the remaining sites excavated yielded any evidence of industrial activities. The proximity of Green Spring and the Challis Site to Jamestown further suggests that they may represent an expansion of such activities outward from Jamestown.

When the industrial areas of Jamestown are examined in terms of their temporal relationship to one another a definite pattern of their placement is apparent. First the earliest industries were scattered east of the church, far removed from any existing houses. A concentration of industries in the northern part of this area appeared about 1630, but was abandoned with the spread of dense settlement. Industries are not found again within the town area until the late seventeenth century when Jamestown was declining in size and much of the inhabited area had been abandoned. It is interesting to note that with the expansion of Jamestown, industrial activities seem always to have been situated on the borders following the Old World pattern of dispersed industry. When seen in this light the industries at Challis and Green Spring represent a mid-seventeenth-century dispersion of such activities at Jamestown in response to its increasing size.

Jamestown then appears to represent the center of the economic subsystem in coastal Virginia in the seventeenth century. Its concentration of industries follows the Old World patterns of dispersal yet, at the same time, exhibits the frontier characteristic of being limited almost exclusively to a single location.

5. When the colony is viewed in a temporal sense it is possible to see the decline of Jamestown as an example of the shift in location of the frontier town in response to the expansion of the colony. The fifth hypothesis states that as a new frontier town arises closer to the moving frontier, replacing the old one as the focus of the economic subsystem, there will be a sudden and marked shift of industrial activities from the latter to the former.

By noting the dates of the sites illustrated in Figure 1 it is possible to trace the approximate limits of the area of colonization archaeologically. This area appears to have first been confined to the territory surrounding those sites on the lower James River. It later expanded upriver and inland from both shores of the James, while at the same time encompassing the lower York River. A settlement assuming the role of a frontier town would be likely to be situated more centrally in this enlarged area with access to both the York and James rivers. Middle Plantation, later called Williamsburg, seems to have arisen to provide a frontier town in the expanded areas of colonization.

In terms of the economic subsystem, Williamsburg, and no other settlement, would be most likely to take on the industrial characteristics which disappeared from Jamestown at the close of the seventeenth century. As mentioned in the previous discussion, most manufacturing activities carried out at Jamestown disappeared by 1700. Even two lime kilns built within the former area of dense occupation of the declining town were closed in the first decades of the eighteenth century, as was the Challis kiln.[63]

At the same time that industrial activities were declining at Jamestown, the archaeological data indicate a concomitant upsurge in such activities at Williamsburg and, to a lesser extent, its port of Yorktown on the York River (Fig. 1). High concentrations of wasters suggest pottery kilns at both settlements, and the identifiable wares of several potters are widespread in Virginia archaeological contexts after 1725.[64] One large kiln dating after 1720 has been excavated at Yorktown.[65]

Apart from ceramic manufacturing, a number of other technological activities have been identified through archaeological investigations at Williamsburg, including gold and silver smithing, furniture-making, and printing.[66] Here, as at Jamestown, the bulk of industrial activity seems to have been situated outside the main part of the settlement, although most of the sites have not been thoroughly investigated.

Archaeological investigations in the coastal region of Virginia have revealed evidence which strongly supports the hypotheses concerning the development of the economic subsystem, as set down in the frontier model. In the following section the documentary evidence will be examined to corroborate the conclusions reached here.

On the whole, documentary sources tend also to confirm the hypotheses. In the case of the first, it is clear that despite occasional borrowing of aboriginal traits, the complexity of Old World technology allowed the English to adapt to the new environment without assimilating a large portion of native technology. Diffusion, in fact, flowed mainly in the opposite direction. Despite the adopting of New World crops and the necessity of utilizing swidden techniques of agriculture owing to the scarcity of draft animals and the presence of extensively forested land,[67] European metal implements were effectively utilized and were eagerly sought after by the aborigines to replace their tools. English manufactured goods, in fact, became the means by which to barter for food or raw materials such as hides and furs.[68]

In other instances English forms were generally maintained in the colony. For example, structures followed English types,[69] town planning paralleled European models,[70] and extractive and finishing industries were similar to those in the Old World.[71] This is not to say that the retained European traits represent actual adaptive responses to the frontier, but rather that they were not maladaptive to the extent that they would seriously threaten the existence of the colony.

In the case of the second hypothesis, the proliferation of small industries is immediately recognizable. Despite the stifling effect of tobacco growing, which provided a very high return on labor and capital investment compared to other agricultural activities, many diversified industries were implemented during the early history of the colony. Brick making and lime burning for mortar were begun at Jamestown not long after the first landing in 1607, and within a decade brick was an integral part of many Virginia structures. It was even occasionally exported as far as the Bermudas.[72] Closely tied to brick is pottery-making. The clays of coastal

Virginia were well suited to the manufacture of earthenware and clay pipes,[73] and by mid-century pottery was listed among products manufactured in Virginia.[74]

Other small industries included smithing, coopering, carpentry, and boatbuilding, the last of which was of moderate significance in this riverine area.[75] Grain mills and saw mills were in operation by the 1620's and small manufacturers such as tailors, hatters, shoemakers, tanners, and hosiers produced goods in the colony, although their production was legally restricted by a government in England ever jealous of protecting home industries.[76]

The ecological advantages of tobacco growing effectively discouraged other industries intended to replace imports from foreign sources. Despite the continued encouragement of the Virginia Company during the early years of the colony, the production of commodities such as pitch, tar, soap ashes, flax, cotton, wine, slat, iron, hemp, and silk failed.[77]

The production of raw materials for home industries was also attempted on the Virginia frontier, but like many of the other small manufacturing ventures encouraged by the Virginia Company, these were generally unsuccessful. The production of naval stores, row glass, and bar iron were beyond the capability of a small colony primarily engaged in commercial monocrop agriculture. It was not until the late eighteenth century, when extensive expansion had greatly increased the size and complexity of the colony, that many of these resources were eventually exploited.

The industrial activities which were successful within the area of colonization were generally associated with the frontier town. In the early years of the colony the threat of attack by hostile aborigines confined manufacturing sites to the immediate vicinity of Jamestown,[78] and, later, laws were enacted encouraging the settlement of technical specialists here.[79] Although many of the seventeenth century plantations housed minor industries, the major part of colonial manufacturing was confined to Jamestown. Industries present there included all of these mentioned above.[80] It is important to remember, however, that because of the dependence upon tobacco as a staple, Virginia remained essentially an enclave throughout the seventeenth century, and most finished goods were still imported from England.

Finally, with the removal of the political capital of Virginia from Jamestown to Williamsburg in 1699, the focus of economic activity shifted inland. Jamestown itself had been nearly destroyed during Bacon's Rebellion two decades earlier, and had never fully recovered. Craftsmen resident there began to situate themselves inland as settlement expanded along the peninsula. By the time the political focus of the colony was moved it appears that industrial activities were already established at Williamsburg.[81] Documentary sources on local manufacturing are vague in the eighteenth century, owing in part to the official opposition to colonial industry by the English government, which was striving to maintain the enclave status of Virginia. Although it sought to keep Virginia industries from competing with other components of its colonial system, accounts indicate that early in the century Williamsburg, and its principal ocean port of Yorktown, formed the focus of considerable economic activity in the Virginia colony.

Conclusions

It is immediately apparent that the conclusions arrived at from an examination of documentary sources agree remarkably well with those reached through an analysis of the archaeological data. This is significant in that it confirms the ability of archaeological methodology as a means of recognizing and describing a process of culture change without recourse to other forms of evidence, and also because it demonstrates the utility of viewing cultural variation in terms of a systemic context. Using analogy based upon an ethnographic model of culture change, it has been possible to predict certain changes of a systemic nature in one aspect of seventeenth-century English culture. As each of these changes is accompanied by variation in cultural patterning, the changes are observable in terms of both the documentary and archaeological evidence.

With regard to the study of frontiers in general, this paper has touched upon several points which may be elaborated briefly here. First, it has dealt with a frontier which occurred as the result of the colonization of an overseas land by a developing industrial state, but not one structured in the same manner as those which launched the modern-day colonies upon which the original frontier model is based. For this reason the precise nature of the changes expected in each of the subsystems will be different, as each of the latter is organized differently. In both cases, however, the colony is set up as an extension of the state in an area in which, for varied reasons, political or economic dominance is desired, and for which highly developed control mechanisms govern the nature of settlement. In the case of Jamestown these mechanisms were chiefly commercial in nature and the

Virginia Company is clearly an outgrowth of London's paramount position in the commercial aspect of the English socioeconomic system. Colonization here also produced a frontier quite unlike those of preindustrial states of both the New and Old Worlds. Indeed, the frontier of a preindustrial state such as Rome involved the articulation of different variables than those present in a commercial frontier of the seventeenth century.

Second, the process of acculturation as it relates to the culture of an intrusive people has been examined in part and been shown to exhibit certain general regularities. These regularities must be seen as the adaptation of components within the sociocultural system to a series of state changes in other components of the general environment, which are occasioned chiefly by the isolation of the colony from the homeland, and by the nature of the connections between the two, in the case of Jamestown principally commercial. The frontier process is much more than a response of culture to environment in that it represents the interplay of a number of variables, which is influenced both by the necessity of adapting to a new environment, and by the organizational structure of complex state societies. If, however, we assume that certain aspects of the frontier situation are similar in most cases involving colonization by commercial or industrial states, then the acculturation by the individual societies involved in such situations should also follow a similar pattern. This pattern appears to be reflected in the systemic characteristics of the frontier model.

In summary, certain similarities in the nature of acculturation among complex societies involved in colonization have been noted. It is possible to view them collectively as a process of culture change which may be applicable to frontier colonization in general. As recent studies of contemporary colonies have tended to confirm the frontier model and broaden our understanding of many aspects of frontier change, an increased emphasis upon the study of acculturation among intrusive societies which are represented in the archaeological record should greatly add to our knowledge of the long-term nature of such change. It is hoped that historic sites archaeology, with its access to documentary as well as archaeological data, will play a key role in the study of this and other processes of sociocultural change.

Notes

1. Lewis R. Binford, "Archeological Perspectives," in *New Perspectives in Archeology*, ed. by Sally R. and Lewis R. Binford (Chicago, 1968), p. 14.

2. Julian H. Steward, "Cultural Causality and Law: a Trial Formulation of the Development of Early Civilizations," *American Anthropologist*, LI (1949), 1–25.; *Theory of Culture Change*, (Urbana, 1955).

3. R. J. C. Munton, "Systems Analysis: a Comment," in *The Explanation of Culture Change*, ed. by Colin Renfrew (London, 1973), p. 689.

4. Walter Buckley, *Sociology and Modern Systems Theory* (Englewood Cliffs, 1967), p. 41.

5. Colin Renfrew, *The Emergence of Civilization: the Cyclades and the Aegean in the Third Millenium B.C.* (London, 1972).

6. Clifford Geertz, *Agricultural Involution* (Berkeley, 1963), p. 10.

7. Lewis R. Binford, "Archaeological Systematics and the Study of Culture Process," *American Antiquity* (1965), p. 205.

8. David L. Clarke, *Analytical Archaeology* (London, 1968), p. 87.

9. James N. Hill, *Broken K Pueblo, Prehistoric Social Organization in the American Southwest*, Anthropological Papers of the Museum of Arizona, No. 18. (1963), p. 104.

10. Stephen I. Thompson, *San Juan Yapacani: a Japanese Pioneer Colony in Eastern Bolivia* (Ph.D. dissertation, University of Illinois, 1970).

11. Joseph B. Casagrande, Stephen I. Thompson, and Philip D. Young, "Colonization as a Research Frontier: the Equadorian Case," in *Process and Pattern in Culture, Essays in Honor of Julian Steward*, ed. by Robert A. Manners (Chicago, 1964), pp. 281–325.

12. Ivor Noël Hume, *Here Lies Virginia* (New York, 1963).

13. Karl Polanyi, "The Economy as Instituted Process," in *Trade and Market in Early Empires*, ed. by Karl Polanyi, Conrad M. Arensberg, and Harry W. Pearson (New York, 1957), pp. 243–270.

14. M. W. Flinn, *An Economic and Social History of Britain, 1066–1939* (London, 1965), p. 130.

15. Harry A. Miskimin, *The Economy of Early Renaissance: Europe, 1300–1460* (Englewood Cliffs, 1969).

16. John Hatcher, *Rural Economy and Society in the Duchy of Cornwall, 1300–1500* (Cambridge, 1970), p. 29.

17. L. Dudley Stamp, *Britain's Structure and Scenery* (London, 1946), pp. 5–6.

18. F. Sherwood Taylor and Charles Singer, "Prescientific Industrial Chemistry" in *A History of Technology, Vol. 2*, ed. by Charles Singer, E. J. Holmyari, A. R. Hill, and Trevor I. Williams (Oxford, 1956), pp. 347–373.

19. Archie Clow, "The Influence of Technology on Environment" in *Ecology in Theory and Practice*, ed. Jonathan Benthall (New York, 1972), pp. 50–80.

20. Hatcher, p. 209.

21. Nevin E. Fenneman, *Physiography of Eastern United States* (New York, 1938), p. 13.

22. Lewis R. Binford, *Archaeological and Ethnohistorical Investigations of Cultural Diversity and Progressive Development among the Aboriginal Cultures of Coastal Virginia and North Carolina* (Ph.D. dissertation, University of Michigan, 1964).

23. Kenneth E. Lewis, *The Jamestown Frontier, an Archaeological View of Colonization* (Ph.D. dissertation, University of Oklahoma, 1975).

24. John L. Cotter, *Archeological Excavations at Jamestown* (Archeological Research Series, No. 4 (Washington, 1958); J. Paul Hudson, *A Pictoral Booklet on Early Jamestown Commodities and Industries* (Jamestown 350th Anniversary Historical Booklet, No. 23 (Charlottesville, 1957).

25. Cotter, *Archeological Excavations at Jamestown*, p. 146.

26. Ivor Noël Hume, "An Indian Ware of the Colonial Period." *Quarterly Bulletin of the Archaeological Society of Virginia*, XVII (1962).

27. Noël Hume, *Here Lies Virginia*, p. 149.

28. John M. Goggin, "Fort Pupo, a Spanish Frontier Outpost," *Florida Historical Quarterly*, XXX (1951), p. 186; Hale G. Smith, "A Spanish Mission Site in Jefferson County, Florida," in *Here Once They Stood*, ed. by Mark F. Boyd, Hale G. Smith, and John W. Griffin (Gainesville, 1951), p. 129; William M. Kelso, "Excavations at the King George Historical Site, Darien." *Archeological Research Series*, No. 1 (Atlanta, 1968), p. 14.

29. Stephen G. Baker, "Colono-Indian Pottery from Cambridge, South Carolina," *University of South Carolina, Institute of Archeology and Anthropology, Notebook* IV (1972), 16.

30. Cotter, *Archeological Excavations at Jamestown*, p. 24.

31. Karl Schmitt, "Archeological Chronology of the Middle Atlantic States," in *Archeology of Eastern United States*, ed. by James B. Griffin (Chicago, 1952), p. 68.

32. Binford, *Archaeological Investigations*, pp. 346–347.

33. Cotter, *Archeological Excavations at Jamestown*, p. 106; Hudson, *Jamestown Commodities and Industries*, p. 29; Floyd Painter, "The Artifacts from the Thoroughgood Site," *The Chesopiean* III (1965), 134.

34. Cotter, *Archeological Excavations at Jamestown*, p. 191.

35. *Ibid.*

36. Louis R. Caywood, *Green Spring Plantation Archeological Report: Excavations at Green Spring Plantation* (Yorktown, 1955), pp. 12–13.

37. Noël Hume, *Here Lies Virginia*, p. 216.

38. Joseph B. Brittingham and Alvin W. Brittingham, Sr., *The First Trading Post at Kecoughton, Hampton, Virginia* (Hampton, 1947), p. 7.

39. Cotter, *Archeological Excavations at Jamestown*, p. 145.

40. J. C. Harrington, "Seventeenth Century Brickmaking and Tilemaking at Jamestown, Virginia," *Virginia Magazine of History and Biography*, LVIII (1950), 25.

41. Cotter, *Archeological Excavations at Jamestown*, pp. 90–91.

42. Worth Bailey, "Lime Preparation at Jamestown in the Seventeenth Century," *William and Mary Quarterly*, series 2, XVIII (1938), 11.

43. Brittingham and Brittingham, *The First Trading Post*, p. 7.

44. J. C. Harrington, *A Tryal of Glasse, the Story of Glassmaking at Jamestown* (Richmond, 1972).

45. D. W. Crossley, "Glassmaking in Bagot's Park, Staffordshire in the Sixteenth Century," *Post-Medieval Archaeology* I (1968), 53.

46. J. C. Harrington, "The Tools of America's First Glassblowers," *The Chronicle of the Early American Industries Association* X (1957), 5.

47. Noël Hume, *Here Lies Virginia*, pp. 204–205.

48. J. Paul Hudson, "The Story of Iron at Jamestown, Virginia," *The Ironworker* XX (1956), 8.

49. Cotter, *Archeological Excavations at Jamestown.*

50. *Ibid.*

51. J. C. Harrington, "Tobacco Pipes from Jamestown," *Quarterly Bulletin of the Archaeological Society of Virginia* V (1951), n.p.

52. Harrington, "Seventeenth Century Brickmaking," p. 35.

53. Cotter, *Archeological Excavations at Jamestown,* p. 193.

54. Bailey, "Lime Preparation at Jamestown," p. 2.

55. Hudson, "The Story of Iron at Jamestown," p. 8.

56. Flinn, *An Economic and Social History,* p. 63.

57. Samuel M. Bemiss, ed., *The Three Charters of the Virginia Company of London 1606–1621,* (Jamestown 350th Anniversary Historical Booklet, No. 4 [Charlottesville: Virginia, 1957]), p. 6.

58. Hudson, "The Story of Iron at Jamestown," p. 5.

59. Cotter, *Archeological Excavations at Jamestown,* p. 110.

60. J. C. Harrington, "Progress Report on the 1941 Excavations in the A.P.V.A. Grounds, Jamestown Island, Virginia," National Park Service Manuscript on file, Colonial National Historical Park, Virginia (1942), p. 11.

61. Hudson, *Early Jamestown Commodities and Industries,* p. 14.

62. Harrington, "Progress Report on the 1941 Excavations," p. 11.

63. Noël Hume, *Here Lies Virginia,* p. 216.

64. C. Malcolm Watkins and Ivor Noël Hume, *The "Poor Potter" of Yorktown,* U.S. National Museum Bulletin No. 249, Contributions from the Museum of History and Technology, Paper 54, (1967), p. 110.

65. Norman F. Barka, "The Kiln and Ceramics of the 'Poor Potter' of Yorktown: a Preliminary Report," in *Ceramics in America,* ed. by Ian M. G. Quimby (Charlottesville, 1973), p. 313.

66. Noël Hume, *Here Lies Virginia.*

67. Philip Alexander Bruce, *Economic History of Virginia in the Seventeenth Century* 2 vols. (New York, 1895), I, 199.

68. William Strachey, *The Historie of Travaile into Virginia Britania,* ed. by Louis B. Wright and Virginia Freund (London, 1953), p. 115.

69. Henry Chandlee Forman, *Jamestown and St. Marys, Buried Cities of Romance* (Baltimore, 1938).

70. John W. Reps, *Tidewater Towns: City Planning in Colonial Virginia and Maryland* (Charlottesville, 1972).

71. Hugh Jones, *The Present State of Virginia* (Chapel Hill, 1956), p. 81.

72. Bruce, *Economic History,* II, 137.

73. Robert Beverley, *History of the Present State of Virginia,* ed. by Louis B. Wright. (Charlottesville, 1947), p. 125.

74. Peter Force, ed., *Tracts and Other Papers, Relating Principally to the Origin, Settlement, and Progress of the Colonies in North America, from the Discovery of the Country to the Year 1776* 4 vols. (New York, 1836–1846), II, No. 8, p. 7.

75. Bruce, *Economic History,* II, 430–435.

76. Bruce, *Economic History,* I, 482.

77. Beverley, *The History and Present State of Virginia,* p. 295.

78. Beverley, *The History and Present State of Virginia,* p. 126.

79. Bruce, *Economic History,* II, 411.

80. Carl Bridenbaugh, *The Colonial Craftsman* (New York, 1950), pp. 14–15.

81. Jane Carson, ed., *We Were There; Descriptions of Williamsburg, 1699–1859* (Charlottesville, 1965), p. 1.

The Fur Trade of the West, 1807–1840:
A Geographic Synthesis

David J. Wishart

A CENTRAL GOAL of both geography and history is synthesis, the attempt to organize the myriad of facts behind a given situation into an interpretable whole. "A historical synthesis," writes Harris, "is usually built around such concepts as events, society, or period; a geographical synthesis around such concepts as region, landscape, or place."[1] The historical geographer strives to weave together these emphases into a hypothetical reconstruction of past reality, but his orientation and presentation are ultimately geographic: the warp is more pronounced than the woof and this may give old material a new appearance.

With the exception of Chittenden's classic study, no encompassing synthesis has been made of the American fur trade of the West.[2] This is not to derogate the historical literature, which is rich in detail and insight. The historical studies, however, have generally been concerned more with the parts of the fur trade than with the whole, and the focus has been more on personality than on place. There is a need for a new synthesis which views the fur trade as a complex of interrelated biological, physical, and cultural environments. In other words, the fur trade of the West may be conceptualized as an ecosystem.

Like all open systems, an ecosystem is characterized by interdependence of the parts, input and output of energy, and feedback mechanisms which regulate the system and produce an ordered process of change.[3] Ideally it should be possible to measure in unambiguous mathematical language the relationships of the parts to each other and of the parts to the whole. Such precision, however, may well be unattainable in complex man-environment systems.[4] This does not negate the value of an approach which provides a framework for synthesis. The systems approach, according to Bertalanffy, provides a "guiding idea" for the study of wholes, and if it achieves nothing more than to focus attention on entireties rather than parts, then the endeavor is worthwhile.[5] Furthermore, in Bertalanffy's opinion, a "verbal model is better

161

than no model at all, or a model which, because it can be formulated mathematically, is forcibly imposed upon and falsifies reality."[6]

The purpose of this chapter is to offer such a "guiding idea" for the study of the American fur trade of the West from 1807 to 1840. No attempt is made to write a definitive historical narrative because that topic is vast and the historical details have been supplied by others. Instead, emphasis is placed upon the changing geographic organization of the fur trade as a system of occupance: emerging through experimentation after 1807, crystallizing into a "steady state" after 1822, and re-adjusting to a new equilibrium after 1834.

Experimental Strategies, 1807–1822

Before 1807, the Saint Louis fur trade was confined to the lower reaches of the Missouri River where traders obtained bison robes and beaver pelts from the Otoe, Osage, Kansas, Ponca, and Omaha Indians. Some Spanish-sponsored expeditions, seeking the elusive route to the Pacific, had reached the Mandan villages in the 1790's, but the upper Missouri fur trade was firmly under the control of the North West Company. The British were also in the process of securing their hold on the fur trade of the Pacific Northwest in the first decade of the nineteenth century, and that grip would not be loosened until the 1840's. The expansion of the American fur trade into the trans-Missouri West after 1807 was, therefore, an economic penetration with important geostrategic implications: it was a means of preventing a possible British dominion over much of the western United States.[7]

A primary purpose of the Lewis and Clark expedition was to discover a route to the Pacific that would serve as an artery for the fur trade and which would be more efficient than any route that the British could establish to the north. The traverse proved more difficult than established geographic lore had suggested, but Lewis and Clark did confirm that the trans-Missouri West offered rich prospects for the fur trade. In 1806 Lewis reported to Jefferson that the upper Missouri was "richer in beaver and otter than any country on earth."[8] Even before the triumphant return of the explorers to Saint Louis on September 23, 1806, American traders had penetrated to the upper Missouri in search of furs. Within six years, most of the Great Plains north of the Platte had been explored and trapped, and John Jacob Astor had attempted to found his trading empire in the Pacific Northwest.

These initial attempts to establish a fur trade of the West may be viewed as geographic experiments, preludes to the emergence of successful strategies in the 1820's. Although the visionary schemes of Manuel Lisa and Astor failed, they served to clarify the details of the biological, cultural, and physical environments of the West and were "models" for the future development of the fur trade.

Manuel Lisa and the Missouri Fur Company, 1807–1812

It was Manuel Lisa, a Saint Louis trader of Spanish heritage, who first instituted a broadly based fur trade on the upper Missouri.[9] As part of his plans to create a cis-Rocky Mountain trading system that would connect the upper Missouri and Santa Fe trades, Lisa ascended the Missouri River in 1807 and built Fort Manuel at the mouth of the Bighorn (Fig. 1). In the following year Lisa formed the Missouri Fur Company and prepared to establish a network of trading posts along the Missouri River. Lisa's strategy was explained by the contemporary trader Thomas Biddle:

> The objectives of this company appear to have been to monopolize the trade among the lower tribes of the Missouri, who understand the art of trapping, and to send a large party to the headwaters of the Missouri capable of defending and trapping beaver themselves.[10]

This would be the model for the fur trade on the northern Great Plains until the mid-1820's. The primary objective was to exploit the large reserve of fur-bearers that Lewis and Clark had discovered at the headwaters of the Missouri River. The Blackfoot, however, who occupied the area from the Three Forks of the Missouri to the Marias River, would not tolerate American trappers or traders in their country.[11] In 1810 Lisa's men were driven out of Blackfoot country with considerable loss of life, and that area remained closed to Americans until 1821, when a treaty was negotiated with the Piegan band.

Lisa's secondary objective—to establish trading posts at the Indian villages on the Missouri—was temporarily successful. Trad-

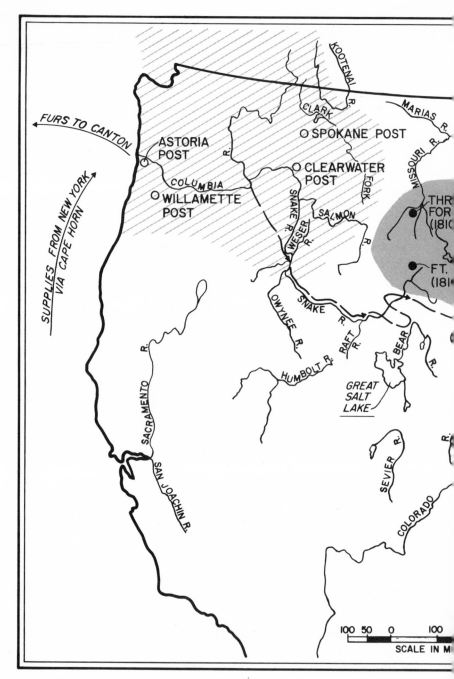

Fig. 1. The attempt of J. J. Astor and Manuel Lisa to develop strategies for the fur trade of the West, 1807–1819 (Sources: Oglesby, note 9; Irving, note 13; and Meinig, note 13)

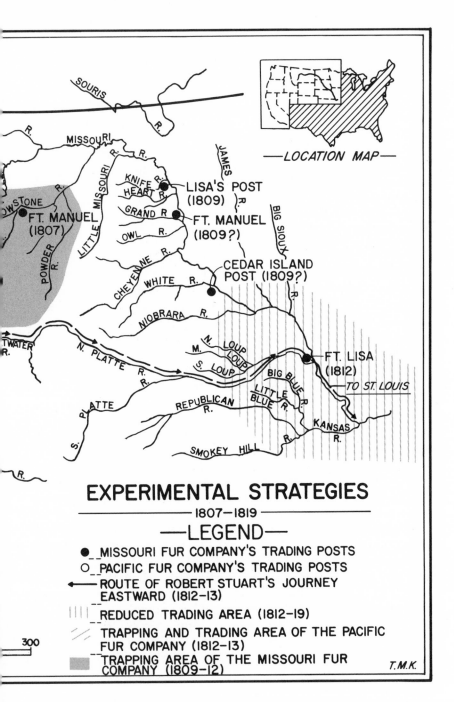

SOURIS R.

MISSOURI R.

LISA'S POST (1809)

KNIFE R.
HEART R.

YELLOWSTONE R.

FT. MANUEL (1807)

POWDER R.

LITTLE MISSOURI R.

GRAND R.

FT. MANUEL (1809?)

OWL R.

JAMES R.

BIG SIOUX R.

CEDAR ISLAND POST (1809?)

CHEYENNE R.

WHITE R.

NIOBRARA R.

SWEETWATER R.

N. PLATTE R.

N. LOUP
M. LOUP
LOUP
S. LOUP

FT. LISA (1812)

TO ST. LOUIS

S. PLATTE

REPUBLICAN R.

BIG BLUE R.
LITTLE BLUE R.

KANSAS R.

SMOKEY HILL R.

R.

—LOCATION MAP—

EXPERIMENTAL STRATEGIES
————— 1807–1819 —————
—LEGEND—

● MISSOURI FUR COMPANY'S TRADING POSTS
○ PACIFIC FUR COMPANY'S TRADING POSTS
◄— ROUTE OF ROBERT STUART'S JOURNEY EASTWARD (1812–13)
|||| REDUCED TRADING AREA (1812–19)
/// TRAPPING AND TRADING AREA OF THE PACIFIC FUR COMPANY (1812–13)
▓ TRAPPING AREA OF THE MISSOURI FUR COMPANY (1809–12)

300

T.M.K.

ing posts were built at the Council Bluffs, Cedar Island, and at the Mandan-Hidatsa and Arikara villages, and a profitable Indian trade commenced. In 1812, however, Lisa's system fell victim to external influences. The price for beaver at Saint Louis fell precipitously from $4 to $2 a pound and the outbreak of the war with Britain disrupted trading operations on the upper Missouri. Fort Lisa, at the Council Bluffs, became the focus of a reduced trading area until 1818 and, according to Biddle, the Saint Louis fur trade during that period was "of little importance from a pecuniary point of view."[12]

The Pacific Fur Company, 1811–1813

The same war that disrupted Lisa's plans for the upper Missouri fur trade, destroyed John Jacob Astor's "magnificent enterprise" in the Pacific Northwest.[13] Astor's plan to establish an international trade network, pivoted at the mouth of the Columbia, was not as original as his chronicler, Washington Irving, suggested. A similar notion had been conceived by Jefferson and Lewis and possibly by Alexander McKenzie before them, but Astor almost made a reality out of the "passage to India."

Encouraged by Thomas Jefferson, Astor founded the Pacific Fur Company on March 24, 1811. Wilson Price Hunt was dispatched overland to the mouth of the Columbia, which he reached, after terrible hardships, in mid-February of 1812. Astor's strategy was to establish a line of trading posts from the upper Missouri to the Columbia for the purpose of the Indian trade. Supplies for this trade would be shipped annually around Cape Horn from New York to Astoria, the trading depot at the mouth of the Columbia. The same ship would be used to transport Rocky Mountain furs to the Canton market and from there Chinese goods would be carried to Europe and North America (Fig. 1). The key to the entire system, particularly when the sea route proved to be impractical, was the discovery of an effective overland route that would allow "rapid" communication between Astoria and New York. This was accomplished by Robert Stuart on an eastward journey from Astoria to Saint Louis beginning on June 29, 1812 and ending on April 30, 1813. Stuart was the first Euro-American to use South Pass and the Platte overland route, but it was not an "effective" discovery, and South Pass had to be re-discovered in 1824.[14]

The initial success of trading activities on the Columbia and the discovery of a direct route to Saint Louis indicate that Astor's visionary scheme was well founded. In 1813, however, the enterprise was aborted when, faced with the prospect of armed encounter with the British, the Astorians sold their trading post and equipment to the North West Company. Nevertheless, Astor's strategy was not forgotten, and Nathaniel Wyeth attempted to institute a similar plan in 1832 and again in 1834–1835.[15] Although Oregon was jointly controlled by England and the United States after 1818, the British were unassailable in the Pacific Northwest as long as the fur trade was the medium of competition, and American trappers rarely ventured to the Pacific except for exploratory purposes.[16]

The Saint Louis fur trade was revitalized in 1819. A new Missouri Fur Company under the control of Joshua Pilcher was preparing to enact Lisa's strategy on the upper Missouri, and there was a new interest in the furs of the central Rocky Mountains stimulated, perhaps, by Major Stephen Long's expedition of 1819–1820. By 1822 a plethora of companies were organizing trapping parties to the northern Great Plains and the Rocky Mountains by way of the Missouri River. In that year, Benjamin O'Fallon, the Indian agent at Fort Atkinson, commented to Ramsey Crooks of the American Fur Company that "it remains for the enterprise of individuals to contend for the wealth of the upper country."[17] The existence of large reserves of fur-bearing animals was proven and there was a lucrative market in Europe and the United States for beaver pelts, which made excellent felting material for hats. What was needed was a viable system for obtaining and marketing the furs.

The Emergence of Successful Strategies, 1822–1826

William Ashley and the Rocky Mountain Trapping System

It was William Ashley, the Missouri politician, who brought the organizing genius to the Rocky Mountain fur trade. As General Henry Atkinson noted in 1822, Ashley's initial strategy was traditional, following closely the precedent set by Manuel Lisa:

Gen. Ashley, Lieut. Governor of this state, and another gentleman by the name of Henry, have organized the company consisting of about a hundred men, for the purpose of ascending the Missouri, the ensuing spring, as high as the Yellowstone to hunt and trap and trade with the Indian Tribes inhabiting that part of the country.[18]

The primary objective was, once again, the headwaters of the Missouri River and the major tributaries, the Yellowstone and the Bighorn, where the Missouri Plateau is interspersed with outliers of the Rocky Mountains (the Black Hills, the Big Belt, Little Belt, Little Rockies, and Big Snowy Mountains). Ashley may even have intended to penetrate the Rocky Mountains proper, to the Three Forks of the Missouri and the Columbia, but the method of approach was the customary Missouri River route, and trading with the Indians of the northern plains was an important part of the strategy.

After some initial success (Andrew Henry established a base for trapping at the junction of the Yellowstone and Missouri rivers in the summer of 1822), Ashley's plans disintegrated. In April, 1823, the two keelboats that Ashley was taking to the mouth of the Yellowstone were attacked by the Arikara and fourteen of his men were killed.[19] This disaster resulted in a change of strategy. Ashley shifted his emphasis from trading to trapping and he dispatched his leading trappers, Jedediah Smith, Tom Fitzpatrick, and William Sublette from Fort Lookout on a direct lateral route to the Rocky Mountains. A decade later, Nathaniel Wyeth described the transition in Ashley's strategy:

> His first attempts were predicated upon the possibility of trading furs from the Indians in the interior for goods. In this he was not successful, and in the event became much reduced in means, and credit, but in the course of this business perceived that there was plenty of Beaver in the country to which he had resorted to trade, but great difficulty to induce the Indians to catch it. After many tyrals of trading voyages he converted his trading parties into trapping parties.[20]

Ashley had instructed Smith's party to proceed overland to the Bighorn River, there to join with a group of Andrew Henry's men who had been trapping on the Yellowstone (Fig. 2). The union did not materialize. Henry continued to concentrate his trappers on the tributaries of the Yellowstone and Bighorn rivers but, constantly threatened by Blackfoot, they obtained few furs.

Henry's retirement from the field in 1824 symbolized Ashley's abandonment of the upper Missouri fur trade.

Jedediah Smith's party crossed the continental divide for the spring hunt and found large reserves of beaver on the small tributaries of the upper Green River. The Crow had shown the trappers the wide depression in the Rocky Mountains, to the south of the Wind River Range and so, in March, 1824, the effective discovery of South Pass was made. Fitzpatrick conveyed the news to Ashley in the summer of that year—not only was there rich beaver country in the central Rocky Mountains but there was a viable access route by way of South Pass and the Platte overland trail. In the course of two expeditions to the Rocky Mountains in the next two years Ashley developed a successful production system based on beaver pelts, Europ-American trappers, the rendezvous, and the Platte supply route.

For a decade after 1824 the Rocky Mountain trapping system flourished. Ashley and his trappers amassed eighty to one hundred packs of beaver in the 1824–1825 season, worth $50,000 in Saint Louis, and one hundred twenty-five packs during the following year, worth more than $60,000.[21] In the summer of 1826 Ashley sold his trapping interests to a new company headed by Jedediah Smith, David Jackson, and William Sublette. Under this new partnership, from 1826–1830, and under their successors, the Rocky Mountain Fur Company, Ashley's system was expanded. The basic structure, however, was unaltered. A condition of dynamic equilibrium was sustained until 1834 when, strained by burgeoning competition and invalidated by the decline in the market for beaver, the Rocky Mountain trapping system collapsed.

The American Fur Company and the Upper Missouri Fur Trade

In 1822 a large number of companies were contesting for the furs of the northern Great Plains. The Missouri Fur Company, which had been revived in 1820, had three hundred trappers in Crow and Blackfoot country. On May 17, 1823, a trapping party led by Michael Immel and Robert Jones was massacred by the Blood band of the Blackfoot and the Missouri Fur Company withdrew from the upper Missouri and disbanded two years later. Two other powerful fur companies were established on the Missouri River by 1822 and they were impediments in the way of

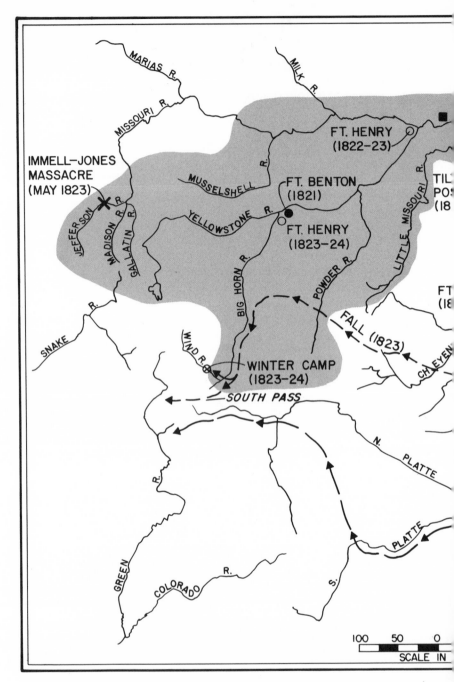

Fig. 2. The emergence of the Rocky Mountain trapping system and the Upper Missouri fur trade, 1822–1826 (Sources: Morgan, note 18; Chouteau Collection, note 17; Ashley Papers, note 25)

POST (1825)

—LOCATION MAP—

AMERICAN FUR TRADE
OF THE WEST
—— 1822 – 1826 ——

—LEGEND—

◄— — WILLIAM ASHLEY'S ROUTE TO THE ROCKY MOUNTAINS (1824-25)

◄- - - JEDEDIAH SMITH'S ROUTE TO THE ROCKY MOUNTAINS (1823-24)

▨ AREA TRAPPED BY HENRY'S MEN AND THE MISSOURI FUR COMPANY (1822-24)

■ COLUMBIA FUR COMPANY'S TRADING POSTS (1822-27)

□ FRENCH FUR COMPANY'S TRADING POSTS (1820-26)

● MISSOURI FUR COMPANY'S TRADING POSTS (1814-25)

○ ANDREW HENRY'S POSTS (1822-24)

⊗ CAMP SITE

✗ MASSACRE SITE

▲ VILLAGE SITE

RA
GES—►

MSEH

JAMES R.

BIG SIOUX R.

FT. LOOKOUT
(1822)

FT. RECOVERY
(1822)

COUNCIL BLUFFS

100

T.M.K.

the American Fur Company's drive to gain control of the upper Missouri fur trade.

The French Fur Company, founded in 1820, was controlled by the powerful Saint Louis merchants Bartholomew Berthold, Bernard Pratte, Sr., and Pierre Chouteau, Jr. By 1826 this company dominated the fur trade on the lower reaches of the Missouri from trading posts at Council Bluffs and Fort Lookout (Fig. 2). They were challenged by the Columbia Fur Company, an amalgam of traders who had been made redundant when the North West Company was merged into the Hudson's Bay Company in 1821. The Columbia Fur Company was oriented to Lake Traverse, which served as a supply base for trading posts on the upper Missouri and the upper Mississippi. By 1826 the Columbia Fur Company had built posts for the Arikara, Mandan-Hidatsa, Teton and Yankton Dakota, Ponca, and Omaha trade, and the network was pivoted at Fort Tecumseh at the mouth of the Teton River (Fig. 2).

In 1822 the American Fur Company created a Western Department and prepared to contend for the fur trade of the upper Missouri. The "Company," as it was called, eliminated opponents in one of two ways: by negotiation, which generally led to the incorporation of the rival company, or by outpricing the opposition and taking short-term losses in order to achieve long-term victory. The French and Columbia Fur companies were eliminated in the former manner.

In December, 1826 Ramsey Crooks placed the affairs of the Western Department in the hands of Bernard Pratte and Company and so the French Fur Company was remodelled as a unit of the American Fur Company. In July of the following year an agreement was reached with the Columbia Fur Company which, in effect, left the American Fur Company in a position of virtual monopoly on the upper Missouri. The Columbia Fur Company agreed to withdraw from the Great Lakes fur trade where it had been challenging the Northern Department of the American Fur Company. On the upper Missouri the Columbia Fur Company was incorporated into the American Fur Company as the Upper Missouri Outfit, with jurisdiction above the mouth of the Big Sioux River. By 1827, therefore, the American Fur Company had acquired a string of trading posts on the upper Missouri and the foundation was laid for a production system that would endure until the 1860's.

In the course of the next seven years a hierarchy of trading posts was established on the central and northern Great Plains (see Fig. 6). At the top of this hierarchy were the major depots, Fort Union, Fort Tecumseh (rebuilt in June, 1832 as Fort Pierre), and Fort William. At the next, lower level of the hierarchy were the regional trading posts, built to serve, and often at the request of, the Indians. Fort Cass, for example, was built for the Crow at the mouth of the Bighorn River in 1833 and Fort Piegan (later, in a slightly different location, Fort McKenzie) was located near the junction of the Marias and Missouri Rivers in 1831 for the Blackfoot trade.[22] The depots and regional posts spawned numerous temporary trading houses each winter, again at the request of the Indians. For example, Cabanné's Post at the Council Bluffs maintained winter posts at the Pawnee villages, at the Otoe, Omaha, and Ponca camps, and in various locations for the Dakota trade.[23] In this way no Indians were unserved by American Fur Company traders.

This trading post network, superimposed on the Missouri River and its tributaries, was a lattice that supported the production system of the upper Missouri fur trade. The main product was bison robes, procured and prepared by the plains Indians, exchanged for manufactured goods at the trading posts, and moved to Saint Louis by water transportation. At Saint Louis the bison robes from the northern Great Plains were gathered with the beaver pelts from the Rocky Mountains and fed into a national and international trade network. The pasts of this entire system (resource base, producers, exchange medium, and market) were united by a flow of furs, goods, and people, and a condition of dynamic equilibrium was maintained by information feedback which converged on Saint Louis, the major decision-making center (Fig. 3).

The Fur Trade of the West, 1822–1834: An Ecosystem Analysis

The Rocky Mountain Trapping System

The most important fur-bearer in the Rocky Mountain trapping system was the beaver, with otter, muskrat, foxes, and other small furs of secondary concern. Beaver occur in a wide range of environments in the Rocky Mountains and on the Great Plains, but the preferential habitat is "sluggish streams and small lakes

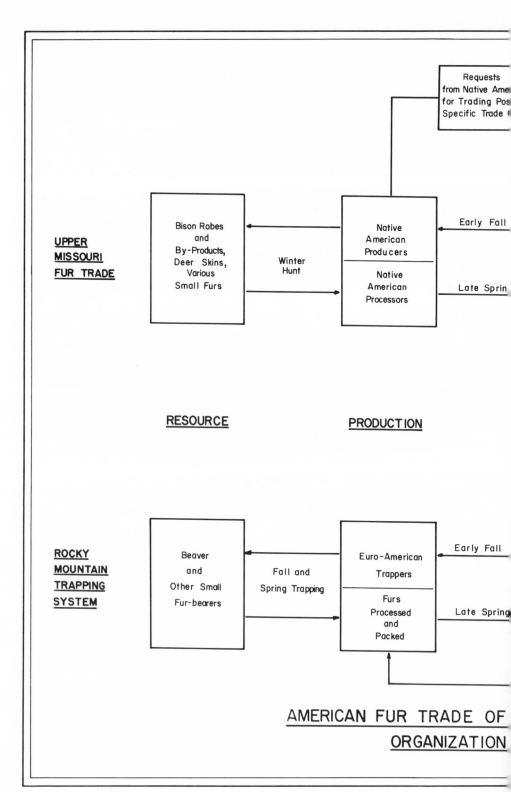

Fig. 3. The organization and regulation c

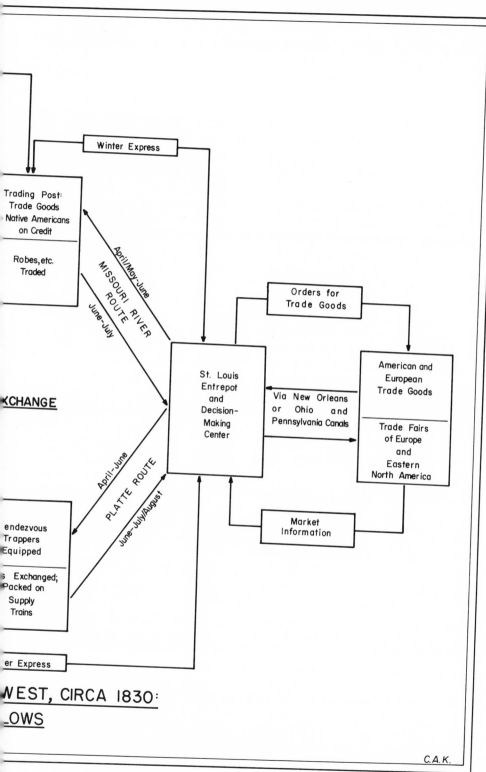

Winter Express

Trading Post:
Trade Goods
Native Americans
on Credit

Robes, etc.
Traded

April/May-June
MISSOURI RIVER
ROUTE

June-July

XCHANGE

Orders for
Trade Goods

St. Louis
Entrepot
and
Decision-
Making
Center

Via New Orleans
or Ohio and
Pennsylvania Canals

American and
European
Trade Goods

Trade Fairs
of Europe
and
Eastern
North America

April-June
PLATTE ROUTE

June-July/August

endezvous
Trappers
Equipped

Exchanged;
Packed on
Supply
Trains

Market
Information

er Express

WEST, CIRCA 1830:
OWS

C.A.K.

he American fur trade of the west, ca. 1830

with clay banks that are well-wooded with aspen and willow."[24] In such locations the beaver constructs a lodge of branches cemented together with mud, or a den hollowed out of the bankside and with underwater access.

The trappers rapidly discovered the areas where beaver colonies were concentrated. When William Ashley first penetrated the Rocky Mountains in the spring of 1825, he found the small tributary streams of the upper Green "richly stocked with beaver."[25] The Bear River and the streams of the Wasatch Range, the upper Snake and its left bank tributaries, the environs of Flathead Lake, the "Parks" of Colorado and, to the east of the Continental Divide, the headwaters of the Missouri, Yellowstone, and Bighorn rivers were the main foci of trapping operations in the 1820's and 1830's (Fig. 4).

The beaver is a stationary mammal, easily trapped, and with a relatively low rate of natural increase. Moreover, like most fur-bearers, beaver are subject to drastic population fluctuations caused by disease or climatic change.[26] These biological cycles and the unbridled exploitation by British and American trappers resulted in a rapid depletion of the beaver reserves in the 1830's. As each reserve was exhausted, the trappers were obliged to spiral out from the most accessible hunting grounds on the Green, Bear, and Snake rivers until, by 1834, only Blackfoot country and the Colorado "Parks" remained worthy of attention.

William Ashley also discovered in 1825 that the Rocky Mountain environment furnished excellent subsistance for his one hundred trappers and their animals. The mountain grasses kept the horses in "a great degree of flesh, strength, and spirits," and the "innumerable herds of Buffaloes, Antelope, and Mountain sheep" provided the meat which, wrote Ashley, "is all our Mountaineers require to ever seem to wish."[27] Provisioning was difficult only in winter, or to the west of the range of the mountain bison in "Starvation country."[28] (Fig. 4)

The Rocky Mountain trapping system functioned only because the trappers were willing to remain in the mountains for extended periods of time.[29] The total reliance on the Euro-American trapper was an innovation in the American fur trade, where the Indian had normally assumed the role of producer. In the Rocky Mountain trapping system the Native American played only a supplementary part, trading furs to the trappers at the rendezvous or providing the trappers with food and shelter during the winter season. There were two main categories of trappers. The "engagés" were supplied and salaried by the company, and the furs which they collected were the sole property of that company.[30] The free trappers, on the other hand, owed allegiance to no single company. They worked alone, or in small groups, and they sold their furs to the highest bidder. In the early 1830's there were several hundred free trappers in the Rocky Mountains and their trade often determined the success or failure of the competing fur companies.

The annual cycle of operations in the Rocky Mountain trapping system commenced in late August or early September when the trappers dispersed for the fall hunt (Fig. 5). At that time of the year the beaver relinquishes his summer mobility in order to concentrate on a home pond, and this sedentariness facilitated trapping. At dusk the traps were placed in shallow water near the entrance to the den or lodge in anticipation of the beaver's nocturnal activity. At dawn the traps were raised, the beaver skinned, and the pelts transported to the camp where they were cleaned, cured, and packed. Frequently the pelts from the fall hunt were "cached" in the ground until the following spring, so reducing the bulk of winter carriage.[31]

The fall trapping season closed in late November when the streams iced over and the beaver was frozen into the lodge. If the fall hunt had been bad the trappers might continue to work throughout the winter using the traditional Indian method of breaking through the roof of the lodge and clubbing the beaver. In general, however, winter was a season of restricted activity when the trappers hibernated in carefully selected sites.

The wintering sites were predominantly located to the west of the continental divide in sheltered valleys that were well stocked with game (Fig. 4). The exposed Great Plains and the desolate country to the west of the bison range were avoided at all costs. The trappers learned through experience, or directly from the Indians, those areas that were most suitable for winter survival: Cache Valley on the Bear River, where, according to trappers' lore, the winter was milder than elsewhere in the mountains;[32] the Colorado Parks; the Blackfoot and Portneuf tributaries of the upper Snake, where the bison herds accumulated in the winter; the Wind River valley; the Salmon River; and the environs of Fort Hall and Flathead Post. In such locations the trapper passed the winter months repairing equipment and clothing, making pemmican, and, if the opportunity arose, trading with the Crow, Flathead, and Shoshone Indians.

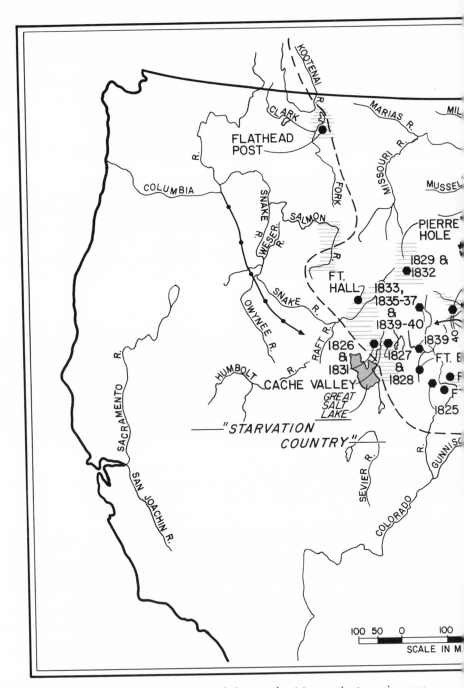

Fig. 4. The spatial organization of the Rocky Mountain trapping system, 1826–1840 (Sources: Ashley Papers, note 25; Russell, notes 31 and 35; Victor, note 31; Ferris, note 32; Morgan and Harris, note 46)

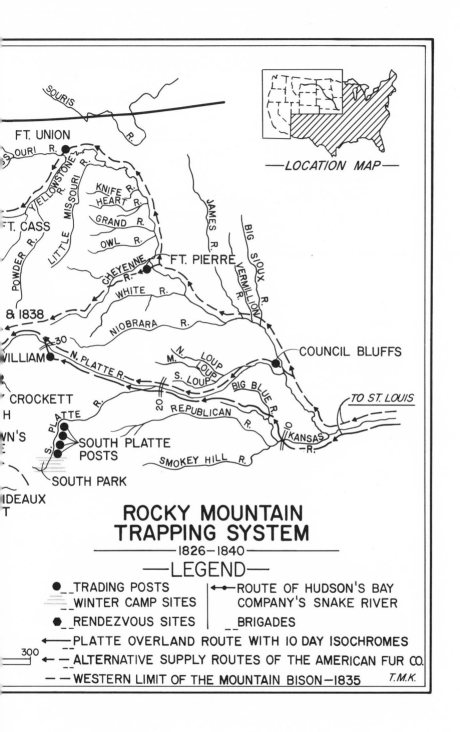

SOURIS R.

FT. UNION

MISSOURI R.

FT. CASS

YELLOWSTONE R.

LITTLE MISSOURI R.

POWDER R.

KNIFE R.

HEART R.

GRAND R.

OWL R.

JAMES R.

BIG SIOUX R.

VERMILLION R.

CHEYENNE R.

FT. PIERRE

WHITE R.

& 1838

NIOBRARA R.

30

WILLIAM

N. PLATTE R.

CROCKETT

H

N. LOUP

M. LOUP

S. LOUP

BIG BLUE R.

COUNCIL BLUFFS

TO ST. LOUIS

WN'S

PLATTE R.

S. PLATTE R.

20

REPUBLICAN R.

KANSAS R.

SOUTH PLATTE POSTS

SMOKEY HILL R.

SOUTH PARK

IDEAUX

T

LOCATION MAP

ROCKY MOUNTAIN TRAPPING SYSTEM
──── 1826–1840 ────
─LEGEND─

● ─ TRADING POSTS
≡ ─ WINTER CAMP SITES
⬣ ─ RENDEZVOUS SITES

←● ─ ROUTE OF HUDSON'S BAY COMPANY'S SNAKE RIVER
─ ─ BRIGADES

←── PLATTE OVERLAND ROUTE WITH 10 DAY ISOCHROMES

300
←─ ─ ALTERNATIVE SUPPLY ROUTES OF THE AMERICAN FUR CO.
─ ─ WESTERN LIMIT OF THE MOUNTAIN BISON─1835

T.M.K.

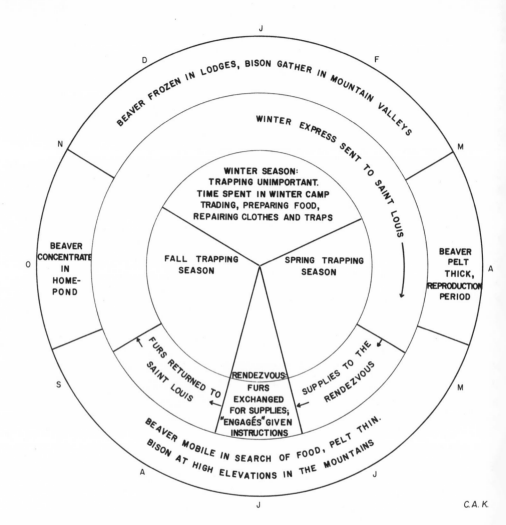

Fig. 5. The annual cycle of operations in the Rocky Mountain trapping system, 1826–1840 (Sources: Russell, note 31; Victor, note 31; Ferris, note 32; Leonard, note 36; Morgan and Harris, note 46; and Devoto, note 59)

The winter season was also the time of year when the express was sent to Saint Louis. The winter express was a tenuous but vital communication link between the producers and the market. The Saint Louis merchants needed mid-season information on the progress of the hunt so that they would inform their agents at the European and East Coast markets of the fur prospects for the following fall. The agents would match these estimates against the orders for furs and, in turn, inform the Saint Louis merchants of the market conditions. In this way a monitor was kept on all parts of the economic system.

The winter express was also used to confirm contracts that had been arranged between the trappers and their suppliers at the previous rendezvous and which were contingent upon the success of the fall hunt. This was the type of agreement that William Ashley made with Smith, Jackson, and Sublette at the 1826 rendezvous. Ashley agreed to supply the partnership with "not less than eight, nor exceeding fifteen thousand dollars" worth of merchandise at the 1827 rendezvous.[33] The arrangement would stand only if the trappers informed Ashley in Missouri by March 1, 1827 that they had taken sufficient furs to justify the contract. David Jackson made a successful hunt on the upper Snake that fall, and William Sublette and Moses Harris crossed the Great Plains in winter and confirmed the agreement.

Trapping re-commenced in spring as soon as the ice melted and the flow of the rivers abated. Spring was the most important trapping season, for the beaver's pelt was still thick from the winter cold. With the progression of the season, however, the quality of the fur deteriorated and trapping became difficult when the beaver began his period of summer mobility. In June or July the trappers moved their furs to a pre-arranged site where they met the annual supply train from Saint Louis.

The rendezvous was an annual trade fair which combined the pragmatism of an economic exchange with the celebration of a social occasion.[34] There the trappers exchanged their furs for provisions, equipment, and, in the case of the company trappers, a salary in the form of a note payable in Saint Louis. Like much of Ashley's system the rendezvous evolved extemporaneously. But from the first informal gathering of Ashley's four trapping parties on Henry's Fork of the Green River in 1825 until the last, diminished meeting in 1840, the rendezvous was the hub and the distinguishing feature of the Rocky Mountain trapping system.[35]

The rendezvous allowed a year's trading to be completed in

a few days without the expense of a fixed trading post. Moreover, unlike a trading post, the rendezvous was flexible and could be held in any location as long as the site provided support for as many as 1,000 trappers and Indians.[36] In the second half of the 1820's the rendezvous was generally held in the environs of Bear Lake, a location that was central to the main area of trapping operations during that period. The rendezvous was moved north-eastward in the early 1830's, symbolizing the shift in trapping emphasis to the east of the continental divide. After 1833 the rendezvous was located in the Green River valley, within easy reach of South Pass and the supply trains which, after 1832, had sacrificed mobility for bulk transportation by replacing horses and mules with wagons drawn by oxen (Fig. 4).

The supply trains followed the route that had been pioneered, if not initially discovered, by Ashley's trappers in 1824. The Missouri newspapers claimed that the Platte overland trail to South Pass was "so broad and easy a way that thousands may travel it in safety, without meeting with any obstruction deserving the name of a mountain" and "better for carriages than any turn-pike in the United States."[37] In reality the route was far more difficult. Wagons had to be hauled with ropes over the dissected terrain on the North Platte and the aridity of the western plains caused the wooden wheels to shrink.[38] Nevertheless, this central route was by far the most effective connection between Missouri and the rendezvous. By the early 1830's, the suppliers Robert Campbell and William Sublette had reduced the time for the outward journey to forty days.

The American Fur Company, which entered the Rocky Moun-tain trapping system in 1830, experimented with alternative supply routes (Fig. 4). Their supplies were taken by steamboat to Council Bluffs, Fort Pierre, or Fort Union, then transported overland by pack-horse to the rendezvous. However, the American Fur Com-pany supply train generally arrived late at the rendezvous and missed the important trade of the free trappers.

This problem of transporting furs and goods over extended distances was the Achilles' Heel of the Rocky Mountain trapping system. Indeed, William Ashley was willing to pay one dollar a pound to have his furs delivered in Saint Louis, where the selling price was rarely more than four dollars a pound.[39] As long as the resource base was sound and the market price remained high, the transportation system sufficed; but when the Rocky Mountain trapping system began to fail after 1834, the costs of operations, and particularly the cost of transportation, became prohibitive.

The Upper Missouri Fur Trade

The most important product of the upper Missouri fur trade was the bison robe, although a diverse array of other furs and skins were traded (Table 1). Beaver pelts had been emphasized in the 1820's but by 1831, according to William Gordon, the beaver had been "extirpated" from the northern Great Plains by over-trapping.[40] Each major trading post continued to employ a trapper, but after 1830 the emphasis clearly shifted to bison robes. From an average of 25,375 robes a year from 1828–1834, production rose to 45,000 robes in 1839 and continued to increase until the 1860's.[41]

The naturalist Seton calculated that the Great Plains had a potential carrying-capacity for forty million bison.[42] The bison subsisted on grama, bluestem, bunch grasses, and, during the winter when the forage was snow-covered, the bark of the sweet cottonwood tree. Ethologists traditionally believed that the bison migrated in large herds following well-defined seasonal patterns, but the current concensus is that the migrations were random movements of small, loosely-knit bands.[43] Edwin Denig, a perceptive trader who was employed at Fort Union from 1837 to 1855 believed that the migrations were erratic and unpredictable: "There is no rule for this" wrote Denig, "the bison migrate and return."[44]

To a great extent the seasonal movements of the bison herds determined both the robe production and the food supply of the upper Missouri fur trade. During mild winters the herds remained on the open plains, remote from the trading posts; but when the winter was severe the bison congregated in the river valleys, seeking the shelter and the forage of the cottonwood groves. In December 1830, for example, Daniel Lamont, the head trader at Fort Tecumseh, informed Pierre Chouteau that the prospects for production were poor because the season was mild and there were no bison herds within reach of the post. The winter worsened in the early months of 1831 and at the end of the season Lamont was able to report an excellent return of robes because "cattle" had been "in the greatest abundance."[45]

The annual cycle of production and, indeed, the entire struc-

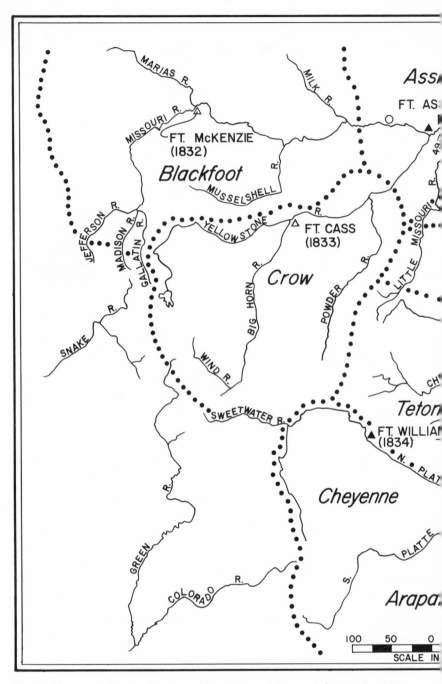

Fig. 6. The spatial organization of the Upper Missouri fur trade, 1826–1840 (Sources: Chouteau Collection, note 13; American Fur Company letterbooks, note 41; Chittenden, volume 3, note 2; A. L. Kroeber,

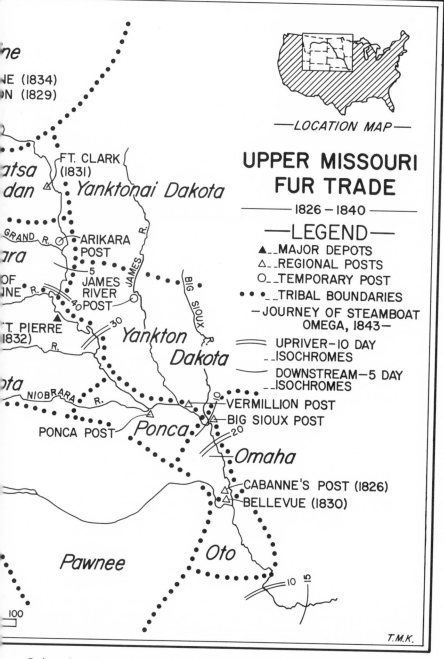

UPPER MISSOURI FUR TRADE

── 1826 – 1840 ──

── LEGEND ──

▲ ── MAJOR DEPOTS
△ ── REGIONAL POSTS
○ ── TEMPORARY POST
• • • ── TRIBAL BOUNDARIES
── JOURNEY OF STEAMBOAT
        OMEGA, 1843 ──
══ UPRIVER – 10 DAY
 ── ISOCHROMES
── DOWNSTREAM – 5 DAY
 ── ISOCHROMES

─ LOCATION MAP ─

T.M.K.

Cultural and Natural Areas of Native North America, University of
California Publications in American Archaeology and Ethnology, 38,
Berkeley, 1939, map supplement)

ture of the upper Missouri fur trade was arranged to accommodate the producers, the Plains Indians (Fig. 6). The fur trade was fitted to the existing patterns of Indian occupancy and the traders worked within those limits to encourage the production of furs. Only winter robes taken from cows and young bulls were sufficiently thick and pliable for the fur trade, although inferior summer robes were produced for the local Missouri market and bison were killed for tongues, tallow, and bones year-round. Robe production was limited not by the number of bison that the Indians could kill but by the number of hides that the Indian women could dress, and twenty robes was a good season's work for one woman. After twenty-one years of observation, Denig concluded that there was no significant decrease in the size of the bison herds. The Indians, Denig wrote, scratched "merely the outskirts of these immense herds," and any reduction in bison population as a result of this hunting was quickly replenished by the high rate of natural increase.[46]

At the fixed trading posts a variety of maintenance, agricultural, and industrial activities was carried on throughout the year, but the production cycle fell clearly into two segments. In fall and winter the Indians were equipped (on credit) and the robes produced; in spring and summer the robes were traded, pressed, and moved to Saint Louis (Fig. 7).

As soon as the ice melted from the Missouri River, trade goods were dispatched by steamboat to the trading posts. The successful introduction of steamboat navigation between Saint Louis and Fort Union in 1831, replacing the onerous and unreliable keelboat, secured the production system for the American Fur Company. Ramsey Crooks wrote to Pierre Chouteau, the man most instrumental in this innovation, "you have brought the Falls of the Missouri as near comparatively as the River Platte was in my younger days."[47] Time-distance was compressed—by 1843 the supply journey to Fort Union took only fifty days, the return trip a mere fifteen (Fig. 6). From the Missouri River trading posts the merchandise and supplies were carried on pack-horses, carts, and keelboats to wherever the Indians requested a trading site.

During the late fall and winter, while the Indians were hunting bison and preparing the robes, the trading posts were isolated and often confronted with serious famine. The only link between the trading posts was by dog-teams, which were used to move food from well-supplied to deficient areas, and the sole communication between the upper Missouri and Saint Louis was the

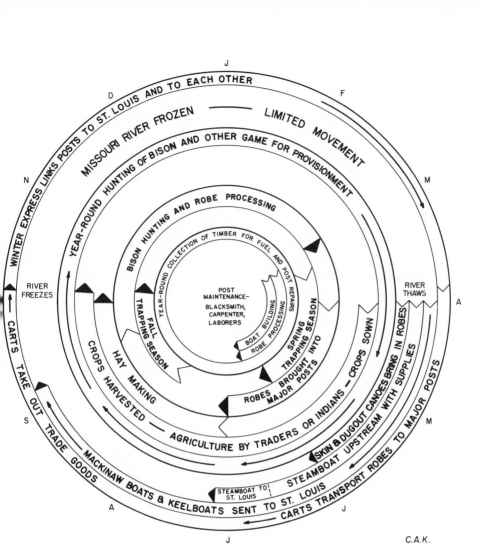

Fig. 7. The annual cycle of operations at the fixed trading posts on the upper Missouri in the 1830's (Sources: Fort Tecumseh and Fort Pierre Letterbooks, and Fort Union Letterbooks, note 17; A. H. Abel, ed., *Chardon's Journal at Fort Clark, 1834–1839*)

winter express. In late December or early January an express, using a dog-sled, was sent from Fort Union to Fort Pierre, there to be met by the express from Saint Louis. The two parties exchanged dispatches and retraced their journeys. Requisitions for trade goods, hunting equipment, seeds, provisions, and employees were returned to Saint Louis, together with detailed estimates of mid-season robe production. The traders on the upper Missouri, in return, were given preliminary market information which would be used to determine the exchange rates for furs in the spring trading.

In the spring, as soon as movement was practical, the robes and furs were transported by the Indians to the regional posts. The Indians were selective and specific in their demands for trade goods, as William Gordon suggested:

> Woolen goods of coarse fabric, such as blue and red strouds, Blankets, etc., constitute the principal and most costly items of trade. . . . The Indians are good judges of the articles in which they deal, and have always given a very decided preference for those of English manufacture—knives, guns, powder, lead and tobacco are also among the primary articles, some of which are of American and some of English manufacture.[48]

Gordon estimated that the exchange of goods gave the trader "a great ostensible profit upon the primary cost, say from two hundred to two thousand per cent."[49] Denig agreed, but he noted that the profit margin was narrowed by the costs and risks of operation:

> The cost of buffalo robes is about $1.35 in cash and we estimate the expenses in men, forts, and animals and other disbursements at $1.20 more each robe which would bring them to $2.25. Now the best sale of a large quantity is $3 each. Therefore, the loss of one or two boats loaded with furs must show a loss on the profits.[50]

Such losses did occur and in 1835, for example, the steamboat *Assiniboine* caught fire just below Fort Clark and a cargo of furs valued between $60,000 and $80,000 was lost. Nevertheless, because the traders derived profits from both the sale of robes and the exchange of goods, because the resource base and market were reliable, and because the transportation system was generally efficient, the upper Missouri fur trade was much more securely grounded than the Rocky Mountain trapping system.

At the Missouri River trading posts the robes were pressed and packed and shipped in mackinaw boats or on the returning steamboat to Saint Louis. There the robes, furs, and skins from the northern Great Plains and the Rocky Mountains were sorted in preparation for transportation to the markets in the eastern United States and Europe.

The National and International Trade Network

In the mid-1830's three routes were used to move the furs to New York (Fig. 8). The traditional method was by steamboat to New Orleans and thence by sea to New York. However, the heat and humidity of the southern summer often damaged the furs, and the "endless, ruinous detention" of quarantine at New Orleans delayed the shipments.[51] Consequently, Ramsey Crooks experimented with alternative routes. In the summer of 1835 the furs were shipped by steamboat on the Ohio River to Pittsburg, then transferred to barges and sent on the Pennsylvania Canal to the east coast. The following summer, the furs were moved from the Ohio River to Buffalo by way of the Ohio Canal, then sent on the Erie Canal to New York.

None of these routes was totally satisfactory. The Ohio and Pennsylvania canals afforded direct passage to New York, but they were often in ill-repair and impassable because of low water or ice. Moreover, the cost of shipment via Pennsylvania was three cents a robe more than on the New Orleans route.[52] A diversified transportation system emerged in the late 1830's. The southern route was preferred in winter, particularly for the high-bulk robes, while the Pennsylvania and Ohio canals were used during the remainder of the year, especially for deerskins and small furs.[53]

The bison robes were marketed in New York, Boston, and Montreal, where they were made into coats, wraps, and blankets. In 1842 Crooks attempted to sell robes in Europe, but they cost 66 per cent more than domestic sheepskins, a comparable product, and the scheme failed.[54] Europe was, however, the primary destination for beaver, muskrat, and other small furs.

In Europe, at the fur marts held each Easter and Michaelmas at Leipzig and London, the American products came into com-

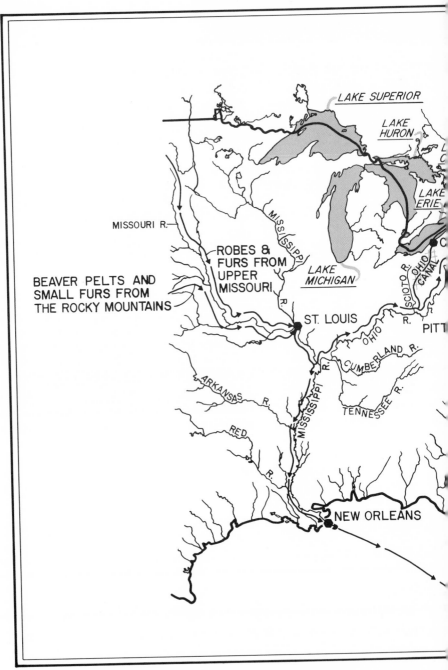

Fig. 8. Routes to the American and European markets, ca. 1835 (Sources: American Fur Company Letterbooks, note 31)

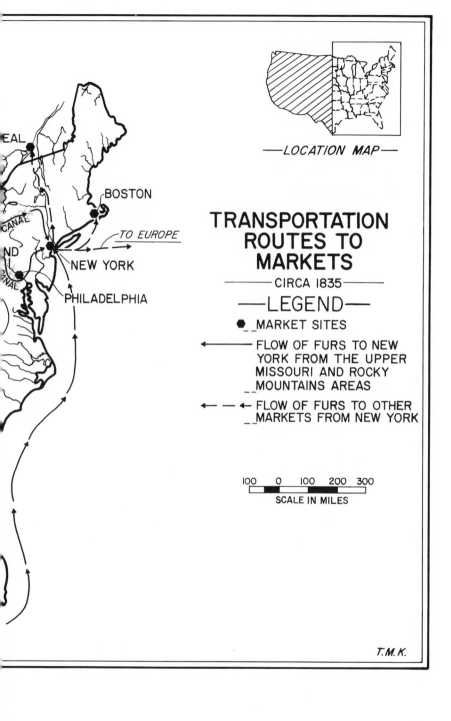

—LOCATION MAP—

TRANSPORTATION ROUTES TO MARKETS

———CIRCA 1835———

—LEGEND—

⬢ _MARKET SITES

⟵——— FLOW OF FURS TO NEW YORK FROM THE UPPER MISSOURI AND ROCKY _MOUNTAINS AREAS

⟵ — ⟵ FLOW OF FURS TO OTHER _MARKETS FROM NEW YORK

```
100    0    100   200   300
████████████████████████
      SCALE IN MILES
```

BOSTON

TO EUROPE

NEW YORK

PHILADELPHIA

EAL

CANAL

ND

NAL

T.M.K.

petition with furs from a wide variety of sources. The Hudson's Bay Company sent beaver, otter, martin, lynx, muskrat, and bear-skins to Europe every year, and nutria were shipped from South America and goat skins from the Cape Colony. Curtis M. Lampson, an independent agent affiliated with the American Fur Company, kept Chouteau and Crooks in perennial contact with the market conditions in Europe. In 1838 and again in 1839, for example, Lampson reported that there would be no demand in Europe for American beaver, otter, and muskrat for the Hudson's Bay Company had inundated the market.[55] Each spring Lampson prepared lists of the furs and skins that were expected to do well at the fall auctions and this information was sent to Crooks and Chouteau. In April 1835, for example, Lampson informed Crooks that there would be a large demand for gray deerskins in London, and in 1837 Lampson reported that the Russian duties on muskrat, raccoon, and bear skins had been reduced and he expected large order for these products from St. Petersburg.[56]

The destination of the furs from the trans-Missouri West was decided only after a thorough, comparative analysis had been made of the market conditions in the Mid-West, on the East Coast, and in Europe. In 1839, for example, there was a large demand for beaver pelts in Missouri. Crooks advised Chouteau to sell only inferior furs locally, for beaver was also in demand in New York, where higher prices could be obtained. A final decision was made to send the pelts to New York where they would be sold if a price of $4.50 a pound was forthcoming; otherwise the furs would be sent to Europe.[57]

The return flow of trade goods through the system began in the factories of Europe, and to a lesser extent New England, and ended with the trapper or the Indian. To fill the orders that the Indians submitted, and to supply the trappers with the tools of their trade, the American Fur Company brought beads and glassware from Trieste, blankets and cloth from Leeds, guns from Birmingham, traps and knives from Sheffield, and vermillion from China.

The entire system was, therefore, closely monitored and tightly organized despite the problems of communication. Consequently, when the Rocky Mountain trapping system began to fail after 1834 Pierre Chouteau responded by withdrawing his investments from that subsystem to concentrate on the robe trade of the Great Plains.

Table 1—Fur Production at Selected Trading Posts, 1834–1835

Post	Production
Fort McKenzie	9000 Robes, 1020 beavers, 40 otters, 2000 muskrats, 180 wolves, 200 red foxes, 1500 prairie dogs, 19 bears, 390 buffalo tongues
Fort Assiniboine	179 red foxes, 1646 prairie dogs, 74 badgers, 269 muskrats, 89 white wolves, 196 white hares, 5 swanskins, 4200 robes, 37 dressed cowskins, 12 dressed calf skins, 450 salted tongues, 3500 lbs. of powdered buffalo meat, 3000 lbs. dried buffalo meat
Fort Union	1970 packs of robes, 4100 lbs. beaver, 4000 fox skins, 9000 muskrats
Fort Cass	450 packs of robes, 1200 lbs. beaver

Sources: Fort Union Letterbooks, Fort Tecumseh and Fort Pierre Letterbooks, op. cit., footnote 17; Larpenteur, op. cit., footnote 22; and Fur Trade Envelope, op. cit., footnote 23.

Note: Fort Assiniboine was a temporary trading site above Fort Union operative only in the 1834–35 season. A pack of robes consisted of ten skins.

Disequilibrium and Re-adjustment, 1834–1840

During the first half of the 1830's the American Fur Company turned its sights to the Rocky Mountains and acquired complete control over the fur trade of the West. Ever conservative, the American Fur Company hesitated before committing itself to the Rocky Mountain trapping system. Chouteau argued against sending an expedition to the mountains in 1828, cautioning that "these enterprises have succeeded well with Gen. Ashley and with him alone."[58] Caution prevailed until 1830. Thereafter the American Fur Company sent annual expeditions to the Rocky Mountains under the capable leadership of Lucian Fontenelle and Andrew Drips, and within a few years they had eliminated the American competitors.

The American Fur Company's strategy was to price the Rocky Mountain Fur Company out of business. Drips and his trappers dogged the footsteps of the Rocky Mountain Fur Company parties, learning the best trapping grounds and luring the trade of the free trappers by offering as much as nine dollars for a beaver pelt that would bring less than half that price in Saint Louis.[59] Chouteau admitted to Astor that "these expeditions have been an annual loss," but, realizing that the Rocky Mountain Fur Company lacked the resources to withstand such competition for long, Chouteau did not "think it politic to abandon this trade."[60]

The strategy was successful. At the 1834 rendezvous, held on Ham's Fork of the Green River, the Rocky Mountain Fur Company merged with Fontenelle, Drips, and Company, the representatives of the American Fur Company. The traveller William Marshall Anderson witnessed this merger and wrote in this diary: "The members of the two rival companies have associated themselves—they hunt and exist now *una anima, uno corpore.*"[61] With Astor's retirement in 1834 the company of Pratte and Chouteau assumed control of the American fur trade of the West, and with Bernard Pratte's withdrawal in 1838 Pierre Chouteau Jr. became the dominant power in both the Rocky Mountain trapping system and the upper Missouri fur trade.

The Rocky Mountain trapping system was, however, a dubious acquisition. The resource base was showing signs of depletion by 1830 and the rapid increase in the number of trappers in the early 1830's hastened the decline in beaver populations. Moreover when the supply train returned to Saint Louis following the 1833 rendezvous, the traders found that the market price for beaver had fallen to $3.50 a pound. This was only the beginning of a precipitous decline that would bring the price down to $2 a pound by 1840.

The core of the Rocky Mountain trapping system, centered on the Green River, had been trapped out in the late 1820's. The Snake River country was deliberately stripped of its furs by the Hudson's Bay Company who wished to create a "fur desert" that would serve as a buffer against American penetration to the Pacific Northwest.[62] Flathead country had been scoured repeatedly by British and American trapping parties and by 1834 was no longer productive. Even Crow country was exhausted by the mid-1830's, the result of continuous trapping by the mountain men and the Crow for more than a decade.

Only Blackfoot country and, to a lesser extent, the Colorado mountains continued to yield furs on a regular basis. In order to ensure safety in the lands of the Blackfoot the trapping parties were expanded into brigades, often consisting of more than 150 men. This raised the overhead costs of trapping operations while the growing distance between the trapping grounds and the rendezvous stretched thin an already extended transportation system. The annual cycle of the Rocky Mountain trapping system was altered as the brigades attempted to cut transportation costs by wintering in Blackfoot country. Jim Bridger continued to lead the Blackfoot brigades until 1838, but by that time the low market price for beaver did not justify the risks and expense of trapping operations.

The trappers recognized the demise of the Rocky Mountain trapping system. In 1835 Warren Ferris observed that "beaver and other kinds of game become every year more rare,"[63] and in 1837 Joe Meek realized that "the beaver was being rapidly exterminated."[64] By the late 1830's the mountain bison had been so seriously depleted that the herds were rarely found west of the continental divide. This compounded the problems of provisioning in the Rocky Mountains.[65] William Ashley had realized that beaver populations fluctuated in regular cycles and he recognized that rest periods of five or six years would replenish the resource base.[66] No attempt was made, however, to place production on a sustained-yield basis. The prevailing frontier attitude to resources and the intense competition between the rival companies prohibited any attempts to conserve the furbearers.

Even if high yields had been sustained the Rocky Mountain trapping system was destined to fail because, after 1834, the market for beaver collapsed. The major reason, as the retiring Astor explained to Chouteau, was that "they now make hats of silk in place of beaver."[67] The increased availability of silk from China, new technologies for felting hats, and the whims of fashion combined to diminish the market for beaver. Lampson's reports from Europe were consistently depressing; even the army cap manufacturers reduced their orders for beaver. The situation was aggravated by the financial panic of 1837 which reduced confidence in American products abroad, and by growing competition from other areas. As Crooks lamented to Chouteau in 1836, "nutria has diminished the consumption of Beaver so much that we fear a decline in the price of that article must be submitted to."[68] In an attempt to offset these losses the suppliers raised the prices of goods at the rendezvous until, in Osborne

Russell's estimation, the trappers were paying 2000 per cent above Saint Louis prices.[69] This was a mere palliative, and in 1838 Chouteau began a systematic withdrawal from the Rocky Mountain trapping system.

At the 1838 rendezvous, held at the confluence of the Wind River and the Popo Agie, "it was rumored among the men that the Company intended to bring no more supplies to the Rocky Mountains and discontinue all operations."[70] The supply trains were sent to the mountains until 1840, but with only one hundred twenty-five trappers in the field the Rocky Mountain trapping system could not, as James Douglas of the Hudson's Bay Company explained, "support such expensive machinery."[71] The system was abandoned and the Rocky Mountain fur trade was left primarily to the British.

A handful of American trappers continued to operate in the Rocky Mountains. They were outfitted from cis-montane trading posts on the South Platte, and from Fort William, Bent's Fort, and Santa Fe. Some short-lived trading posts were established in the Colorado Rockies and served as wintering sites for the trappers. Symbolically, Jim Bridger's establishment in southwest Wyoming was primarily a road-ranch for the emigrants of the 1840's.

The upper Missouri fur trade experienced periodic stress in the 1830's. The devastation of the village tribes on the Missouri River by smallpox, famine, and the constant conflict with the Dakota nomads, reduced the profitability of the trading posts below Fort Pierre. This was more than offset, however, by the extension of trading operations into Blackfoot country in 1831. Thereafter, Fort McKenzie, the Blackfoot post, became the most lucrative trading site on the northern Great Plains.

The upper Missouri fur trade continued to prosper. The transportation system was efficient, the resource base sound, and the market sure. Bison robes were worth six dollars each in 1839 compared to the standard price of three dollars in the early 1820's, and production rose to 90,000 robes a year in the 1840's and 100,000 robes a year in the 1850's and 1860's.[72]

Pierre Chouteau, by withdrawing the American Fur Company from the Rocky Mountains had re-established an equilibrium in the fur trade of the West. The structure of the upper Missouri fur trade, established in the 1820's, remained essentially unchanged until after 1860, when the northern Great Plains were opened for settlement and the bison herds were wantonly exterminated.

Notes

1. R. C. Harris, "Theory and Synthesis in Historical Geography," *Canadian Geographer*, 15 (1971), 163.

2. H. M. Chittenden, *The American Fur Trade of the Far West*, 3 vols. (New York, 1902). In this paper the fur trade of the West includes American trapping and trading operations on the Great Plains north of the Platte River and in the central and northern Rocky Mountains. The upper Missouri is here defined as the Missouri River system above the mouth of the Platte.

3. The information on the use of systems analysis in geography is taken from E. A. Ackerman, "Where is a Research Frontier?," *Annals, Association of American Geographers*, 53 (1963), 81–85; and D. R. Stoddart, "Organism and Ecosystem as Geographical Models," in *Integrated Models in Geography* [ed. by R. J. Chorley and P. Haggett] (London, 1970), pp. 511–48. For a cogent discussion of the uses of systems analysis in history, see R. F. Berkhofer, Jr., *A Behavioral Approach to Historical Analysis* (New York, 1969), pp. 169–210.

4. R. J. Chorley, "Geography as Human Ecology," in *Directions in Geography* [ed. by R. J. Chorley], (London, 1973), pp. 155–169.

5. L. Von Bertalanffy, *General System Theory* (New York, 1968), p. 24.

6. Bertalanffy, p. 24n.

7. H. N. Smith, *Virgin Land: The American West as Symbol and Myth* (New York, 1950), pp. 16–19.

8. M. Lewis to T. Jefferson, September 23, 1806, in *Original Journal of the Lewis and Clark Expedition, 1804–1806* [ed. by R. G. Thwaites] (New York, 1905), 7, p. 335.

9. R. E. Oglesby, *Manuel Lisa and the Opening of the Missouri Fur Trade* (Norman, 1963).

10. T. Biddle to H. Atkinson, 1819 (no exact date), *Indian Trade Papers* (Saint Louis: Missouri Historical Society).

11. A member of the Lewis and Clark Expedition had killed two Piegan in 1806 and, by allying themselves with the Crow (traditionally enemies of the Blackfoot), the American trappers antagonized the Blackfoot.

12. Biddle, footnote 10.

13. The accolade is Washington Irving's and his study of Astoria is the best source of information on that subject. W. Irving, *Astoria* (New York, 1909), p. 362. See also, D. W. Meining, *The Great Columbia Plain: A Historical Geography, 1805–1910* (Seattle, 1968), pp. 1–124.

14. Stuart did not, seemingly, appreciate the significance of South Pass. It is quite possible that a number of trappers knew of the existence of this pass by 1812, but its discovery was not publicized.

15. See N. J. Wyeth, "The Correspondence and Journals of Captain Nathaniel J. Wyeth, 1831–6," *Sources of the History of Oregon* [ed. by F. J. Young] (Eugene, Ore., 1899), Vol. 1, Parts 3–6.

16. The Conventions of 1818 provided for a ten-year joint occupation of the disputed territory to the west of the continental divide and between latitudes 42° north and 54°40′ north. In 1828, Britain and the United States agreed to an indefinite extension of joint occupation.

17. B. O'Fallon to R. Crooks, July 10, 1822, *Chouteau Collection* (Saint Louis: Missouri Historical Society).

18. H. Atkinson to J. C. Calhoun, Secretary of War, January 25, 1822, in *The West of William H. Ashley* [ed. by D. L. Morgan] (Denver, 1964), p. 1. Andrew

Henry had been a partner in Lisa's first Missouri Fur Company. Between 1808–11, Henry had trapped the headwaters of the Missouri and he even crossed the continental divide to the Snake River where he built a short-lived trading post. The fur trade of the west was characterized by a continuity of trappers, who were much more permanent than their companies.

19. For details of this disaster see D. L. Morgan, *Jedediah Smith and the Opening of the West* (Lincoln, 1904), pp. 42–77.

20. Wyeth, footnote 15, pp. 73–4.

21. *The Missouri Republican* (Saint Louis), October 3, 1825; and *The Missouri Intelligencer* (Fayette), September 28, 1826. A pack of beaver generally weighed from ninety to one hundred pounds (40.5 to 45 kg.) and contained about seventy or eighty pelts.

22. An accommodation was finally arranged with the Blackfeet in 1831 when Kenneth McKenzie, the head trader at Fort Union, negotiated a treaty with the Piegan using the old trapper Jacob Berger as a go-between. See C. Larpenteur, *Forty Years a Fur Trader on the Upper Missouri*, ed. by E. Coues (New York, 1898), I, 109–16.

23. J. Dougherty to L. Cass, Secretary of War, November 19, 1831, *Fur Trade Envelope* (Saint Louis: Missouri Historical Society).

24. E. T. Seton, *Life Histories of Northern Animals* (New York, 1910), I, 453. The aspen is the beaver's main source of food and beaver are found at elevations above 10,500 feet in Colorado wherever aspen is available. The optimal gradient of a stream for lodge construction is 0–6%. See E. R. Warren and E. R. Hall, "A New Species of Beaver from Colorado," *Journal of Mammalology*, 20 (1939), 358–67; and A. E. Shaler, "Beaver Food Utilization Studies," *Journal of Wildlife Management*, 2 (1938), 215–22.

25. W. Ashley, Diary, 1825, *Ashley Papers* (Saint Louis: Missouri Historical Society). It is difficult to ascertain the density of beaver populations in these areas. Some idea, however, may be gleaned from a survey of beaver colonies on the upper Snake in 1953–54 which counted 309 colonies on 1593 stream miles (2564 km.). Utah Department of Fish and Game, *Utah Fur-Bearers Management Recommendations and Harvest Report* (Boise, 1953–4).

26. J. M. Cowan, "The Fur Trade and the Fur Cycle: 1825–1857," *British Columbia Historical Quarterly*, 2 (1938), 19–30. A mild winter, for example, would result in a high survival rate of beaver cubs and a large population increase. High population densities would, in turn, leave the beaver vulnerable to the rapid diffusion of epidemics.

27. Ashley, *op. cit.*

28. The Trapper, Tom Fitzpatrick described the distribution of the mountain bison to John C. Fremont, as of 1824: bison were found "in immense numbers over the Green and Bear River valleys, and through all the country lying between the Colorado . . . and the Lewis Fork of the Columbia." J. C. Fremont, *The Expeditions of John Charles Fremont*, ed. by D. Jackson and M. L. Spence (Urbana, 1970), 1, 490–91. See also G. M. Christman, "The Mountain Bison," *American West*, 8 (1971), 44–47.

29. For example, when Jim Bridger returned to Saint Louis for a brief visit in 1839 it was after an uninterrupted stay in the Rocky Mountains of seventeen years.

30. Salaries averaged between $100 and $200 a year, although experienced trappers would command as much as $1000 for a year's work.

31. For detailed descriptions of the trapping process see F. F. Victor, *River of the West* (Hartford, 1870), pp. 64–65; and O. Russell, *Journal of a Trapper, 1834–1843*, ed. by A. L. Haines (Lincoln, 1968), pp. 149–52.

32. W. A. Ferris, *Life in the Rocky Mountains*, ed. by P. C. Phillips (Denver, 1940), pp. 46–47. Climatic data tend to substantiate the trappers' choice of wintering sites. Average January temperatures near Cache Valley and Flathead Lake, for example, are 21°F and 24°F respectively.

33. W. H. Ashley to B. Pratte and Co., October 14, 1826.

34. W. E. Washburn, "Symbol, Utility, and Aesthetics in the Indian Fur Trade," *Aspects of the Fur Trade: Selected Papers of the 1965 North American Fur Trade Conference* (Saint Paul, Minnesota, 1967), pp. 50–54. The rendezvous probably drew from an Indian precedent, for the Shoshone trade fair was held in the valley of the Green River. See J. G. Ewers, "The Indian Trade on the Upper Missouri before Lewis and Clark: An Interpretation," *Bulletin, Missouri Historical Society*, 10 (1954), 429–46.

35. C. P. Russell, "Wilderness Rendezvous Period of the American Fur Trade," *Oregon Historical Quarterly*, 42 (1941), 1–47.

36. Zenas Leonard, for example, estimated that there were 400 white trappers at the Pierre's Hole rendezvous of 1832. Z. Leonard, *Narrative*, ed. by W. E. Wagner (Cleveland, 1904), p. 109.

37. *Saint Louis Enquirer*, March 11, 1826; and the *Missouri Herald and Saint Louis Advertiser*, November 8, 1826.

38. Captain Benjamin Bonneville was the first to take wagons across the continental divide. For an account of the 1832 expedition and the associated problems of transportation, see W. Irving, *The Adventures of Captain Bonneville* (New York, 1886), pp. 24–50.

39. Morgan, p. 308.

40. W. Gordon to H. L. Cass, October 3, 1831.

41. Pratte, Chouteau and Co. to R. Crooks, March 28, 1835. *American Fur Company Letterbooks, 1831–1849* (New York: New York Historical Society).

42. Seton, 1, 259n.

43. See, for example, E. Park, *The World of the Bison* (Philadelphia and New York, 1969).

44. E. T. Denig, *Indian Tribes of the Upper Missouri*, ed. by J. N. B. Hewitt. Forty-Sixth Annual Report of the Bureau of American Ethnology, 1928–29 (Washington, D.C., 1930), p. 463.

45. D. Lamont to P. Chouteau Jr., December 30, 1830; and D. Lamont to P. Chouteau Jr., April 4, 1831. *Fort Tecumseh and Fort Pierre Letterbooks*.

46. Denig, p. 462n. This issue is controversial. William Marshall Anderson, a traveller with Sublette's supply train to the 1834 rendezvous, was told by experienced mountaineers that the "diminution of the buffaloe" was "very considerable." It is possible that the erratic migrations of the herds might have resulted in such conflicting conclusions. D. L. Morgan and E. T. Harris (Eds.), *The Rocky Mountain Journals of William Marshall Anderson* (San Marino, 1967), p. 178.

47. R. Crooks to P. Chouteau Jr., November 16, 1832, *Fort Pierre Letterbooks*.

48. W. Gordon to General W. Clark, October 17, 1831.

49. *Ibid*.

50. Denig, p. 460n.

51. R. Crooks to Pratte, Chouteau and Co., June 15, 1835.

52. *Ibid.*

53. Pratte, Chouteau and Co., to R. Crooks, July 1, 1835.

54. M. F. Klauche to R. Crooks, May 3, 1842.

55. R. Crooks to W. Brewster, December 31, 1839.

56. C. M. Lampson to R. Crooks, April 23, 1835; and C. M. Lampson to B. Clapp, January 28, 1837.

57. R. Crooks to P. Chouteau Jr., Aprill 22, 1839; and P. Chouteau Jr. to R. Crooks, July 5, 1839.

58. P. Chouteau Jr. to K. McKenzie, April 25, 1828, *Fort Union Letterbooks.*

59. For a brilliant and readable analysis of the Rocky Mountain trapping system in its waning years, see B. DeVoto, *Across the Wide Missouri* (Boston, 1947).

60. Quoted in Russell, p. 26n.

61. Morgan and Harris, p. 173n.

62. According to James Douglas of the Hudson's Bay Company, the Snake River country was "no longer capable of supporting a numerous body of hunters" by 1839. E. E. Rich (ed.), *McLoughlin's Fort Vancouver Letters* (Toronto, 1941–44), p. 225.

63. Ferris, p. 229n.

64. Victor, p. 237n.

65. Fremont, p. 491n.

66. W. Ashley to T. H. Benton, November 12, 1827, in Morgan, p. 178n.

67. Quoted in Chittenden, p. 364n.

68. R. Crooks to Pratte, Chouteau and Co., July 6, 1836.

69. Russell, p. 60n.

70. *Ibid.*, p. 91n.

71. Rich, p. 256n.

72. J. E. Sunder, *The Fur Trade on the Upper Missouri, 1840–1865* (Norman, 1965), p. 17.

Frontier Settlement in Eastern Ontario in the Nineteenth Century: A Study in Changing Perceptions of Land and Opportunity

Brian S. Osborne

THE PRIMARY PURPOSE of this study is to investigate the progress of settlement and development of a specific region in eastern Ontario.[1] But apart from illustrating the factors operating in an unique region, it is also hoped that principles of more general application and relevance will also be underscored. To this end, particular attention will be focussed upon the various levels of decision making and their motives; contemporary evaluations of success or failure of the various policies; and the influence of changing assessments of the environment upon the determination of the potential for settlement. In order that some of the propositions may be examined in the context of a specific frontier experience, the progress of settlement in the counties of Frontenac, Lennox, and Addington will be examined. The latter may be taken as constituting the hinterland of an important nineteenth-century Ontario urban center, Kingston.

Initial Assumptions

Frontier areas are usually defined in terms of their isolation, the absence of linkages with the metropolis, the general underdevelopment of the region and low population densities.[2] Given a combination of these factors, it is to be expected that the general experience of occupying such areas and making them productive was a demanding one, requiring much human effort and sacrifice. It was these demands which made the experience so distinctive for the participants. Indeed, it could be argued that settlers on the frontier experienced a recapitulation of the general social development from the state of "barbarism" to that of "civilization," a recapitulation which was often unique to each specific region.

Success or Failure

The progress of such a region from the condition of peripheral

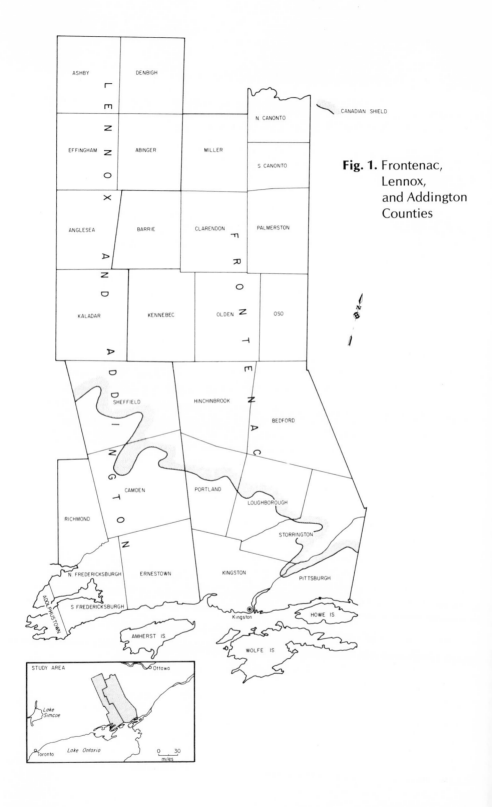

Fig. 1. Frontenac, Lennox, and Addington Counties

"wilderness" to that of economic development and social maturity has often been represented as being marked by a series of stages.[3] The initial evaluation of the region as a potential field for colonization is followed by deliberations whether or not to exclude, temporarily to reserve, or to maximize the distribution of land and resources to potential settlers and developers. Given a decision in favor of development, continuity of occupance suggests that the pioneers have successfully established a diversified subsistence system, have linkages with external markets for their economic staples, or some combination of both. With these demands met, the integration of the nuclear family settlements into communities and the development of various social, economic, and political institutions to serve the region is allowed to proceed.

Implicit in many evaluations of this process is that continuity of occupance is the prime indicator of success and that population density is its best measure.[4] But measures of an increase in population or the expansion of the settled area may be inadequate surrogates of successful settlement. Perhaps more pertinently, any evaluation of the success or failure of settlement and colonization schemes should take into consideration the original objectives of the colonization and the welfare of the settlers who participated.[5]

The interpretation here is that the continued vitality of the settled area suggests that the needs of both the sponsoring agency and the settlers are being met. The interests of the latter could be economic, cultural, social, political, or even spiritual; but they must always be accompanied by the attainment of an adequate basis for subsistence. Failure to attain these objectives, therefore, would be attended by abandonment and depopulation of the area. In making this point it is noted that a common denominator of frontier areas, even those considered to be successful, is a high rate of individual failure and consequent personal loss and suffering. Indeed, it may be taken as the definitive feature of the frontier settlement experience. However, a low rate of retention of settlers and an associated high rate of turnover was not incompatible with a successful scheme. The survival of a small demographic nucleus could provide for the future infilling of the area being colonized. Moreover, any assessment of mobility rates in frontier areas must take into consideration the rates of mobility characteristic of the other rural and urban areas of the society.

In other cases, however, the objectives were not necessarily pro-settlement and cannot, therefore, be evaluated by demographic indicators. Policies for the development of resources were concerned with maximizing production of primary products and were frequently opposed to settlement promotion. Moreover, since lumber and minerals were susceptible to depletion, they were usually transitory experiences. Assessment of the effectiveness of policies for these enterprises in frontier areas are better effected with reference to revenues generated, yields and outputs of commodities, and the adequacy of resource management rather than in terms of population increase. Finally, the developers of such resources were often antipathetic to the promotion of agrarian settlement which was often represented as being in conflict with the effective development of their interests.

The investigation of the settlement of the study area will concern itself with the expressed objectives of the settlement policies and will take as measures of the implementation of these policies the evidence provided by land patenting and population data. By plotting the location of lands patented from the Crown, an indication of the periodicity and spread of settlement is possible (see Figs 2–5). But patenting often took place several years after initial location on the land, while in other cases it was never attended by occupation of the land and was more an indication of speculation than settlement. The patent maps must be considered as only a general indicator of the settlement process, therefore, although their interpretation allows some insights into interests other than settlement in the region. The effective settlement of a region is a problem of actually locating people on the lands rather than a legal process of merely distributing titles and the latter must be evaluated in the context of information on the number of people introduced into the area and the length of their tenure. But while any critical evaluation of the development of a frontier must be concerned with measures of success or failure, it is insufficient to assign simple demographic criteria alone. Rather, these must be evaluated in the context of the specific objectives of the day, taking into account the various motives and aspirations of the parties involved.

Levels of Decision Making

At each stage of development, decisions were made with regard to the viability of any potential development and the direction which this should take according to the contemporary perceptions of the land, the needs of society in general, and the aspirations of

specific groups and individuals. Three major levels of such decision making may be recognized: the state, local municipalities
and business interests, and individual citizens.

First, ideally the state was concerned with national best interests and was motivated by considerations of national strength,
political security, economic well being, and, in some cases, cultural heritage. The frontier, being by definition an undeveloped
region, constituted a veritable *tabula rasa* upon which the contemporary models of the ideal development could be developed
and which may be taken as indicators of the objectives of the
state. The extent to which these objectives were less concerned
with the ideals of "national good" and were manipulated to the
advantage of more precisely defined groups is another dimension
of this question.

Second, operating within the general development policies
established by the state, and frequently attempting to direct it to
their own best interests, were the entrepreneurs, business men,
and "men of capital."[6] While these "mercantile capitalists" were
enthusiastic advocates of the opportunities for investment afforded by the frontier, the actual mode of development favored
depended upon the specific resources and the period of development. Metropolitan based, their influence is often identifiable in
the rhetoric and boosterism of railroad promotion, land speculation ventures, and advocacy of programs of general expansion
and national progress.

Finally, the individual citizen, as a pioneer and settler, was
generally motivated by opportunities for bettering his own material, social, or spiritual lot. His evaluations of the system however, were seldom verbalized or, at least, recorded for posterity.[7]
For the most part, he remains a faceless, anonymous factor, and
one with which the state and entrepreneurial interests were concerned only as the means by which their ends of national or corporate strength could be attained. He was always referred to in
terms of gross numbers or overall contribution to national or
regional progress, and attention was seldom paid to the actual
conditions to be expected by the settler. If described at all, the
experience was described as a morally and economically salutory
one, with but little concern for the actual hardships to be encountered. The rhetoric of promotion was seldom countered by
any more objective evaluation to which the prospective settler
could turn for advice.

The interests of the three levels may be discerned in the study area during the 1783–1880 period. As part of British North America, the region was subjected to controls and directives from imperial, national, and provincial centers, each having a characteristic emphasis in its policies. Moreover, the presence of an urban center, Kingston, added the dimension of local municipal interests in developing the hinterland. Functioning as a military, commercial, and administrative center, Kingston was an important element in Ontario society for much of the nineteenth century. Its relative decline in the nineteenth century occasioned a strident concern for ventures which promised to develop the hinterland and thus benefit local business interests and the community in general.[8] Finally, the settlers themselves have left but little record of their attitudes and sentiments although the evidence of their actions is to be found in the actual extent and intensity of the settlement which they affected.

The Environment

In any settlement study, but most especially that of a frontier area, the nature of the physical environment is most important. While attention must be focussed on the human agencies involved in the process of settling the frontier, the nature of the land being developed must also be taken into consideration. A passive element in the decision-making process, evaluation of its significance varied according to the attitudes and interests of the various parties involved. In some cases, the concern was simply whether or not the land could accommodate the settlers at a subsistence level, so providing a demographic core for later growth. In other cases, the evaluation was a more precise one specifically related to particular crops and products and based upon assumptions of market demands and technology of production. Finally, contemporary reports of the potential for settlement varied from the one extreme of first-hand accounts and observations by surveyors and settlers to the more interpretative, and often deceptive, writings of those attempting to proselytize the settlement opportunities.

The study area consists of a unique juxtaposition of the two primary elements of the Ontario environment, the glaciated lowland and the Canadian Shield.[9] Located at the eastern end of the Great Lakes, the counties extend inland a hundred miles to the north of Lake Ontario. The southern lake littoral of the region consists of a low-lying limestone plain which alternates between extensive sections of lacustrine-glacial deposits and bare outcrops

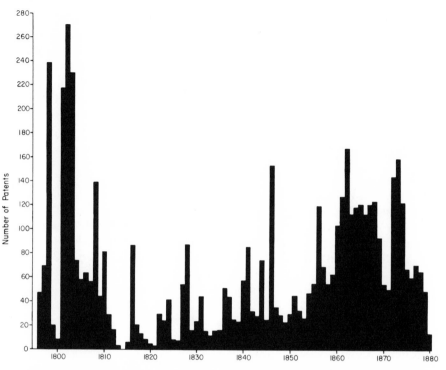

Fig. 2. Land Patenting in Frontenac, Lennox, and Addington Counties, 1792–1880

of limestone pavement. Of some significance to the settlement history of the area is the fact that within a dozen miles of the lake shore, this plain is limited by a southern extension of the Canadian Shield which is here known as the Frontenac Axis. Consisting of igneous and metamorphic outcrops of granites, gneisses, and schists, the topography is one of local high relief with rocky outcrops separated by low-lying swamps. Whereas for much of the province, the contact with the Shield was delayed until the second half of the nineteenth century, settlers in the study area had the dubious distinction of encountering this region of "ridges and swails" at an early date. It is the changing evaluations and associated strategies for development of these lands which is a central theme of this study.

The Settlement Process

The chronological and spatial distributions of patenting suggest three distinct periods in the spread of settlement throughout Kingston's hinterland. Each of these periods experienced changing emphases in the land policy and, moreover, were associated with markedly different environments locally.

1783–1814: Relocation, Reward, and Preservation

The initial settlement of the study area was associated with the American War of Independence and the defeat of the British Loyalist cause, an event which greatly influenced the ensuing policy of development. As early as 1784, of the 50,000 Loyalists and military personnel who had been forced or impelled to migrate to the rump area of British North America, some 6,152 were located in the western part of Quebec with nearly 4,000 of these being located around Kingston and the adjoining Bay of Quinte of Lake Ontario.[10]

The initial concern was finding suitable lands to accommodate these displaced persons and the British policy was very much concerned with both relocating and rewarding the loyalists. With the partition of the former province of Quebec into Upper and Lower Canada in 1791, this principle was extended to those still resident in the United States in an attempt at luring population to the new colony. In the words of the new Lieutenant Governor, Sir John Graves Simcoe:

> The great mutual blessings of superior soil and of climate, British freedom, British Union and the experienced loyalty of those who inhabit this province will speedily raise it up to an unexampled height of prosperity and permanent security.[11]

Not only were free grants made to the military and the loyalists but whole townships were also allocated in an attempt at sponsoring a resident squirearchy on the British model. Furthermore, the support of the government and the established church was provided for by the reservation for rental of two-sevenths of the lots of each township as Crown and Clergy reserves.[12] For the first generation of settlement, therefore, the colonial objective was clearly articulated: the establishment of a new colony, loyal to the British crown, in the western lands of British North America.

Its characteristic features were the relocation of a population loyal to the Crown, the rewarding of this population's loyalty by land grants, and a concern for establishing the social and political fabric of a British society.

The lands in the southern section of Frontenac, Lennox, and Addington, fronting onto Lake Ontario, were chosen as one of the locales for the reception of the loyalists. Military surveyors had been dispatched to discover lands conducive to settlement and a propitious evaluation reported that ". . . the (climate) is very mild and good, and I think the Loyalists may be the happiest in America by settling the country from Long Sou to Bay of Quinty . . . ," while the lands fronting onto Lake Ontario were said to be "Of an excellent Quality fit for the production of Wheat, Oats, Indian Corn, Hemp, Timothy, and Clover."[13] Thus, the front ranges of townships were opened for settlement and at the very outset severence of lands proceeded apace with the initial allocations being made by lottery according to the military rank and social status of the recipient.[14] Moreover, the Simcoe policy continued the practice of extensive and free grants to prospective settlers, provided they were "loyal." For some of these "Simcoe loyalists," allegiance to the Crown was realized a trifle late and possibly prompted by the generosity of the land grants. Figure 2 demonstrates the rapid severence of land during this period while Figure 3 illustrates the concentration in the front townships along the Lake Ontario littoral.

With regard to the extent of the area being made available to settlement at this time, the restriction of activity to some twenty miles inland reflected both the contemporary transport system and also the nature of the lands being encountered in the interior. Communications were focussed on the Great Lakes–St. Lawrence water routeway and land transport linkages with the main metropolis, Montreal, were but poorly developed. Furthermore, contact with the interior was much neglected and settlers within a dozen or so miles of the lake front were quite isolated.[15] Moreover, this isolation was also exacerbated by another factor, the presence of the Shield. The initial surveys of the region reported that the lands to the east of Kingston were ". . . exceeding bad, being a constant succession of stoney Ledges and sunken Swamps altogether unfit for Cultivation,"[16] and, accordingly, these lands were not laid out for settlement. While the next decade witnessed their inclusion in the area made available for settlement, the surveyor of the rear of Pittsburgh abandoned his task in 1792

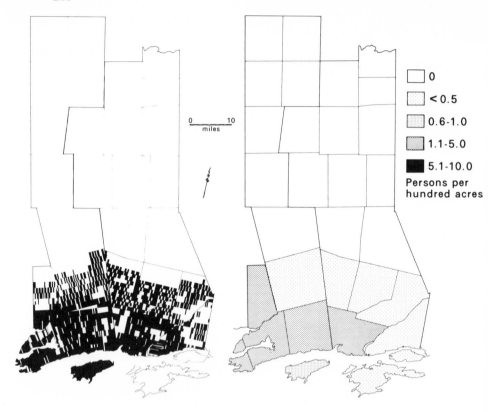

Fig. 3. Patenting, 1792–1814   **Fig. 4.** Population, 1819

because the land was so bad that "I would be putting government to a useless expense to Survey lands that never will be settled."[17] Similarly, an 1808 survey reported that ". . . at least two thirds of the Land in Camden and Portland cannot settle, being either Swamps or Rocks, in many places there is nothing growing except small Ironwood and Elm Timber with Juniper Berries."[18] These lands were, therefore, witheld from settlement and the initial distribution of lands was confined to those townships laid out over the glaciated limestone plain.

If the legal severence of land was substantial, much of the land was left unimproved and even unoccupied. Large quantities fell into the hands of members of the new social hierarchy and both

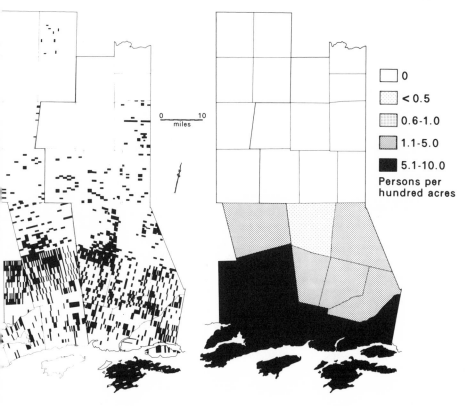

Fig. 5. Patenting, 1815–1852   **Fig. 6.** Population, 1851

absentee landlords and speculators flourished.[19] Furthermore, the
checkerboard pattern of the patent maps underscores the ubiquity
of the reserved lands which continued as wild and undeveloped
units, contributing but little revenue to the support of the church
and state. It was characteristics such as these which served to
make the initial period of settlement a "hollow frontier," more
real on paper than on the ground. Certainly the population of the
area had increased from the 3,776 persons of 1784 to approximately 17,000 by 1815.[20] However, while much of the land had
been allocated to individuals, population densities of less than 5
persons per hundred acres throughout the region, and even less
than 0.5 persons per hundred acres in the second range of town-

ships emphasize the high land-to-man ratios of the period. (See Figure 3.)

But while not experiencing spectacular growth, the initial policy objectives had been realized with a new and viable outpost of the British empire established in North America. Moreover, the basic concept of land use had been established with an agrarian, pro-settlement policy being developed for those areas deemed suitable for grain production. Elsewhere, in the undivided extent of Crown lands to the north, it had been declared that timber, gold, silver, coal, tin, iron, lead, and, in fact, all "singular advantages of a common and public nature," were protected for the Crown.[21] In the Kingston area, these Crown domain lands severely restricted the available area of settled land.

1815–1852: Settlers or Lumber

While politico-military decisions regarding the defense and security of the colony continued to be important considerations for another half century, increasingly the concern of both the imperial and domestic administrations was the promotion of settlement and the nurturing of a viable economy and community. This period, therefore, witnessed the progress of the new colony from a state of government-sponsored settlement to a more spontaneous growth associated with the expansion of the occupied area and an involvement in the export of staple commodities as part of the imperial mercantilist system.[22] In particular, the burgeoning population and the ever-increasing involvement in the wheat staple occasioned pressure upon the lands surveyed and available for settlement. Moreover, in the areas already opened for settlement, it was widely recognized that the benevolence of the Dorchester and Simcoe years had approached extravagance. Patenting had not been accompanied by proportionate settlement and development, much land being held by speculators and absentee owners.[23] These factors, therefore, motivated a demand for an expansion of the entire system and a reform of the land distribution process.

The reaction to the former abuses and deficiencies of the old system was to establish a new policy which taxed wild lands as an inducement to improvement, created land boards throughout the various districts to advertise the lands and encourage settlement, and to emphasize the sale of lands rather than the awarding of free grants.[24] Finally, both Crown and Clergy reserves which had been witheld for settlement and which accounted for two-sevenths of the area of each township were made available to settlers. With these developments, the existing area of settlement experienced an overall population increase, a greater density of population, and a general infilling of the available lots. These developments are illustrated by the pattern of distribution of the dates of first patents for the period in Figure 3. First, a clear component is the infilling of the "chequerboard" pattern as the Clergy and Crown reserves were settled. Second, the settlement of Wolfe and Howe islands represents the surrendering of a relict seigneurial claim to these areas and their granting in "free and common socage" tenure.

The demands for extending the total area available for settlement were met by the surveying of new townships out of the residual lands to the north which were held by the Crown and leased to the lumber interests. In the Kingston area, the need for an extension of the settled area was recognized by the grand jury which recommended the construction of four roads to Hinchinbrooke, Kennebec, Kaladar, and Madoc respectively, "the more effectually to arrive at some plan for opening the back Townships . . ."[25] Such developments would extend the potential settled area some twenty miles inland and open up an area which had been "long since surveyed but no settlement has hitherto been attempted."[26]

Figure 4 represents the patenting of new lands throughout the interior townships to the north of Storrington, Loughborough, Portland, and Camden during this period, especially in those sections which had benefited from the construction of new roads. Other more isolated lots away from these clusters reflect more adventurous pioneers or, in some cases, speculators in lumber. One identifiable group acquiring land in advance of the frontier line, and not necessarily involved in agriculture, consisted of the surveyors who received grants of land as their ". . . share of Land according to Contract for the survey of the said Township."[27] Thus, one Samuel Benson patented some 2,800 acres in the township of Bedford and 3,050 acres in the township of Sheffield, the allocated acreage being 3 3/4 per cent of the area surveyed.[28] Obviously not involved in actively farming these 6,000 acres, men such as these became important speculators in land and possibly lumber. Finally, it should be noted that, while not represented by patenting, "squatting" was taking place in areas not opened for settlement and which were reserved as accommodation lands for the native peoples and revenue-generating lands for lumber activity. Such was the extent of such pre-emption that the provincial government passed, in 1839, "An Act for the Protection of the Lands of the Crown in this Province from Trespass and Injury."[29]

But while both infilling of the existing, and extension of the new, settled areas occurred, and while the population of the study area continued to increase, the Kingston area did not experience the growth of other sections of the province. Between 1815 and 1853, the population of the province increased from approximately 100,000 to close to one million people. In the same period, the population of Kingston's hinterland grew from 17,000 to over 90,000.[30] Moreover, by the close of this period, the lake littoral townships appeared to be approaching the point of complete settlement. Not only had most of the land been patented and severed, but assuming an average family size of five persons and a model farm unit of 100 acres, the population densities of between 5 and 10 persons per hundred acres suggest that maximum occupation was being reached. The range of township platted along the Shield boundary continued to display lower densities, however, while others to the north of the Bedford, Hinchinbrook Sheffield line were witheld from settlement. The proximity of the Shield was increasingly asserting itself as an influential factor in limiting the extent of settlement in the region.

With continued contact with this demanding environment, government surveyors could report that while much of the land was ". . . entirely unfit for settlement being very hilly, rocky, and much broken with Lakes,"[31] settlement was thought to be possible on the pockets of good land throughout the region. Surveyor Elmore's report on Oso township in 1826 may be regarded as typical of the prevailing evaluations of such lands which were being submitted to the provincial government:

Oso cannot be considered to possess any or at least not many advantages superior to those of Olden and Kennebec. . . . as the principal part of the land in it is particularly rocky and uneven, especially the high lands, the low lands are principally swamps and generally dead and sunken nature. There are, however, some lots which will admit of improvement and are well adapted to agricultural pursuits, but being in general surrounded with rough rocky and uneven land, and in some instances with impassable swamps, no very extensive improvements or settlement can ever be anticipated.[32]

But some settlement was possible in such areas and another report of an adjoining township, Hinchinbrook, stated that

> Notwithstanding so large a portion is unfavorable to settlement, there are numerous small tracts of good land scattered here and there in different parts which from an acquaintance with what is now occupied, I believe would be settled upon if the class of settlers who usually locate these back parts had access to them.[33]

That this surveyor could report that there were "upwards of seventy families, actual settlers" located in Hinchinbrook and the surveyor of Bedford that there were "many persons desirous of settling"[34] were testaments to the possibility of selective, if arduous, pioneering throughout the shield.

Promotional interests based in Kingston arrived at even more optimistic evaluations of the potential of their local area. Arguing from the premise that "The extensive trade carried on at Toronto is maintained by the rich country in the rear of it," promoters claimed that a "well settled back country would greatly promote the prosperity of this City."[35] In 1835, the formation of the Midland District Land Company had as its objective the stimulation of local settlement[36] while contributors to the local newspapers waxed enthusiastic and poetic on the attributes of the local region:

> But let emigrants to equal distances from Kingston for good lands that they do there (Toronto), and they shall find such as would surprise them. Let them pass the gloomy woods of Portland, and open their eyes on the fine lands in Hinchinbrooke, Holden etc. not forgetting many parts of Loughborough, with their small crystal lakes of countless numbers, their rivers and rivulets, and springs, not of muddy and stagnant waters, but clear as Ferentosh, and all abounding with fish. The very sight of the timber itself, without putting a spade in the ground, is sufficient to convince any judge of the fertility of the soil.[37]

It was rhetoric such as this that was directed at the potential settlers passing through the region during the period. But having observed the nature of the environment while travelling along the Rideau Canal, and having in mind the model of a wheat-producing farm, few were induced to stay, and the main stream of immigration moved to more amenable areas to the west.

The official government attitude towards the allocation of lands

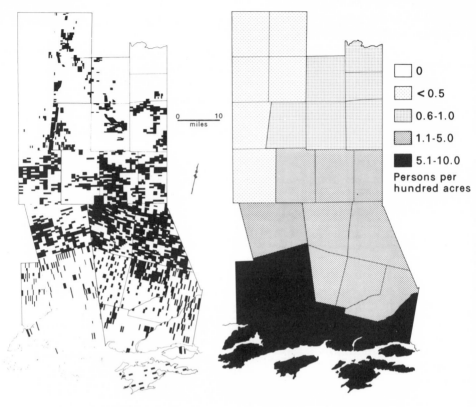

Fig. 7. Patenting, 1853–1880   **Fig. 8.** Population, 1881

for development during this period, therefore, reflected the dominance of agrarian interests in the society. The undeveloped Crown Lands were allowed to remain the realm of the lumbermen and miners so long as they were not required to accommodate agricultural settlers. The separation of the two systems was formalized by the line separating the surveyed from the unsurveyed, a line which was constantly being pushed inland to the north. A local variation of this policy was experienced by the Kingston area, however. In it, unlike other areas of the province to the west, the expansion of the agricultural area encountered the Canadian Shield and the problems associated with settling it at an early date. The initial reaction was to conclude that much of it was inimical to effective agricultural occupation and production. At a time when extensive areas conducive to commercial agriculture were still available elsewhere throughout the province, the Shield lands were thought to be best reserved for lumber and mineral exploitation. Settlement of the Kingston hinterland, therefore, was severely curtailed. It was of some interest for the ensuing period, however, that both the rhetoric of local business interests and the more prosaic actions of pioneer squatters throughout the Shield argued for the possibility of the selective settlement of the Shield by farmers.

1853–1880: Settlement of the Shield

With continued population growth and immigration, demand for farms increased throughout the province in the second half of the nineteenth century. Accordingly, attention was directed to the lands of the Shield, lands which had originally been rejected but which were now reappraised in terms of their potential for settlement. The passage of the Public Lands Act of 1853 provided for the construction of colonization roads into the interior and the granting of free lands to those who chose to settle along their route.[38] Continued pressure for agricultural land resulted in the Free Grants and Homestead Act of 1868 which further expanded the colonization road scheme and also opened a further forty townships throughout the Shield country to settlement.[39] Whereas the former policy had been one of separating the two land uses of agriculture and lumbering by assigning them to the southern and northern sections of the province respectively, the new policy, therefore, was one of integrating them into a symbiotic relationship. This, together with the provision of transport linkages with the markets to the south, would ensure the success of such an agrarian policy for the Shield lands.

The actual survey and exploration of these northern townships had reported that the rear townships were generally "uneven and much broken by rocky hills and swamps interspersed however with cultivable and fertile tracts of land."[40] The surveyors noted that where settlement had already occurred, crops of wheat, oats, corn, potatoes, turnips, and so forth, were grown but that the land was generally "better adapted for grazing and pasture than other kinds of farming."[41] Particular attention was directed to the many natural meadows of "Beaver Hay" that fringed the lakes and rivers. These were used by lumbermen and settlers for summer pasture and winter fodder and it was anticipated that "A large portion of this tract will no doubt be purchased for the meadow alone, besides these only small patches of arable land are to be met with in this section."[42] Even so, in 1864 a report described half of Palmerston, the northern two-thirds of Clarendon, and the western half of Miller and Canonto as being suited to settlement.[43] The pockets of potentially productive land throughout the Shield had been recognized earlier but had been considered unsuited to settlement because of their isolation. The construction of roads and the increase in lumbering activities in these townships made the settlement of the suitable land an economically viable proposition. The decision regarding the potential of Frontenac's most northerly township, Miller, may be taken as representative of the attitude towards these rear townships:

> The facilities which will be afforded for transport by the Mississippi and Frontenac roads when completed, passing through a healthy section of country; the land tolerably good, building materials in abundance; a sufficient supply of water power for manufacturing purposes; a ready market for the surpluses produced of the settlers, and employment for themselves and teams during the winter months at the lumbering settlements; serve to render Miller and the adjacent townships as desirable a field for settlement, as this part of the country affords.[44]

As may be expected, the Kingston-based interests echoed these positive appraisals and anticipated significant benefits from the development of the lands to the rear. Lands would be made productive, immigrants attracted, new communities formed and "Kingston, being one of the foremost markets in the province, such a tract of land would be of great value if it were brought under cultivation."[45] Throughout the period, letters to the editor and editorials in the local newspapers reiterated the view that "The people of Kingston and in fact of the United counties are deeply interested in the opening up of . . . a tract of the finest land in Central Canada."[46] With such concurrence between provincial and local interests, the northern townships of Kingston's hinterland experienced the introduction of agrarian interests into an area formerly reserved for lumbermen.

The pattern of settlement revealed by the distribution of patents in the period following 1853 clearly demonstrates the opening up of the rear townships, to the north of the Bedford, Hinchinbrook, and Sheffield line (see Figure 5). The initial concentration was along the route of the Addington colonization road running through Barrie, Abinger, and Denbigh and the Frontenac road through the townships of Olden, Clarendon, and Miller. These north-south roads to the headwaters of the Ottawa River system were complemented by the east-west running Lavant road through Palmerston and Clarendon. Patenting of lands away from the roads was effected under the aegis of the 1868 Act. But while Sheffield, Hinchinbrook, and Bedford experienced a significant burgeoning of their population by the close of the study period to 2591, 1322, and 2019 respectively, none of the dozen townships to the north attained populations of more than a thousand people and all were featured by densities of less than 1 person per 100 acres.[47] Indeed, most of them were to experience much abandonment and accompanying loss of population over the next two decades with population peaks being reached in the early twentieth century.[48] For many of the pioneers of this section of the Shield of Eastern Ontario, one generation of clearing the land and attempting to establish a livelihood was enough to underscore the essential limitations of isolation and the environment. More remarkable than the abandonment, in fact, is the continued presence of others throughout the region in the face of the same obstacles.

The move to settle the rear townships of the Ottawa-Huron tract manifests the synchronization of several institutional agencies. The provincial government's concern for extending the ecumeme of the province was in harmony with, and was largely generated by, the popular demand for land. Moreover, this move north was to be facilitated by a change in emphasis in the allocation of land between the two major economic enterprises, agriculture and lumber. Previously separated into two distinct zones of the province, they were now to be integrated into one economic system to the mutual advantage of both. The demands of the lumberman for produce, livestock, and labor could be accommodated by an agricultural population while the pioneer's search for supplementary income and local markets could be met by the lumber camps. Both pioneers and lumbermen benefited from the associated improvements in communication with the lake-front townships. But the whole rationale for the northern expansion was only as attainable as the model of a symbiotic relationship was viable. In fact, the reality of the community of interest between pioneers and lumbermen in the Shield was not as apparent as the rhetoric would suggest. Lumbering in the nineteenth century was not concerned with the renewal of the resource and was essentially a transient phenomenon, and any dependence upon it by pioneers could only be expected to last as long as the timber lasted in any area. Moreover, while claiming a symbiotic relationship between the two enterprises, increasingly it was argued that agriculture and lumbering were actively antipathetic to one another. Specifically, it was argued that fires were caused by uncontrolled clearing, that much settlement was artificial and concerned only with "poaching" lumber, and that an agrarian policy removed from the public domain land which was best suited to lumbering.[49]

The latter half of the nineteenth century, therefore, witnessed the energetic promotion of the idea of categorization of the Shield country according to its capabilities and the allocation of areas to specific activities. The traditional argument that the lumberman preceded the farmer, clearing the land for agriculture, was challenged and the government was urged by the lumbermen to maintain "a fair line of separation between the lumbering and agricultural regions, as nature has laid down."[50] No amount of optimism could disguise the fact that much of the settlement had been a failure, attended by much human misery, and with the passage of the Forest Reserves Act in 1899, the dominance of lumbering, and later mineral extraction, throughout the Shield was ensured.[51]

Conclusion

One recent student of the process of development of Ontario's frontier resources places much emphasis upon the way in which the environment influenced the course of events:

> In Canada, the interaction between political values and geographic environment did not permit one conception of land use to dominate the entire framework of resource alienation. The liberal, philosophical foundations for agrarianism were weaker, and the rocky margins of the Shield clearly limited the very conditions of its existence, namely prime arable land . . . The Shield itself and the economic interests dependent upon it challenged a unitary, agrarian view of the environment.[52]

The environment, therefore, cannot be assumed to be an objectively determined element upon which was imposed the frontier development process. The inventory of its resources varied according to the current technology and economic system. Moreover, the interpretation of its capabilities which was disseminated to the settlers often reflected the interests of those directing the settlement process. Since these determinants of the evaluation changed through time, the generally held assessment of the environment also changed and this had a profound effect upon the progress of events in frontier areas.

The state, business interests, and the individual, all looked to the frontier as a region of much opportunity, albeit opportunity attended by considerable challenge. When all three of these vested interests in developing frontier areas were in harmony, the movement to occupy and develop the "New Lands" proceeded apace and "spontaneous settlement" could thrive. When, however, disharmonies of interests occurred, initiatives were taken by each party to advance their own ends. Thus, government promotion and even sponsorship of settlement occurred at times when investors and settlers were disinterested or opposed to development schemes. Similarly, while "boosterism" and the "promotional rhetoric" in nineteenth-century newspapers, journals, and pamphlets were common, municipal and corporate interests sponsored it when settlement lagged or was not increasing rapidly enough. This end was also attained by lobbying for legislation favoring the interests of various resource developers. Finally, when pro-settlement pressures from the popular sectors ran counter to, or in advance of, the state's interests, individuals often had recourse to their own strategy of pre-empting and "squatting" on lands in advance of the policy and without the benefit of legal title to their claims.

All three levels operated within the terms of reference of the general credo of progress which was manifest in the world around them and which may be argued as being the ethic of the nineteenth century.[53] It was on the frontier that the most dynamic expression of the ideal of progress could be found. Here the application of manpower and contemporary technology to the task of developing a mature society and productive economy out of the wilderness set the stage for the several dimensions of economic, social, political, material, and even moral progress. If Nature abhorred a vacuum, the nineteenth-century advocates of progress knew how to fill one and such was the socioeconomic vacuity of the frontier that it challenged the ethic of the day. There was less unanimity, however, in terms of the best means of attaining the optimal development of the frontier and it was here that the interests of the state, capital, and the individual were often in conflict. In the Kingston area between 1783 and 1880, the opportunities and limitations peculiar to the development of the Shield exacerbated this conflict.

Notes

1. For more on this thesis see B. Osborne, "The Settlement of Kingston's Hinterland," *To Preserve and Defend: Essays on Kingston in the Nineteenth Century*, ed. by G. J. Tulchinsky (Montreal, 1976); L. A. Johnson, "Land Policy, Population Growth and Social Structure in the Home District, 1851–1973," *Ontario History*, 13 (1971), 41–60; J. H. Richards, "Lands and Policies: Attitudes and Controls in the Alienation of Lands in Ontario During the First Century of Settlement," *Ontario History: Papers and Records*, 50 (1958), 193–211. During the period being studied in this paper, the study area was variously part of the colony of Quebec, the province of Upper Canada, Canada West in Ontario. For the sake of clarity, the term Ontario is used for the whole period.

2. For other definitions of the term "frontier" see K. D. Kristoff, "The Nature of Boundaries and Frontiers," *Annals*, Association of American Geographers, 49 (1959), 269–282.

3. For consideration of these stages, apart from Turner, see also R. Mitchell, "The Commercial Nature of Frontier Settlement in the Shenandoah Valley of Virginia," *Proceedings*, Association of American Geographers, 1 (1969), 109–112; and D. J. Wishart, A. Warren, and R. Stoddard, "An Attempted Definition of a Frontier Using a Wave Analogy," *Rocky Mountain Social Science Journal*, 6 (1969), 73–81.

4. Apart from Turner's use of densities of two persons per square mile, see also W. A. Mackintoch, "The Spread of Settlement," *Canadian Frontiers of Settlement, 1: Prairie Settlement, the Geographical Setting*, ed. by W. A. Mackintosh and W. L. G. Joerg (Toronto, 1954); and J. F. Hart, *The Look of the Land* (Englewood Cliffs, 1975), pp. 62–63.

5. E. A. Wilkenning and S. Iutaka, *Sociological Aspects of Colonization as viewed from Brazil* (Land Tenure Center, 37 [Madison, 1967]); . . . S. I. Thompson, "Success and Failure in Colonization: the Human Factor," *Papers in Anthropology*, 16.1 (1975), 1–9.

6. For a discussion of the role of the "mercantile capitalist," see J. Steffen, "Some Observations of the Turner Thesis: A Polemic," *Papers in Anthropology*, 14.1 (1973) 16–30.

7. An interesting use of records left by settlers themselves is to be found in J. C. Hudson, "Migration to an American Frontier," *Annals*, Association of American Geographers, 66 (1976), 242–265.

8. Osborne, "Kingston in the Nineteenth Century: A Study in Urban Decline," *Perspectives on Landscape and Settlement in Nineteenth Century Ontario,* ed. by J. D. Wood (Toronto, 1975).

9. For more details, see D. F. Putnam and L. J. Chapman, *Physiography of Southern Ontario* (Toronto, 1966).

10. G. M. Craig, *Upper Canada, The Formative Years, 1784–1841,* (Toronto, 1963), 6.

11. *Ibid.*

12. G. Patterson, *Land Settlement in Upper Canada, 1783–1840* (Sixteenth Report of the Department of Archives for the Province of Ontario [1921]), p. 45; see also A. Wilson, *The Clergy Reserves of Upper Canada: A Canadian Mortmain* (Toronto, 1968); L. Gates, *Land Policies of Upper Canada* (Toronto, 1968).

13. John Collins' Survey of Kingston Township, October 27th, 1783, quoted in R. A. Preston, *Kingston Before the War of 1812* (Toronto, 1959), 3.40.

14. Patterson, pp. 22–24. The allocations were:

	Combattants	
Field Officers	1,000 acres	(5,000 acres)*
Captains	700 acres	(3,000 acres)
Sublaterns, staff, warrants	500 acres	(2,000 acres)
Non commissioned	200 acres	(500 acres)
Privates	100 acres	(200 acres)
	Non-Combattants	
Master of Family	100 acres	(200 acres)
Each person in family	50 acres	
Single man	50 acres	

*After 1788.

15. The inhabitants of Loughborough township petitioned Government that ". . . the poor devils in the rear can only get to town with their produce about three months out of twelve which is shocking encouragement for actual settlement," Public Archives of Canada, RG5, ff. 20940–20941, Petition of Geo. Medley to Lt. Governor re: Kingston market and supplies, April 26, 1818.

16. Quoted in E. A. Cruikshank, *The Settlement of the United Empire Loyalists on the Upper St. Lawrence and Bay of Quinte in 1784: A Documentary Record* (Toronto, 1934).

17. Department of Lands and Forests, Surveyors' Letters, Vol. 9, folio 2, Alex Aitken to D. W. Smith, Surveyor General, 26 Dec., 1792.

18. *Ibid.,* Vol. 35, folio 68, 11 March, 1809.

19. For a discussion of the significance of the controlling elite, see R. E. Saunders, "What Was the Family Compact?," *Ontario History,* 49 (1957) 165–178; for land speculation, see J. Clark, "The Role of Political Position and Family and Economic Linkage in the Western District of Upper Canada, 1788–1815," *Canadian Geographer,* 19 (1975), 18–34; as a local example, one Richard Cartwright of Kingston had by 1815 come into possession of some 28,632 acres.

20. Public Archives of Canada, R.G.5, B. 26, Vols. 1, 2, 3, 4. Population Returns, 1805–1850.

21. T. Southworth and A. White, *A History of Crown Timber Regulations from the date of the French Occupation to the Year 1899,* Dept. Lands and Forests, Annual Report, 1907, pp. 156.

22. For the development of Ontario Agriculture, see R. L. Jones, *History of Agriculture in Ontario, 1613–1880* (Toronto, 1946); also K. Kelly, "Wheat Farming in Simcoe County in the Mid-Nineteenth Century," *Canadian Geographer*, 15.2, (1971), 95–112; for lumber see A. R. M. Lower, *The North American Assault on the Canadian Forest* (Toronto, 1938), *Great Britain's Woodyard: British America and the Timber Trade, 1763–1867* (Montreal, 1973).

23. Gates, p. 131, notes that by 1824, of the eight million acres granted, only three million were occupied with only half a million being cultivated.

24. For specifics, see Gates, *ibid.*

25. Kingston *Chronicle and Gazette*, 8 August, 1835.

26. Public Archives of Canada, RG5, A1, pp. 82063–82065, Petition of inhabitants of Midland District re: roads to rear of Portland.

27. Department of Lands and Forests, Surveyors' Letters, Vol. 2, folio 910, Neil MacDonald to Thomas Ridout, 10 Oct., 1822.

28. *Ibid.* and also Department of Forests, Field Note Book 626, Survey of Sheffield, 1822.

29. 2nd Vict., Chapter 15, 1839.

30. *Census of the Canadas*, 1851–2, Quebec, 1853–55, Vol. 1.

31. Department of Lands and Forests, Survey Notes.

32. Department of Lands and Forests, Field Notes, Vol. 846, Surveyor P. Elmore's report on Oso Townships, 18th Dec., 1826.

33. *Ibid.* Field Notes, Vol. 1304, 30 May, 1836.

34. *Ibid.*, Surveyors' Letters, Vol. 37, B. Tett of Newborough to S. Wilmot of Kingston, 29 August, 1836.

35. Kingston *Chronicle and Gazette*, 4 July, 1842.

36. *Ibid.*, 23 Dec., 1835.

37. *Ibid.*, 11 July, 1835.

38. Province of Canada. Journals of Assembly, 1847, Appendix (L.L.) Quoted in G. W. Spragge, "Colonization Roads in Canada West, 1850–1867," *Ontario History*, 49.1, 1–17.

39. See Jones, p. 298; also, N. V. Nelles, *The Politics of Development: Forests, Mines and Hydro-electric Power in Ontario, 1849–1941* (Toronto, 1974), 44.

40. Department of Lands and Forests, Field Notes, Book 1605, T. F. Gibbs' report on the resurvey of Oso, 1862.

41. *Ibid.*, Field Notes, Book 1599, T. F. Tibbs' resurvey of Olden, 30 Jan., 1861.

42. *Ibid.*, Field Notes, Book 1051, J. A. Snow's report on Claredon, 11 Aug., 1862.

43. Kingston *Chronicle and News*, 9 Sept., 1864.

44. Department of Lands and Forests, Field Notes, Book 1479, J. S. Harper's report on Miller, 27 Oct., 1860.

45. Kingston *Chronicle and News*, 31 July, 1857.

46. *Ibid.*, 18 April, 1862.

47. Census of Canada, 1881.

48. In fact, the southern townships ranging from Pittsburgh across to Adolphustown all attained population peaks before 1881. The opening of the western prairies, the collapse of local wheat production, and the rise of urban opportunities initiated a rural emigration that was to continue into the next century.

49. An Act to Preserve the Forest from Destruction by Fire, 1878. Also an item in a Department of Lands and Forests Field Notes Book, 1599, reported

that many of the lands were not patented for their agricultural capabilities but rather "for the purpose of Disposing of, or cutting the timber."

50. Quoted in Nelles, p. 17.

51. Some later settlement would be sponsored by the Volunteers Land Grant Act of 1891, the Ontario Returned Soldiers and Sailors Land Settlement Act of 1917 and the Veterans Land Grant Act of 1922, but the latter specified that such settlement would only be allowed where it could be shown that the lands were suitable for agriculture.

52. Nelles, pp. 44–45.

53. See L. S. Fallis, "The Idea of Progress in the Province of Canada, 1841–1867," Ph.D. thesis, University of Michigan, 1966; W. Wager, *The Idea of Progress Since the Renaissance* (New York, 1969).

Nineteenth-century Land Use and Settlement on the Canadian Shield Frontier

Geoffrey Wall

DURING the middle of the nineteenth century, the government of Upper Canada became increasingly concerned at the difficulties of attracting and retaining permanent settlers.[1] The view was widely entertained that the commercial and industrial development of Canada depended upon a large population and a growing domestic market. Many forces contributed to this attitude: the desire of the landed proprietor to increase the value of his land, the patriotism of the United Empire Loyalists, the political desire of the British element, the fears of the militarists, and the desire to develop new country all stimulated a favorable attitude towards immigration.[2]

However, immigration to Canada was at a relatively low level during the middle years of the nineteenth century. Various causes contributed to this situation. The demands of the Crimean War resulted in a marked improvement in the British economy and, during the 1840's, the rural districts of Ireland and Scotland were depleted of much of their surplus manpower. Both causes combined to remove the usual incentives to emigration from Britain. A further deterrent to emigration was the Imperial Passenger Act of 1856 which brought more ships within the scope of the navigation laws, reduced the number of passengers any ship could legally carry, increased the quantity of compulsory provisions for the needs of the passengers, almost doubled the fares for adult passengers, and made emigration more difficult for poor people with large families. In addition, 1857 saw commercial and financial depression throughout North America.[3]

A major factor frustrating Canadian immigration policy throughout the nineteenth century, was the strong competition for emigrants from other receptor countries, particularly the United States. Both Canada and the United States undertook extensive advertising campaigns in Europe, and the United States not only lured settlers who might otherwise have gone to Canada, but also attracted many former residents of Canada to the growing

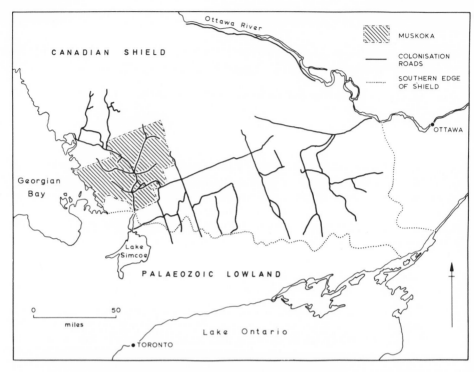

Fig. 1. The Location of Muskoka

industrial cities in the east and the newly opened prairies farther
west. For instance, of the arrivals in Canada in 1856, 41 per cent
were reported as being transients to the United States, including
almost all of the Scandinavians, 50 per cent of the Irish and
Germans, and one-sixth of the English and Scots.[4]

It was in this difficult immigration climate that new lands were
opened in a desperate attempt to attract immigration to Canada.
By the middle of the nineteenth century the better crown lands
in Upper Canada had been settled, there remained only the "Ottawa-Huron tract," the territory between the Ottawa River and
Georgian Bay, to the north of existing settlements (Figure 1). A
colonization scheme was devised to facilitate settlement on this
southern margin of the Canadian Shield.[5] Muskoka, the most
westerly part of the "Ottawa-Huron tract," was the first area to
be opened to settlement under the colonization scheme and the

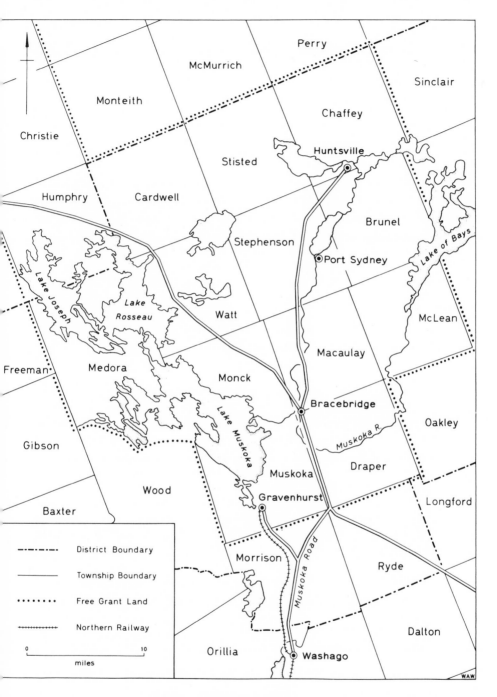

Fig. 2. Muskoka in 1875

remainder of the paper will concentrate upon settlement and land use there (Figure 2). However, Muskoka is reasonably typical of the Shield fringe in Ontario, and similar problems of settlement and land-use were found throughout the Ottawa-Huron tract.

The Study Site

Muskoka is an area of lakes and forests on the southern margin of the Canadian Shield, approximately one hundred miles north of Toronto. The area, like the rest of the Canadian Shield, is characterized by low biological productivity. Acidic soils formed on the granitic bedrock are generally shallow podzols or gleys. Rock outcrops fragment the limited cultivable areas, and, with the exception of a small number of isolated pockets, Muskoka has never been an area conducive to agriculture.[6] However, it once contained extensive stands of marketable timber, and its attractive scenery has contributed to its development as a major recreational area for residents of Toronto.

Early Evaluations of Muskoka

Explorers and surveyors were among the first white men to enter Muskoka,[7] and their reports include the earliest evaluations of the natural wealth of the area. The major task of the explorers was to discover a water route between the Ottawa River and Georgian Bay which would provide an alternative route to that via the lower Great Lakes which had been threatened by the war of 1812. However, the explorers' reports also contained comments concerning the suitability of the land for agriculture. The report of F. H. Baddeley, 1835, was typical:

> On the whole, everything I have seen or heard enables me at least to state that in this, hitherto unnoticed part of Canada, a fine habitable country will be found, to the extent of millions of acres; and I have now only to express my hope that it will, ere long, be rendered accessible to population.[8]

Only Henry Briscoe, writing in 1826, came out strongly against the suitability of the area for settlement, and he commented that,

"The country through which we passed was uniformly, with very few exceptions, of a sterile nature."[9] Most explorer reports were either favorable or noncommital. Collectively, they did little to discourage hopes that the area could support a large number of permanent settlers.

The explorers were followed by surveyors who were to undertake a resource inventory and thereby prepare the way for settlement. Their instructions were as follows:

> to describe the land, whether level, rolling, broken, hilly or mountainous. The quality and character of the soil, and whether first, second or third rate. The several kinds of timber and undergrowth with which the land may be covered, naming each kind of timber in the order in which it is most prevalent.[10]

These instructions, in their references to both soil and timber, provide an early precursor of later conflicts between farming and lumbering interests.

The surveyors' reports were similar to those of the explorers in that the government was able to interpret the reports in the way that it had hoped and an official scheme of settlement was devised and implemented.

It is interesting to speculate concerning the reasons for the surveyors' over-estimates of the quality of the land for agriculture. At least three possibilities can be suggested. It is common for unexplored lands to be viewed with optimism and the American West and the interior of Australia provide comparable examples where settlements had been extended into agriculturally marginal areas. Second, it is possible that surveyors with Southern Ontario experience viewed trees as indicators of good soil and felt that large stands of timber could be replaced by high yields of crops. However, large pines can thrive on thin sandy soils which are not conducive to agriculture. Finally, perhaps the favorable reports were motivated by self-interest on the part of the surveyors who may have felt that future work depended upon the maintenance of government interest in these unmapped areas.

Colonization Policy 1858–1868

The keystone of the colonization policy was the construction of a network of colonization roads which were to serve the Ottawa-

Huron tract and link it to the lowland to the south (Figure 1). Construction began in 1858 with the intention of imposing a grid of roads across the southern margins of the Canadian Shield, similar to that which had been constructed in Southern Ontario. The rugged topography and numerous lakes made construction difficult and costly and it proved impossible to build an efficient road network. Nevertheless, the Muskoka Road, of plank and gravel construction, reached Bracebridge in 1859 and the townships of Morrison, Muskoka, Draper, and Macaulay were opened for settlement (Figure 2). Lots were laid out on each side of the road, with a frontage of twenty chains (440 yards), and, in their optimism, government spokesmen expected that the new area would be popular since land was cheap and the roads ensured a line of communication to the south.

For several years after the colonization roads program was begun the reports of the agents for the various roads were optimistic. In the first year, 1859, R. J. Oliver, the Crown Lands Agent, reported that fifty-four locations had been taken up, and that most of the locatees had taken possession of their lots, had built shanties, and had made small clearings.[11] However, the initial rate of colonization was not maintained. In 1860, a total of forty-one settlers on the Muskoka Road had cleared one hundred-seventy acres. By 1862, seventy-six settlers had cleared only two hundred-seventy-five acres and half the population was still living in temporary shanties.[12] In 1862, seventy-one emigrants left the townships of Draper, Macaulay, Morrison, and Muskoka,[13] representing a loss of 10 per cent of the population in one year, and in 1864 only two new locations were taken out.[14] Clearing land covered with pine was difficult, the rigors of the Canadian winter were sufficient to discourage many settlers, and there were few alternative opportunities for earning capital on the Shield frontier.

The initial inflow of settlement was followed by a period of stagnation accompanied by a withdrawal of a considerable proportion of the population. If hopes for the future of Muskoka were to be realized a means had to be found by which settlers could be induced to come to the area in competition with the richer lands of the American West which had become especially attractive with the passage of the Homestead Act, 1862.

DOMINION OF CANADA.

EMIGRATION

TO THE

PROVINCE OF ONTARIO.

To Capitalists, Tenant Farmers, Agricultural Labourers, Mechanics, Day Labourers, and all parties desirous of Improving their Circumstances by Emigrating to a New Country.

The attention of intending Emigrants is invited to the great advantages presented by the Province of Ontario. Persons living on the Interest of their Money can easily get EIGHT PER CENT. on first-class security.

TENANT FARMERS WITH LIMITED CAPITAL,

Can buy and stock a Freehold Estate with the money needed to carry on a small farm in Britain. Good Cleared land, with a Dwelling and good Barn and out-houses upon it, can be purchased in desirable localities, at from £4 to £10 sterling per acre.

Farm hands can readily obtain work at GOOD WAGES.

Among the inducements offered to intending Emigrants, by Government, is

A FREE GRANT OF LAND!

WITHOUT ANY CHARGE WHATEVER.

Every Head of a Family can obtain, on condition of settlement, a Free Grant of TWO HUNDRED ACRES of Land for himself, and ONE HUNDRED ACRES additional for each member of his family, male or female, over eighteen years of age.

All persons over Eighteen years of age can obtain a Free Grant of ONE HUNDRED ACRES.

The Free Grants are protected by a Homestead Exemption Act, and are not liable to seizure for any debt incurred before the issue of the patent, or for twenty years after its issue. They are within easy access of the front settlements, and are supplied with regular postal communication.

REGISTERS OF THE LABOUR MARKET

And of Improved Farms for sale, are kept at the Immigration Agencies in the Province, and arrangements are made for directing emigrants to those points where employment can be most readily obtained. Several new lines of Railway and other Public Works are in course of construction, or about being commenced, which will afford employment to an almost unlimited number of labourers.

Persons desiring fuller information respecting the Province of Ontario

Are invited to apply personally, or by letter, to the Canadian Government Emigration Agents in Europe, viz: WM. DIXON, 11 Adam Street, Adelphi, London, W. C.; J. G. MOYLAN, Dublin; CHARLES FOY, Belfast; DAVID SHAW, Glasgow; and E. SIMAYS, Continental Agent at Antwerp.

Also to the Immigration Agents in Canada, viz:—JOHN A. DONALDSON, Toronto; R. H. RAE, Hamilton; WM. J. WILLS, Ottawa; JAS. MACPHERSON, Kingston; L. STAFFORD, Quebec; J. J. DALEY, Montreal; E. CLAY, Halifax, Nova Scotia; ROBT. SHIVES, St. John, and J. G. G. LAYTON, Miramichi, New Brunswick,—from whom pamphlets, issued under the authority of the Government of Ontario, containing full particulars in relation to character and resources of, and the cost of living, wages, &c., in the Province, can be obtained.

JOHN CARLING.

Commissioner of Agriculture and Public Work for the Province of Ontario

DEPARTMENT OF IMMIGRATION
Toronto, March, 1871.

Fig. 3. Advertisement for Free Land Grant

Table 1. Locations and Patents in the Free Grant Lands 1874–1886

	1874	1875	1876	1877	1878	1880	1881	1882	1886
New locations made	919	1387	1463	1914	2115	1292	1077	932	1149
Old locations canceled	453	381	462	691	1118	870	781	624	607
Patents received		570	546	542	472	487	487	502	706

Source: N. H. MacKenzie, "Economic and Social Development of Muskoka, 1855–1888" (M.A. thesis, Department of Political Economy, University of Toronto, 1943), p. 19.

Free Grant and Homesteads Act, 1868

In an attempt to lure more settlers to the Ottawa-Huron tract, the Free Grant and Homesteads Act was passed in 1868 (Figure 3). Under this Act, any settler over the age of eighteen years, and on agreement that it was his intention to settle, clear, and cultivate the land, could receive a Free Grant of one hundred acres. Owing to the unsuitable nature of much of the territory for agriculture, the settler could often find only a few acres in his hundred which he could cultivate. Within a year, as a result of an Order in Council, married settlers were granted two hundred acres and were permitted to buy more land at fifty cents per acre. On evidence that he had fulfilled the minimum settlement duties, and after five years of residence, the pioneer farmer could receive a patent to the land. It was cynically suggested that the government bet the settler that he could not remain on the land for five years.

The first year saw a rapid influx of settlers and the number of new locations rose to a peak in 1878. However, signs of difficulty were soon encountered. After 1878 there was a gradual decline in the number of new settlers, patents were slow to be received, and a large number of the locations were canceled (Table 1). Even in 1881 only 11.9 per cent of the occupied land was actually cultivated.[15]

Government Reactions

The government was slow to recognize the failure of its policy. Even in 1863, five years before the passage of the Free Grant and

Homesteads Act, realistic observations of the nature of Muskoka had been made. At that time the Select Committee on the State of the Lumber Industry reported as follows:

> settlement has been unreasonably pushed in some localities quite unfit to become the permanent residence of an agricultural population. Especially has this been the case of some of the Free Grant roads and adjacent country between the waters of the Ottawa and Lake Huron. Your committee would recommend that the government should, in all cases, ascertain positively the character of the country before throwing open any tract of land for settlement.[16]

Residents of Muskoka produced propaganda to attract new settlers to their District,[17] but, by 1870, favorable comments were becoming increasingly rare. For example, the *Montreal Witness* published an article entitled "Cruelty of sending newly arrived immigrants to worthless Free Grant Lands,"[18] and Joseph Dale wrote a book on the Free Grant Lands of Canada which was devoted to condemning Government policy and pointing out the foolishness of attempting to people the Ottawa-Huron tract with farmers.[19]

Gradually the dream of agricultural settlement faded. The colonization roads were allowed to grow over. By the 1880s the government had been forced to recognize that the Ottawa-Huron tract was an area with only a few limited pockets of fertile soil and that any scheme to people Muskoka with farmers was doomed to failure.

Lumbering

At the same time as Muskoka was being opened to settlers, lumbermen were pushing northwards into the Ottawa-Huron tract in search of white pine (*pinus strobus*). From 1860 to 1900, with the exception of a number of minor recessions, the market for pine was flourishing. There was an increasing demand from the northeastern United States because of the depletion of the Michigan forests[20] and because of the rapidly expanding urban markets, especially New York and Chicago. In addition, as settlement pushed westward the pioneers found themselves in the prairies where timber was in short supply and thus the North American market was further augmented. This period of favorable market conditions coincided with the period of active cutting in Muskoka.

The lumber industry of the 1850s and 1860s concentrated on the production of square timber and required wood of high quality. Cutting was selective and because of the rapidity with which a square timber "gang" covered a large section of wooded country, the industry was essentially of a transitory nature and did not promote settlement to any great degree. The square timber trade was gradually superseded in importance by the production of saw logs which could utilize timber of lower quality. Thus saw log production tended to deforest larger areas than square timber production, was less transitory, and its shanties tended to provide a more stable market for the agricultural produce which was grown along the colonization roads.

Lumbering was regarded by the government as a temporary phenomenon which could provide an income through the sale of timber leases, provided that the limits were sold before settlers had destroyed the forest cover. The money thus gained was to be used to promote agricultural settlement which it was hoped would be the permanent land utilization of the area.

Interrelationships between Agriculture and Lumbering

From the earliest days of settlement in Muskoka lumbering and agriculture were interdependent.[21] The two activities were compatible seasonally; the peak demand for shanty labor was in the winter when little could be done on the farm. This employment opportunity was especially valuable in the early years of settlement when the settler was likely to have only a limited amount of capital and little agricultural produce to sell.

Furthermore, the shanties provided a local market for farm products. Muskoka was remote from urban markets and it was difficult and costly for farmers to get their products to "the front." The lumbermen would have had to pay high prices for food and fodder "imported" from the south because of the transfer costs involved, and thus the agricultural production of the settler coincided in space and time with the demands of the lumbermen to their mutual benefit. However, the construction of the Northern Railway, which reached Muskoka in 1875, by reducing the isolation of Muskoka, undermined the sheltered shanty market and acted to the detriment of Muskoka farmers. The situation was graphically described in a despairing letter sent to a local news-paper, *The Bobcaygean Independent*, in 1880:

> Before the railway opened I could sell all I could raise at a good price for the lumberers could not bring anything here except at great ex-pense in teaming. Now, if I wont take half the price I used to get for my oats, the lumbermen bring oats by railway from Chicago. If I wont sell my hay at just the price the lumberman chooses, presto, he bring in hay from the Front or from Toronto, or from Jericho or somewhere, and I can't sell a ton.[22]

Most farms could only operate profitably while the shanties bought their produce, but with the exhaustion of the pine the lumbermen closed their camps and moved elsewhere. In the ab-sence of alternative markets many farmers had little choice but to abandon their holdings or operate at a bare subsistence level.[23]

Although there were important reasons for cooperation be-tween farmers and the lumbermen, causes of conflict were soon apparent. The settlers' fires often went out of control and de-stroyed the lumberman's valuable timber resource, and these fires were aggravated by the timber slash left by the lumbermen them-selves. Large quantities of timber were destroyed by fire and repeated burnings laid open the thin soils to erosion. Firing of timber became such a problem that in 1878 an "Act to Preserve the Forests from Destruction by Fire" was passed and fire dis-tricts were created.[24] The lumbermen complained of settlers filling the rivers with rubbish from their clearings which impeded efforts to drive logs in the spring. Settlers retorted that the timber booms made navigation difficult, the lumberman's dams caused the flooding of areas of settled land, and the heavy lumbering traffic destroyed the colonization roads.

The above causes of friction were minor irritations in compari-son with the resentment resulting from the government policy of giving Free Grant Lands to settlers and selling timber limits on the same plots of land. The problem was exacerbated by the con-trasting attitudes towards the forest which were held by the lum-bermen and the farmers. To the former, the timber was a valuable resource to be harvested, but to the latter the forest was a barrier standing in the way of successful cultivation. The inevitable result of this system was that keen competition developed between the lumberman and the settler. The former attempted to cut the pine before the latter had completed his settlement requirements and recieved his patent, thus "inciting the one to slash down and the other to burn up."[25] It seemed very hard to the settler, who was at liberty to burn up his pine while performing his settlement duties, that he was unable to sell timber without first paying the government a tax of seventy-five cents per thousand feet.

The forest was regarded by the government as a quick source of revenue which could be used to foster agricultural settlement. Regulations were directed towards protecting and increasing timber revenues and towards the control of timber stealing and illicit operations undertaken under the guise of settlement. There was little concern over the future availability of timber in Muskoka for lumbering was regarded by the government as an ephemeral activity which would be supplanted by agriculture as the major form of land use.

However, as early as 1854 a parliamentary enquiry had indicated that the supply of pine was not inexhaustible and that the settler, by attempting to clear and farm poor soil often did more harm than good to the land.[26] There were occasional pleas that lumbermen and settlers should be kept apart. For example, Burke in 1855 criticized

the wanton, foolish and insane policy of the Crown Lands Department in surveying a township where nothing but pine and rock exist. . . . We go for keeping a fair line of separation between the lumbering and agriculture regions as nature has laid it down.[27]

Similarly, the Commissioner of Crown Lands, in his report of 1866, advocated a strict distinction between lands which were agricultural and those which were not, with the prohibition of settlement in the latter. The report states that, "It needs a careful discrimination between pine-lands exclusively, and lands fit for settlement, to place it in the power of the government to conserve this valuable source of national wealth."[28] However, little attention was paid to these early opinions and, with the exception of fish and game laws, the conservation of resources and the necessity for land management were scarcely considered until the 1880s.[29]

Thus the government schemes intended to open up the Ottawa-Huron tract for agricultural settlement proved to be not only misdirected, but also wasteful of a considerable quantity of high-quality timber.

Conclusions

Efforts to develop Muskoka in the second half of the nineteenth century failed because they were not based upon an accurate evaluation of the available resources, and because of misplaced attitudes towards those resources. Agricultural settlement was largely unsuccessful because, in spite of the optimism which existed in the 1850s and 1860s, there simply was an insufficient area of land suitable for large numbers of farmers. Lumbering was more soundly based; at least the resource was available. But, although the lumbermen made a handsome profit in the short run of two decades, in their belief that the forest was unlimited they gave little thought to forest conservation and consequently destroyed the resource. The ill-conceived policy of agricultural settlement, and the ruthless destruction of the forest by the lumbermen, left in their wake problems of rural poverty, abandoned farmsteads, and desolated areas.

In the long run both agriculture, and to a lesser extent lumbering, have failed to prosper on a large scale in Muskoka. This lack of permanence need not have been the case. In the short run lumbering and agricluture were compatible, and could have remained so if agriclutural settlers had been directed and restricted to the limited fertile areas, and if the lumbermen had not rejected the possibility of long-term profits for short-term gains. The animosity between lumbermen and farmers could have been greatly reduced, if not eliminated, if the government had adopted a more straightforward land policy. However, the requirements of agricultural settlement and lumbering did result in the construction of a railway connecting Muskoka with Toronto. This facilitated the development of the recreation industry and outdoor recreation has now supplanted agricluture and lumbering as the major economic activity in Muskoka and the greater part of the Shield margin in Ontario.[30]

Notes

1. Based on a paper presented at the Second Oklahoma Symposium on Comparative Frontiers, University of Oklahoma, Norman, Oklahoma, March, 1976.

2. H. M. Morrison, "The principle of free grants in the Land Act of 1841," *Canadian Historical Review*, 14 (1933), 392–407.

3. N. Macdonald, *Canada: Immigration and Colonization 1841–1903* (Toronto, 1966), pp. 78–9.

240

4. *Ibid.*

5. G. Wall, "Pioneer settlement in Muskoka," *Agricultural History*, 44 (1970), 393–400; F. B. Murray, "Agricultural settlement on the Canadian Shield: Ottawa River to Georgian Bay" in *Profiles of a Province*, ed. by E. G. Firth (Toronto, 1967), pp. 178–86; G. W. Spragge, "Colonization roads in Canada West 1850–1867," *Ontario History*, 49 (1957), 1–17; and K. A. Parker, "Colonization roads and commercial policy," *Ontario History*, 67 (1975), 31–8.

6. W. G. Dean and E. B. MacDougall, "Toronto into Muskoka: A Geographic Traverse," Department of Geography, University of Toronto, 1966. (Mimeographed.)

7. Many key documents have been reprinted in F. B. Murray, *Muskoka and Haliburton 1615–1875: A Collection of Documents* (Toronto, 1963).

8. Quoted in H. R. Cummings, *Early Days in Haliburton* (Toronto, 1962), p. 6.

9. Great Britain, Public Records Office, W. O. 55/864, quoted in Murray, p. 52.

10. Canada, Department of Crown Lands, *Remarks on Upper Canada Surveys and Extracts from the Surveyors' Reports, Containing a Description of the Soil and Timber of the Townships in the Huron and Ottawa Territory . . . Appendix No. 26 to the Report of the Commissioner of Crown Lands for 1861* (Quebec, 1862), VIII.

11. Canada, Department of Crown Lands Report 1859, reprinted in Murray, p. 243.

12. Canada, *Sessional Papers, 1860–1863*, quoted in N. H. MacKenzie, "The Economic and Social Development of Muskoka, 1855–1888" (M. A. thesis, Department of Political Economy, University of Toronto, 1943), p. 56.

13. Canada, Department of Crown Lands Report 1862, reprinted in Murray, p. 249.

14. Spragge.

15. Canada, Dominion Bureau of Statistics, *Census of Canada* (Ottawa, 1881).

16. Ontario Royal Commission on Forestry, *Report* (Toronto, 1947), quoted in R. S. Lambert, *Renewing Nature's Wealth* (Toronto, 1967), p. 91.

17. For example, W. E. Hamilton, *Guide Book and Atlas of Muskoka and Parry Sound Districts* (Toronto, 1879), and Captain Mac (J. T. McAdam), *The Muskoka Lakes and the Georgian Bay* (Toronto, 1884).

18. Ontario, Department of Agriculture and Public Works, *Emigration to Canada; the Province of Ontario* [1869?], quoted in Murray, p. 257.

19. J. Dale, *Canadian Land Grants in 1874* (London, 1875).

20. Dean and MacDougall, p. 45. (An alternative opinion concerning the role of Michigan timber is presented in W. A. Mackintosh, "The Laurentian Plateau in Canadian Economic Development," *Economic Geography*, 2 [1926], 537–50).

21. G. Wall, "Land Use Interrelationships in Nineteenth Century Muskoka" (M.A. thesis, Department of Geography, University of Toronto, 1968).

22. *Bobcaygeon Independent*, February 20, 1880, quoted in Cummings, p. 164.

23. The implications of lumbering for the decline of Shield agriculture have been discussed by H. E. Parson, "Rural Land Use Change in Gatineau County, Quebec" (Ph.D. dissertation, Department of Geography, University of Toronto, in progress).

24. J. H. Richards, "Land Use and Settlement Patterns on the Fringe of the Shield in Southern Ontario" (Ph.D. dissertation, Department of Geography, University of Toronto, 1954).

25. A. R. M. Lower and H. A. Innis, *Settlement and the Forest and Mining Frontiers* (Toronto, 1936), p. 56.

26. A. R. M. Lower, *The North American Assault on the Canadian Forest* (Toronto, 1938), pp. 161–2.

27. Quoted in Lambert, p. 156.

28. Canada, *Sessional Papers, 1866*, quoted in MacKenzie, p. 6.

29. Lambert.

30. G. Wall, "Transport in a pioneer area; a note on Muskoka," *Transport History*, 5 (1972), 54–66; and G. Wall, "Recreational land use in Nineteenth Century Muskoka," paper presented to the Annual Meeting of the Canadian Association of Geographers, Quebec, May, 1976.

Ethnic Differences on the Southwestern United States Frontier, 1860

David T. Bailey and Bruce E. Haulman

ETHNIC DIFFERENTIATION AND CONFLICT were among the dominant social phenomena characterizing the United States' Southwestern frontier during the mid-nineteenth century.* The diaries of traders, soldiers, and other Anglo travelers generally reflect a considerable degree of expressed prejudice for the Mexican population, and at least in New Mexico, the attempted revolts of the New Mexicans after the United States conquest indicate that the opinion was at least in part reciprocal. Beyond these diaries, a few scattered reports, and the revolts themselves, we know little about the nature and extent of the ethnic differentiation on the frontier. From the above indications, the general picture is fairly clear—a military, social, political, and economic conquest of a quasi-indigenous people (the Tejanos, Nuevo Mexicanos, Californios, etc.) by a powerful invading group (the U.S. Army and traders)—but the sociological details are sketchy or nonexistent.

Our problem is compounded by the fact that not only do we as social scientists know little about the Southwestern frontier experience, but we have generally neglected the phenomenon of the frontier. This is due to the fact that empirical sociology has tended to focus on the readily available contemporary United States society. It is only as we broaden our space and time dimensions, as we are now doing, that we encounter such phenomena as the frontier which are not present in contemporary United States society.

If sociology offers no clues about the frontier per se, what does it offer of value in related areas? The obvious answer is the sociology of ethnic relations, specifically the sociology of the Mexican American, but even this is relatively ahistorical, and the historical knowledge offered is hazy and impressionistic. Because few sociologists were studying Mexican American-Anglo relations before about 1960, we have very little empirical data on earlier times, especially on the past century. Extrapolating from the present, we might expect to find the same specific patterns of

243

differentiation operating in 1860 as are predicted from the sketchy historical data: namely, a domination of the Mexican Americans by the Anglos in every aspect of social life, and the resulting characreristics generally associated with majority or minority status.

This chapter has two major goals: (1) to provide some information about the ethnic configuration of the populations of two major Southwestern frontier cities in 1860; and (2) to test informally some of the vague hypotheses concerning the historical relations of the Anglo and Mexican-American groups in the Southwest. The data used are from the United States Census of 1860 for San Antonio, Texas, and for Santa Fe, New Mexico.

Historical Description

San Antonio and Santa Fe were chosen for this examination of the ethnic configuration of the Southwestern frontier because of their striking similarities. Yet there are also a number of major differences which enable us to see some of the emerging patterns of ethnicity which may have determined the ethnic configuration of the Southwest today.

Both San Antonio and Santa Fe were founded as political and military centers by the Spaniards as they expanded into North America. San Antonio was founded in 1718 as part of a system of missions in Texas (Bancroft, 1890: 618). By the 1730's, only the Mission San Antonio de Valero remained and, in conjunction with the Presidio and Villa de Bejar, formed the nucleus of what would become San Antonio (Wheeler, 1968: 7–8). In 1773, it became the official capital of the Province of Texas, and remained a significant political and military center under the Spanish regime (Wheeler, 1968: 10). Santa Fe was founded much earlier (in 1610) and developed into military and political prominence from the beginning. With the exception of the period of the Pueblo Revolt and the Reconquest, it remained an active center of Spanish control in New Mexico (Writer's Program, 1940). Throughout this period, it served as the major presidio in New Mexico.

With the move toward Mexican independence from Spain in the early nineteenth century, both cities underwent significant transformations. Santa Fe began to develop as a major trade center with the opening of the Santa Fe Trail in 1821. This event placed Santa Fe in the position of a commercial terminal with the

Chihuahua Road leading south to Mexican markets, and with developing trade routes to the expanding colonies in California (Moorhead, 1958). San Antonio was caught up in the flood of migration which brought Americans and Europeans into Texas and laid the foundations for the Texas Revolution. Although San Antonio remained largely on the periphery of these developments, they could not but affect the future and growth of the city. Following independence and the establishment of the Texas Republic, San Antonio remained a predominantly Spanish city. It was believed by Texans in other cities to be somewhat ambivalent about independence; and, being so isolated from the rest of Texas and on the edge of the frontier, it remained stable in size during the years of independence (Wheeler, 1968: 5, 35). The city's primary lines of trade and communication continued to run to Mexico. The continued hostility of the Mexicans and the isolation of San Antonio from the rest of Texas meant that it did not follow the pattern of the remainder of the Republic in becoming rapidly Anglicized. An indication of the continuing Spanish domination of the city can be seen in the city elections of 1837, in which all but one of the candidates were Spanish-surnamed (Wheeler, 1968: 5).

The 1840's saw rapid changes occurring in the growth and ethnic composition of both cities. San Antonio began to change from a Spanish-Mexican outpost to a more cosmopolitan entrepot. The Mexican-American War in the late 1840's brought prosperity to San Antonio with large payments by the United States government to merchant-contractors to supply the United States Army (Wheeler, 1968: 111). In addition, large numbers of immigrants began to flood into San Antonio during this period. In 1843, the *Adelsverein* was founded to encourage and protect German immigration. It was responsible for the immigration of thousands of Germans (Fehrenbach, 1968: 292–296). Americans also arrived in large numbers, mostly from the Southeastern United States. There were also significant numbers of Irish and French immigrants into Texas and the San Antonio area (Wheeler, 1968: 142–146). These changes were reflected in the city elections of 1847 in which only five of the twenty-one candidates were Spanish-surnamed (Wheeler, 1968: 5). In only ten years the ethnic balance had radically shifted. Santa Fe was undergoing similar changes, but not as rapidly nor to the degree that occurred in San Antonio. American merchants involved in the Santa Fe trade began to establish themselves, or their proxies, as merchants in Santa Fe in an attempt to eliminate the Spanish middlemen. This brought increased numbers of Americans into the city although it retained a predominantly Spanish population (Moorhead, 1958; Loyola, 1939). The waves of immigration which altered the ethnic makeup of San Antonio did not really reach Santa Fe, but the opening of the California gold fields meant that new demands were placed on the city as one of the primary trade centers of the Southwest. Major trade developed to supply cattle and sheep to California, increasing the role of Santa Fe as a trade terminal and bringing in new elements which began to alter the ethnic composition of the city.

During the next decade, these trends continued with San Antonio redirecting its trade toward the growing areas of Texas and toward the larger growth patterns of the United States. A mail route and a stage line were established between San Antonio and San Diego, providing a link to the west, and plans were made for the construction of a railroad link with the Gulf coast (Fehrenbach, 1968: 319). Santa Fe was beginning to feel the impact of new migrations. It was during this period that the first major influx of Protestants began to be felt in New Mexico, and congregations were formed in Santa Fe. Also, some of the overflow of European immigration began to filter through to the far Southwest. The major migration came from Americans from the Middle West, which meant that as the Civil War approached, New Mexico would remain loyal to the Union while Texas, peopled largely by Southern Americans, would secede.

Both of these cities went through similar patterns of growth and change during their early history, yet significant differences remained by the 1860's. San Antonio began rapidly to lose its Spanish character and became a more cosmopolitan city with extensive economic and cultural ties throughout the Southwest. Santa Fe felt these influences but remained largely a Spanish city with a relatively small Anglo population. Although it was a major trade center, it did not develop the extensive links with other areas and with its hinterland that occurred in San Antonio. The fact that San Antonio was located in a state and was much more deeply involved in the larger pattern of American growth may help to explain this. Santa Fe remained in a territory and, although it played a significant role in the pattern of westward expansion, remained on the periphery of those developments.

Data and Methods

A. *The Data*

Our data are taken from copies of the enumeration schedules of the United States Census of 1860 for the two cities. The official report of the 1860 census was published in 1865 and was of limited value to sociologists for several reasons: (1) the tables were obviously not prepared with sociologists in mind, and few cross-tabulations were provided; (2) the geographical units most often used were for regions consisting of several states; and (3) most important, the Civil War was just ending, and apparently little effort was put into the publication.

Fortunately, however, microfilm copies of the original census enumerator's schedules are available, more than making up for the deficiencies of the original publication. The enumerators were United States Marshals and their employees, and the schedules remain in the original longhand. This makes data processing somewhat tedious, but individuals are listed by name, and any combination of variables is possible.

Because of this unique form of the data, the quality of the data varies. The enumerators sometimes made misspellings or wrote in a sloppy hand, making deciphering necessary. Also, in spots, the ink has faded, reducing legibility. Some enumerators were less zealous than others, so that gaps exist in the recording of certain variables. While these deficiencies must be taken into account, we do not feel these are shortcomings. Such weaknesses surely appear in every early census, and, in this case, the decisions were made under our control, rather than by an uninterested clerk.

B. *The Sample*

Because our main purpose is to explore and describe the social makeup of these historical populations in an informal as well as a statistical way, we wanted to include as many cases as possible in our sample. At the same time, we were limited in resources. For these reasons, we decided to include in our sample the entire work force (that is, every case for which an occupation was listed). This technique produced a sample of about 4400 cases (Santa Fe, N = 4635; San Antonio, N = 8235). This includes almost every adult male in the population, as well as those females with listed occupations (generally not including housewives and unpaid family farm workers), and a substantial number of children (mainly servants). Information on these individuals was copied from the microfilm, coded, and punched onto cards.

C. The Variables

The enumeration forms listed the following categories: name, age, sex, color, occupation, value of real and personal property, birthplace, marital status, number of servants, and literacy. Combinations of these, plus information given for individuals living in the same household as the subject, allowed us to infer values for several additional variables, producing a total of fourteen. Unfortunately, given the limitations of our format, an adequate treatment of all of these is not possible in this study. We have chosen for this analysis ethnicity, occupation, marital status, family size, literacy, and birthplace.

The choice of ethnicity is obvious. This variable is a composite, constructed from the census categories of color, name, and birthplace. The general code used by the enumerators was blank for White, and Black, Mixed, and Indian. The Black and Indian categories were recoded in the same form. Cases in the "Mixed" category were coded Indian or Black, depending upon the birthplace of the individual. The "White" category was divided into non-Spanish-surname and Spanish-surname depending upon surname, and, in difficult cases, birthplace.

Occupation was coded into the eleven categories of the Edwards occupational classification currently used by the United States Census Bureau.

Marital status on the original forms was simply indicated by a check mark. We made no attempt to determine if unmarried people had always been single or if they were divorced, widowed, or separated. Thus, the unmarried category includes all four.

Family size of the subject was inferred from the listing of other people with the same surname living in the same household with (and including) the subject, also from the marital status of the subject, excluding apparent siblings and parents of the subject.

Literacy was coded directly from the original schedule, which required a check mark if the subject would not "read and write."

Birthplace was listed on the original schedule. Our coding attempted to introduce relevant sociological distinctions: North-

ern United States/slave states; Anglo-Saxon Protestant Europe–
Southern, Eastern Europe, and Ireland. For our purposes,
birthplace was taken as an indication of social origins and
migration.

D. *Methods of Analysis*

Since our major purpose is simply to describe, the method of
analysis is a simple presentation of the data in tabular form (the
independent variable, ethnicity, correlated with each dependent
variable) for each city, with comparisons between the cities, and
appropriate interpretation.

Analysis of the Data

Table 1 presents an overall distribution of ethnicity for the two
cities. There are some significant differences which reflect the
patterns of growth and migration which affect these cities. San
Antonio is by and large an Anglo city by 1860, while Santa Fe
remained predominantly Spanish by roughly the same percentage.
An interesting, and perhaps significant, absence is the lack of any
data for Blacks and Indians in San Antonio. This would indicate
that those groups were not considered part of the work force, or
else were not considered worth enumerating by the individual
census takers. Santa Fe had only a very small number of Blacks
and Indians. This may reflect the isolation of New Mexico from
the more eastern Southwestern states that seceded in 1861 while
New Mexico remained loyal to the Union. The small number of
Indians indicates that most were probably coded as Spanish-

Table 1. Ethnic Distribution, Per Cent, Santa Fe and San Antonio, 1860

Ethnicity	Santa Fe	San Antonio
Non-Spanish Surname White	18.3 (316)	73.7 (1963)
Spanish Surname	79.3 (1366)	26.3 (701)
Indian	1.7 (29)	0.0 (0)
Black	0.7 (11)	0.0 (0)
Total	100.0 (1722)	100.0 (2664)

Table 2a. Occupation by Ethnicity, Per Cent, Santa Fe, 1860

Occupation	Ethnicity			
	Non-Spanish Surname White	Spanish Surname	Indian	Black
Professional, Technical	21.2 (67)	2.6 (36)	0.0 (0)	0.0 (0)
Managers, Officials, Proprietors	14.9 (47)	1.8 (25)	0.0 (0)	0.0 (0)
Farm Owners and Managers	1.6 (5)	14.3 (195)	6.9 (2)	0.0 (0)
Clerical and Kindred Workers	12.6 (40)	1.2 (16)	0.0 (0)	0.0 (0)
Sales Workers	0.6 (2)	1.7 (23)	0.0 (0)	0.0 (0)
Craftsmen, Foremen, and Kindred Workers	29.1 (92)	16.7 (227)	3.4 (1)	0.0 (0)
Operatives and Kindred Workers	2.5 (8)	3.9 (53)	0.0 (0)	0.0 (0)
Private Household Workers	3.2 (10)	21.9 (298)	75.9 (22)	75.9 (22)
Service Workers, Except Private Household	6.6 (21)	6.5 (88)	6.9 (2)	0.0 (0)
Farm Laborers	0.3 (1)	9.5 (130)	3.4 (1)	0.0 (0)
Laborers, Except Farm	7.3 (23)	19.9 (271)	3.4 (1)	27.3 (3)
Total	100.0 (316)	100.0 (1362)	100.0 (29)	100.0 (11)

Table 2b. Occupation by Ethnicity, Per Cent, San Antonio

Occupation	Non-Spanish Surname White	Spanish Surname
Professional, Technical	11.0 (215)	1.0 (7)
Managers, Officials, Proprietors	14.0 (274)	3.4 (24)
Farm Owners and Managers	4.3 (85)	6.6 (46)
Clerical and Kindred Workers	8.1 (159)	2.7 (19)
Sales Workers	1.0 (19)	0.4 (3)
Craftsmen, Foremen and Kindred Workers	31.9 (624)	23.2 (162)
Operatives and Kindred Workers	1.8 (35)	1.6 (11)
Private Household Workers	8.5 (167)	6.0 (42)
Service Workers, Except Private Household	2.2 (44)	0.4 (3)
Farm Laborers	2.6 (50)	2.6 (18)
Laborers, Except Farm	14.6 (286)	52.0 (363)
Total	100.0 (1958)	100.0 (698)

surname whites, or else there were actually very few allowed to
live within the city and participate in the work force.

Table 2 presents the distribution of occupations (Edwards'
classification) for both cities. These figures are fundamental to
explaining the nature of the ethnic relations of the 1860's and to
demonstrating the roots of the pattern of occupational discrimination which we have in the Southwest today. The Spanish-
surnamed work force in both cities falls largely into the unskilled
and service categories while the Anglo work force is found mainly
in the skilled crafts and in the higher occupational categories.
In Santa Fe, for example, the number of professionals and man-
agers of Spanish descent is extremely small, while more than a
third of the Anglos are in these classifications. Further, in the
clerical classification, the Anglos have ten times a greater percentage than the Spanish-surnames, and the craftsman category
Anglos nearly double the percentage of Spanish-surnamed individuals. On the other hand, in the classifications of household
worker, farm laborer and laborer the percentage of Spanish-
surnamed individuals far outnumbers the percentage of Anglos.
What this means is that the skilled occupations, the "white collar"
positions, and the professions are the almost exclusive preserve
of the Anglos; while the Spanish-surnamed, the Blacks, and the
Indians are relegated to the lower occupational classifications.
This is in a city that has a majority of Spanish-surnamed population, outnumbering the Anglos more than four to one. In San
Antonio, with a larger Anglo population (almost three Anglos to
every Spanish-surnamed individual), these trends and patterns
are seen even more clearly. The pattern would seem to indicate
that as Anglos increased in numbers, the relative position of those
of Spanish descent in the work force began to decline. The
relatively large number of Anglo household workers in San Antonio reflects the number of European immigrants rather than a
rebalancing of the occupational distribution. What may actually
have occurred was a displacement of a significant number of
Spanish-surnamed servants by higher status European servants.

Table 3 shows marital status by ethnicity, and demonstrates
some interesting patterns. For both cities, the work force is
largely unmarried. Significantly, the Indians and Blacks in Santa
Fe were for the most part unmarried, perhaps reflecting their
extremely low status and the fact that most were attached to white
households as servants. For both the Anglos and the Spanish-
surnamed, most were unmarried, which might reflect the frontier

Table 3. Marital Status by Ethnicity, Per Cent, Santa Fe and San Antonio, 1860

Marital Status	Santa Fe				San Antonio	
	Non-Spanish Surname White	Spanish-Surname	Indian	Black	Non-Spanish Surname White	Spanish-Surname
Unmarried	85.4 (270)	58.3 (797)	100.0 (29)	90.9 (10)	62.0 (1216)	60.6 (425)
Married	14.6 (46)	41.7 (569)	0.0 (0)	9.1 (1)	38.0 (746)	39.4 (276)
Total	100.0 (316)	100.0 (1366)	100.0 (29)	100.0 (11)	100.0 (1962)	100.0 (701)

nature of the two cities and a more transient population than would be found in established eastern cities. The frontier would attract the unattached and provide a temporary residence. It may also reflect the lack of available females, a problem on many frontiers. It is significant, however, that the Anglos tend to be less often married, while the Spanish-surnamed are fairly balanced. This would reflect the more permanent and stable nature of the Spanish-surnamed population, while the Anglo population would be more transient and less tied to locality.

Those that were married tended to have relatively small families (Table 4) with only one or two dependents. Again, this might reflect the frontier nature of the two cities. The Anglo residents of San Antonio tended to consist of more families, indicating that more may have intended to settle in the area and to make a more permanent residence. It might also demonstrate the frontier nature of Santa Fe with a relatively small number of Anglo families planning to settle and become permanent residents. Significantly, the majority of Spanish-surnamed in Santa Fe tended to be married and to have families, which reflects the permanence of their residence within the city. These data also attack the myth of the large frontier family. For the most part, at least in these two cities, the large family was the exception rather than the rule.

Table 5 demonstrates differential patterns of literacy which may explain some of the occupational patterns seen in Table 2. By far the majority of non-Spanish-surname whites were literate. For the Spanish-surnamed, the Blacks, and the Indians, this pattern is reversed, with the majority being illiterate (San Antonio's Spanish-surnamed being an exception to this by 0.8 percentage points). It may well be that the vicious circle of illiteracy, the lack of educational opportunities, and the resulting limitations of

Table 4. Family Size by Ethnicity, Per Cent, Santa Fe and San Antonio, 1860

| Family Size | Santa Fe | | | | San Antonio | |
	Non-Spanish Surname White	Spanish-Surname	Indian	Black	Non-Spanish Surname White	Spanish-Surname
Single	85.7 (269)	49.2 (672)	79.3 (23)	63.6 (7)	58.2 (1138)	57.2 (394
One or Two Dependents	7.6 (24)	26.7 (365)	17.2 (5)	27.3 (3)	18.7 (366)	21.8 (150
Three to Five Dependents	6.0 (19)	19.6 (268)	3.4 (1)	9.1 (1)	19.1 (373)	15.5 (107
Six or More Dependents	0.7 (2)	4.4 (60)	0.0 (0)	0.0 (0)	4.1 (80)	5.5 (38)
Total	100.0 (314)	100.0 (1365)	100.0 (29)	100.0 (11)	100.0 (1957)	100.0 (689

economic opportunities was well founded by 1860, and had set a pattern that limited minority group mobility in the Southwest through the middle of the twentieth century.

Finally, Table 6 tells us a great deal about the origins of the two major ethnic groups in these two cities. The Anglos of Santa Fe for the most part migrated from the United States or from Northern Europe, with a smaller, yet significant, migration from Southern Europe. Very few Anglos were native-born New Mexicans, reflecting the isolation of the city from the United States well into the 1820's. The Spanish-surnamed in Santa Fe, however, were largely native born, with most of the rest migrating from Mexico. In San Antonio, a similar pattern can be seen, yet with significant differences. The largest group of Anglo migrants came from Northern Europe reflecting the major waves of German migration of the 1840's and '50's. Most of the rest of the Anglo population came from the United States with a slight edge going to those from the South. Yet, there was an almost equal number of Southern European migrants, reflecting the large numbers of Irish who were coded into that category because of their predominantly Roman Catholic religious preference. For the Spanish-surnamed in San Antonio, the majority migrated from Mexico. The fact that the city was virtually deserted for periods of time between the 1820's and the 1840's may explain this pattern. How-

Table 5. Literacy by Ethnicity, Per Cent, Santa Fe and San Antonio, 1860

	Santa Fe				San Antonio	
Literacy	Non-Spanish Surname White	Spanish-Surname	Indian	Black	Non-Spanish Surname White	Spanish-Surname
Literate	93.7 (296)	34.7 (474)	34.5 (10)	18.2 (2)	98.8 (1939)	50.8 (356)
Illiterate	6.3 (20)	65.3 (892)	65.5 (19)	81.8 (9)	1.2 (24)	49.2 (345)
Total	100.0 (316)	100.0 (1366)	100.0 (29)	100.0 (11)	100.0 (1963)	100.0 (701)

ever, a significant number were native-born Texans and far out-numbered the native-born Anglos.

Summary and Conclusions

1. A pattern of occupational discrimination is quite apparent as early as 1860, a pattern that may have been instrumental in establishing a system of economic exploitation of Spanish-surnamed individuals.

2. San Antonio was a much more Anglicized city, and reflected the new waves of migration and the larger patterns of national development, while Santa Fe retained its Spanish character and remained isolated from those broader developments.

3. Individuals of Spanish descent were more likely to be married and tended to have larger families, perhaps reflecting the more permanent nature of the Spanish residents of these cities.

4. The occurrence of illiteracy among the Spanish-surnamed reflects patterns similar to those found in the occupational data. The basis for a systematic pattern of discrimination was already well founded by 1860.

5. Most Spanish-surnamed individuals were native born or migrated from Mexico, while the Anglo population was comprised almost entirely of Americans and new Northern European immigrants.

Table 6. Birthplace by Ethnicity, Per Cent,
Santa Fe and San Antonio, 1860

	Santa Fe		San Antonio	
Birthplace	Non-Spanish-Surname White	Spanish-Surname	Non-Spanish-Surname White	Spanish-Surname
New Mexico	3.2 (10)	89.3 (1216)	0.0 (0)	0.7 (5)
Texas	0.3 (1)	0.2 (3)	3.6 (69)	30.8 (216)
Mexico	0.0 (0)	9.9 (135)	0.6 (12)	67.3 (472)
Southern U.S.	18.4 (58)	0.0 (0)	12.8 (243)	0.0 (0)
Northern U.S.	21.9 (69)	0.0 (0)	11.6 (220)	0.0 (0)
Other N. Am.	5.4 (17)	0.2 (2)	2.3 (44)	0.0 (0)
Northern, Western Europe	38.4 (121)	0.0 (0)	46.4 (881)	0.2 (2)
Southern, Eastern Europe	12.2 (38)	0.2 (3)	22.6 (429)	0.7 (5)
Other	0.3 (1)	0.2 (2)	0.1 (2)	0.1 (1)
Total	100.0 (315)	100.0 (1361)	100.0 (1900)	100.0 (701)

These findings are fairly modest, and at best tentative; yet they do demonstrate some of the patterns of ethnic relations that seem to have been well established by 1860. They present an opportunity to describe the nature of ethnicity in two Southwestern frontier cities, and may provide the beginning of a broader examination of the sources and roots of the present pattern of ethnicity we find in the Southwest today.

References

Bancroft, Hubert H.
1890   History of Texas and the North Mexican States,
       Volume I. San Francisco: The History Company.
Fehrenbach, T. R.
1968   Lone Star: A History of Texas and Texans. New York:
       The MacMillan Co.
Loyola, Sister Mary
1939   "The American occupation of New Mexico: 1821–1852."
       New Mexico Historical Review 14 (January, April, July):
       34–75, 143–199, 230–286.
Moorhead, Max L.
1958   New Mexico's Royal Road. Norman: University of Oklahoma
       Press.
Wheeler, Kenneth W.
1968   To Wear a City's Crown: The Beginnings of Urban Growth in
       Texas, 1836–1865. Cambridge: Harvard University Press.
Writers' Program
1940   New Mexico. Works Projects Administration.
       New York: Hastings House.

*This paper is a revision of a paper presented at the annual meetings of the Southwestern Social Science Association, Spring, 1973. The research was in part supported by a grant from the Faculty Research Committee, the University of Oklahoma.

Social Change on the Latin American Frontier

Emilio Willems

A PROBE into the changes that frontier conditions presumably bring to an emerging society cannot really succeed without a careful redefinition of a term which has been known, at least in the United States, for its normative and emotional connotations. The attributes that, rightly or wrongly, have been ascribed to the North American frontier, have tended to gain acceptance as universal criteria by which frontier status has been bestowed upon or denied to other areas of the world. Few anthropologists, I believe, would go along with the idea that, to qualify as a frontier, social life on freshly occupied lands should necessarily generate individualism, democracy, inventiveness, materialism, entrepreneurship, or whatever real or mythological traits are associated with North American frontier life. As an anthropologist I refuse to impose ethnocentric criteria on a process the component aspects of which are fairly uncomplicated and truly universal. By frontier I mean an area of highly variable size into which migrants have moved to exploit some of its known resources. The process of appropriating these resources is competitive and requires the establishment of a system of rules by which the new society proposes to live. The migrants of course attempt to transplant their own cultural traditions, but these do not always fit the situation and require changes. However, changes which may be agreeable to some are resisted by others. Antagonisms and conflict are aggravated if, as it happens most of the time, the cultural traditions of the migrants are at variance with each other. The frontier society is thus characterized by anomie and social disorganization, meaning that differing value systems and modes of behavior are pitted against each other. Once the resources are distributed and the emergent society has found a *modus vivendi*, the area begins to lose its frontier character.

I

There are cases of highly cohesive groups—mostly religious sects—that migrate to frontier areas as single bodies, whose internal solidarity would seem to preclude anomie. Although such groups may be able to avoid internal strife, they still have to face the (potentially antagonistic) competition of all those frontiersmen who do not share their persuasion and cannot be kept out of the general area. In fact, sectarian intransigence tends to become a divisive factor in the eventual development of community structures. The concept of the frontier does not imply that its resources have never been touched by human hands, or that it is totally uninhabited. The existence of a native population tends further to intensify the problems the migrants have to face. Needless to say, there are several ways of solving the problem of the "natives," and not all of these are mutually exclusive. The society emerging out of the frontier conditions may be relatively egalitarian or seigneurial, it may be composed of small holders or large estates, or of a mixture of both. It may be based on pastoral, agricultural, mineral, or other resources, but to qualify as frontier it does not have to be an economic "success." The frontier areas of Latin America that have come to the attention of social scientists have almost invariably been identified with some economically significant export crops, such as sugar, coffee, cotton, wheat, cacao, rubber, tobacco, beef, and so forth, or with the discovery of major mineral resources.

The conceptual restriction of the frontier to such characteristics seems totally unwarranted. I propose to study the "unsuccessful" frontier unsung by economists and historians. Oriented towards markets and international trade, the "successful" frontier has bestowed wealth on the upper classes, but it has proved quite unsuccessful in apportioning an adequate share of that wealth to the rural working class. The unsuccessful or anonymous frontier, on the other hand, is the frontier of the little man, who has not found wealth, but merely conditions of survival superior to those that prevailed in the area or country whence he came.

Frontier areas, particularly those linked to the development of mineral resources and commercial crops, have been known to generate their own forms of urbanization. While the distinction between rural and urban frontier seems neither new nor objectionable, my suggestion that the sprawling shantytowns surrounding numerous urban centers of Latin America be considered as a version of the urban frontier will probably come as a shock to many adherents of traditional frontier ideology.

It seems difficult indeed to think of squatter settlements except in terms of "social cancer," "incubators of rebels and gangsters," and "urbanistic monstrosities" (cit. apud Leeds 1968: 41). One suspects judgments of this sort to come from middle- and upper-class people, but I venture to suggest that the indigenous peoples of North and South America judged the European frontier invading their homeland and appropriating or destroying its resources with the same abhorrence the established urban classes nowadays exhibit with regard to the proliferating squatter settlements.

II

No matter whether urban or rural, the anonymous frontier seems to have generated deeper and more comprehensive changes than economically successful frontier areas, at least in Latin America. More or less isolated in remote areas, the anonymous settler depended on his ability to use the resources of his immediate environment in order to stay alive. This might include the selective adoption of indigenous technology and custom, perhaps a complete amalgamation with local Indian groups, a rather common process manifest in the rapid emergence of a mestizo society with a hybrid culture. While on the anonymous frontier radical culture change was a question of survival, the wealth of the plantation and mining frontiers made it possible to maintain a European style of life by massive culture transfer from Portugal and Spain.

Paraguay in the sixteenth and early seventeenth century may be regarded as the prototype of the anonymous frontier. Originally, the few hundred Spaniards who moved into Paraguay were hardly different from any other group of conquistadores, but the complete failure to discover the expected mineral wealth forced the survivors of many fruitless expeditions to take up subsistence agriculture as a last resort. These three or four hundred Spaniards were a thousand miles away from the La Plata estuary, their numbers were not replenished by new settlers and, to complete isolation, trade restriction virtually closed the La Plata region to the rest of the world.

Under these conditions some kind of close association with the tractable Guaraní Indians became imperative. "Instead of attempting to force the Indians to become adapted to the Spanish system, the Spanish soldiers expediently adjusted themselves to hative habits by bringing Indian women to Asunción as wives and concubines and living by the contributions in food and services which their Indian relatives and allies freely provided" (Service: 1954: 30–31). It seems that most Spaniards lived in polygymous marriages, and already by the middle of the sixteenth century the number of mestizo children was estimated to be about six thousand (Service 1954: 34). Not surprisingly, native crops and agricultural techniques were added to European domestic plants and animals, and food preparation acquired a distinctive indigenous flavor. From their Indian mothers the mestizo children learned Guaraní rather than Spanish, and up to this day Guaraní still is spoken by most Paraguayans (in addition to Spanish). The economy was based on barter rather than money exchange and, to the rare visitor, the Spanish settlers died out, the mestizo population proliferated and took over the frontier tradition by founding many new settlements in Paraguay.

The processes that changed Iberian, as well as the indigenous, culture occurred in many frontier areas of Latin America. In the Amazon and São Francisco river basins, in São Paulo, in northern Argentina, in large sections of Colombia, and in many parts of Central America, early frontier conditions led to large-scale miscegenation and cultural hybridization. In many of these areas indigenous groups almost ceased to exist as distinct biological and cultural entities, and so did the Portuguese and Spanish settlers. The more these were forced to rely on local resources and indigenous technology and custom, the profounder the changes their Iberian traditions underwent.

More often than not life in anonymous frontier areas involved the loss of significant elements of Iberian culture. Paradoxically, the disappearance of particular cultural elements proved adaptive in that the preservation of such elements would have jeopardized the viability of the frontier. The adaptive value of culture loss was even more forcefully demonstrated in certain frontier areas opened by European immigrants during the nineteenth century. Many early settlements established in the subtropical rain forests of Southern Brazil, mainly by German, Italian, and Polish immigrants, had to face two major problems: The extreme scarcity of capital and credit, combined with the remoteness of markets capable of absorbing agricultural surpluses. The new settler had to use farming techniques producing the highest yields within the shortest possible time, and at the lowest possible cost. As I have shown in my earlier studies of German immigration to southern Brazil, settlers who attempted to clear their jungle patches of the felled trees and tree roots, in order to use cultivation techniques brought over from Europe, often failed before the first year was over. They might have a nicely cleared field, but they had nothing to eat because the strategically crucial planting seasons were lost in preparatory tasks. However, those settlers that took over the indigenous slash-and-burn agriculture, and planted their first food crops among the partly carbonized tree trunks, survived the critical first year and stayed on. Since markets were distant and poor, there was no point in preserving or improving the intensive farming methods then prevailing in Europe. In other words, the adoption of primitive, indigenous agricultural methods, and indigenous crops, mainly maize and manioc, turned out to be adaptive in the frontier areas of Rio Grande do Sul and Santa Catarina (Willems, 1946: 329ff). It is true that in time some of these settlements modernized as new groups of immigrants arrived, and urban markets expanded and became more accessible, but in many settlements, slash-and-burn agriculture associated with a predominance of native crops remained, and eventually outgrew their original usefulness.

Needless to say, in most earlier settlements established by European immigrants frugality became a way of life. Still in the nineteen thirties, I found the settlers of the Alto Itajaí Mirím frontier (Brusque, Santa Catarina) living in a barter economy and practicing indigenous agriculture. Their only tools were the hoe, the ax, the billhook, and the machete. Men, women, and children walked barefoot all year round, and their clothes were made of the cheapest available materials. They lived on a diet of corn bread, manioc, rice, black beans, jerked beef, and occasional salt pork.

While most people in Alto Itajaí Mirím were native-born of German descent, a few were immigrants, and one of these, a man from Pomerania, had discovered a way of linking local agricultural resources to the market economy. He had established a rendering plant to fatten hogs with low-priced corn brought from local settlers. In contrast to corn (or any other agricultural product) lard could be sold in the next town at a price which made the whole operation quite profitable, in spite of the fact that the lard had to be transported by pack train on a jungle trail, parts of which were flooded by heavy rainfalls most of the time. The settlers could demand cash for their corn, but since there was little opportunity to spend money, they preferred to exchange it for cloth, salt, kerosene, tools, or other articles from the local store.

Obviously the whole set-up involved a radical break with German peasant traditions. Technology, food habits, dress, and housing patterns had changed almost beyond recognition; instead of a peasant village there were widely scattered farmsteads, transportation was by ox cart of mule train, and the settlers' participation in the money economy was marginal at best. The Alto Itajaí Mirím area was not part of a broad pioneer "front" advancing slowly from east to west, but like so many Latin American frontiers, a small enclave which had been opened in the nineteen twenties by a landowner desirous of selling his holdings in small parcels.

The extent to which the anonymous frontier participates in the market economy varies considerably. In a recent study of black frontiersmen in the Pacific lowlands of Ecuador and Colombia, Norman E. Whitten, Jr., emphasizes strong temporary demands for resources partly controlled by the black settlers. Such short-lived "booms" account for the temporary role the frontiersmen play in the market, over and above the level of their traditional subsistence agriculture (Whitten, 1974: 74ff).

III

The structure of the frontier society may be described as "loose," in contrast to the structures of the migrants' society of origin. This means, among other things, that wider range of alternate ways of behavior is open to the individual frontiersman. He may, if he chooses to do so, engage in economic pursuits which will eventually move him or his children into a "higher" social class. Upward social mobility has, of course, been considered as the most desirable, and also the most common change characterizing a frontier society, but it has been associated almost exclusively with the economically successful frontier. Even there, data about the social origin of the settlers tend to be vague. In my own study on social mobility I found that of 900 landowners in northern Paraná, Brazil, less than one-third acquired land shortly after arrival in the area. This simply means that most of them could

not afford to make the requisite down payment on a small piece
of land. At any rate, these settlers did not belong to the poorest
stratum of migrants. Two-thirds of those who were landowners
in 1967 had worked their way up from the level of rural laborers,
tenant farmers, or sharecroppers. These agricultural activities
were often combined with wage-earning jobs. But of course,
northern Paraná has been one of the most successful frontiers of
the twentieth century, and upward mobility has been so common
that it is taken for granted by the local population (See also Margolis, 1973: 214.)

Unfortunately, the role of the frontier in the process of social
mobility has often been underrated or misunderstood, particularly
with regard to earlier frontiers.

First of all, one could argue, if there is a history of frontiers
reaching back to the very Conquest, social mobility must have
been rare or nonexistent, because the social structure of Spanish
and Portuguese America remained essentially unchanged until
the late nineteenth century. Actually, while social mobility was
slow and difficult elsewhere, it was common in frontier areas.
But it was also temporary, because, as frontier conditions began
to fade, the social structure assumed the customary rigidity and
eventually became indistinguishable from that of other traditional
structures of Ibero-America. This process was particularly visible
in the colonial cities where the founding families initiated their
social ascent by becoming recipients of land grants. If the new
settlement proved viable, the first settlers, owning the choicest
pieces of real estate, constituted the nucleus of a new upper class,
although their family genealogy or past history rarely justified
their status aspirations. Their social ascent was contingent on
frontier conditions, but once the land had been allocated the new
structure became as rigid as elsewhere in traditional urban society.
Both in Spanish America and Brazil this process was common
enough to constitute a cultural pattern (Morse, 1965: 38).

IV

It has been said that in Latin America "genuine" frontier conditions have been rare because the latifundio monopolized all available land and deprived the mass of potential pioneer settlers of
the social advantages of the North American frontier (Lambert,
1963: 59). Actually, most Latin American frontiers generated

social structures far more complex than the alleged dominance of the latifundio implies.

In the first place, pioneer migrants who succeeded in becoming owners of large estates in frontier areas, and thus members of the land-holding upper class, were frequently of modest origin. A case in point is the coffee frontier in Brazil between 1800 and 1830. The beginnings were primitive indeed. The first settlers of the Vassouras region, for example, had to settle for "small-scale cultivation carried on by a few slaves, when coffee was slowly, hesitatingly adapted to the highland" (Stein, 1957: 23). The main thing was to produce food crops and to become self-sufficient. Large estates and wealth appeared gradually after 1830. The great planters of Vassouras, many of whom were raised to the non-hereditary nobility of the Brazilian empire, were of "modest origin." They had been traders or small holders; some had made money in mining, and others were military men (Stein, 1957: 120). In other words, social mobility was the rule rather than the exception. There was no prevalence of the large estate while Vassouras was frontier. Later, many small holdings were absorbed by the latifundios, but they never completely disappeared (Stein, 1957: 225).

As the coffee frontier moved to and through the state of São Paulo, it continued to further upward mobility involving an increasing percentage of the population of the newly settled regions. By the middle of the nineteenth century the social composition of the pioneer settlers changed so far as an increasing number of immigrants from various European and Asian countries participated in the opening of the western regions of São Paulo. The moving coffee frontier attracted Italians, Spaniards, Japanese, Syrians, Lebanese, and smaller numbers from many other nations. Cultural pluralism became one of the major characteristics of the new settlements, quite in contrast to the more homogeneous composition of the older frontier areas. Actually, the interaction of different cultural traditions in an atmosphere of general tolerance tended to generate changes of various kinds. While the technology of earlier frontiers was hemmed in by routine, the frontiers of western São Paulo, and its extensions thoughout northern Paraná, proved highly receptive to experimental innovations. Cultural pluralism is further reflected in a high degree of religious differentiation. Along with the ethnic churches, a variety of Protestant denominations found a fertile field for missionary endeavor. There may be as many as five or six different Protestant churches, along with a Buddhist temple, a Ukranian sanctuary, and the usual Roman Catholic church, in a single community.

The frequent occurrence of non-Portuguese names among the owners of coffee farms suggests substantial upward mobility among immigrants, the majority of whom started out as rural laborers or sharecroppers. While only a minority moved to the top, a great many became proprietors of medium-sized or small holdings (*sítios*). In 1937, in four different frontier areas of São Paulo, the proportion of coffee farms with less than 25,000 trees— *sítios* or small holdings rather than *fazendas*—amounted to 88.8, 83, 71, and 64 per cent, the percentages being inversely proportional to the quality of the soil (Monbeig, 1952: 241).

Perhaps the most common way for an impecunious pioneer to acquire his own property was the *empreitada*, or contractual obligation assumed towards a landowner to clear a piece of jungle, to plant coffee trees, and tend them during the first four or five years. At the same time the *empreiteiro* had the right to plant food crops in between the rows of young coffee trees. At first no monetary compensations were involved in these contracts, but as labor became scarcer, the landowner had to pay a stipulated amount of money for each coffee tree found to be in satisfactory condition at the end of the contractual period. A hard-working and frugal *empreiteiro* was able to save enough money to make at least a down payment on a small piece of land.

While on the Brazilian coffee frontier the large estate predominated in terms of production and size of cultivated land, the Colombian coffee frontier typically generated small and medium-sized holdings. Even the largest coffee farms are merely *sílios* by Brazilian standards.

V

The conditions under which the anonymous frontier develops do not seem to justify expectations of upward mobility. As a matter of fact, far too little is known about this sort of frontier to support generalizations. Among the black frontiersmen of the Ecuadorian coast, an unspecified number of people apparently rise to a middle-class level (Whitten, 1965: 148ff). Some information has become available on the frontier of Caquetá, one of the Amazon territories belonging to Colombia. The population of Caquetá rose, from an estimated 77,510 in 1959, to approximately 300,000 in 1972. In 1963 about 100 families per month entered the Intendencia de Caquetá through Florencia, the regional capital (Tinnermeyer, 1964: 35).

The Caquetá frontier generated a land-tenure pattern different from that found in the rest of Colombia. 71.1 per cent of all settlers owned holdings from 5 to 100 hectares, totaling 34.17 per cent of the total land area under cultivation. 19.9 percent owned farms larger than 100 hectares, representing 65.68 per cent of all cultivated land, and no more than 9.0 percent owned less than 5 hectares, totaling 0.15 per cent of the land. In Colombia as a whole, 50 per cent of all farms measured less than three hectares, covering only 4 to 5 per cent of the land area. Farm units with more than 100 hectares represented 2.3 per cent of all farms and 50 per cent of all land (Tinnermeyer, 1964: 47–48).

The Caquetá frontier produces cattle, rice, corn, bananas, manioc, hogs, and wood, but, of the crops, only rice could be sold. As on most anonymous frontiers of Latin America, agricluture is of the slash-and-burn type, and primarily for subsistence. In spite of these obvious limitations, out of a sample of 184 settlers, who could be intensively interviewed, 164 or 89 per cent wanted to stay (Tinnermeyer, 1964: 63). Whatever the disadvantages of the Caquetá frontier, they could not be attributed to the size of the holdings. The mean size for the spontaneous settler was 75 hectares, and 60.4 hectares for the directed settlers (Tinnermeyer, 1964: 92). Not unexpected is the high percentage of squatters among the spontaneous settlers, of whom 35 per cent had no legal title at all, while another 43 per cent had only a bill of sale, but no registered title (Tinnermeyer, 1964: 97). To judge from the educational level of the colonists composing the sample, they all were of lower-class extraction, but the data do not support definite statements about upward mobility. However, there can be no doubt that nowhere outside the frontier areas of Colombia would these settlers have found a way to acquire or take possession of 60 or 70 hectares of cultivable land.

VI

One of the most far-reaching changes in Latin America, and many other parts of the world, may be seen in the fact that the modern city has been competing with rural frontier areas as the "land of opportunity," attracting hundred thousands of migrants who cannot immediately be absorbed by the physical and social structure of any given city. Frequently, these migrants take possession of land that does not belong to them, and in doing so they merely follow a pattern as old as European colonization in America. Beginning in the sixteenth century countless Spanish and Portuguese settlers seized land without paying attention to the rights of the native population. The *composición*, a jural device to legalize ownership of such land for a fee, was instituted by the Spanish crown, and since then virtually all legal systems of Latin America include established procedures to convert squatters into lawful owners. This is, of course, the hope of the modern shantytown dweller: Based on known precedents he perceives a chance to become the legitimate owner of the piece of land where he builds his temporary shack.

As a rule, these migrants are not inexperienced peasants freshly arriving from some remote village. Those who settle in large metropolitan areas have often been exposed to similar experiences in provincial cities, and participated in more than one attempt to establish themselves in a shantytown (Mangin, 1967: 68–69, Cardona Gutierrez, 1968: 70). There is enough evidence to support the assumption that most squatters understand the risks involved in their undertakings, and many have had opportunity to acquire the political skills necessary to deal with such risks.

What are the resources the shantytown settler intends to exploit? The answer is simple: the land he settles on and the labor market of the nearby city. They are interconnected: without an advantageous location in the vicinity of the city, the chances of engaging in some gainful economic activity remain slim. And without some sort of income, however uncertain, the possibility of improving the dwellings, or the squatter settlement in general, is practically nonexistent.

The most serious problem the squatter has to cope with is the hostility of the "native" population, which more often than not seems determined to thwart the migrants' attempts to settle on vacant land. Unlike the settlers of the jungle frontier, the urban squatters face an immensely superior enemy which cannot be overpowered, driven off, or enslaved like the indigenous populations. The squatters must proceed with extreme caution to avoid open confrontation. It is always preferable to choose marginal land on steep hillsides or swampy terrain usually considered unfit for urban development. If, in addition, it is public domain or of uncertain or unknown ownership, the chances are that occupation by squatters will not immediately be challenged by urban authorities. Effective squatter strategy further demands that occupation be a concerted action of a large number of families who build their first shacks at once, to confront the city with a *fait accompli* (See Mangin, 1967: 69.) Such strategy is not always successful of course, but one of the impressive qualities of these frontiersmen is their persistence in the face of defeat. They try time and again, and not always for the same reason. A new settlement may survive the hazards of the social environment, but, if it fails to live up to expectations, the most ambitious settlers join some more promising venture.

One of the most urgent requirements to be met by emerging shantytowns is social organization. Since urban institutional resources are not available to the settlers, they must find a *modus vivendi* by themselves. Virtually nothing is known about the earliest phases in the life of a new squatter settlement, but one may assume that a considerable amount of conflict is almost inevitable. Furthermore, to consolidate its existence, a new settlement must fight for almost everything other city dwellers take for granted. And this includes physical stability of the settlement, water, transportation, electricity, schools, police protection, hospitals, and so forth. Gradually, the almost amorphous mass of settlers acquires a structure, and becomes increasingly articulate. In the barrios of Caracas, for example, a junta is "elected" from among the first squatters, and one of the major tasks of the junta is to create an informal legal system concerning rights in land and housing. Since the majority of the squatters does not have legal title to the land they occupy, ownership of the house is separated from land ownership. Ownership then means the "rights to undisturbed possession" (Karst, 1971: 562). It is an unwritten law that the owner has the right to sell his house, or to give it away, but, if it remains vacant for several months, the junta may assign it to another family. Houses may be rented too, but the junta "prevents the landlord from evicting the tenant for nonpayment of rent" (Karst, 1971: 565–566). Furthermore, the junta arbitrates conflicts between neighbors and in extreme cases may try to expel troublemakers.

The spontaneous emergence of such legal systems seems relevant because it illustrates the settler's ability for innovation. Although relatively few data are available about the legal systems of other urban frontiers, we may assume that no squatter settlement could possibly survive for any length of time without some such informal structure.

Essential for the permanence of any squatter settlement appear to be the perception of dissidence in the society at large and the development of strategies designed to take advantage of disagreements among the urban holders. So far very little attention has been paid to the fact that many shantytowns are allowed to survive, and to expand year after year, in spite of periodical outbursts of public indignation and political opposition, because they are inexhaustible sources of cheap labor. Numerous maids, gardeners, washerwomen, chauffeurs, janitors, porters, paper boys, and assorted repairmen, serving most city districts come from nearby *favelas, barriadas, tugurios*, or whatever the local version of the squatter settlements may be.

Party politics, and the electoral system of most Latin American countries, also tend to further the permanence of the squatter settlements. What the settlers want is legal title to their house sites and all those improvements which would integrate the settlement into the urban service structure. Their expectations are reflected in the promises made by the party candidates running for municipal office. To make the most of the fierce competition among the different parties constitutes one of the major skills the settlers and their local leaders have to acquire. In one of the rare studies of political behavior in the favelas of Rio de Janeiro, it was found that, for the squatter, "universal suffrage is vital; it is an instrument of vindications and survival. It is through the ballot that he becomes clearly conscious of his needs and tests his representatives" (SAGMACS, 1960: 35).

To the settler of the anonymous urban frontier, exploitation of the political resources of the city is as vital as his struggle for economic survival. There are two major avenues open to the squatters: They may choose between seeking jobs and starting some independent enterprise. Often enough both avenues are exploited by different members of the same family including children. Neither wage earners nor independent operators can expect stability and continuing success in whatever field of endeavor is chosen, and wages and profits seldom cover more than the barest necessities. Whenever there is a small surplus it is probably invested in ameliorating or replacing the original shack with a more solid and larger structure. This is the advantage of the squatter settlement: it is highly adaptive under conditions of extreme economic instability. The settlers are not burdened with property taxes or any other kind of payment. No matter how long it takes, many families are capable of improving their housing conditions, and at the end of several years—usually from five to eight—they may own a modest brick house with a tile roof.

The risks and uncertainties the squatter of the urban frontier has to face are comparable to those confronting the rural frontiersman. Floods, droughts, pests, maladies of man and beast, lack of credit and markets constantly threaten the survival of the rural frontiersman as much as the urban squatter is imperiled by the spectre of coercive eviction, job instability, irregular income, low wages, and a host of problems associated with the lack of urban services. With luck and enormous effort both types of anonymous settlers may eventually rise to a level of relative stability. In the urban squatter settlement this point is reached when ownership of the lot is regulated, most original shanties have been replaced by permanent structures, and urban services have been made available to the population. Examples of this rather complex process exist in most major cities of Latin America.

Little is known about the social mobility in shantytowns. In the aforementioned study of several favelas of Rio de Janeiro, social mobility, upward as well as downward, was found to be "intense." Five "social strata" of settlers were described, the "highest consisting of people who had made it" and could afford to leave the favela. The members of the next lower stratum had improved their dwellings, and their way of life was somewhat above the level of mere survival. Next came the families who had to struggle hard to satisfy their most elementary necessities. The two lowest strata were barely distinguishable from each other, consisting of families living in the sort of squalor and social disorganization usually associated with life in shantytowns (SAGMACS 1960: 3). Similar levels of social mobility may be observed in most shantytowns and some are quite visible, even to the casual visitor, in the way the houses differ from each other. However, it should be added that the dimensions of social change on the anonymous urban frontier go way beyond social mobility. Actually, they encompass all those processes by which the shantytown dweller acquires the outlook, attitudes, and skills that make it possible for him to survive in an extremely difficult urban environment.

Bibliography

Cardona Gutierrez, Ramiro, "Migración, Urbanización y Marginalidad," in Ramiro Cardona Gutierrez, ed. *Urbanización y Marginalidad.* Bogotá: Publicación de la Asociación Colombiana de Facultades de Medicina, 1968.

Karst, Kenneth L., "Rights in Land and Housing in an Informal Legal System: The Barrios of Caracas," *The American Journal of Comparative Law* 9 (3): 550–574, Summer 1971.

Lambert, Jacques, "Requirements for Rapid Economic and Social Development: The View of the Historian and Sociologist," in Egbert de Vries and José Medina Echavarria, eds. *Social Aspects of Economic Development in Latin America*, Vol. I. Paris: UNESCO, 1963.

Leeds, Anthony, "The Anthropology of Cities: Some Methodological Issues." In Elizabeth M. Eddy, ed. *Urban Anthropology. Research Perspectives and Strategies* (Southern Anthropological Society, Proceedings, No. 2) Athens: University of Georgia Press, 1968.

Mangin, William, "Latin American Squatter Settlements: A Problem and a Solution." *Latin American Research Review*, 2, No. 3, 1967.

Margolis, Maxine L., *The Moving Frontier. Social and Economic Change in a Southern Brazilian Community.* Gainesville: University of Florida Press, 1973.

Monbeig, Pierre, *Pionniers et Planteurs de São Paulo.* Paris: Librairie Armand Colin, 1952.

Morse, Richard, "Recent Research on Latin American Urbanization: A Selective Survey with Commentary." *Latin American Research Review*, 1, Fall 1965.

SAGMACS, *Aspectos Humanos da Favela Carioca.* São Paulo: Estado de S. Paulo, Suplemento Especial 2, 1960.

Service, Elman R., *Spanish-Guarany Relations in Early Colonial Paraguay* (Anthropological Paper, No. 9, Museum of Anthropology, University of Michigan). Ann Arbor: University of Michigan Press, 1964.

Stein, Stanley, *Vassouras: A Brazilian Coffee County 1859–1900.* Cambridge: Harvard University Press, 1957.

Tinnermeyer, Ronald I., *New Land Settlements in the Eastern Lowlands of Colombia.* University of Wisconsin unpublished Ph.D. Dissertation, 1964.

Whitten, Norman E. Jr., *Class, Kinship, and Power in an Ecuadorian Town.* Stanford: Stanford University Press, 1965.

Whitten, Norman E. Jr., *Black Frontiersmen: A South American Case.* New York: John Wiley and Sons, 1974.

Willems, Emilio, *A Aculturacão dos Alemães no Brasil.* São Paulo: Companhia Editora Nacional, 1946.

Social Relations of Production on the Brazilian Frontier

Martin T. Katzman

RURAL SOCIAL STRUCTURE plays a key role in the economic development of newly settled regions. Those regions where plantation economies arose generally have remained poor, overwhelmingly rural, technologically stagnant, and socially hierarchic, while regions which have become prosperous, industrialized, and egalitarian have generally evolved out of family-farming societies.[1] The links between the egalitarian social structure and long-run development are: the broad base of demand, which facilitates the attainment of "threshholds" for import-substituting industrialization; a political system which is responsive to the welfare of all, and which therefore invests heavily and equally in education, health care, and transportation facilities; and a scarcity of cheap labor that encourages technological innovation, especially of the labor-saving kind.[2]

The purpose of this chapter is not to explore the links between rural social structure and industrialization, but to explain variations in time and space within the rural social structure and the former, in the context of a nation still undergoing frontier settlement. Within Brazil, different social structures have coexisted in adjacent regions; for example, plantations, sharecroppers, and commercial family farmers currently occupy different parts of the coffee region. Furthermore, some coffee zones have undergone the transition from slavery, to wage labor, to sharecropping, to family farming, back to other forms of dependency.

Ideally, one would like to obtain answers to the following questions concerning the social relations of production, from which rural social structures emerge: is the *control of the work* process vested in the worker, a manager, or the landowner; what are the *rules for distributing* output among factors of production—that is, do the workers receive a wage, a share of output, or a fixed payment in kind; is the *organization of work* on an individual or team basis, and if the latter is there a hierarchical division of labor; how is the *ownership* of complementary factors of production—capital and land—distributed among the workers?

Traditionally, neoclassical economic theory has taken the social relations of production, the patterns of land tenure, and distribution of land rights within the proper domain of the historian or sociologist. Especially in the last decade, several classes of neoclassical models have been developed to explain variations in the social relations of production. Such relations are viewed as a "social technology" that can be adopted or discarded as they facilitate or hinder the maximization of the landlord's profits. One class of models focuses on the parameters of the agricultural production-function, another on the risks and transactions costs of agriculture in various regions, and a third on the impact of factor endowments, that is, land-labor ratios, on the opportunities to exploit labor.

We should first review these neoclassical theories of the social relations of production. The spatial emphasis is upon newly settled regions, where the inertia of tradition may have less importance than in the European metropolis. The lack of inertia as an explanatory force would be least important for the tropics where natural conditions were quite different from the metropolis and where unique relations of production arose, that is, slavery. The conceptual dichotomy of greatest interest here is between plantations and family farms. Following Taylor, we define a plantation as any large and continuous tract under unified ownership and management, operated commercially on the basis of some form of dependent labor, be it slavery, wage labor, fixed-rent tenancy, or sharecropping.[3] The distinguishing feature is whether or not the land is owned, the work process is controlled, and the yield of the land is appropriated by the worker-family unit. On plantations, the owner of the land factor of production controls the work process and shares in the output to a greater or lesser degree depending upon the specific relations of production: slavery, serfdom, sharecropping, fixed rent tenancy, or wage labor.

Second, we attempt to explain variations over time and space in two frontier regions of Brazil. One particular focus is the coffee frontier of São Paulo and Paraná, where planned development schemes have allegedly given rise to a rural middle class. Another regional focus is the former frontier of Goiás, which has undergone rapid and "spontaneous" settlement in the last fifty years.

Production-Function Approach

The production-function approach attempts to derive the social relations of production in a newly settled region from the technological conditions under which the regional staple is produced. The relevant technological parameters are: (1) the output elasticities of the various factors of production—land, capital, and labor intensities; (2) the elasticity of substitution between capital and labor; and (3) the returns to scale.[4]

It is hypothesized that crops grown in the tropics are highly capital and labor intensive, have a low elasticity of substitution between capital and labor, and are characterized by substantial economies of scale. Consequently, production must take place in large units, employing considerable capital and labor. Since capital and labor are not easily substituted, an increase in wages will not result in further mechanization: thus, the proletariat is not easily liquidated as a class.

A variant of the production-function model holds that tropical crops require considerably more transformation or beneficiation than temperate crops, and that these forward-linked industrial processes enjoy considerable economies of scale. Processing *in situ* is desirable if the crop is perishable in its raw state, as is sugar, or if processing reduces shipping weight, as does rice milling or cotton ginning.

While it is not obvious that temperate crops, such as wheat, require less processing than tropical crops, the existence of scale economies in processing does not imply that all operations must be organized within a single agricultural enterprise. Economies of scale in beneficiation is an argument for the rarity of mills and refiners, and perhaps their proximity to raw materials, but not for vertical integration.

Another variation of the argument is that large-scale organization is necessary to support research and to facilitate the diffusion of innovation. In family farming zones, however, the same function is performed by agricultural experiment stations, extension services, and 4-H clubs.

For the moment, let us accept these assumptions about the agricultural production functions for tropical crops. If they faced identical costs of labor and capital, then the large unit could outbid the smaller for the land, and a plantation society would come into being. These factor-costs are not likely to be equal, because the wage the plantation would have to pay the laborers would exceed the imputed value of the labor when working for oneself.[5] This wage difference must compensate the worker for his loss of independence, and may be high enough to eliminate the technological benefits from the economies of scale. The inutility of plantation work accounts for the inability of many plantations in newly settled areas to induce the indigenous population to abandon their peasant culture, and the resultant importation of aliens.

If the wage differences paid by the plantation owner (pecuniary diseconomy of scale) more than offsets the technological economies of scale, plantation owners as a class have an incentive to create restrictions on labor mobility, via serfdom or slavery. If slave labor were available, so long as the maintenance and supervision costs of slaves did not exceed the imputed cost of free labor, the plantation owner could not be outbid for land by family farmers. If legal restraints prohibited the alienation of land from the original (large) grantees, then workers would have no choice but to work for the plantation owner.

If workers had a great disutility to working in a dependent status on the plantation, why does the landowner not capture some of the benefits of the workers' demand for independence by selling the land to them instead of exploiting it directly? While noneconomic goals, such as prestige and power maximization may be important, the nature of the capital markets may be more so.[6]

An institutional factor favoring the plantation is the imperfection of the markets in both financial and human capital. Financial capital in a newly settled region is likely to be unequally distributed, severely rationed, and highly immobile. Those who already possess considerable capital are most likely to be able to offer collateral and reasonable down payments for the purchase of frontier land. Transactions costs for sellers are minimized by selling large blocks of land. Since the absolute amount of capital needed to operate a tropical plantation is also high, relatively few workers will be able to afford both the land and the labor necessary to operate one.

In the temperate region, the relatively low optimum farm size requires smaller amounts of capital and permits a wider distribution of ownership. Because there are no significant economics of scale in production, those with large amounts of capital will not continually displace smaller farmers. On the contrary, larger operators will be at a disadvantage because of the wage gap they will have to meet. The high elasticity of substitution between capital and labor implies that small increases in wages lead to mechanization and the reduction of hired labor or the increase in the amount of land utilized. The result is a society of owner-operators with no permanent rural proletariat or tenantry. Dependent workers tend to be individuals who work a few years to accumulate enough savings to purchase their own farm.[7]

In summary, the production-function approach suggests that the plantation provides the optimum social relation of production in the tropics; the family farm, the optimum in the temperate zones, both systems time-tested by natural selection. It is noteworthy that the approach is robust to the extent of being ahistorical. Since technology determines the social relations of production, it is not important whether a region is newly settled or not. Perfecting the capital market may change the odds of a peon becoming a planter, but technology dictates that the social relations in the tropics remain essentially hierarchic.

There is considerable evidence that family-farm and plantation crops cannot be easily distinguished on the basis of economics of scale or factor-intensity. Output elasticities of land, labor, and capital have been obtained by econometric studies of a wide range of crops in both tropical and temperate countries (Table 1). The regional variations in these parameters for a given crop suggests that these functions are somehow misspecified, that the data are of uneven quality, the crops are of different varieties, or crop production functions truly vary among regions. Nevertheless, we may hazard the following conclusions. Tropical and temperate crops on the average seem to employ similar amounts of labor per unit output. Conforming to hypothesis, tropical crops indeed seem more labor-intensive; therefore, as indicated by the ratio of land to labor coefficients, tropical crops would induce greater concentrations of farm workers than temperate crops. The capital coefficient, however, is higher for temperate rather than tropical crops; therefore, more capital, per unit of land and of labor, should be employed in the temperate zones than in the tropics. Together these results imply that the absolute capital requirements for the optimum farm are greater in temperate than in tropical zones; that temperate-zone agriculture should operate on a large scale, with considerable mechanization, and a dependent labor force; and that the tropics should be characterized by small-scale, lightly capitalized agriculture.

Perhaps the most glaring counterevidence is that wheat, the family-farm crop *par excellence* in the American and Canadian Prairies,

Table 1. Factor Intensities for Various Tropical and Temperate Crops

Crop	Land	Labor	Capital	Total	Region
Tropical (mean)	(.57)	(.24)	(.12)	(.93)	
cotton	.46	.03	.28	.78	Brazil
cotton	.46	.20	.05	.71	Brazil
coffee	.50	.27	.14	.91	Brazil
coffee	.70	.32	.01	1.03	Brazil
sugar	.57	.19	.06	.82	Brazil
sugar	.93	.08	.01	1.02	Brazil
sugar	.57	.26	.05	.88	Brazil
sugar	.46	.62	.00	1.08	Brazil
sugar	.37	.69	.03	1.09	Asia
sugar	.36	.25	.34	.95	Asia
rice	.76	.00	.42	1.18	Brazil
rice	.70	.07	.07	.84	Brazil
Temperate (mean)	(.68)	(.05)	(.46)	(1.19)	
corn	.91	.08	.16	1.15	U.S.
corn	.79	.09	.39	1.27	U.S.
wheat	.50	.04	.58	1.12	U.S.
wheat	.50	.00	.69	1.19	U.S.

Source: William Cline, *The Economic Consequences of a Land Reform in Brazil* (Amsterdam: North Holland, 1970), pp. 68–70.

has been cultivated by tenant farmers and harvested by migrant workers in Argentina. In contrast to rural North America, where wheat is supposed to have generated rural democracy and industrialization, the Argentine landlord created a pattern of worker dependence and insecurity similar to that of plantation society. In his social history of Argentine wheat, Scobie writes: "The result was pampas without settlers—a frontier filled with migrants. One class which increased markedly after 1890 was totally migratory. . . These were European laborers . . . who made the long Atlantic crossing in October or November of each year to earn high wages as harvest workers. . . . Almost as migratory in a social sense were the work-horses of Argentina's agricultural greatness; the sharecroppers and tenant farmers. These were the agricultural laborers and little capitalists, who cultivated Argentina's boom crops, who planted the alfalfa pastures, who conquered the pampas economically, but who in reality left those plains as empty as in the 1850's. Behind them they left no houses, no schools, no churches, no roads, no villages."[8]

The Property Rights Paradigm

Another line of neoclassical thought investigates the efficiency of alternative forms of property rights and the contractual exchanges of these rights. According to North and Thomas, those institutional changes were selected which "improve the efficiency and output of society by equating the private and social profitability of an activity." Opportunities for institutional innovation are especially propitious when there are efficiency gains to be exploited, due to increasing returns to scale, the correction of externalities, risk aversion, the reduction of information or transaction costs, or the redistribution of income.[9]

In the areas of land tenure, this paradigm has been applied to the existence of permanent land rights in primitive societies, to the rise and fall of the manorial system, to American slavery, and to sharecropping in contemporary societies. While in principle the paradigm pretends to explain the conditions under which landlords might sell land to workers, and even to slaves, in practice it has focused on the efficiency of various contractual and coercive arrangements between landowners and landless workers. The original (unequal) distribution of land is taken as given, and thus skirts the dichotomy of interest between independent and dependent farmers.

The several ideal types of contractual arrangements between landlord and tenant—fixed rent, fixed wage, sharecropping—differ in their risks to the contracting parties and in their transactions costs. Under fixed rent contracts, the farm worker controls the production decisions and bears all risks of variability of yields and output prices. Transaction costs are minimal although the landlord must guard against the tenant's despoliation of the land. Under fixed-wage contract, the landlord controls the production process and thus transactions costs are high in insuring that the worker does not shirk his duty. For a given

season, the landlord bears all the risks of yield and price variability.

Under sharecropping, risks are split between landlord and tenant. If the tenant completely controls the production process,
he will work until the marginal disutility of effort equals *his share*
of the marginal value product of labor. This undersupply of effort
and, by similar argument, other variable inputs provides the traditional argument against sharecropping as an efficient contractual arrangement. In practice, however, share contracts specify
labor and other inputs required of the tenant; therefore, in taking
control of the production process out of the hands of the tenant,
efficiency is assured.

Regardless of the contractual arrangement, both the landlord
and tenant bear the risks of long-term changes in agricultural
prices. Cheung has shown that the expected return to the landlord, and presumably to the worker, is invariable under alternative contractual arrangements.

What determines those social relations of production actually
contracted in a given region? In Taiwan, Cheung has shown
that where yields are highly variable—that is, where agriculture
is risky—crop sharing as a method of mutual risk reduction is
more common than fixed rent or fixed wage contracts. Georgescu-
Roegen speculates that in "labor-surplus" economics, where the
marginal product of labor is below the subsistence level, wage
contracts would lead either to unemployment or mass starvation;
therefore, sharecropping under feudalism is the only benign form
of dependency.[10]

On an individual plane, the distribution of attitudes towards
risk and independence will determine the contractual arrangement of individual workers, wage labor, fixed rent tenancy, sharecropping, or even land owning. In order to compensate him for
his employment risk, dependence, and social inferiority, the landless labor might realize an even higher return on his labor than
the landowner!

Such a picture is hardly constant with the facts of Brazilian
agriculture, as no one has even pictured dependent rural workers
as a high-income class. In Paraná, which has been heralded as
middle-class rural society, Nicholls found the following income
hierarchy on coffee farms: owner-operators, $763; resident share-
croppers, $597; colonos, a form of resident wage laborer, $357;
and nonresident seasonal workers, $214. Indeed, it may be taken
as axiomatic that every Brazilian sharecropper, tenant, or field

hand would like to own his own land regardless of the risks involved. Vergara, for example, found that immigrants to two frontier counties in Goiás experienced little increase in gross income, but migrated to achieve their own land and independence. It is possible to impute a value of independence by finding that increase in income sufficient to induce migration across an equivalent distance, approximately three hundred miles. Using Sahota's migration equations, one finds that independent status for the landless is as attractive as a 10 per cent increase in volume.[11]

Since our main interest is in the spatial and temporal variations along the dependence-independence dimension, the property rights paradigm seems to offer little insight. It is clear from both the North and South American experience, that such dramatic changes as the abolition of slavery on sugar, coffee, or cotton plantations do not automatically eliminate dependency. In describing the process on the Northeastern sugar plantation, Eisenberg comments: "Summarizing the various modes of free labor employment brings the realization that abolition did not change the high dependency of most of the rural proletariat on the planter class."[12]

Factor Proportions

A third neoclassical explanation of the social relations of production focuses on the population density of a newly settled region. In densely settled regions, the marginal productivity of labor is low and that of land high, while the opposite is true in a sparsely settled region, the frontier. The analysis assumes that in both types of regions, land ownership is relatively concentrated, whether because of the initial distribution of political power, say the grant of land by a king to his vassals, or because of the type of capital market imperfections mentioned earlier.

If factor returns were determined by marginal productivity, landlords in the densely settled region could extract high rents, whether units of production were peasant families or plantations. Landlords in the empty region, on the other hand, enjoy such low returns that they may not even bother to enforce their property rights.

In order to increase his return, the landlord in the empty region has a strong incentive to recruit labor either through a contractual arrangement (free immigration) or through coercion (slavery);

or to violate the marginal productivity principle of distribution, by eliminating a competitive labor market (serfdom).

The voluntary recruitment of labor to empty regions will succeed when the psychic and material benefits of migration exceed their costs. The Brazilian historian Caio Prado has noted that European migrants have generally gone to the temperate zones in the New World rather than the tropics, and that these former zones developed later.[13]

At the time of initial settlement, temperate zones were quite similar to Europe in their natural endowments (soils, climate) and, after the initial extraction of furs and timber, the production possibilities were much less conducive to trade than those of the tropics. Although the temperate zones may have been unattractive to landlords seeking a commercial crop, they were clearly attractive to subsistence farmers, who had been displaced by the English enclosures. This landless mass of humanity eagerly reestablished themselves on the temperate frontiers of North America and on the subtropical highlands, such as the Southern Piedmont.

Why did European peasants not flock to the tropics in order to establish family farms, since the headright system encouraged the immigration of small holders to Latin America? Prado argues that the advantages of the tropics over the temperate zone in offering more lucrative staple crops was offset by tropical climate and diseases to which the European had not yet acquired immunity. Furthermore, the unfamiliar ecology imposed greater costs to prospective farmers. While these conditions were no obstacle to Europeans who wished to establish themselves as *latifundistas,* the explorations, and the denigration of agricultural labor in Portugal, created a paucity of Europeans available for colonization in Brazil. In sum, the supply of land in Brazil was great and the supply of labor low.

If laborers were free to migrate, the opening of the frontier would force rents down regardless of the ownership of land. Where land is monopolized by the few, however, Domar suggests it is also possible that the existence of the frontier increases repression in *both* the metropolis and the frontier regions. The imposition of serfdom, which restricts movement from one estate to another, prevents competition in the labor market and enables the landlord in the metropolis to keep wages down and rents up, despite the existence of the frontier. While serfdom on the frontier forces wages below and rents above their competitive levels, it does not alleviate the frontier landlord's labor shortage.[14]

The linkage between the man-land endowment and the social relations of production depends upon whether the landlords can offset labor's market power with their own political power in order to enforce serfdom. The factor endowment model, then, ultimately depends upon a non-economic variable, a political decision in favor of the landlords, to explain the rise of serfdom. An equally plausible result of labor scarcity is: (a) a frantic competition among landlords for labor; and (b) the rise of an independent yeomanry as a powerful class. The *Turner frontier thesis* argues that the latter result is more plausible, at least in the temperate frontier regions. Population sparseness increases the bargaining power of rural, and even urban labor, while increasing the landlords costs of enforcing their property rights. Below we suggest that this hypothesis has some validity in Brazil.[15]

The absence of sufficient voluntary migration is the third alternative for the frontier landlord: the introduction of slavery. Presumably, slavery would be profitable in any region where the marginal productivity of labor exceeded maintenance costs of the slave, plus those of the system itself (policing, etc.). A logical question at this point is why the temperate zones were never organized on the basis of slave labor or plantations, which is really our original problem.

The Role of Initial Political Power

In emphasizing the advantages of large-scale enterprise, the production-function approach ignores the possibilities of cooperative alternatives. In examining the optimal contractual arrangement between landlord and tenant, the property-rights paradigm assumes that some exogenous force determines that the owners of land and of labor be different people. In emphasizing the advantages of exploitation to the landlord, under conditions of land abundance, the factor endowments approach cannot explain the counter-examples of family farming in the American and Canadian prairies.

It is therefore tempting to assume that the relations of production on the frontier are determined by legal norms and political power in the metropolis, rather than determined endogenously on the frontier. The existence of latifundia in the tropics might be explained by the initial distribution of political power at the time when land policy was being formulated. For example, in commenting on the nature of latifundia in Latin America, Barraclough and Domike aver: "These land tenure institutions are a product of the power structure." Presumably, the powerful classes surrounding the Crown shaped institutions of land tenure to maximize their advantages, which may be extra- and even anti-economic. In addition, Barraclough and Domike assert: "the fundamental difference between this migration toward the frontier in Latin America and the settlement of American frontier land in the last century is that in the United States . . . these lands belonged to no one, while in Latin America almost all land already has an owner."[16]

Experience in both the United States and Brazil suggests that this is not the essential difference. Although the Homestead Act of 1862 provided free land to those satisfying certain residency requirements, the major waves of pioneering preceded the Act. Previously, government land was available in plots of 640 and later 320 acres at a minimum price of $1.25 per acre at auction, or at a flat $1.25 under pre-emption. Free or low-priced land, however, can also be effectively worthless land if it is too arid, too distant from transport facilities, or too difficult to clear. Most farmers purchased land at higher prices per acre from canal or railroad companies who provided financing and transport facilities, from speculators who subdivided the land into smaller plots, or from "professional" pioneers who took the risk of preparing and testing the land.[17]

The original distribution of political power is not a sufficient explanation for regional differences in the social relations of production on the frontier. For example, it is difficult to find much regional difference in the motivations, pretensions, and world view of the aristocrats who organized the settlement of the English colonies in North America. With the exception of the Puritans in New England, the colonizers sought huge land grants in order to duplicate a feudal order which was already moribund in England. The headright system of granting land employed in the middle and southern colonies encouraged the latifundia-minifundia pattern of land distribution common in Latin America. Despite the similar interests of the ruling classes of all but the New England colonies, family farms emerged as the dominant form in the North; plantations based upon slave labor in the

South. The family farm could hardly be considered a traditional English institution, the relations of production in the metropolis having traditionally been hierarchical.[18]

Brazilian institutions of land tenure were also shaped by a small group of rich and powerful men surrounding the Court. The aspirations and institutional forms initiated by these men were not so different from those of the organizers of North American settlement. In the early colonial period, huge holdings were granted to noblemen on condition that a permanent rural population be attracted to generate production taxable by the crown; that is, the same headright system attempted in North America. Most of these grants expired, without their conditions being fulfilled. During the empire, those with means could purchase huge holdings from the crown, a policy continued under the republic. Since the wealthy and powerful helped determine public land policy, it is not surprising that they attempted to establish institutions that would further their self-interest. When immigrants were considered by the crown as a solution to the labor shortage in the coffee frontier, the plantation owners blocked the granting of freeholds in all but the most inaccessible and exhausted lands, compelling most immigrants to work in some form of dependent status on the plantations.[19]

The ability of a small ruling class to shape institutions of land tenure does not give us much insight into the behavior of this class. Why did the maximization of wealth, power, and status on the part of this oligarchy generate such a wide range of institutions in various circumstances: plantations based upon slaves, tenants, or wage labors in some circumstances; the voluntary fragmentation of the estates for sale to laborers, in others. How did a family-based society arise in the southern temperate region of Brazil, which never experienced the dominance of plantations?

A Capital Market Hypothesis

In most developing countries, capital markets are poorly developed because financial intermediaries are monopolistic and poorly articulated from one sector or region to another. In addition, the range of financial instruments is narrow, and transactions costs are high. Because of high transactions costs and collateral requirements, as well as for the weakness of secondary mortgage markets, low-income laborers are unable to borrow money for land purchases. The effective demand for land purchases on the part of landless laborers, then, would be basically limited by their savings. Because of the paucity of financial instruments, landlords may be unable to find profitable outlets from receipts of land sales. Where inflation is chronic, moreover, land is a fairly safe investment, whose prestige value is of additional benefit.[20]

It may be noted in passing that many of the large-scale land purchases on the American frontier were financed by British investors, who could dispose of their assets on the well-developed secondary markets in London. It is perhaps not a coincidence that the most successful Brazilian colonization scheme, which involved the financing of small holders, was also initiated by the British.

When agriculture is still a profitable field for investment in the long run, short-term fluctuations in the prices and yields of commercial crops can create great risks of bankruptcy for the original landowners. In São Paulo, import-export houses financed the expansion of coffee cultivation in the latter part of the nineteenth and early part of the twentieth century. When world coffee markets crashed in the 1890's, the short-term indebtedness of the landowners forced the fragmentation of their estates, which were purchased by both the exporters and some tenants. More recently, in the Paraná coffee frontier, more prosperous farmers have been buying out small holders, who are temporarily indebted.[21]

As emphasized by the property rights paradigm, imperfections in the capital market are not immutable. If there are gains to be enjoyed by the dominant classes, the appropriate financial institutions will be developed. When investment opportunities are superior outside the agricultural sector, landowners will attempt to liquidate some of their land assets. The industrial-urban development of São Paulo, for example, seems to have encouraged the voluntary fragmentation of coffee estates for sale to their tenants. Similarly, when a superior agricultural frontier opens, landowners may be more willing to sell their exhausted estates in small parcels.[22]

Imperfections in the capital market have several implications for spatial variations in the social relations of production. First, the lower the absolute value of land (owing to inaccessibility or to infertility), the greater the likelihood that purchases can be financed out of savings by dependent workers. Second, the lower the value of land, the less likely it will be that the landlord will enforce his property rights against squatters. A corollary is that as land values arise because of improved transportation, or rising demand, squatters will be forced out by one or more "legitimate" claimants to the land, an event which is commonplace on the modern Brazilian frontier. Third, in areas where urban-industrial opportunities are favorable, voluntary fragmentation may occur.

In this section, we will attempt to test three models that explain the relations of production on the frontier: the production-function model, the factor-proportions model, and the capital-market model. The tests utilize evidence from the coffee frontier and the rice frontier.

São Paulo–Paraná Coffee Frontier

The coffee lands of the Paulista plateau were developed under a wide variety of historical and economic circumstances. Ribeirão Preto was developed by large landowners in the 1880's. First utilizing slaves, the landowners switched to European immigrants serving as wage laborers and sharecroppers. After a collapse in the coffee markets in the 1890's, many indebted landowners subdivided their plantations for sale to these immigrants. Marília was opened up by the Paulista railway company in the 1920's and 1930's. To generate traffic, the railway sold plots to small holders for 50 per cent down.

Parts of northern Paraná were developed by a British land company beginning in the late 1920's. The company surveyed the area in small plots; cleared titles; built a railroad, feeder roads, and cities; and provided financing for a maximum of four years, with a 30 per cent down payment. Other parts were developed by voluntary fragmentation of estates.

If the production-function hypothesis is correct, then all coffee regions should show similarities by indicators of size of farm, structure of the labor force, and patterns of land tenure.

The factor-proportions approach suggests that dependency is less on the newer frontiers. The Doman version suggests that the opening of new frontiers should lead to repression, or greater dependency on the older ones. On the other hand, the Turner version suggests that the opening of the frontier should liberate the older zones.

The capital-markets approach suggests that lands should be more evenly distributed and dependency less in company lands in northern Paraná and perhaps Marília than in other coffee lands. Second, as land values rise over time, squatting should diminish. Third, rising urban-industrial opportunities should encourage fragmentation in the older coffee zones near the manufacturing center, that is, Marília or Ribeirão Preto.

While the production function approach predicts spatially uniform relations of production in all coffee zones, the factor proportions and capital market approaches predict less dependency on the newer frontiers. Over time, however, Domar predicts greater dependency in the older zones while Turner and the capital markets predict the opposite. In the long run, the capital-markets approach recognizes the possibility of concentration in the newer frontier zones, as small holders face problems of cyclical indebtedness.

Evidence. For the years 1940, 1950, and 1960, the following statistics are computed for each coffee region: (a) mean hectares per establishment; (b) Gini coefficient of inequality of size distribution of holdings; (c) share of labor force who are employees; (d) share of labor force who are owner-operators; (e) share of operators who are sharecroppers; and (f) share of farm operators who are squatters.

While there has been a fragmentation of operating units in all coffee zones, the inequality in the size of establishments seems to be increasing in Ribeirão, stabilizing in Marília, and declining somewhat in the two Paraná zones. While the share of the labor force comprised of owner-operators and their families has remained fairly stable in each zone, this share varies among zones. These patterns suggest that technological imperatives are not driving all coffee farms inexorably toward some optimum size, labor-force structure, or tenure pattern.

Dependency in any form is less frequently encountered in the Paraná zones than in Ribeirão or Marília, which may suggest the liberating effect of the frontier. While squatting is relatively unimportant in any of these zones, there is an increase in squatting in non-company northern Paraná, which underwent the most rapid settlement in the later 1950's.

In the period, 1940–60, all zones underwent a decline in the share of the labor force employed for wages. Underlying this decline was a tremendous decrease in permanent-wage employment and an increase in the less secure day-wage employment. Although sharecropping is not particularly significant in any of the coffee zones, there has been an increase in the share of operators

Table 2. Relations of Production in Four Coffee Zones, 1940–1960

	Ribeirão Preto	Marília	Northern Paraná	
			Company	Non-Company
MEAN HA./FARM				
1940	149	53	74	100
1950	205	68	56	73
1960	170	28	27	37
INEQUALITY				
1940	.79	.69	.69	.74
1950	.78	.73	.89	.79
1960	.89	.75	.60	.62
% LABOR FORCE EMPLOYEE				
1940	83	85	40	65
1950	71	55	40	50
1960	68	34	31	29
% LABOR FORCE OWNER-OPERATOR FAMILIES				
1940	12	9	47	24
1950	13	21	35	34
1960	14	18	27	32
% OPER. SHARECROPPER				
1940	n.a.	n.a.	n.a.	n.a.
1950	13	11	8	6
1960	10	13	15	5
% OPER. SQUATTER				
1940	0	0	4	2
1950	1	2	7	8
1960	2	1	2	23

Sources: Paraná, *Censo Agricola,* 1940, 1950, and 1960; São Paulo, *Censo Agricola.*

renting, as opposed to owning, land. These trends suggest a decreasing security and control for workers in the coffee zone which are not inconsistent with the Domar hypothesis.

The importance of capital-market improvements is less than that hypothesized. The share of owner-operators in Marília, where financing was offered by the railroad company, is no higher than in the most traditional region, Ribeirão Preto. Second, while owner-operators were originally more numerous on company lands in northern Paraná, the share on non-company lands has exceeded this amount in recent years.

Goiás and the New Rice Frontier

Largely composed of savanna, the state of Goiás is the northward continuation of frontier settlement radiating from São Paulo. Especially since the 1940's this state's growth has been propelled by the export of rice to industrial centers of the south. Goiânia, the major marketing center, is located in the southern part of the state, in a zone of rich forest soils.

The production function hypothesis would predict no systematic spatial variation in the relations of production on the savanna, since rice is the common staple.

The factor proportions hypothesis would predict that worker dependency would decline with distance from the market center, as the frontier exerts its liberating influence. While the Domar version would suggest that frontier expansion would lead to greater repression near the market center, over an extended time, the Turner version would predict the opposite.

The capital-imperfection model predicts greater dependency where land is more valuable; that is, near the market, and on more valuable forest soils.

Evidence: For the years 1940, 1950, and 1960, several measures of labor dependence by *municipio* are regressed against distance from Goiânia and soil quality (a dummy variable $= 1$ for forest soils). The measures of dependency are percentage of the labor force as sharecroppers, the percent of employees (total), and the percent as permanent and temporary employees.

The proportion of the farm-labor force in dependent status as sharecroppers and employees varies inversely with distance from the market center. This result is consistent with the factor-proportions and capital-market hypothesis.

Table 3. Labor Dependency on the Goiás Rice Frontier, 1940–1960

	1940		1950		1960	
	Distance	Forest	Distance	Forest	Distance	Forest
% Workers sharecrop	——	——	−.0269*	.8609	−.0260*	1.3804*
			(.0049)	(.5598)	(.0048)	(.5469)
				R² = .48		R² = .51
% Workers employee, total	−.0075*	−.1728	−.0044*	−.3157*	−.0046*	−0.1322
	(.0022)	(.2476)	(.0016)	(.1892)	(.0019)	(.2171)
		R² = .20		R² = .13		R² = .11
% Workers employee, permanent	−.0054*	.0982	−.0116*	0.1648	−.0034	0.5597
	(.0027)	(.3112)	(.0042)	(.4779)	(.0037)	(0.4158)
		R² = .09		R² = .16		R² = .08
% Workers employee, temporary	−.0115*	−.3173	−.0031	−0.4483*	−.0047*	−.3213
	(.0053)	(.5985)	(.0020)	(.2321)	(.0021)	(.2441)
		R² = .09		R² = .09		R² = .10

Source: Goiás, *Censo Agricola*, 1940, 1950, 1960
*significant .05 (one-tail)

Second, the proportion of the labor force used as sharecroppers is higher in the forest soil than in the savanna. Conversely, the percentage used as employees (total) is somewhat less on the forest soils, but not significantly so. The proportion of the labor force in all forms of dependency (as sharecroppers plus employees), however, is greater on forest soils, which is consistent with the capital markets hypothesis.

Conclusion

The social relations of production on the Brazilian frontier have been examined as consequences of the technology of production, factor endowments, and capital-market imperfections. Contrary to the predictions of the production-function approach, there are wide variations in the relations of production in regions that produce a common staple. In general, those regions which are newer and less accessible to market, and hence are less valuable, tend to have less dependency. This suggests that the existence of the frontier exerts a relatively liberating effect for the landless.

Notes

1. Exceptions to these generalizations come readily to mind. While England and Japan had highly hierarchical rural social structures, France after the Revolution had a structure more closely approximating the ideal-type family farming society, yet was retarded in its industrialization. See A. Whitney Griswold, *Farming and Democracy* (New York: Harcourt, 1948).

2. Douglass C. North, "Location theory and regional economic growth," *Journal of Political Economy*, 63 (June 1955), 243–258; Robert Baldwink "Patterns of development in newly settled regions," *Manchester School*, 24 (May 1956), 161–179; and George L. Beckford, "The economics of agricultural resource use and development in plantation economies," *Social and Economic Studies*, 18 (Dec. 1969), 321–347.

3. Paul S. Taylor, "Plantation agriculture in the United States, 17th-20th century," *Land Economics*, 30 (May 1954), 141–152, includes large-scale dairying in Rhode Island as well as irrigated wheat farming in California, both of which are oriented toward the domestic market. Cf. the more restrictive definitions of W. O. Jones, "Plantations," in David L. Sills, *International Encyclopedia of the Social Science*, Vol. 12, 1968; Lloyd Best, "Outlines of a model of pure plantation economy," *Social and Economic Studies*, 17 (Sept. 1968), 283–326; and George Beckford, "Toward an appropriate theoretical framework for agricultural development planning and policy," *Social and Economic Studies*, 17 (Sept. 1968), 233–242.

4. Robert Baldwin, "Patterns of development"; and, "Export technology and development from a subsistence level," *Economic Journal*, 73 (March 1963), 30–92; and Antonio Barros de Castro, "O modelo historico latino-americano," in *Sete Ensaios Sobre a Economia Brasileira*, ed. by A. Barros de Castro (Rio, 1972), I, 19–75.

5. A. B. Chayanov, *The Theory of Peasant Economy*, ed. Daniel Thorner et. al. (Homewood, Ill., 1966); Stanley Engerman, "Some considerations relating to property rights in man," *Journal of Economic History*, 33 (Mar. 1973), 43–65.

6. Harold Demsetz, "Toward a theory of property relations," *American Economic Review*, 56 (May 1967), 346–359. The argument that landowners are largely motivated by nonpecuniary benefits is made by Solon Barraclough and Arthur Domike, "Agrarian structure in seven Latin American countries," *Land Economics*, 42 (Nov. 1966), 391–424, and Eugene Genovese, *The Political Econ-*

17. Fred Shannon, "The Homestead Act and the labor Surplus," *American Historical Review*, 41 (July 1936), 637–651; Paul Gates, "The Homestead Law in an incongruous land system," *ibid*, 65–168; Martin Primack, "Land clearing costs in the 19th century," *Journal of Economic History*, 22 (Dec. 1962), 484–497; and Allen Bogue, *From Prairie to Corn Belt*, chap. 4.

18. Marshall Harris, *The Origin of the Land Tenure System in the United States* (Ames, 1953).

19. Richard R. Beeman, "Labor force and race relations: a comparative view of the colonization of Brazil and Virginia," *Political Science Quarterly*, 86 (Dec. 1971), 609–636; Warren Dean, "Latifundia and land policy in nineteenth century Brazil," *Hispanic American Historical Review*, 51 (Nov. 1971), 606–626; and Viotti da Costa, *De Senzala a Colonia*.

20. Bogue, *loc. cit*; and Nicholas and Paiva, "Northern Parana."

21. Pierre Monbeig, *Pionniers et Planteurs de Sao Paulo* (Paris, 1952).

22. Warren Dean, *The Industrialization of Sao Paulo, 1880-1945* (Austin, 1969).

The Cultural Ecology of Pioneer Agriculture in Contemporary South America

Stephen I. Thompson

WITH the possible exception of Siberia, virtually the only ing major frontier area in the contemporary world l' Amazon Basin and adjacent regions of lowland South In recent years, each of the nations which controls a this territory has embarked upon a scheme to color velop it; the Brazilian program has been the most licized, but similar projects have been inaugurated Chile, Peru, Ecuador, Colombia, Venezuela, Boli guay.[2] This situation offers an abundance of rese ties for students of comparative pioneer coloniz fact already generated a considerable literature work of cultural geographers.[3] The present p' some of the problems and prospects of these vantage point of anthropology, and, more s the eyes of the theoretical approach general' ecology.

In spite of the multidisciplinary nature of a safe supposition that most of its readers would perhaps be appropriate to begin explicit statement of its theoretical assu'

Cultural ecology has been defined by "the adaptive processes by which the unpredictable number of features of basic adjustment through which ma ment."[4] The fundamental premise of a direct relationship between the e' very broadly to encompass both r example, neighboring societies) environment is exploited, on the pects of the culture, on the othe cultural ecologist involves a th is to determine "the interrelatic technology and environment

Index

319

omy of Slavery (New York, 1967). The distinction between plantations and haciendas has been made on the basis of commercial vs. nonpecuniary orientations of the landowners by Eric R. Wolf and Sidney W. Mintz, "Haciendas and plantations of Middle America and the Antilles," *Social and Economic Studies*, 6 (Sept. 1957), 380–412.

7. Paul A. David, "Mechanization of reaping in the ante-bellum Midwest," in *Industrialization in Two Systems*, ed. by Henry Rosovsky (New York, 1966), pp. 3–39; Don Kanel, "Size of farm and economic development," *Indian Journal of Agricultural Economics*, 22 (April/June 1967), 26–44; Allen Bogue, *From Prairie to Corn Belt: Farming on the Illinois and Iowa Prairies in the Nineteenth Century* (Chicago, 1963), chap. 4.

8. James R. Scobie, *Revolution on the Pampas: A Social History of Argentine Wheat*, 1860–1910 (Austin, 1964), p. 53.

9. Douglass C. North and Robert P. Thomas, "The rise and fall of the manorial system," *Journal of Economic History*, 31 (Dec. 1971), 777–803; Lance E. Davis and Douglass C. North, *Institutional Change and American Economic Growth* (Cambridge, Eng., 1971); Armen Alchian and Harold Demsetz, "The property rights paradigm" *Journal of Economic History*, 33 (Mar. 1973), 17–27; Steven N. S. Cheung, *The Theory of Share Tenancy* (Chicago, 1970); Frederic L. Pryor, "Property institutions and economic development: some empirical tests," *Economic Development and Cultural Change*, 20 (April 1972), 406–437; Robert Fogel and Stanley Engerman, *Time on the Cross: The Economics of American Negro Slavery* (New York, 1974).

10. Steven N. S. Cheung, "Private property rights and sharecropping," *Journal of Political Economy*, 74 (Nov./Dec. 1968), 1107–1122, and "Transaction costs, risk aversion, and the choice of contractual arrangements," *Journal of Law and Economics*, 12 (April 1969), 23–42; and Nicholas Georgescu-Roegen," Economic theory and agrarian economics," *Oxford Economic Papers*, 12 (Feb. 1960), 1–40.

11. William H. Nicholls and Ruy Miller Paiva, *Ninety-nine Fazendas: The Structure and Productivity of Brazilian Agriculture*, Chapter VI, "The North of Parana: Maringa;" Otto Vergara, "Analise socioeconomica das migracoes inter-rurais: Ceres e Rubiataba, Goias," unpublished master's thesis, Universidade Rural, Vicosa, M.G., 1968; and Gian Sahota, "An analysis of internal migration in Brazil," *Journal of Political Economy*, 76 (Mar. 1968), 218–245.

12. Peter Eisenberg, "Abolishing slavery: the process on Pernambuco's sugar plantations," *Hispanic American Historical Review*, 52 (Nov. 1972), 580–597, J. H. Gallaway, "The last years of slavery on the sugar plantations of Northeast Brazil," *Hispanic American Historical Review*, 51 (Nov. 1971), 586–605; and Emilia Viotti da Costa, *De Senzala a Colonia* (Sao Paulo, 1966) cf. Taylor, "Plantation agriculture in the U.S."

13. Caio Prado Junior, *Colonial Background of Modern Brazil* (Berkeley, 1967). Cf. Ida C. Greaves, "Plantations in the world economy," in *Plantation Systems in the New World* (Washington, D.C.); Beckford "Toward an appropriate theoretical framework," and Best, "Outlines of a model."

14. Evsey Domar, "The causes of slavery or serfdom," *Journal of Economic History*, 30 (Mar. 1970), 18–32.

15. Frederick Jackson Turner, *The Frontier in American History* (New York, 1920 and 1962).

16. Barraclough and Domike, "Agrarian structure," p. 398, 408.

17. Fred Shannon, "The Homestead Act and the labor Surplus," *American Historical Review*, 41 (July 1936), 637–651; Paul Gates, "The Homestead Law in an incongruous land system," *ibid*, 65–168; Martin Primack, "Land clearing costs in the 19th century," *Journal of Economic History*, 22 (Dec. 1962), 484–497; and Allen Bogue, *From Prairie to Corn Belt*, chap. 4.

18. Marshall Harris, *The Origin of the Land Tenure System in the United States* (Ames, 1953).

19. Richard R. Beeman, "Labor force and race relations: a comparative view of the colonization of Brazil and Virginia," *Political Science Quarterly*, 86 (Dec. 1971), 609–636; Warren Dean, "Latifundia and land policy in nineteenth century Brazil," *Hispanic American Historical Review*, 51 (Nov. 1971), 606–626; and Viotti da Costa, *De Senzala a Colonia*.

20. Bogue, *loc. cit*; and Nicholas and Paiva, "Northern Parana."

21. Pierre Monbeig, *Pionniers et Planteurs de Sao Paulo* (Paris, 1952).

22. Warren Dean, *The Industrialization of Sao Paulo*, 1880-1945 (Austin, 1969).

The Cultural Ecology of Pioneer
Agriculture in Contemporary South America

Stephen I. Thompson

WITH the possible exception of Siberia, virtually the only remaining major frontier area in the contemporary world lies in the Amazon Basin and adjacent regions of lowland South America.[1] In recent years, each of the nations which controls a segment of this territory has embarked upon a scheme to colonize and develop it; the Brazilian program has been the most widely publicized, but similar projects have been inaugurated by Argentina, Chile, Peru, Ecuador, Colombia, Venezuela, Bolivia, and Paraguay.[2] This situation offers an abundance of research opportunities for students of comparative pioneer colonization, and has in fact already generated a considerable literature, much of it the work of cultural geographers.[3] The present paper will examine some of the problems and prospects of these programs from the vantage point of anthropology, and, more specifically, through the eyes of the theoretical approach generally known as cultural ecology.

In spite of the multidisciplinary nature of this volume, it seems a safe supposition that most of its readers will be historians, so it would perhaps be appropriate to begin this paper with a fairly explicit statement of its theoretical assumptions.

Cultural ecology has been defined by its founder as the study of "the adaptive processes by which the nature of society and an unpredictable number of features of culture are affected by the basic adjustment through which man utilizes a given environment."[4] The fundamental premise of the approach is that there is a direct relationship between the environment (which is defined very broadly to encompass both natural and social factors—for example, neighboring societies) and the ways in which that environment is exploited, on the one hand, and the remaining aspects of the culture, on the other. The research procedure of the cultural ecologist involves a three-stage analysis. The first step is to determine "the interrelationship of exploitative or productive technology and environment . . . Second, the behavior patterns involved in the exploitation of a particular area by means of a particular technology must be analyzed . . . The third procedure is to determine the extent to which the behavior patterns entailed in exploiting the environment affect other aspects of the culture."[5] The ultimate aim of the approach, once such analyses have been accomplished in a number of specific cultures, is to identify and describe broad cross-cultural regularities—processes which recur regularly in cultures exploiting similar (or functionally equivalent) environments in similar ways.

The most successful applications of this method in anthropology have dealt with societies at a subsistence or near-subsistence level. It has enabled us, for example, to perceive the adaptive value of apparently irrational cultural behavior as the East African "cattle complex" or the potlatch system of the Northwest Coast Indians.[6] Such cases lend themselves readily to this sort of analysis because of the relative intimacy of the relationship between physical environment and man in primitive society. Cultural ecological studies of more complex cultures have been relatively rare,[7] not because the approach is inherently inapplicable to such situations, but because of the staggering methodological difficulties involved. No matter how broadly one defines environment, it is not easy to demonstrate direct causal relationships between environment and culture when one is dealing with an industrialized society.

The anthropological study of historical and contemporary cases of pioneer colonization offers at least a partial solution to this methodological dilemma.[8] Most pioneers, in the modern world and in the recent past, have been drawn from relatively complex sociocultural systems. The frontier experience has often thrust them into environments strikingly different from those of their mother areas. Transportation and communications facilities have usually been primitive at best. These factors have frequently necessitated sweeping, innovative alterations in the total way of life of the pioneers in order to ensure their survival.[9] The pace of social change has been rapid, and it has been social change in which the role of the environment has been clear-cut and unequivocal. In short, the comparative study of pioneers' communities offers a veritable laboratory for the ecological anthropologist. Hypotheses concerning the effect of environment upon culture can be tested here with other variables controlled to an extent which is rare in social science.

For frontier areas in contemporary South America, the physical environment, in spite of the vast territorial range involved, is quite homogeneous. Although there are a few expanses of open savanna, the region is predominantly one of tropical rain forest. Its aboriginal inhabitants, while extremely diverse linguistically, display considerable cultural homogeneity. Their settlements tend to be located as close as possible to one of the many rivers which interlace the region. The typical community consists of one or more large, multi-family dwellings, with each family occupying a specific space demarcated by posts to which its sleeping hammocks are attached at night. Almost all tropical forest Indians are primarily horticulturists; in spite of North American stereotypes, the Amazon basin is not rich in wild game, and archaeological evidence indicates both antiquity for agriculture in the region and a very small pre-agricultural population.[10] The staple crop through most of the area is manioc (*Manihot esculenta*), a tuber which is probably most familiar to North Americans as cassava, the source of tapioca.

Although botanists recognize only one species of manioc, many varieties exist. The anthropological literature usually distinguishes between "bitter" and "sweet" manioc. The distinction is based upon the amount of prussic acid (HCN) present in the tuber in the form of cyanogenetic glucosides. All varieties are potentially poisonous, but those known as "sweet" contain relatively low concentrations of poison which can be driven off merely by boiling, whereas the "bitter" varieties must be grated and the resulting pulp squeezed in a flexible basket before cooking (this, at least, is the conventional anthropological view; one botanist, however, has suggested that boiling is sufficient to detoxify *all* manioc, and that differences in techniques or preparation are purely cultural in nature[11]). Manioc is usually converted into flour and then baked into flat cakes which are eaten at every meal.

The typical inventory of cultivated plants in the tropical forest also contains other root crops (e.g., sweet potatoes, New World yams), sugar cane, peppers, various tree crops, tobacco, and/or one or more hallucinogens, and occasionally maize. The usual division of labor is such that most agriculture, apart from the initial clearing of the plot, is performed by women. The primary subsistence activity of men in most groups is fishing; fish normally is the chief source of protein.[12]

A rather heated debate has developed during the past few years over the question of the agricultural potential of the Amazon basin. The most outspoken pessimist has been the archaeologist

Betty Meggers, whose position is indicated by the subtitle of her book on the topic, *Amazonia: Man and Nature in a Counterfeit Paradise*.[13] Meggers' pessimism is based on the unique nature of the natural ecosystem in the tropical forest. This has been summarized as follows in a recent statement by a botanist:

The properties of the humid tropical ecosystem that are basic to an understanding of what is not happening are: (1) the rapid leaching out of the soluble bases and other nutrient elements from the soils; (2) the resulting low fertility of the soil proper and the lack of weatherable mineral compounds, e.g., silicates; (3) the concentration of the greater part of the available nutrient supply in the biomass of the tropical forest; (4) the frequent accumulation of nutrients in the lower subsoil zones; (5) the tendency of the sesquioxide mixture dominant in laterized soils to harden to ironstone on exposure to sun and air; and (6) accelerated erosion that starts immediately when bare soil is exposed to the often torrential tropical rains.[14]

Meggers points out that the primary forest of the Amazon basin[15] provides a virtually continuous canopy of foliage which is of crucial importance in nutrient capture, nutrient storage, and protection of the soil from erosion and solar radiation. Twenty-five per cent of the precipitation is absorbed before reaching the ground, and the remainder is broken up into a fine spray. Furthermore, litter fall from the trees is an important source of nutrients. "Whereas in temperate climates nutrients can be accumulated in the soil until needed, under tropical conditions all elements not recovered immediately are vulnerable to leaching and permanent loss. The spectacular growth rate and vast bulk of tropical vegetation are adaptations for the rapid recapture and storage of nutrients."[16]

In contrast, in cleared areas, whether natural or man-made, the unshielded ultraviolet rays of the sun produce chemical changes in the soils, resulting in the conversion of nitrogen and carbon dioxide into gas which escapes into the air. The increase in soil temperature as a result of exposure to direct sunlight is also harmful; humus formation does not take place if the soil temperature exceeds 77 degrees Fahrenheit, and each degree of temperature rise above 77 leads to an increased nitrogen loss of fifteen to twenty pounds per acre per year.[17] The erosive effects of rainfall are also greatly intensified in clearings.

It is unlikely that anyone would take serious issue with Meggers' conclusions so far as they refer to the potentially disastrous effect of permanent, intensive agriculture in the Amazon region. There is room for skepticism, however, concerning their applicability to the shifting, extensive agricultural practices which constitute the primary aboriginal adaptation in the area.

Shifting ("swidden," "slash-and-burn"[18]) cultivation is the most common horticultural system in the world's tropical forest areas, in Africa and Southeast Asia as well as South America, and is practiced in some temperate regions as well. While there are many differences in technical detail, its fundamental characteristics are quite uniform. A plot, either virgin forest or secondary growth, is selected for cultivation and, at the beginning of the local dry season, preparation begins. Smaller trees and underbrush are felled; larger trees are either girdled and left standing or are simply ignored by the cultivator. The accumulated debris is left for a considerable period to dry, sometimes *in situ* and sometimes after having been spread more evenly over the plot. Then, shortly before the onset of the rains, the area is burned, and the resulting residue of ash provides a natural fertilizer. Normally for the first year fertility is high, but it diminishes rapidly, and the plot is usually abandoned after two to four years. Often, weed encroachment is as significant a motivation for abandonment as loss of fertility. It is left fallow for at least eight, and more often fifteen to twenty-five, years before the cycle begins again.

The topic of shifting cultivation has spawned an enormous literature, by geographers, agronomists, agricultural economists, and colonial administrators as well as anthropologists. Conklin in 1963 compiled a bibliography of more than 1400 items which could now be greatly augmented by subsequent publications.[19] The tone of this discussion has undergone a change through the years. Early accounts tend to be negative and somewhat ethnocentric; aboriginal agricultural techniques struck Western observers as chaotic and "unscientific," and as leading inevitably to environmental degradation.[20] Recently, however, more and more attention has been paid to the adaptive advantages of these techniques, both in terms of their relatively low labor requirements and their effect on the natural environment.[21]

When a people's entire livelihood depends on a particular technological adaptation to a specific environment, their knowledge of that environment necessarily tends to be intimate and sophisticated. The Hanunóo, shifting agriculturalists from the island of Mindoro in the Philippines, recognize 40 different soil categories and distinguish 1500 useful plant types, including 430 cultigens.[22]

Given the peculiarities of tropical forest environments, and the potential for disaster inherent in attempting to utilize the techniques of temperate-zone agriculture therein, the most effective adaptation appears to be for man to imitate nature as closely as possible. In the words of Netting,

> . . . the best strategy is to keep the field protected with a series of differentially maturing crops in dense stands. The shifting cultivator in a rain forest may have, all in one place, food plants with subterranean tubers and root systems, ground vines, bushy vegetables, stalked plants, and trees with climbing vines. Forty separate crops have been seen growing in one Hanunóo swidden at the same time. These successive levels break the force of the rain and shield the soil in the same way as would the natural vegetation. All are not harvested at once, and the field is allowed to revert gradually to the original cover.[23]

Netting goes on to quote Clifford Geertz's succinct comment: "A natural forest has been transformed into a harvestable forest."[24]

With specific reference to shifting agriculture in lowland South America, the most eloquent spokesman for the optimistic view has been Robert Carneiro. Carneiro worked in the early fifties with the Kuikuru Indians of the upper Xingú River in the Matto Grosso region of Brazil.[25] A total of 145 Kuikuru inhabit a single community of nine houses. The cultivation of eleven varieties of bitter manioc provides 80 to 85 per cent of the food supply. Other cultigens supply another 5 per cent, and fishing 10 to 15 per cent. Hunting is practiced but is relatively insignificant economically, yielding less than 1 per cent of the diet.

Plots averaging one and one-half acres in size are cultivated by slash-and-burn methods utilizing hoes as primary tools. Manioc is utilizable five to six months after planting, but the Kuikuru prefer to wait eighteen to twenty months before beginning to harvest it (one advantage of root-crop over seed-crop agriculture in the humid tropics is that, within limits, plants can be stored in the ground). Each plot produced four to five tons of manioc per year. Almost half of this is lost to the depredations of peccaries and leaf-cutter ants. The gardens are replanted gradually as tubers are harvested, so that the second harvest is staggered. Occasionally, a third crop is planted; after this, the plot is abandoned.

According to a traditional anthropological stereotype, hunting and gathering and primitive horticultural societies did not develop complex civilizations because of an absence of leisure time; virtually every waking moment had to be devoted to the food quest. This notion has recently been demolished with reference to hunters and gatherers—for example, the !Kung Bushmen of the Kalahari desert of Southwest Africa, one of the world's most inhospitable environments, spend an average of sixteen hours a week on subsistence activities, are almost never short of food, and have a nutritionally more than adequate diet.[26] The work of Carneiro and others has now gone far toward similarly exploding the stereotype with regard to horticulturalists. The Kuikuru spend an average of three and one-half hours a day in food production, including hunting and fishing as well as farming. Food is always abundant; more land is planted than necessary because of the peccaries and ants.

Carneiro has estimated that the manioc agriculture of the Kuikuru produces approximately four million calories per acre per year. Even after subtracting half of this, which is consumed by animals and insects, more than two million remain for human consumption. He contrasts this statistic with a comparable productivity figure for Inca maize cultivation in highland Peru, where the yield was about twenty-five bushels per acre. On the Peruvian coast, where lower altitude and milder climate permitted double cropping, aboriginal maize productivity was fifty bushels per acre per year. Fifty bushels of maize contain approximately 700,000 calories. Inca maize agriculture involved extensive cultivation of permanent plots. Tools and techniques were much more "advanced" than those of the Kuikuru, labor input per unit of land was substantially higher, and yet, measured in terms of calories alone, productivity per unit of land was less than half (less than one-fifth if we ignore the inroads of ants and peccaries on the Kuikuru crop). A thorough analysis should, of course, take into account nutritional factors other than calories; for example, maize is a much richer source of protein than manioc. However, the Kuikuru, like most other tropical-forest societies in South America, were able to obtain an adequate protein supply by utilizing fish, turtle eggs, and other riverine resources.[27]

Meggers fails to mention Carneiro's Kuikuru material in her book, nor does she cite other authorities whose conclusions tend to corroborate Carneiro's.[28] In order to understand these omissions, it will be instructive to take a brief excursion into the history of Meggers' own research.

In 1954 she published a paper in which she propounded what she called "the law of environmental limitation on culture," to the effect that "the level to which a culture can develop is dependent upon the agricultural potentiality of the environment it occupies."[29] Perhaps in order to protect herself against accusations that she was advocating a simplistic environmental determinism, Meggers added the qualification that "as this potentiality is improved, the culture will become stabilized at a level compatible with the food resources."[30] In other words, technological change may lead to an increase in agricultural potential. This evoked the following critical comment: ". . . note that the second quotation indicates that the agricultural potentiality of a region depends on the technology of the culture. The statement then becomes one to the effect that the level to which a culture can develop depends upon the culture. Although this may be true, it is neither interesting nor useful."[31]

To Meggers, the archetypal area of limited agricultural potential is the South American tropical forest. As she sees it, the low fertility of the soil and the necessity of maintaining an uncultivated land reserve several times as large as the area under cultivation impose severe constraints on population density, sociopolitical complexity, and general cultural development.

In 1948–49 Meggers and her husband had conducted archaeological research on Marajó, a large (165 by 110 miles) island at the mouth of the Amazon, and on the adjacent Brazilian mainland.[32] The archaeological sequence on Marajó culminated in the Marajoara phase, which was, judging from the material remains, a technologically advanced and socially complex culture. Given Meggers' view of the limitations of tropical-forest environments, Marajoara was an anomaly; therefore, she and Evans concluded that it must have been intrusive in the area, probably the result of a migration down the Amazon from the Andean region, and that it underwent a gradual cultural decline upon reaching Marajó. Tropical-forest environments cannot support complex cultures; Marajoara was a complex culture; *ergo* Marajoara must have developed elsewhere and decayed after entering the tropical forest. Yet to a considerable extent Meggers and Evans' own data belie their conclusions. An earlier, much more technologically primitive and therefore, presumably, more "typical" occupation at Marajó was the Ananatuba phase. The people of this phase apparently lived in villages of one or two communal houses, the average village population being estimated at about 150.[33] A formula was derived in an attempt to calculate the approximate average length of occupation of Ananatuba phase sites on the basis of depth of refuse accumulation. This led to some unexpected results:

> The application of this formula to the sherd totals per standard cut of 1.5 by 1.5 meters from sites of the Ananatuba Phase gives estimates of village duration ranging from 4.9 years at (site) J-8 to 147.7 years at J-7, Mound 2. However, J-8 is the only village with a duration of under 98.9 years. . . . This is an unparalleled degree of permanency for villages of the Tropical Forest Pattern, as attested by the ethnographical evidence, but since the formula was designed to err on the conservative side, there seems to be no way to avoid attributing this duration to the Ananatuba phase sites. If anything, they may have been occupied considerably longer.[34]

The "ethnographical evidence" cited here indicates that a village population of one hundred fifty is about average for tropical-forest peoples but that where permanency is concerned, the Tupinamba move every four to five years, Montaña villages every two to three years, the Jívaro at least every six years, the Cubeo every three to five years, and the Tapirape every four to five years.[35]

Other cases not mentioned by Meggers and Evans, however, indicate that the Ananatuba phase was perhaps not so unique. Lathrap has pointed out that ". . . the earliest European explorers in the Amazon basin . . . consistently noted dense populations, extensive political units, powerful chiefs or kings, priests, temples, and idols along the mainstream of the Amazon from its inception to its mouth."[36] Because these groups were the first to come into contact with Europeans, they were also the first to be exterminated, either deliberately or through exposure to new diseases.

Carneiro's Kuikuru study is once again illuminating in this regard; of the many ethnographies of tropical-forest Indian groups, his presents the most thorough analysis of subsistence and land-use patterns. The Kuikuru, he tells us,[37] are willing to walk up to four miles to their manioc plots. Within a four-mile radius of the village there are a total of 13,500 acres of usable forest. Only ninety-five acres of this are under cultivation at any one time. Each year about forty acres are abandoned and another forty acres cleared. Combining these statistics with the period of time required for an abandoned plot to become re-usable (about twenty-five years), Carneiro concludes that the Kuikuru are never faced with the necessity of moving their village because of soil depletion. They have occupied the same locality for about ninety years. They have moved the village four times during this period, but the move in each case was motivated by supernatural considerations (e.g., the belief that a particular site had become unlucky). Each of these relocations, however, involved a shift in site of only a few hundred yards.

Carneiro calculates that the territory currently occupied by the Kuikuru could support, with no change in agricultural technology, a population of two thousand—almost fourteen times their number in 1953–54. However, political factionalism usually leads to schism in tropical forest communities when they reach the size of five to six hundred people.

Carneiro attempts to explain the discrepancies between his data and Meggers' conclusions by pointing out that shifting agriculturalists in general must weigh two inconveniences against each other; that of walking an increasingly long distance to cultivate a plot, and that of building a new village near the plot. Most of the groups cited by Meggers as frequent movers build relatively flimsy houses; it is for them, therefore, easier to relocate the entire village than to walk long distances to the fields. The Kuikuru, on the other hand, build much more elaborate, substantial dwellings, and for them the former inconvenience is the lesser of the two evils.

Data on shifting cultivation of dry rice in tropical-forest areas of Southeast Asia tend to support Carneiro's relatively optimistic conclusions. Conklin estimates that, given the subsistence technology of the Hanunóo, a population density of one hundred thirty persons per square mile could be supported without environmental damage.[38] Shifting agriculturalists in northern Thailand have inhabited the same village sites for at least as long as forty years, and others on the China-Burma border for centuries.[39]

A distinction is made by ecologists between "complex" and "simple" ecosystems.[40] The former are characterized by the presence of relatively small numbers of individuals of many different species; in the latter, there are fewer species but more representatives of each. In nature, homeostasis is more easily preserved in complex ecosystems because of the wider variety of ecological niches available. The tropical rain forest constitutes the world's most complex natural ecosystem.

Modern, temperate-zone agriculture tends to create extremely simple ecosystems; the aim is to grow in a single field the maximum possible number of optimum-sized individuals of one or two species. On the other hand, traditional agricultural systems are more complex, raising diverse assemblages of crops in interdependent relationships. As we have seen, this is particularly true of aboriginal shifting cultivation in the South American tropical forest.

The major implications of this rather lengthy discussion for the process of agricultural colonization in the Amazon Basin are, it is hoped, apparent. The author is in agreement with Meggers and others that any attempt to introduce intensive cultivation of the temperate-zone type would lead inevitably to environmental disaster. This, indeed, has already occurred in some regions; for example, an area of some 30,000 square kilometers of what was originally lush tropical forest in the Zona Bragantina near Belém, Brazil, was devastated by the effects of an ill-conceived colonization scheme around the turn of the century.[41]

On the other hand, if such projects are carefully designed with an eye toward disturbing the natural ecosystem as little as possible—toward the imitation rather than the alteration of nature—then, in spite of the very real limitations of the region, a substantially larger population could be supported on the basis of shifting agricultural techniques similar but not identical to those employed by the aboriginal inhabitants.[42] Harald Sioli, a German limnologist whose general view is quite as pessimistic as Meggers', cites with approval two such cases from Brazil. One of these was the work of a Japanese colonist in the Rio Uaicurapá region of the Central Amazon. An area of about twenty-five hectares was cut and burned in the traditional manner, then planted with a number of different crops which matured at different rates:

> ... rice (was planted) as densely as possible, manioc 1.5 meters apart, guaraná (*Paullinia sorbilis*) 6 meters apart, and Brazil nut trees (*Bertholetia excelsa*) 18 meters apart. The rice grew quickly, fertilized by the ash of the burned jungle, and produced a sufficient harvest within three months to pay the whole expense of preparation of the area. After 1½ years, the manioc was harvested, paying the expense of maintaining the planatation clean of invading capoeira vegetation.

The guaraná started to bear fruits in about 6 years, and finally, after about 15 years, the Brazil nut trees began to produce. The result was a new, planted, and productive forest replacing the original jungle, covering and protecting the soil, and yielding annually a good return for the human settler.[43]

A second example involves a combination of shifting cultivation of pepper as a cash crop with animal husbandry on the farm of a German colonist east of Belém. Twenty thousand pepper plants are raised on about eighty hectares, in addition to 20,000 chickens, 500 pigs, and 200 cattle. Fodder for the animals is imported from southern Brazil. Animal manure is used as fertilizer in the pepper fields. Animals products cover the expenses of the farm, and the sale of pepper provides the margin of profit. Manuring, which is not a characteristic of aboriginal agriculture in the area, helps to compensate for the low level of inorganic nutrients in tropical-forest soils and both to maintain the fertility of an individual plot for a longer time and to shorten the duration of the necessary fallow period.[44]

It might be thought that cultural conservatism on the part of the intensive agriculturalists who are the most likely colonists in contemporary South America would militate against a ready acceptance of shifting techniques. In fact, however, there are a number of cases on record of the opposite being true—Italian and German pioneers in Brazil have easily made the transition,[45] and Japanese immigrants in Bolivia with a tradition of intensive cultivation of irrigated rice have turned to shifting cultivation of dry rice with no difficulty.[46]

An instructive case from the aboriginal world is that of the Kofyar of northern Nigeria.[47] Until recently, the Kofyar inhabited a small territory of approximately two hundred square miles in the southern portion of the Jos plateau in the interior. This rather inaccessible area provided a sanctuary from slave raids and other incursions by the more numerous and better organized Fulani and Hausa to the south. A population density of three hundred per square mile was supported on a base of intensive agriculture involving an elaborate system of terracing and permanent cultivation of heavily manured and composted fields. Sorghum and millet were the staples, but were supplemented by some thirty or more additional crops, varying according to local conditions.[48]

Beginning in the 1920's the peace imposed by the colonial

regime permitted some Kofyar to migrate out of their somewhat marginal homeland and move into an unoccupied but potentially fertile lowland forested area to the south. The basic crop inventory underwent no major alteration in this new region, but traditional labor-intensive agricultural techniques were abandoned and shifting cultivation was adopted. The closer proximity of the new territory to arteries of a gradually improving transportation network led the colonists to become seriously involved, for the first time, in the production of a sizable surplus for the market.

Netting provides some interesting statistics on the relative productivity of the two types of Kofyar farming—the traditional intensive farms and the migrant swidden farms. The former average only 1.54 acres in size, the latter 7.75 acres. As might be expected, the traditional type gives a somewhat higher yield per acre—an average total of 996 pounds of the three major crops, sorghum, millet, and cowpeas, versus 747 pounds per acre on the lowland swidden plots. In terms of overall productivity, however, the average for traditional farms is 1,534 pounds as opposed to 5,793 pounds in the lowlands.[49]

The Kofyar data provide substantiation for the general proposition that labor intensive agriculture, as exemplified by, say, wet rice cultivation in East Asia, is an effective adaptation to conditions of land shortage and labor surplus, since it maximizes productivity per unit of land. On the other hand, when land is abundant and labor scarce, as is the case in most frontier areas, extensive techniques, as epitomized by shifting cultivation, constitute a much more efficient pattern of land use.

Carneiro has couched his analysis of Kuikuru subsistence, as we have seen, in terms of the potential population increase which could be supported given the current technology in the present territory. Another way of looking at the same data, however, would be to attempt to calculate the potential surplus which could be produced by the Kuikuru if they were willing to devote eight hours a day to subsistence activities in place of the present three and a half hours. This would entail more than doubling the amount of land under cultivation, but the Kuikuru could manage this with no difficulty. The Kuikuru, it will be recalled, produce some four to five tons of manioc per household garden per year. If the working day were expanded to eight hours, they could presumably produce as much as ten tons. Actually, this is a conservative estimate; Carneiro states that only two of the three and a half daily hours devoted to subsistence are spent in gardening; the remainder is expended in fishing, hunting, and processing activities.

With no access to the market, the Kuikuru clearly have no incentive to produce any surplus. However, a century ago the Mundurucú of the Rio Tapajós region were producing an annual surplus of 90 to 150 tons of manioc flour for sale to traders.[50]

Certain reservations are, of course, necessary before we can extrapolate from statistics based on aboriginal horticulture and make confident forecasts concerning potential productivity for pioneer agriculturalists. The nature of bitter manioc is such that the most intensive labor requirement is not in cultivation or harvesting, but in processing. The tasks involved in removing the prussic acid from the tubers and manufacturing flour are performed exclusively by women in tropical-forest South America, and have the effect of doubling the length of the female working day as compared with that of the males. On the other hand, these are presumably processes which could be performed more easily and quickly by machines. The utilization of domestic animals, not a significant part of the aboriginal agricultural complex, would not only provide a source of fertilizer which would increase potential soil fertility and thereby decrease the length of fallowing time necessary, but would also constitute a reliable and readily available protein source and thereby reduce or even eliminate the period of time now expended in hunting and fishing.

Shifting agriculture as an ecological system, however, has certain ramifications with regard to settlement pattern and social organization. In areas of low population density in general and pioneer areas in particular, labor is at a premium. Each of the governments involved in contemporary South American colonization schemes has adopted some sort of land policy comparable to the Homestead Act in the United States; land in the pioneer region is either given away or sold to settlers at very low prices. Because of this ready availability of free or cheap land, few settlers are willing to work as wage laborers on the farms of others. While the labor input per acre is low, acreages tend to be large. It is therefore advantageous if a household is able to mobilize as large a family labor force as possible.

When I undertook field research in a Japanese pioneer colony in Bolivia in 1964, one of my initial hypotheses was that the abundance of free land (123.55 acres per family) would lead to a rapid breakdown of the traditional Japanese practice of primogeniture and to the fragmentation of extended families. With so much land available, I reasoned, each son would set up an independent household of his own at marriage. I found, however, that the reverse was true. There were more cases of fusion of related nuclear families to form new extended family households than of fragmentation of extended families into their nuclear components.[51] The same process has apparently been a regular occurrence in frontier areas. In Massachusetts Bay colony, "children were seen as a definite economic asset as a labor source,"[52] in French Canada, "a basic competition of the Old World was turned upside down in the New World. Here it was a competition between seigniors for tenants, whereas there it was between peasants for land owned by seigniors."[53] In contemporary Brazil, more than half of the Japanese immigrant family heads interviewed by Seiichi Izumi told him that they wished to have at least six children so that their family labor supply would be increased.[54] In the Kofyar case, traditional intensive agriculturalists average 3.50 workers per household while migrant shifting agriculturalists average 5.03.[55] A rapid increase in family size is facilitated through the mechanism of polygynous marriages.

The process of shifting agriculture does require larger allotments of land than do more intensive techniques; one hundred to one hundred fifty acres probably represents about the minimum size of a viable holding for the South American tropical forest, of which a maximum of twenty to twenty-five acres might be under cultivation at any given time. Local transportation facilities are primitive at best, and are likely to remain so for the foreseeable future. These factors result in a settlement pattern of isolated homesteads, often arrayed in a linear pattern along a road or trail or river bank. This may seem logical and normal to the North American accustomed to the individual farmsteads which characterize the rural United States, but in most of Latin America, as well as in traditional Europe and Asia, the more common rural settlement pattern is one of nucleated villages or hamlets, with each community surrounded by the farm land of its constituent households. An individual family's land is often scattered in several small plots; each farmer must walk every morning to the land he will work that day, but the distances involved are usually short. On the other hand, the compactness of the settlement facilitates social interaction and interfamily cooperation at those points in the agricultural cycle when a large-scale labor input is necessary.

The dispersed settlement pattern of the frontier leads to a social isolation and fragmentation which may disastrously affect community solidarity. When one's nearest neighbor lives a kilometer or so away, it is difficult to maintain traditional systems of labor cooperation. Whatever the disadvantages for settlement of the open, virtually treeless terrain of the North American Great Plains, it at least enabled people to travel relatively rapidly to the market town or the neighbor's homestead; this is not the case in the South American tropical forest.

This physical isolation combines with an absence of pre-existing kinship ties and other integrative mechanisms in contemporary pioneer communities to generate an endemic factionalism which can prove seriously disruptive. If, as is often the case, the settlers are drawn from heterogeneous backgrounds in religious or ethnic terms, this situation can be exacerbated.[56] It is likely, in short, that governmental colonization schemes in modern South America will incur a considerable human cost; the aboriginal inhabitants of the tropical forest who face imminent extinction may not be the only victims.[57]

On a purely pragmatic level, however, it is difficult to avoid the conclusion that the Amazon basin, while hardly the paradise depicted by a few overenthusiastic viewers,[58] could support a substantially larger population than it now contains without any catastrophic environmental consequences. The question of whether current colonization programs are worthwhile is one that properly falls within the domain of ethics rather than that of ecology or social science.

Notes

1. Some of the data on which this paper is based is drawn from the author's anthropological field work in eastern Ecuador during the summer of 1962 (reported in Joseph B. Casagrande, Stephen I. Thompson, and Philip D. Young, "Colonization as a Research Frontier: The Ecuadorian Case," in *Process and Pattern in Culture*, ed. by Robert A. Manners [Chicago, 1964], pp. 281–325), which was supported by the Carnegie Foundation and the National Science Foundation, and in Bolivia from 1964 through 1966 (reported in Stephen I. Thompson, *San Juan Yapacaní: A Japanese Pioneer Community in Eastern Bolivia*, Ph.D. dissertation, University of Illinois, 1970), supported by research grant #MH 10095, United States Public Health Service. The assistance of those agencies is gratefully acknowledged.

2. Robert C. Eidt, *Pioneer Settlement in Northeast Argentina* (Madison, 1971), p. 4.

3. An annotated bibliography of sources published prior to 1968 is in T. Lynn Smith, "Studies of Colonization and Settlement," *Latin American Research Review*, 4 (1968), 115–123. This is supplemented by *Colonization and Settlement: A Bibliography*, a mimeographed publication of the Land Tenure Center, University of Wisconsin, which was originally issued in 1969 and is periodically updated, and by Stephen I. Thompson, "The Contemporary Latin American Frontier," *Comparative Frontier Studies: An Interdisciplinary Newsletter*, 1 (1975), 2–3.

4. Julian Steward, discussant, in *An Appraisal of Anthropology Today*, ed. by Sol Tax, *et al.* (Chicago, 1953), p. 243.

5. Julian H. Steward, *Theory of Culture Change* (Urbana, 1955), pp. 40–41.

6. For a discussion of these specific cases as well as what is perhaps the best general exposition of cultural ecology, see Robert McC. Netting, *The Ecological Approach in Cultural Study* (Addison-Wesley Modular Publications, 6 [Reading, Mass., 1971]).

7. Two excellent examples of such studies, however, are Julian Steward, ed., *The Peoples of Puerto Rico* (Urbana, 1956), and Clifford Geertz, *Agricultural Involution: The Processes of Ecological Change in Indonesia* (Berkeley, 1966).

8. This point is discussed in greater detail in Stephen I. Thompson, *Pioneer Colonization: A Cross-cultural View* (Addison-Wesley Modular Publications, 33 [Reading, Mass., 1973]).

9. An eloquent exposition of this point is, of course, Walter Prescott Webb's *The Great Plains* (Boston, 1928). While Webb's classic work is, regrettably, little read by anthropologists, it is a precursor if not a progenitor of the cultural ecological approach.

10. See Donald W. Lathrap, "The 'Hunting' Economies of the Tropical Forest Zone of South America: An Attempt at Historical Perspective," in *Man the Hunter*, ed. by Richard B. Lee and Irven DeVore (Chicago, 1968), pp. 23–29

11. Karl H. Schwerin, "Techniques of Manioc Preparation and the Identification of Manioc Types," paper presented at the 70th annual meeting, American Anthropological Association, New York, 1971.

12. The most comprehensive survey of tropical forest cultures is Julian Steward, ed., *Handbook of South American Indians, 3: The Tropical Forest Tribes* (Bureau of American Ethnology, Bulletin 143 [Washington, 1948]). A number of excellent monographic studies of particular groups are available; one of the best is Irving Goldman, *The Cubeo: Indians of the Northwest Amazon* (Urbana, 1964).

13. Betty J. Meggers, *Amazonia: Man and Nature in a Counterfeit Paradise* (Chicago, 1971).

14. F. R. Fosbert, "Temperate Zone Influence of Tropical Forest Land Use: A Plea for Sanity," in *Tropical Forest Ecosystems in Africa and South America: A Comparative Review*, ed. by Betty J. Meggers, *et al.* (Washington, 1973), p. 346. More recently, however, two prominent soil scientists have persuasively argued that the fertility of tropical soils has been consistently underestimated in the literature and that the danger of laterization of soils in cleared areas has been grossly exaggerated (P. A. Sanchez and S. W. Buol, "Soils of the Tropics and the World Food Crisis," *Science*, 188 [1975], 598–603).

15. The phrase "primary forest" here may be inaccurate; according to the author of a recent ethnography on the Sharanahua Indians of eastern Peru, ". . . there is probably not a single square foot of the Amazon Basin that has not at

one time or another been cultivated . . ." (Janet Siskind, *To Hunt in the Morning* [New York, 1973], p. 39).

16. Meggers, *Amazonia*, p. 17.

17. *Ibid.*, p. 18.

18. For a discussion of these and other virtually synonymous terms, see George L. Barney, *An Analysis of Swidden Cultures in Southeast Asia*, Ph.D. Dissertation, University of Minnesota, 1970, pp. 1–2.

19. Harold C. Conklin, *The Study of Shifting Cultivation* (Washington, 1963).

20. Perhaps the best-known and certainly one of the most sophisticated examples of this point of view is Karl J. Pelzer, *Pioneer Settlement in the Asiatic Tropics* (American Geographical Society Special Publication No. 29 [1945]).

21. The most eloquent case for the low labor requirements of shifting agriculture has been made by the economist Ester Boserup in her provocative and influential book, *The Conditions of Agricultural Growth: The Economics of Agrarian Change under Population Pressure* (Chicago, 1965). Recently, however, there have been some indications that the pendulum is beginning to swing back in the direction of pessimism; see John W. Bennett, "Ecosystemic Effects of Shifting Agriculture," in *Annual Review of Anthropology 1973*, ed. by Bernard J. Siegel, Alan R. Beals, and Stephen A. Tyler (Palo Alto, 1973), pp. 36–45.

22. Harold C. Conklin, "An Ethnoecological Approach to Shifting Cultivation," *Transactions of the New York Academy of Sciences*, ser. 2, 17 (1954), 133–142.

23. Netting, *Ecological Approach*, p. 19.

24. Geertz, *Agricultural Involution*, p. 25.

25. The following discussion of the Kuikuru is taken from Robert Carneiro, "Slash-and-Burn Cultivation among the Kuikuru and its Implications for Cultural Development in the Amazon Basin, *Antropologica*, supplement 2 (1961), 47–67.

26. Richard B. Lee, "What Hunters do for a Living, or, How to Make Out on Scarce Resources," in *Man the Hunter*, ed. by Richard B. Lee and Irven DeVore (Chicago, 1968), pp. 30–48. A number of the other papers in this source provide comparable data on subsistence activities of other hunting and gathering groups.

27. Indeed, protein availability rather than agricultural potential may have been the primary limiting factor on aboriginal cultural development in Amazonia; for an exposition of this point, see Daniel R. Gross, "Protein Capture and Cultural Development in the Amazon Basin," *American Anthropologist*, 77 (1975), 526–549. In many areas, the once-rich riverine resources have been seriously depleted in recent years. However, it should be pointed out that the aboriginal population made virtually no use whatsoever of domesticated animals, unlike recent agricultural colonists.

28. E.g., Goldman, *The Cubeo*; William M. Denevan, "Campa Subsistence in the Grand Pajonal, Eastern Peru," *Geographical Review*, 61 (1971), 496–518.

29. Betty J. Meggers, "Environmental Limitations on the Development of Culture," *American Anthropologist*, 56 (1954), 801–824.

30. *Ibid.*

31. Richard I. and Joan F. Hirshberg, "Meggers's Law of Environmental Limitation on Culture," *American Anthropologist*, 59 (1957), 890–891.

32. Betty J. Meggers and Clifford Evans, *Archeological Investigations at the Mouth of the Amazon* (Bureau of American Ethnology Bulletin 167 [Washington, 1957]).

33. *Ibid.*, pp. 245–248.

34. *Ibid.*, pp. 252–253.

35. *Ibid.*, p. 21.

36. Donald W. Lathrap, *The Upper Amazon* (New York, 1970), p. 47.

37. Carneiro, *Slash-and-Burn Cultivation.*

38. Harold C. Conklin, *Hanunóo Agriculture: A Report on an Integral System of Shifting Cultivation in the Philippines* (FAO Forestry Development Paper No. 12 [Rome, 1957]), p. 32.

39. Lucien M. Hanks, *Rice and Man: Agricultural Ecology in Southeast Asia* (Chicago, 1972), p. 32.

40. The argument of the next two paragraphs is based on David Harris, "The Origins of Agriculture in the Tropics," *American Scientists*, 60 (1972), 32.

41. Harald Sioli, "Recent Human Activities in the Brazilian Amazon Region and their Ecological Effects," in *Tropical Forest Ecosystems*, ed. by Meggers *et al.*, pp. 321–334.

42. There is, of course, a serious moral problem involved here—the effect of colonization schemes on the indigenous population of the region. Entire cultures and populations have already been exterminated, and many more will almost certainly follow. A discussion of this situation is beyond the scope of this paper; however, documented information is available from a number of sources: the International Workshop for Indigenous Affairs, Copenhagen, Denmark; the Documentation and Information Center for Indigenous Affairs in the Amazon Region, Geneva, Switzerland; INDIGENA and the American Friends of Brazil, both in Berkeley, California.

43. Sioli, "Recent Human Activities," p. 332.

44. *Ibid.*, p. 333.

45. Boserup, *Conditions of Agricultural Growth*, p. 63.

46. Thompson, *San Juan Yapacaní.*

47. Robert McC. Netting, *Hill Farmers of Nigeria: Cultural Ecology of the Kofyar of the Jos Plateau* (Seattle, 1968).

48. *Ibid.*, p. 68.

49. *Ibid.*, p. 201.

50. Henry Walter Bates, *A Naturalist on the River Amazon* (London, 1864), p. 273, cited in Carneiro.

51. For a fuller discussion, see Stephen I. Thompson, "Changes in Family and Household Organization in an Overseas Japanese Pioneer Community," *Journal of Comparative Family Studies*, 2 (1971), 165–177.

52. James G. Leyburn, *Frontier Folkways* (New Haven, 1935), p. 14.

53. A. L. Burt, "If Turner had looked at Canada, Australia, and New Zealand when he wrote about the West," in *The Frontier in Perspective*, ed. by Walker D. Wyman and Clifton B. Kroeber (Madison, 1957), p. 61.

54. Seiichi Izumi, *Imin* (Tokyo, 1957), p. 61.

55. Netting, *Hill Farmers*, p. 208.

56. This point is elaborated in Thompson, "Changes in Family and Household Organization." Religious factionalism in pioneer communities is discussed in Stephen I. Thompson, "Religious Conversion and Religious Zeal in an Overseas Enclave: The Case of the Japanese in Bolivia," *Anthropological Quarterly*, 41 (1968), 201–208.

57. For a consideration of the human cost of contemporary colonization for the pioneers themselves, see Stephen I. Thompson, "Success and Failure in

Colonization: The Human Factor," *Papers in Anthropology*, 16 (1975), 1–9.

58. Henry Nash Smith devotes a lengthy section of *Virgin Land,* his classic study of the impact of the frontier on American literature (Cambridge, 1950), to an analysis of what he calls the "Myth of the Garden." There is ample evidence that a comparable myth is emerging with reference to the Amazon frontier. For a recent example of romantic overoptimism on the part of two otherwise level-headed cultural geographers, see the preface in Raymond E. Crist and Charles M. Nissly, *East from the Andes: Pioneer Settlements in the South American Heartland* (Gainesville, 1973).

The Contributors

DAVID T. BAILEY is Assistant Professor of Sociology at Sam Houston University, Huntsville, Texas

WILLIAM S. COOTER is a recent graduate of the Department of History, University of Oklahoma

JOHN W. EADIE is Professor of History at the University of Michigan

BRUCE E. HAULMAN is a management analyst for King County (Seattle) Washington

JOHN C. HUDSON is Associate Professor of Geography at Northwestern University

MARTIN T. KATZMAN is Associate Professor of City and Regional Planning at Harvard University

H. LEEDOM LEFFERTS, JR. is Assistant Professor of History at Drew University, Madison, New Jersey

KENNETH E. LEWIS, JR. is Research Archaeologist in the Institute of Archaeology and Anthropology at the University of South Carolina

DAVID HARRY MILLER is Associate Professor of History at the University of Oklahoma

BRIAN S. OSBORNE is Associate Professor of Geography in the Queen's University, Kingston, Ontario

WILLIAM W. SAVAGE, JR. is Assistant Professor of History at the University of Oklahoma

STEPHEN I. THOMPSON is Associate Professor of Anthropology at the University of Oklahoma

GEOFFREY WALL is Associate Professor of Geography at the University of Waterloo, Waterloo, Ontario

EMILIO WILLEMS is Professor Emeritus of Anthropology at Vanderbilt University

DAVID J. WISHART is Assistant Professor of Geography at the University of Nebraska

Index